CW01662640

DR. ALI ALBARGHOUTHI

THIS IS LOVE

FORTY HADITHS ON THE MEANING OF LOVE, ITS PATH, AND HOW IT CAN CHANGE OUR LIVES

DAKWAH CORNER
BOOKSTORE

Published by:

Dakwah Corner Bookstore (M) Sdn. Bhd.
No. 7, Jalan Dato Abdul Aziz, Section 14,
46100 Petaling Jaya, Selangor Darul Ehsan,
MALAYSIA
T: +60 3 7956 4664

2nd Edition Published:
2021

Title:
This is Love

Author:
Dr. Ali Albarghouthi

ISBN:
978-967-5699-73-3

Director:
Farid Ullah Ahmed Hussain

Cover Design:
Norashikin Yussof

Typesetting:
Every Edition Sdn. Bhd.

Printed by:
Fussian Advertising & Printing Sdn. Bhd.

For suggestions and comments:
dakwahcornerpublications@gmail.com

Showroom Outlets

MALAYSIA

Dakwah Corner Bookstore
7, Jalan Dato Abdul Aziz, Section 14, Petaling Jaya
Tel: +60 3 7956 4664

Dakwah Corner Bookstore
Ampang Point Shopping Centre, Ampang
Tel: +60 3 4266 9692

SAUDI ARABIA

Dawah Corner Bookstore
Makkah Commercial Center, Holy Makkah
Tel: +966 125311 895

NIGERIA

Dawah Islamic Bookshop
UAC Building , Abuja
Tel: +234 805 603 7779

PHILIPPINES

Dakwah Corner Bookstore
Falcatan Street, Tetuan, Zamboanga City
Tel: +63 926 5384

Distributors

Darussalam Australia
Australia
Tel: +61 2 9740 7188

Salaam Media International
Singapore
Tel: +65 63964121

Darussalam Publishers
USA
Tel: +1 860 224 2400

Darussalam Books
(London Central Mosque)
UK
Tel: +44 2077231234

TABLE OF CONTENTS

PART ONE

Loving Allah

PART TWO

Loving His Prophet

PART THREE

Loving His Creation

PUBLISHER'S NOTE

All Praise be to Allah the Almighty, and peace and blessings be upon the Messenger of Allah and upon his family and companions.

It is easy to talk lyrical about love and passion, but the path of true love is more often difficult and demanding. Walking the talk is not easy and love is not a bed of roses as many portray. The great English writer, William Shakespeare once said, "The course of true love never did run smooth."

Volumes upon volumes of books have traversed the axis of the emotion of love in all forms. Theologians and philosophers from different faiths and ideologies had a principal role in this endeavour and have addressed the phenomenon of love throughout centuries. Some have praised it, some have hated it, and some disapprove of it.

When we look at Islamic revealed knowledge, our pious predecessors and the generations who followed their footsteps, we find that they have left us with rich literary masterpieces to explain passion and love in all their respective shades and forms in light of the authentic teaching of Islam. Their legacy and heritage shows us how Islam considers the emotion of love as a sacred and an utmost important element in human life; so much so that Islam has placed having sincere and true love as a condition to succeed in attaining the pleasure of Allah and a precursor of gaining acceptance of any acts devoted to Him.

On the other hand, we find certain individuals within this caravan of Islam who mixed the truth with falsehood and explaining this powerful emotion of love in a tainted manner, heavily influenced by the wayward thoughts of logicians as well as Persian and Greek philosophies in addressing the matter. But the glorious scholars of Islam have exposed these individuals and their misguided works from time to time and warned the Ummah regarding their evil actions and intentions.

Today we are in dire need of restoring this priceless, intellectual, and authentic heritages. We need to shed light on the literary body of work that can show us how to look at this immensely powerful emotion of passion and love in light of authentic prophetic teachings.

Dr. Ali AlBarghouthi (author of the bestselling title, *The Heart Therapy*) provides us with another valuable contribution to the Islamic publishing industry under the title, 'This Is Love' by linking the emotion of love to the divine wisdom to stimulate the noble intentions upon which the creation was established, and creatures naturally believed in. He also talks, in his initial lines, about the different kinds of lovers and their situations. He has explained this matter to the public as well as the advanced readers in a way that suits everyone's taste, is easy to understand, rectify one's actions, and apply what they read in their daily lives.

We at Dakwah Corner Bookstore Malaysia believe that this work will help everyone to understand this powerful emotion that many human minds find hard to fathom instead of just relegating it to being very complicated. If one devotes this emotion of love to one who is truly deserving it, a very positive transformation can be achieved. Indeed this can only happen when the direction of our love compass is directed to our Creator, Allah The Almighty and to love Him according to His revealed guidelines.

As the saying goes, "Every true love is a story of unexpected transformation. If we are the same person before and after we loved, that means we haven't loved enough..."

Allah said in the Quran:

قُلْ إِن كَانَ ءَابَآؤُكُمْ وَأَبْنَآؤُكُمْ وَإِخْوَٰنُكُمْ وَأَزْوَٰجُكُمْ وَعَشِيرَتُكُمْ
وَأَمْوَٰلٌ ٱقْتَرَفْتُمُوهَا وَتِجَٰرَةٌ تَخْشَوْنَ كَسَادَهَا وَمَسَٰكِنُ تَرْضَوْنَهَآ أَحَبَّ
إِلَيْكُم مِّنَ ٱللَّهِ وَرَسُولِهِۦ وَجِهَادٍ فِى سَبِيلِهِۦ فَتَرَبَّصُوا۟ حَتَّىٰ يَأْتِىَ ٱللَّهُ
بِأَمْرِهِۦ ۗ وَٱللَّهُ لَا يَهْدِى ٱلْقَوْمَ ٱلْفَٰسِقِينَ ﴿٢٤﴾

Say, [O Prophet], "If your parents and children and siblings and spouses and extended family and the wealth you have acquired and the trade you fear will decline and the homes you cheris (if all these) are more beloved to you than Allah and His Messenger and struggling in His Way, then wait until Allah brings about His Will. Allah does not guide the rebellious people.

At-Tawbah (Q9:24)

Farid Ullah bin Ahmed Hussain
Chief Executive Officer

INTRODUCTION

Love is complicated. It is our most powerful emotion, yet we do not understand it. We give it to those who do not deserve it, and deny it those who do. Some spend their whole lives looking for it, while others run away from it when it finds them. We feel this basic need to love and be loved but do not know whom to love, how, and to what end. It has the power to make us the happiest and the saddest, and gives us the greatest hope and the bleakest despair. Poems were written to extol it as the noblest pursuit, while others ended their lives because of it. Love is, indeed, complicated.

These complications grow more serious when it comes to our conception of the divine. Some religious paths ignore love to produce a harsh and distant Creator, while others exaggerate love to undermine the transcendence of the Creator and His laws. Both create an imbalance with grave consequences for individuals and society. The first brings draconian laws and promotes cruelty, while the second is overly permissive. Avoiding these extremes demands that we understand the place of love in Islam. This need grows direr with the assumption some non-Muslims have that Islam is a violent religion without love and compassion. Unfortunately, some Muslims believe this to be the case too. Growing up, those Muslims were introduced to the fear of Allah but not His love. They have also seen terrible violence committed and justified in the name of Islam. This has led to a rift between their experience of Islam and their need for a loving Creator. And they are right to feel this rift. But as shall become clear in this book insha-Allah, loving Allah is the most important motivation to worship Him. There is no Islam without love, and there is no complete love without Islam.

The modern search for love

The world today is desperately seeking love. Collectively, we are experiencing stubborn systemic problems that are plunging the world into greater uncertainty and chaos. Economic inequality, racial discrimination, political corruption, and social alienation have planted the seeds of suspicion and hostility in the world. We are witnessing the growth of xenophobia and populism, and the collapse of trust. There is an almost complete breakdown of communication between people on opposite sides of an issue. We demonize each other and are uninterested in listening to anyone but ourselves. We are at the point of not knowing what news to believe anymore. Information-manipulation (i.e. deception) has made the world more cynical, more divided, and more dangerous. We have made significant technological and scientific advances but seem to have lost ourselves along the way.

Individually, we are also looking for love. More of us today feel alone, disconnected, and misunderstood. The social bonds that offered emotional and social support in the past have evaporated. The demands of modern life distance us from our loved ones and exact psychological and physical tolls. We work longer hours, hop from one city or country to the next, and feel the pressure to prioritize the material over everything else. On top of that, technology made us more solitary and devoured time that used to go to family and friends. All of this has left a gaping hole in our lives and hearts.

We are living in a love-deficient world. Our desperate need for love pushes us to look for it wherever we can find it, sometimes in all the wrong places. Songs and movies offer us constant doses of love stories because they know it sells. Novels make romantic love the purpose of life itself, creating a fantasy destined to make real-life seem disappointing and empty. They distort love, demean it, and turn it into a cheap commodity. Their flawed conception of love seeps into our hearts and minds. When the love they sell us disappoints us—and disappoint it must—we fill the emptiness with anything at hand. We feed the body to drown out the cries of the soul. We eat, we travel, we shop, and collect more money. Some numb the pain with intoxicants (alcohol and drugs), while some mistake illicit sex for an emotional connection. But our need for love remains, stubbornly unwilling to disappear, reminding us that we need more.

We require comprehensive solutions that address all of our needs. Partial and temporary answers will not do. Our problems originate from a lack of love and compassion in our lives and the broader systems around us (economic, political, and social). And no matter how hard we try, we will not find love unless we go back to its source: Allah. When we removed the divine from our life, we impoverished it. We lost the very thing that gave it meaning and direction. When Allah is absent, love is absent too (this is one of the main points of the book). Many accuse religion—especially Islam—of spreading hate, and may be incredulous to hear of love's dependence on Allah. But it is Allah who grants us all that we have, including and especially love. Humanity's medicine is to understand the meaning of love as Allah intended and to reestablish it in our lives. Our need for love beckons us to Allah.

We may have heard the shibboleth that "love is the answer." It is attractive and catchy. Yet, when some point to love as "the answer," they do not explain it. What does it mean for love to be an answer? What do we mean by love? Is loving another a blanket approval of their beliefs and actions? Does love have its own moral compass, or does it need guidance and parameters? Is love a destination or a vehicle? The slogan may give us fuzzy feelings, but it says nothing concrete. It is sparse on details to accommodate any conception of a solution. Since it is ambiguous, it can encompass good as well as bad means and ends. Love cannot be an absolute good that justifies everything in its path (see *Hadith Thirty-One*). It is one answer that—when combined with other answers—guides us to Allah and a nobler life.

The centrality of love in Islam

This may come as a surprise to some. But as love is central to life itself, it is central to Islam. Allah's creation and revelation are connected since they both come from the same source. Allah joined the two when He said:

...أَلَا لَهُ ٱلْخَلْقُ وَٱلْأَمْرُ... ﴿٥٤﴾

Indeed, all creation and command belong to Him.

Al-A'raf (Q7:54)

Since Allah created all, He knows what is best for His creation. And He commands them with the best. The link between creation and revelation goes even further. The motive behind both is the same, and that is love. Ibn al-Qayyim رَحِمَهُ ٱللَّهُ wrote:

العالم العلوي والسفلي إنما وجد بالمحبة ولأجلها وأن حركات الأفلاك والشمس والقمر والنجوم وحركات الملائكة والحيوانات وحركة كل متحرك إنما وجدت بسبب الحب.

روضة المحبين (ص٨٨)

The upper and lower realms [i.e. the heavens and the earth] were created with love and for it. And the movement of celestial bodies in orbits, the sun, the moon, the planets, the angels, the animals, and the movement of every mover is because of love.

Rawdat al-Muhibbin (p. 88)

Allah created us and everything else because of love, with it, and for it. Everything that Allah does, He does out of love. This is discussed further in *Hadith Three*. But for now, note how, in Islam, the act of creation is inseparable from love. And it is the same for religious commands, which are the basis of worship. In Islam, the word for worship is 'Ubudiyyah. Ibn al-Qayyim رَحِمَهُ ٱللَّهُ explained that though the word linguistically means submission and humility, this is done out of love. He wrote:

وأما التعبد فهو غاية الحب بغاية الذل... المحب قد ذلله الحب ووطأه.

روضة المحبين (٨٣)

> Worship is utmost love with utmost humility... Love has humbled the lover and made them submissive.
>
> *Rawdat al-Muhibbin* (p. 83)

Putting it differently, he also wrote:

> الْعِبَادَةُ الَّتِي هِيَ الْمَحَبَّةُ وَالتَّعْظِيمُ.
>
> مدارج السالكين (ج٣ ص٢٢)
>
> Worship is love and glorification.
>
> *Madarij al-Salikin* (vol. 3, p. 22)

When we understand the boundless Glory of the Creator, we love Him. And based on that, we lovingly surrender to Him. Love is an essential ingredient. Worshipping Allah without love is not worship at all. Ibn al-Qayyim رَحِمَهُ ٱللَّهُ explained:

> وَالْعِبَادَةُ تَجْمَعُ أَصْلَيْنِ غَايَةُ الْحُبِّ بِغَايَةِ الذُّلِّ وَالْخُضُوعِ... فَمَنْ أَحْبَبْتَهُ وَلَمْ تَكُنْ خَاضِعًا لَهُ لَمْ تَكُنْ عَابِدًا لَهُ وَمَنْ خَضَعْتَ لَهُ بِلَا مَحَبَّةٍ لَمْ تَكُنْ عَابِدًا لَهُ حَتَّى تَكُونَ مُحِبًّا خَاضِعًا.
>
> مدارج السالكين (ج١ ص٩٥-٩٦)
>
> Worship is comprised of two principles: utmost love with utmost humility and submission... So, if you loved someone but did not submit to him, you are not worshipping him. And if you submitted to someone without love, you are not worshipping him until you love him and submit to him.
>
> *Madarij al-Sulikin* (vol. 1, pp. 95–96)

It is not worship if you are strong-armed into submission. It must happen willingly, and it must be done out of love.

As worship is founded on love, so is Tawhid. Ibn al-Qayyim رَحِمَهُ ٱللَّهُ said:

حَقِيقَةُ الْإِلَهِيَّةِ كَوْنُهُ مَأْلُوهًا مَحْبُوبًا بِغَايَةِ الْحُبِّ الْمَقْرُونِ بِغَايَةِ الذُّلِّ وَالْخُضُوعِ.

مدارج السالكين (ج١ ص١١٢)

The essence of [Tawhid] al-Uluhiyyah is that He be worshipped and loved with utmost love coupled with utmost humility and submission.

Madarij al-Salikin (vol. 1, p. 112)

And this is why Shirk is the absence of love. In interpreting the following *ayah*:

﴿قُلْ تَعَالَوْا أَتْلُ مَا حَرَّمَ رَبُّكُمْ عَلَيْكُمْ أَلَّا تُشْرِكُوا بِهِ شَيْئًا... ١٥١﴾

Say: "Come. I tell you what your Rabb has forbidden you. Do not associate anything with Him."

Al-An'am (Q6:151)

Mujahid, the famous Tabi'i and exegete of the Quran, explained avoiding Shirk in the *ayah* by saying:

قَالَ مُجَاهِدٌ فِي قَوْلِهِ تَعَالَى ﴿أَلَّا تُشْرِكُوا بِهِ شَيْئًا﴾ [الأنعام: ١٥١]: لَا تُحِبُّوا غَيْرِي.

جامع العلوم والحكم (ص٥٢٥)

Do not love someone other than Me.

Jami' al-'Ulum wa al-Hikam (p. 525)

According to Mujahid, Shirk is loving someone more than Allah. It is giving the love that Allah deserves to someone else. Ibn al-Qayyim رَحِمَهُ ٱللَّهُ confirmed the connection of Shirk to love by writing:

وَأَمَّا الشِّرْكُ فَهُوَ نَوْعَانِ أَكْبَرُ وَأَصْغَرُ فَالْأَكْبَرُ لَا يَغْفِرُهُ اللَّهُ إِلَّا بِالتَّوْبَةِ مِنْهُ وَهُوَ أَنْ يَتَّخِذَ مِنْ دُونِ اللَّهِ نِدًّا يُحِبُّهُ كَمَا يُحِبُّ اللَّهَ وَهُوَ الشِّرْكُ الَّذِي تَضَمَّنَ تَسْوِيَةَ آلِهَةِ الْمُشْرِكِينَ بِرَبِّ الْعَالَمِينَ وَلِهَذَا قَالُوا

لِآلِهَتِهِمْ فِي النَّارِ {تَاللَّهِ إِنْ كُنَّا لَفِي ضَلَالٍ مُبِينٍ إِذْ نُسَوِّيكُمْ بِرَبِّ الْعَالَمِينَ} [الشعراء: ٩٧–٩٨] مَعَ إِقْرَارِهِمْ بِأَنَّ اللَّهَ وَحْدَهُ خَالِقُ كُلِّ شَيْءٍ وَرَبُّهُ وَمَلِيكُهُ وَأَنَّ آلِهَتَهُمْ لَا تَخْلُقُ وَلَا تَرْزُقُ وَلَا تُحْيِي وَلَا تُمِيتُ وَإِنَّمَا كَانَتْ هَذِهِ التَّسْوِيَةُ فِي الْمَحَبَّةِ وَالتَّعْظِيمِ وَالْعِبَادَةِ كَمَا هُوَ حَالُ أَكْثَرِ مُشْرِكِي الْعَالَمِ بَلْ كُلُّهُمْ يُحِبُّونَ مَعْبُودَاتِهِمْ وَيُعَظِّمُونَهَا وَيُوَالُونَهَا مِنْ دُونِ اللَّهِ وَكَثِيرٌ مِنْهُمْ بَلْ أَكْثَرُهُمْ يُحِبُّونَ آلِهَتَهُمْ أَعْظَمَ مِنْ مَحَبَّةِ اللَّهِ.

مدارج السالكين (ج١ ص٣٤٨)

There are two types of Shirk: major and minor. The major is the one that Allah does not forgive except by repenting from it. This Shirk happens when one adopts rivals besides Allah whom he loves as he loves Allah. This Shirk includes equating what the polytheists worship with the Rabb of all beings. And this is why they will say to their idols in the Fire, ﴾By Allah, we were in clear error when we made you equal to the Rabb of all beings﴿ [Al-Shu'ara' 97–98]. They will say this despite admitting [previously] that Allah alone is the Creator of everything and its Rabb and King, and that their idols do not create, do not provide, do not bring life, and do not cause death. But they made them equal [to Allah] in love, glorification, and worship. This is the reality of most of the people who commit Shirk in this world, nay, all of them love what they worship, glorify it, and champion it besides Allah. And a lot of them, nay, most of them love what they worship more than Allah.

Madarij al-Salikin (vol. 1, p. 348)

How much love one gives to Allah or His rivals determines whether they are Muslim or not. When love is misdirected, it leads to Shirk and sin. This is why it is vital to understand love better, to understand what is worthy of love and how to love it. This is one of the primary goals of this book.

Ibn al-Qayyim رَحِمَهُ ٱللَّهُ—the brilliant physician of the hearts—

has some powerful words to summarize how spiritually and Islamically essential love is. He wrote:

اعْلَمْ أَنَّ أَنفَعَ الْمَحَبَّةِ عَلَى الإِطْلَاقِ وَأَوْجَبَهَا وَأَعْلَاهَا وَأَجَلَّهَا مَحَبَّةُ مَنْ جُبِلَتِ الْقُلُوبُ عَلَى مَحَبَّتِهِ وَفُطِرَتِ الْخَلِيقَةُ عَلَى تَأْلِيهِهِ وَبِهَا قَامَتِ الأَرْضُ وَالسَّمَاوَاتُ وَعَلَيْهَا فُطِرَتِ الْمَخْلُوقَاتُ وَهِيَ سِرُّ شَهَادَةِ أَنْ لَا إِلَهَ إِلَّا اللَّهُ فَإِنَّ الإِلَهَ هُوَ الَّذِي تَأَلَّهُ الْقُلُوبُ بِالْمَحَبَّةِ وَالإِجْلَالِ وَالتَّعْظِيمِ وَالذُّلِّ وَالْخُضُوعِ وَالتَّعَبُّدِ وَالْعِبَادَةُ لَا تَصْلُحُ إِلَّا لَهُ وَحْدَهُ وَالعِبَادَةُ هِيَ كَمَالُ الْحُبِّ مَعَ كَمَالِ الْخُضُوعِ وَالذُّلِّ وَالشِّرْكُ فِي هَذِهِ الْعُبُودِيَّةِ مِنْ أَظْلَمِ الظُّلْمِ الَّذِي لَا يَغْفِرُهُ اللَّهُ وَاللَّهُ تَعَالَى يُحَبُّ لِذَاتِهِ مِنْ جَمِيعِ الْوُجُوهِ وَمَا سِوَاهُ فَإِنَّمَا يُحَبُّ تَبَعًا لِمَحَبَّتِهِ وَقَدْ دَلَّ عَلَى وُجُوبِ مَحَبَّتِهِ سُبْحَانَهُ جَمِيعُ كُتُبِهِ الْمُنَزَّلَةِ وَدَعْوَةُ جَمِيعِ رُسُلِهِ وَفِطْرَتُهُ الَّتِي فَطَرَ عِبَادَهُ عَلَيْهَا وَمَا رَكَّبَ فِيهِمْ مِنَ الْعُقُولِ وَمَا أَسْبَغَ عَلَيْهِمْ مِنَ النِّعَمِ فَإِنَّ الْقُلُوبَ مَفْطُورَةٌ مَجْبُولَةٌ عَلَى مَحَبَّةِ مَنْ أَنْعَمَ عَلَيْهَا وَأَحْسَنَ إِلَيْهَا فَكَيْفَ بِمَنْ كل الإِحْسَانُ مِنْهُ وَمَا بِخَلْقِهِ جَمِيعِهِمْ مِنْ نِعْمَةٍ فَمِنْهُ وَحْدَهُ لَا شَرِيكَ لَهُ كَمَا قَالَ تَعَالَى {وَمَا بِكُم مِنْ نِعْمَةٍ فَمِنَ اللَّهِ ثُمَّ إِذَا مَسَّكُمُ الضُّرُّ فَإِلَيْهِ تَجْأَرُونَ} [سُورَةُ النَّحْلِ: ٥٣] وَمَا تَعَرَّفَ بِهِ إِلَى عِبَادِهِ مِنْ أَسْمَائِهِ الْحُسْنَى وَصِفَاتِهِ الْعُلَا، وَمَا دَلَّتْ عَلَيْهِ آثَارُ مَصْنُوعَاتِهِ مِنْ كَمَالِهِ وَنِهَايَةِ جَلَالِهِ وَعَظَمَتِهِ وَالْمَحَبَّةُ لَهَا دَاعِيَانِ الْجَمَالُ وَالإجمال وَالرَّبُّ تَعَالَى لَهُ الْكَمَالُ الْمُطْلَقُ مِنْ ذَلِكَ فَإِنَّهُ جَمِيلٌ يُحِبُّ الْجَمَالَ بَلِ الْجَمَالُ كُلُّهُ لَهُ وَالإجمال كُلُّهُ مِنْهُ فَلَا يَسْتَحِقُّ أَنْ يُحَبَّ لِذَاتِهِ مِنْ كُلِّ وَجْهٍ سِوَاهُ قَالَ اللَّهُ تَعَالَى {قُلْ إِنْ كُنْتُمْ تُحِبُّونَ اللَّهَ فَاتَّبِعُونِي يُحْبِبْكُمُ اللَّهُ} [سُورَةُ آلِ عِمْرَانَ: ٣١] ... وَبِهَذَا التَّوْحِيدِ فِي الْحُبِّ أَرْسَلَ اللَّهُ سُبْحَانَهُ جَمِيعَ رُسُلِهِ وَأَنْزَلَ جَمِيعَ كُتُبِهِ وَأَطْبَقَتْ عَلَيْهِ

دَعْوَةُ جَمِيعِ الرُّسُلِ مِنْ أَوَّلِهِمْ إِلَى آخِرِهِمْ وَلِأَجْلِهِ خَلَقَ السَّمَاوَاتِ وَالْأَرْضَ وَالْجَنَّةَ وَالنَّارَ فَجَعَلَ الْجَنَّةَ لِأَهْلِهِ وَالنَّارَ لِلْمُشْرِكِينَ بِهِ فِيهِ.

الداء والدواء (طبعة دار عالم الفوائد ص٥٣٢-٥٣٤)

Know that the most useful love of all, and the most obligatory, the highest, and the most beneficial is the love of the One whom the hearts were created with His love in them, and creation was made possessing the fitrah of worshipping Him [or of lovingly esteeming Him]. It is because of it [i.e. loving Allah] that the heavens and the earth came into existence, and all creatures have it in their nature. It is the secret of *La ilah illa Allah*, for the meaning of *ilah* is the one who attracts the hearts [or supremely resides over the hearts] with love, majesty, exaltation, humility, submission, and worship. And to Him alone does worship belong. Worship is complete love with complete submission and humility. Shirk committed in this worship is the greatest injustice which Allah does not forgive. Allah is loved for Himself, in every way. Everyone else is loved out of loving Him. The proof that His love is a must—Glory be to Him—is in all of His revealed books, the message of all of His Messengers, the fitrah which he created people with, the minds He instilled in them, and the blessings He bestowed upon them, since the hearts have the fitrah and nature to love the one who gifts them and is kind to them. So, how about the One from whom all favors come, and there is no blessing that any of His creation enjoys except that it is from Him alone without a partner, as Allah said, ﴾And there is no blessing you have except that it is from Allah. And when harm touches you, you cry out to Him﴿ [Al-Nahl 53]. [And from the proofs] is how He reveals Himself to His creation through His Beautiful Names and Lofty Attributes, and that what He created points to His Perfection and His Supreme Greatness and Majesty. Love has two causes: beauty and kindness. And Allah has absolute perfection of both. He is Beautiful, and He loves beauty, nay all beauty is His and all kindness is from

> Him. So, no one deserves to be loved for himself in every way except Him. Allah said, ﴿Say, "If you love Allah, then follow me and Allah will love you﴾ [Ali 'Imran 31]... Allah sent all of His Messengers with this Tawhid of love and revealed it in all of His books. And the messages of all the Messengers-from the first to the last-agreed on it. And it is because of [the Tawhid of love] that Allah created the heavens and the earth and Heaven and Hell, and He made Heaven for the people of love and Hell for those who associate others with Him in it.
>
> *Al-Da' wa al-Dawa'* (pp. 532–534)

There is so much to unpack in this quote, and we will do so together insha-Allah throughout the book. For now, note how the love of Allah is central to all the revealed books and is the message of all the Prophets of Allah. It is the reason Allah made this universe and the afterlife. It is Tawhid and its secret, and it is our fitrah. It is why some head to Jannah and others to Hell. It is the most logical, natural, and necessary love there is, and all other loves emanate from it. It is the beginning and the end. It is how we relate to Allah and what He asks of us. After all this, can we say that there is no love in Islam?

Love is the superior emotion in Allah's worship, and its highest station. Al-Ghazali رَحِمَهُ ٱللَّهُ wrote:

> فإن المحبةِ لله هي الغاية القصوى من المقامات والذروة العليا من الدرجات فما بعد إدراك المحبة مقام إلا وهو ثمرة من ثمارها وتابع من توابعها كالشوق والأنس والرضا وأخواتها ولا قبل المحبة مقام إلا وهو مقدمة من مقدماتها كالتوبة والصبر والزهد وغيرها.
>
> إحياء علوم الدين (ج٤ ص٣١٦)
>
> The love of Allah is the ultimate end of all the stations and the highest level of all degrees. There is no station after that of love except that it is one of its fruits and subsidiaries, such as longing, feeling happy with keeping Allah's company, contentment, and the rest. And there is no station before love except that it

> is one of the introductions that lead to it, such as repentance, patience, disinclination for the world, and others.
>
> *Ihya' 'Ulum al-Din* (vol. 4, p. 316)

All of our worship of Allah points to it, and every reading of the Quran leads to it.

Erroneous conceptions of love

Islam not only emphasizes and elevates love but guides it and protects it. Just as there is righteous and beautiful love, there is also destructive and iniquitous love. To stop the latter, both the object of our love and its means have to be noble. Sometimes, we love the wrong thing. And sometimes, we love the right thing in the wrong way. Islam rescues our love and sublimates it. It refines what and how we love, differentiates between worthy and unworthy love, and saves us from harmful attachments. Love can run to the opposite ends of the spectrum: too much of it or too little. The straight path in Surah al-Fatihah lies between the extremes of the misguided and those with whom Allah is angry. Only Allah's guidance can reveal true love.

The Quran and Sunnah present a holistic and balanced view of love, something that will become clearer throughout the book. The early Muslims absorbed this love and exemplified it. This is why their transformation was so incredible, and they were the best generation. As subsequent generations moved away from the purity and clarity of Allah's revelation, they veered away from implementing the divine guidance. Their decline in understanding and practice of Islam meant a decline in their spirituality and love of Allah. A couple of other factors exacerbated the decline.

First, the expansion and furcation of knowledge. Branches of Islamic knowledge started to sophisticate and accrete, and then separate. Specializations emerged in each field, so there were scholars of jurisprudence, of *Hadith*, of the Quran, and so on. With time, the separation distanced these disciplines from each other and from the organic holism of Islam. As it became more mechanical and procedural, Fiqh and other similar fields focused less on spirituality, the state of the heart, and emotions. In response to this move, a similar development happened on the opposite side. Attention to the soul and heart grew as a path of practice and then as a discipline of study. But its development was marred with exaggerations and imbalance, like the development of Fiqh on the other end. Undue attention and weight were given to emotions, practice, and experiential knowledge at the expense of revealed knowledge. As love was deemphasized on one end, it was exaggerated on the other.

The second factor that widened the gap between revealed guidance and reality was the contact with other civilizations and religious communities. Their alternate views and traditions were adopted, especially as the attachment to the Quran and Sunnah grew weaker. Hence, external exaggerations met internal ones and accelerated the decline.

Without love, certain corners of Islamic study and teaching felt soulless and empty of love. This may help to explain some of the contemporary imbalance that focuses on outward performance and adherence to the law but not the more profound meaning that underlies this practice. In a sense, the love of Allah and how essential it is to worship was lost or neglected. The higher purpose of Fiqh is to gain the love of Allah by following His Law (see *Hadith Forty-One*), but this was rarely integrated into the study of Fiqh. On the other end, there was an even more serious development. The emphasis on divine love pushed some beyond the bounds of the Quran and Sunnah. Love became a tool of liberation. If you loved Allah enough, then the laws of Islam did not apply to you anymore. Some took it even further. They envisioned loving Allah as loving another human, and they desired unity with Him. Thus, some promoted the idea of union with the divine as a consequence of love. Others went further and explained that love removes all barriers revealing the unity of existence: there is nothing but Allah in reality. In other words, we and all of creation are not separate from Allah;

we are Him. This pantheistic belief overturns all of Islamic doctrine and revelation. And it is done in the name of love. Interestingly, the western academy is keen on studying and promoting these conceptions of love (e.g. Rumi).

Our modern world developed similar attitudes towards love. The point of difference is the secular reality, which empties society of love and so intensifies people's need and search for it. The other difference is the global dominance of the Western model and culture. There is also a Far Eastern (i.e. Buddhist) influence that left an impact on Western religion and spirituality. The weakness of Muslims today makes them more open to borrowing from other models and cultures than in the past.

Love has emerged in the West as an absolute. This idea is not part of a coherent belief system but a popular belief in love as all-good, as the solution, as the goal, and the means. I discuss in *Hadith Thirty-One* how love cannot function as an absolute. But it is so prevalent today that it may be counterintuitive to try to debunk it. You hear it in statements like "All we need is love" and "Love is the answer." You see it in how love justifies all life choices: if love is all-good, then any two in love cannot be denied. You see it in the idea of the soulmate who makes your life complete and worthwhile. Since divine love was removed as an option, the soulmate replaces God in receiving our absolute and undivided love. Finding that soulmate has become the pursuit of our life and its ultimate meaning and fulfillment. This was previously reserved for God.

We are emotionally-deprived and impoverished in this age. We are looking for love wherever we can find it. We need so much of it. And there is no better place to receive it than from the One who created love, taught us what it is, and asked us to spread it. Some do not think of Islam when they think of love. But as this book will show, love and Islam are synonymous. If we understand Islam more profoundly, we will learn what love is. We need this now more than ever. The world needs it. And the world needs you to share this love with it.

This book

This book is an introduction to the love of Allah. It is a rediscovery of the supremacy of love in Islam and restoration of the holism of Islamic revelation. It is a corrective, a bolster of *Iman*, and a reviver of hope. It is contemplation into the nature of love and the self. It is the first step towards worship that rests on the love of Allah and views the rest of creation with that lens.

The love of Allah is the basis of all the love we experience, and it is the purpose of our lives. This is the first part of the book. It explores the meaning of Allah's love, the reasons He deserves our utmost love, and what Allah's love says about Him, Glory be to Him. The second part of the book focuses on loving the Prophet ﷺ, the Messenger who delivered and exemplified the message of love. All of Allah's revelations conveyed and taught the His Love, but Islam is the perfection of all of these messages. Hence, Islam expounds on love in such depth, detail, and balance, reflecting its finality. Since the Prophet ﷺ is the most beloved to Allah, loving him introduces us to how love can be realized. The third and last part of the book focuses on what Allah loves. To attain the love of Allah, it is paramount to follow what Allah loves. Not only will this bring us the greatest physical/material benefit, but it will also fill our hearts with peace and content. And we will receive through it the love of Allah Himself.

The book is organized into forty-two authentic *hadiths* of the Prophet ﷺ. Those who had read my previous book, *Heart Therapy: Forty Hadiths in Tazkiyah and Soul Purification* (Dakwah Corner: 2018), will see a familiar format. I explained there the history behind the forty *hadiths* collections in Islamic scholarship, so I will not repeat it here. Presenting the topic through the *hadith* of the Prophet ﷺ grounds our understanding of love in the guidance of the revelation. This makes it easier to detect error and protect from it. Allah's revelation is the quickest and safest—indeed only—way to receive Allah's love.

The book has three appendices that I reserved for lengthier

discussions. Most of the conclusions in them are in the main text, and you will find me referencing them when relevant to give you the chance to examine further evidence and arguments. These are their contents:

Appendix I

- The definition of love
- Is unconditional love possible
- Why Allah alone deserves to be loved for Himself
- The problem with Ishq

Appendix II

- Is all hate contradictory to love?

Appendix III

- Is it permissible for Muslims to love non-Muslims?

I hope this work will help many of us reconnect with Allah on a deeper level. I hope that it will also help us properly understand love in all of its forms—religious, worldly, and romantic—and to form better connections with the world around us. We need more of Allah's Love in our lives. We need more love in the world. If we see the beauty in what Allah made and learn to love Allah's creation, we will cure ourselves of arrogance, greed, and envy. We could end diseases like racism, xenophobia, animal cruelty, and environmental destruction.

This book promotes knowledge and action (علم وعمل), or as some put it (معرفة وسلوك). It is not simply an invitation for us to understand love but to start translating our knowledge into practice. The love of Allah is not an academic inquiry that remains captive in books and our heads. It is how we are supposed to live and feel. Knowledge-based practice of this love will teach us more about it than mere reading. And this practice will change our lives. This book, in a sense, is a continuation of *Heart Therapy*.

It is what we fill our hearts with after we have cleansed them. Both books ask us to implement what we read. Only then could we truly say that we have learned something new.

Among the many things I hope this book will achieve is to inspire someone to write the encyclopedia of love in Islam: a collection of all *ayahs*, *hadiths*, Islamic stories, and sayings related to love. This encyclopedia must also document errors in the conception and practice of divine and human love. I believe the world has a lot to learn about love. And we should give that to them.

I ask Allah to open our hearts and minds to the truth, and to make His love the greatest love in our lives. May you find this book beneficial. May it bring you closer to Allah, comfort your heart, and answer your questions. May Allah love you, guide you, and protect you from all harm.

PART ONE

Loving Allah

HADITH ONE

الحديث الأول

Iman is Love

قال رسول الله ﷺ «ثلاثٌ مَنْ كُنَّ فيه وجَدَ حلاوَةَ الإيمانِ أنْ يكونَ اللهُ و رسولُهُ أحبَّ إليه مِمَّا سِواهُما و أنْ يُحِبَّ المرْءَ لا يُحبُّهُ إلَّا للهِ و أنْ يَكْرَهَ أنْ يَعودَ في الكُفرِ بعدَ إذْ أنقذَهُ اللهُ مِنْهُ كما يَكرَهُ أنْ يُقْذَفَ في النارِ.»

رواه البخاري (١٦) ومسلم (٦٧)

The Messenger ﷺ said, «Whoever has the following three will taste the sweetness of Iman: when Allah and His Messenger are more beloved to them than all else, when they love a person only for the sake of Allah, and when they hate to return to disbelief after Allah had saved them from it as they hate to be thrown in fire.»

Reported by al-Bukhari (16) and Muslim (67)

Commentary

Love is the path to tasting the sweetness of *Iman*. It is the beginning of *Iman* and its culmination. When our love for Allah grows, it reshapes our priorities and brings us the pleasure of this life and the next.

The sweetness of Iman

If you happen to enjoy food, you do so because of its taste and aroma. The flavor and smell of our favorite dish, especially if it brings some fond memories, bring pleasure and transport us to a different plane of sensory experience. Like appetizing food, *Iman* has a taste that we feel in our hearts: it is the real soul food that brings the greatest joy. (Think about this connection between food and *Iman* the next time you are enjoying your favorite dish. As you are finding joy in your meal, remember that *Iman* has a greater potential for joy.) Every act of worship is a meal that brings additional sweetness to our lives. It is not sugary sweetness but contentment and calm that permeate our whole being, a sense of peace that all is right or will be soon. In that state, obeying Allah turns from a chore to pleasure; the burden changes to joy because it leads to the ultimate happiness of being near to Allah. Thabit al-Binani said:

قال ثابت البناني: كابدت الصلاة عشرين سنة وتنعمت بها عشرين سنة.

صفة الصفوة (ج٢ ص١٥٤)

> I struggled in performing Salah for twenty years, and then I enjoyed it for twenty years.
>
> *Sifat al-Safwah* (vol. 2, p. 154)

The soul is not able to taste this sweetness until it has conquered its weaknesses and is elevated in its love of Allah. This is why it took him twenty years, yet he never gave up. Once the soul is there, it will find its greatest happiness and comfort in its proximity to its Maker. The body and tongue of a sick person do not crave or enjoy their favorite food. It is not the fault of the food but a body that is too infirm and a tongue that has turned bitter. When we are addicted to bad food and habits—junk food, smoking, and drugs—we grow unable to enjoy healthy food and a wholesome lifestyle, craving instead what harms us. *Iman* feeds the soul like good food nourishes the body, and sin, like bad food, kills it. When the soul is fed the sweetness of *Iman*, it will not need sin or think it sweet. Sin is what keeps us from tasting the sweetness of *Iman*. But when we break free, we will find it. And when the sweetness of *Iman* is intense, one can almost taste it on their tongue and feel it in their body.

The three conditions to finding the sweetness of *Iman* in the *hadith* are all about love, even the last one. They represent the pinnacle of *Iman* (فتح الباري لابن رجب ج١ ص٥٠) (*Fath al-Bari* by Ibn Rajab, vol. 1, p. 50). Love, it turns out, is the height of *Iman* and the path to its sweetness. Al-Nawawi رَحِمَهُ ٱللَّهُ emphasized the significance of this *hadith* when he said:

هَذَا حَدِيثٌ عَظِيمٌ أَصْلٌ مِنْ أُصُولِ الْإِسْلَامِ.

شرح مسلم للنووي (ج٢ ص١٣)

> This is a great hadith, a pillar of the pillars of Islam.
>
> *Sharh Muslim* by al-Nawawi (vol. 2, p. 13)

It is no wonder that this pillar is all about love. Islam is built on it.

Loving Allah and His Prophet

The first and the foundational condition for the sweetness of *Iman* is for the love of Allah and His Prophet ﷺ to be greater than any other love. This is the the origin of all love and, in reality, the greatest form of love. It is the greatest realization, and from it, all other realizations flow.

As Ibn Rajab رَحِمَهُ ٱللَّهُ explained in *Fath al-Bari* (vol. 1, p. 51), the love of Allah develops from knowing Him better and beholding His bounties upon us. We tend to love others for these two reasons: for admirable qualities they possess that draw us to them and for a good that they have done to us (see also *Appendix I*). When it comes to Allah, He has more of those than anyone else. We learn about Allah's Perfection through His Names and Attributes and the greatness of His creation. The more we study Allah's Names and Attributes, the more we would know Allah to be the Merciful, the Wise, the Forgiving, the Powerful, and the Beautiful. Observing His actions and His creation only confirms these conclusions. The beauty, wisdom, and justice found in creation and the grandeur of what He created are a reflection of His Beautiful Names and Attributes. In addition, Allah is the One who blessed us with everything good in our lives. Realizing the Beauty of Allah, in Himself and His actions, propels people to love Him. Loving Allah for His bounties leads to loving Allah for Himself. Ibn Taymiyyah رَحِمَهُ ٱللَّهُ wrote:

وأصل المحبة هو معرفة الله سبحانه وتعالى ولها أصلان أحدهما وهو الذي يقال له محبة العامة لأجل إحسانه إلى عباده وهذه المحبة على هذا الأصل لا ينكرها أحد فإن القلوب مجبولة على حب من أحسن إليها وبغض من أساء إليها والله سبحانه هو المنعم المحسن إلى عبده بالحقيقة فإنه المتفضل بجميع النعم وإن جرت بواسطة إذ هو ميسر الوسائط ومسبب الأسباب ولكن هذه المحبة في الحقيقة إذا لم تجذب القلب إلى محبة الله نفسه فما أحب العبد في الحقيقة إلا نفسه وكذلك كل من أحب شيئا لأجل إحسانه إليه فما أحب في الحقيقة إلا نفسه وهذا ليس بمذموم بل محمود وهذه المحبة هي المشار إليها بقوله صلى الله عليه وسلم «أحبوا الله لما يغذوكم به من نعمه وأحبوني لحب الله وأحبوا أهلي بحبي» والمقتصر على هذه المحبة هو لم يعرف من جهة الله ما يستوجب أنه يحبه إلا إحسانه إليه وهذا كما قالوا إن الحمد لله على نوعين حمد هو شكر وذلك لا يكون إلا على نعمته و حمد هو مدح وثناء عليه ومحبة له وهو بما يستحقه لنفسه سبحانه فكذلك الحب فإن الأصل الثاني فيه هو محبته لما هو له أهل وهذا حب من عرف من الله ما يستحق أن يحب لأجله وما من وجه من الوجوه التي يعرف الله بها مما دلت عليه أسماؤه وصفاته إلا وهو يستحق المحبة الكاملة من ذلك الوجه حتى جميع مفعولاته إذ كل نعمة منه فضل وكل نقمة منه عدل ولهذا استحق أن يكون محمودا على كل حال ويستحق أن يحمد

على السراء والضراء وهذا أعلى وأكمل وهذا حب الخاصة وهؤلاء هم الذين يطلبون لذة النظر إلى وجهه الكريم ويتلذذون بذكره ومناجاته ويكون ذلك لهم أعظم من الماء للسمك حتى لو انقطعوا عن ذلك لوجدوا من الألم ما لا يطيقون وهم السابقون.

مجموع الفتاوى (ج١٠ ص٨٤-٨٥)

The foundation of love is knowing Allah, Glory be to Him, and it has two sources. The first—which some call the love of the laymen—is [love] for His favors to His slaves. No one denies this love that is based on this cause, for the hearts were created to love the one who is kind to them and to hate the one who harms them. Allah is the true Benefactor and Bestower to His slave, for He is the one who gifted all bounties even if they occur through a medium, for Allah is the Facilitator of mediums and the Causer of causes. But this love, in reality, if it does not pull the heart to love Allah for Himself, then the slave only loves himself. And anyone who loves another because of their kindness to him has in truth only loved himself. And this is not condemnable but praiseworthy. This love is the one referred to when he ﷺ said, «Love Allah because of the bounties by which He nourishes you, love me because of Allah, and love my family because of me.» The one who only knows this love does not know from [the multitude of] reasons for which Allah should be loved except the benefit they receive from Him. And this is as they say that *hamd* is of two kinds: *hamd* that is thanks, and this is only for a bounty, and *hamd* that is praise and exaltation and love because of what He deserves for Himself. And so is love, for the second cause is loving Allah for what He deserves. This is the love of someone who knows why Allah should be loved. And there is no way from the ways by which Allah is known, that His Names and Attributes have guided to, except that He deserves complete love from that way, even His Actions. For every bounty from Him is a favor, and every affliction is justice. And this is why He deserves to be praised all the time, and He deserves to be praised for ease and difficulty. And this is a higher and more complete [love]. This is the love of the chosen. They are the ones who seek the joy of looking at His Honorable Face and enjoy remembering Him and privately conversing with Him, and this would be more important to them than water is for fish. And if they were to stop that, they will find unbearable pain. They are the first and the closest [to Allah].

Majmu' al-Fatawa (vol. 10, pp. 84–85)

Though the *hadith* he quoted is weak, the principles he laid out are sound. Most people love Allah for the sake of what they receive from Him. And this is how we are first introduced to Allah and how we begin to know Him. But Allah is a lot more than the new child or job we got. Still, these bounties guide us to love Allah and want to know Him more. When we do, we move from love only for the sake of worldly gifts to love for the sake of the Giver Himself. This love is unaffected by worldly fortunes and status. It is pure and noble. Allah then becomes the greatest comfort to the heart. Thu al-Nun said:

قَالَ ذو النُّونِ: دَلَائِلُ أَهْلِ الْمَحَبَّةِ لِلَّهِ أَنْ لَا يَأْنَسَ بِسِوَى اللَّهِ وَلَا يَسْتَوْحِشَ مَعَ اللَّهِ لِأَنَّ حُبَّ اللَّهِ إِذَا سَكَنَ فِي الْقَلْبِ آنَسَ بِاللَّهِ لِأَنَّ اللَّهَ أَجَلُّ فِي صُدُورِ الْعَالِمِينَ مِنْ أَنْ يُحِبُّوهُ لِغَيْرِهِ.

الزهد الكبير للبيهقي (ص٧٨).

The mark of the people who love Allah is that they do not find peace except with Allah, and they do not feel estranged while with Allah. This is so because once the love of Allah settles in the heart, it becomes comfortable with Allah, for Allah is greater in the hearts of the knowledgeable than them loving Him for the sake of another.

Al-Zuhd al-Kabir (p. 78)

The believers draw near to Him each day not because they have to but because they want to and need to. They need Him more than they need food, and they rely on Him more than they rely on their bodies and wealth. They love Him to such a degree that they cannot bear separating from Him, and their greatest reward would be to finally see Him. This is the love of Allah, available to all to seek and rejoice in.

The first step in the love of Allah is a must for all believers: to love Him enough to obey His commands, avoid His prohibitions, and be patient with the afflictions and hardships that He destines. Failure here signals insufficient love. If one commits a sin, they do so because they put its love before that of Allah. If one complains about Allah's decisions in their life, they do so because they still love the world more than Allah.

The second step in the path of Allah's love is recommended. Here, one's greater love for Allah prompts them to perform voluntary worship on top of the obligations; avoid the prohibitions, the disliked (*makruh*) acts, and suspicious matters (*shubuhat*); and is content with what Allah destines of hardship and affliction (see *Hadith Forty-One*). 'Amir ibn Qays used to say:

كَانَ عَامِر بن عَبدِ قَيْسٍ يَقُولُ: أَحْبَبْتُ اللهَ عَزَّ وَجَلَّ حُبًّا سَهَّلَ عَلَيَّ كُلَّ مُصِيبَةٍ وَرَضَّانِي فِي كُلِّ قَضِيَّةٍ فَمَا أُبَالِي مَعَ حِبِّي إِيَّاهُ مَا أَصْبَحْتُ عَلَيْهِ وَمَا أَمْسَيْتُ.

حلية الأولياء (ج٢ ص٨٩).

> I loved Allah, the Most Exalted, a love that made [enduring] every disaster easy for me, and made me contented in every matter, so I do not care while loving Him, in what state I will be in the morning or the evening.
>
> *Hilyat al-Awliya'* (vol. 2, p. 89)

Loving the Prophet ﷺ is part of loving Allah, and it increases as the love of Allah increases. Similar to the conditions that create the love of Allah, loving the Prophet ﷺ happens through knowing him better and realizing how much he has benefited us. When we read his biography and go through his teachings, we understand his sacrifice ﷺ, the nobility of his character, and the beauty of what he taught. We will then realize that there is no other human who has done us more good than him ﷺ. And if we add to this that Allah chose him above all else specifically to be the Last Prophet, that Allah loves him more than any other, we would not be able to feel but the greatest love for this incredible man.

In the same vein as the love of Allah, loving the Prophet ﷺ has an obligatory and a recommended level. The necessary love is to love him enough to obey the obligations he commanded and steer clear of the prohibitions. In addition, it includes seeking and accepting his guidance and finding no discomfort with his judgments and counsel. The recommended part is a love that moves one to follow his recommended guidance, etiquette, character, spirituality, and devotion to Allah.

Loving another for Allah's sake

Loving Allah entails loving what He loves. This, as the Prophet ﷺ explained, is of the best and highest stations of *Iman*.

سَأَلَ مُعَاذ بن أنس النَّبِيَّ صَلَّى اللهُ عَلَيْهِ وَسَلَّمَ عَنْ أَفْضَلِ الْإِيمَانِ فقَالَ «أَنْ تُحِبَّ لِلَّهِ وَتُبْغِضَ لِلَّهِ وَتُعْمِلَ لِسَانَكَ فِي ذِكْرِ اللهِ.»

رواه أحمد (٢٢١٣٠) وصححه شعيب الأرناؤوط

Mu'adh ibn Anas asked the Prophet ﷺ about the best of Iman, so he said, «That you love for the sake of Allah, hate for the sake of Allah, and engage your tongue in the remembrance of Allah.»

Reported by Ahmad (22130) and Shu'ayb al-Arna'ut declared it sahih

Why is love for the sake of Allah one of the best acts of *Iman*? Because it is an honest and strong indicator. When you love someone, you would naturally want them to be happy and would hate any harm to come their way. When our love is strong, the likes and dislikes of our beloved become our own, a state only those who have experienced intense love would know. Consider, for example, how we start liking our child's favorite food, story, or toy because it makes them so happy, or how we hold tight to heirlooms from deceased parents simply because they used to love them. Loving what Allah loves is the mark of *Iman*.

Ibn Rajab رَحِمَهُ ٱللَّهُ wrote:

الْمَحَبَّة لَا تَتِمُّ بِدُونِ الطَّاعَةِ وَالْمُوَافَقَةِ قَالَ الْحَسَنُ قَالَ أَصْحَابُ رَسُولِ اللَّهِ صَلَّى اللَّهُ عَلَيْهِ وَسَلَّمَ يَا رَسُولَ اللَّهِ إِنَّا نُحِبُّ رَبَّنَا حُبًّا شَدِيدًا فَأَحَبَّ اللَّهُ أَنَّ يَجْعَلَ لِحُبِّهِ عَلَمًا فَأَنْزَلَ اللَّهُ هَذِهِ الْآيَةَ ﴿قُلْ إِنْ كُنْتُمْ تُحِبُّونَ اللَّهَ فَاتَّبِعُونِي يُحْبِبْكُمُ اللَّهُ﴾ [آل عمران: ٣١] وَمِنْ هُنَا قَالَ الْحَسَنُ اعْلَمْ أَنَّكَ لَنْ تُحِبَّ اللَّهَ حَتَّى تُحِبَّ طَاعَتَهُ وَسُئِلَ ذُو النُّونِ مَتَى أُحِبُّ رَبِّي قَالَ إِذَا كَانَ مَا يُبْغِضُهُ عِنْدَكَ أَمَرَّ مِنَ الصَّبْرِ وَقَالَ بِشْرُ بْنُ السَّرِيِّ لَيْسَ مِنْ أَعْلَامِ الْحُبِّ أَنْ تُحِبَّ مَا يُبْغِضُهُ حَبِيبُكَ قَالَ أَبُو يَعْقُوبَ النَّهْرَجُورِيُّ كُلُّ مَنِ ادَّعَى مَحَبَّةَ اللَّهِ عَزَّ وَجَلَّ وَلَمْ يُوَافِقِ اللَّهَ فِي أَمْرِهِ فَدَعْوَاهُ بَاطِلٌ وَقَالَ رُوَيْمٌ الْمَحَبَّةُ الْمُوَافَقَةُ فِي كُلِّ الْأَحْوَالِ وَقَالَ يَحْيَى بْنُ مُعَاذٍ لَيْسَ بِصَادِقٍ مَنِ ادَّعَى مَحَبَّةَ اللَّهِ وَلَمْ يَحْفَظْ حُدُودَهُ وَعَنْ بَعْضِ السَّلَفِ قَالَ قَرَأْتُ فِي بَعْضِ الْكُتُبِ السَّالِفَةِ مَنْ أَحَبَّ اللَّهَ لَمْ يَكُنْ عِنْدَهُ شَيْءٌ آثَرَ مِنْ رِضَاهُ وَمَنْ أَحَبَّ الدُّنْيَا لَمْ يَكُنْ عِنْدَهُ شَيْءٌ آثَرَ مِنْ هَوَى نَفْسِهِ.

جامع العلوم والحكم (ج١ ص٢١٢-٢١٣)

Love is incomplete without obedience and agreement. Al-Hasan said, "The Companions of the Messenger ﷺ said, 'O Messenger of Allah, we love our Rabb immensely,' so Allah loved to establish a sign for love, and so He revealed this ayah ﴿Say, 'If you love Allah, then follow me and Allah will love you.'﴾" And it is because of this that al-Hasan said, "Know that you will not love Allah until you love obeying Him." And Thu al-Nun was asked, "When would I have loved my Rabb?" He answered, "When what He hates is bitterer to you than the bitterest plant." Bishr ibn al-Sariyy said, "It is not one of the marks of love for you to love what your beloved hates." Abu

> Ya'qub al-Nahrajuri said, "Anyone who claims to love Allah but does not follow His commands, then their claim is false." Ruwaym said, "Love is agreement in all conditions." Yahya ibn Mu'adh said, "The one who claims to love Allah but does not observe His laws is dishonest." Some of the predecessors said, "I read in some of the books of the past, 'If one loves Allah, nothing would be dearer to them than pleasing Him. And if one loves the world, nothing would be dearer to them than their own desire.' "
>
> *Jami' al-'Ulum wa al-Hikam* (vol. 1, pp. 212–213)

One may love Allah, but their love could be weak, unable to love what Allah loves. When one's heart is (partially) captive to this world or to Haram, they will love what Allah hates or hate what Allah loves. But when one's love for Allah grows, it chases away all inferior lovers that try to compete with Him for our hearts. When one liberates themselves from their personal inclinations and ascend to what Allah loves, Allah's choices and preferences become their own. When they encounter someone close to Allah, they will naturally love them because Allah loves them. They are close to Allah, and their heart is drawn to what pleases Allah, their Supreme Love.

Hating to return to disbelief

Loving what Allah loves is incomplete without hating what He hates. Some may find it off-putting that Allah may hate and that they are required to hate. But hate here is not the dark, irrational, and destructive hate that we have seen so much of in modern times (see also *Appendix II*). This is not hate guided by human whims and biases but one that reflects the Divine Wisdom. There is harm and corruption in what Allah hates, like murder, rape, theft, and so on. Knowing the harm, we naturally hate it and try to stop it whenever we can. Additionally, anyone who loves Allah loathes anything that steals them away from Him. Since sin distances us from Allah, it is hateful for that reason too. Every good thing we love has a harmful opposite we should hate. Thus, hate in this context is not there to destroy but to save us from destruction.

Disbelief is the greatest disconnection between Allah and his creation, the greatest ingratitude, and the greatest corruption on earth. Since the believer cannot bear the idea that they could be separated from Allah's love, Kufr becomes so loathsome that they would prefer death. Even being burnt alive. The sweetness of love cannot tolerate the bitterness of separation. Prophet Yusuf عَلَيْهِ ٱلسَّلَامُ said:

...رَبِّ ٱلسِّجْنُ أَحَبُّ إِلَيَّ مِمَّا يَدْعُونَنِيٓ إِلَيْهِۖ... ﴿٣٣﴾

O My Rabb, prison is more beloved to me than what these women invite me to do.

Yusuf (Q12:33)

How could staying in a dingy jail be more pleasing to anyone than comfort, luxury, money, power, and sexual fulfillment? What is the thing that Yusuf عَلَيْهِ ٱلسَّلَامُ had that many of us are still looking for? What prompted the People of the Ditch to choose to be burnt to death in a great fire over polytheism, as recorded in Surah al-Buruj?

When the love of Allah is firmer in the hearts than any other love, it would be possible to give up everything for it. His love is the greatest discovery in this life. But we need to know Allah more to love Him. This is what the rest of the book is inviting you to do.

HADITH TWO

الحديث الثاني

Allah loves beauty

قال رسول الله ﷺ «إنَّ اللهَ تعالى جميلٌ يحبُّ الجمالَ ويحبُّ مَعاليَ الأمورِ ويكرهُ سَفسافَها.»

رواه الطبراني في المعجم الأوسط (٦٩٠٦) وابن عساكر في تاريخ دمشق (٤٥٩٦) وصححه الألباني (صحيح الجامع ١٧٤٣ وانظر الصحيحة ١٦٢٦)

وفي حديث «إنَّ اللهَ كريمٌ يُحبُّ الكُرَماءَ جوادٌ يُحبُّ الجَوْدَةَ يُحبُّ معاليَ الأخلاقِ ويكرَهُ سَفْسافَهَا.»

صحيح الجامع (١٨٠٠)

وفي حديث «إنَّ اللهَ جميلٌ يحبُّ الجمالَ و يحبُّ أن يَرى أثرَ نعمتِه على عَبدِه و يُبغِضُ البُؤْسَ و التَّباؤسَ.»

صحيح الجامع (١٧٤٢)

The Prophet ﷺ said, «Allah is Beautiful and He loves beauty. And He loves lofty matters and hates lowly ones.»

Reported by al-Tabarani in al-Mu'jam al-Awsat (6906) and Ibn 'Asakir in Tarikh Dimashq (4596) and al-Albani it declared it sahih (Sahih al-Jami', 1743 and al-Sahihah, 1626)

In another hadith, «Allah is Generous and He loves the generous [who give without being asked], He is Generous and loves the generous [who give when they are asked], and He loves lofty matters and hates lowly ones.»

Sahih al-Jami' (1800)

And in another hadith, «Allah is Beautiful and He loves beauty. And He loves to see the impact of His bounty on His slave and hates the display of poverty or pretending to be poor.»

Sahih al-Jami' (1742)

Commentary

Allah is Beautiful. When we ponder this, it will open the door to the love of Allah and inspire us to act with beauty in all that we do.

Allah is Beautiful

There is probably no better introduction to explain the Beauty of Allah than what Ibn al-Qayyim رَحِمَهُ ٱللَّهُ wrote:

من أعز أَنْوَاع الْمعرفَة معرفَة الرب سُبْحَانَهُ بالجمال وَهِي معرفَة خَواص الْخلق وَكلهمْ عرفه بِصفة من صِفَاته وأتمهم معرفَة من عرفه بِكَمَالِه وجلاله وجماله سُبْحَانَهُ لَيْسَ كمثله شَيْء فِي سَائِر صِفَاته وَلَو فرضتَ الْخلق كلهم على أجملهم صُورَة وَكلهمْ على تِلْكَ الصُّورَة ونسبت جمَالهمْ الظَّاهِر وَالْبَاطِن إِلَى جمال الرب سُبْحَانَهُ لَكَانَ أقل من نِسْبَة سراج ضَعِيف إِلَى قرص الشَّمْس وَيَكْفِي فِي جماله أَنه لَو كشفَ الْحجابَ عَن وَجهه لأحرقت سُبُحَاتُهُ مَا انْتهى إِلَيْهِ بَصَره من خلقه وَيَكْفِي فِي جماله أَن كل جمال ظَاهر وباطن فِي الدُّنْيَا وَالْآخِرَة فَمن آثَار صَنعته فَمَا الظَّن بِمن صدر عَنهُ هَذَا الْجمال وَيَكْفِي فِي جماله أَنه لَهُ الْعِزَّة جَمِيعًا وَالْقُوَّة جَمِيعًا والجود

كُله وَالْإِحْسَان كُله وَالْعلم كُله وَالْفضل كُله ولنور وَجهه أشرقت الظُّلُمَات كَمَا قَالَ النَّبِي فِي دُعَاء الطَّائِف أعوذ بِنور وَجهك الَّذِي أشرقت لَهُ الظُّلُمَات وَصلح عَلَيْهِ أَمر الدُّنْيَا وَالْآخِرَة وَقَالَ عبد الله بن مَسْعُود لَيْسَ عِنْد ربكُم ليل وَلَا نَهَار نور السَّمَوَات وَالْأَرْض من نور وَجهه فَهُوَ سُبْحَانَهُ نور السَّمَوَات وَالْأَرْض وَيَوْم الْقِيَامَة إِذا جَاءَ لفصل الْقَضَاء تشرق الأَرْض بنوره.

الفوائد لابن القيم (ص٢٦٤-٢٦٥ دار عالم الفوائد)

Of the most special and seldom accessed types of knowledge is knowing Allah the Most High, through beauty. This is the knowledge of the select among creation, where each knows Him through an attribute of His. But the ones who know Him best are those who know Him through His Perfection, Grandeur, and Beauty—glory be to Him, there is no one like Him in all of His attributes. If you were to suppose that all of creation had the most beautiful images, each one of them had this beautiful image. And you were to compare their outer and inner beauty to the Beauty of Allah, glory be to Him, their [combined] beauty would be less than [the light of] a faint lamp compared to the sun. And it is enough [in appreciating] His Beauty that if He were to remove the Veil away from His Face, then His Splendor and Beauty would burn His creation as far as His Sight would reach. And it is enough [in appreciating] His Beauty that all external and internal beauty in this world and the Hereafter is His creation, so what would one think about the One who produced all this beauty? And it is enough [in appreciating] His Beauty that all Honor is His, all Might is His, all Generosity, all Ihsan, all Knowledge, and all favor, and the Light of His Face shined away all darkness as the Prophet ﷺ said in the du'a of al-Ta'if, "I seek refuge in the Light of Your Face, which shined all darkness away and by which the affairs of the world and the Hereafter were set straight." And Abdullah ibn Mas'ud said, "There is no night or day where Allah is, the light of the

> heavens and the earth is from the Light of His Face." He, glory be to Him, is the Light of the heavens and the earth, and when He comes for judgment on the Day of Judgment, the earth will shine with His Light.
>
> *Al-Fawa'id* by Ibn al-Qayyim (pp. 264–265, Dar 'Alam al-Fawa'id)

What about all the ugliness that we see in the world, one may ask? As we engage in deep and complete contemplation of the universe, we will find that beauty in it overwhelms ugliness. Ugliness on earth is of two kinds. There is (relative) ugliness that Allah created—like the ugliness of Shaytan (see Surah As-Safat, *ayah* 65)—but its creation serves a purpose in Allah's general plan, an important part of the ultimate beauty Allah intends. Its creation also demonstrates Allah's power to create what He wills, and the contrast only highlights the beauty that Allah made and wants us to pursue (e.g. the presence of lies and deceit only enhances our love and desire for honesty and truth). The second type of ugliness is one that Allah allows: human disobedience and their spreading of corruption. This ugliness is a necessary consequence of granting humans free will to obey or disobey Allah, an important piece of the puzzle that ends in Jannah and eternal bliss. So, ugliness on earth is consequently beautiful, and this is why Allah's Actions are all Beautiful.

Allah's Beautiful Actions lead us to understand His Names and Attributes, especially His Beauty, Splendor, and Magnificence. This is what Ibn al-Qayyim رَحِمَهُ ٱللَّهُ described as an often-neglected path in knowing and worshipping Allah. Many of us approach Allah and worship Him through Blessed Names such as the Most Forgiving, the Merciful, and the Bestower. Our sins and our needs pull us towards Him, and we know Him through our requests for forgiveness and assistance. When our needs are met and requests fulfilled, we become grateful and draw nearer to Allah. But only a few contemplate the beauty of His creation and revelation and start approaching Allah through His Attribute of Beauty while also embracing beauty in their lives.

(The *hadiths* of this section make a direct connection between this worship and embrace, as shall become clear shortly.) Since contemplating His Beauty comes out of choice, not need, few among us do it. But those who do are the ones who will know Allah the best.

Ibn al-Qayyim رَحِمَهُ ٱللَّهُ (*Al-Fawa'id*, p. 265) explained that Allah's Beauty has four levels: His Beauty in Himself, the Beauty of His Names, the Beauty of His Attributes, and the Beauty of His Actions. We get a glimpse of the Beauty of His Attributes and Names through the Beauty of his Actions, and we get a glimpse of the Beauty of Allah Himself through the Beauty of His Names and Attributes. But no one can fathom the extent and the magnitude of the Beauty of Allah except Allah Himself. Ibn al-Qayyim رَحِمَهُ ٱللَّهُ gave this incredible example. If each human, from the beginning of creation until the end of time, were as beautiful as the most beautiful human, and we added up all this beauty, it would be less than the faint light of a lamp trying to compete with the light of the sun. Another *hadith* explains that all the bounties of Jannah pale in comparison to Allah's Beauty. The Prophet ﷺ said:

«إذا دَخَلَ أهْلُ الجَنَّةِ الجَنَّةَ، قالَ: يقولُ اللّٰهُ تبارَكَ وتَعالى: تُرِيدُونَ شيئًا أزِيدُكُمْ؟ فيَقولونَ: ألَمْ تُبَيِّضْ وُجُوهَنا ألَمْ تُدْخِلْنا الجَنَّةَ وتُنَجِّنا مِنَ النّارِ؟ قالَ: فَيَكْشِفُ الحِجابَ فَما أُعْطُوا شيئًا أحَبَّ إليهِم مِنَ النَّظَرِ إلى رَبِّهِمْ عزَّ وجلَّ.»

رواه مسلم (١٨١)

When the people of Jannah enter Jannah, Allah will ask them, "Do you want more?" So they will reply, "Did you not brighten our faces? Did you not admit us into Jannah and protect us from Hell?" So the Veil [between them and Allah] will be lifted, and they will not be given something more beloved to them than to behold their Rabb, glory be to Him.

Reported by Muslim (181)

Can we appreciate that all the unimaginable beauty and luxury of Jannah cannot compete with Divine Beauty? We can make another comparison with what is familiar to us on this earth, and it would still be incredible. Take the best food that you ate, the best day of your life, your favorite clothes, your favorite pastime, your favorite person, your favorite memory, and all that makes you smile and put all these together—beholding Allah will bring more joy and contentment than all of these combined. Imagine your most beloved person/thing that entrances you and moves your heart, and think how the experience of seeing Allah in Jannah will be greater, sweeter, and happier. It is for this reason that the pious cannot wait to see Allah: they know that seeing Him will be the greatest joy they can experience. May Allah make us among them.

We love others because of their outer and/or inner beauty. We love them because of their beautiful deeds. If you think about it, it is Allah who enabled all this beauty. And Allah's Beauty—the Beauty of His Face, His Attributes, what He does, being close to Him, mentioning His name—is greater than any other beauty you have seen or imagined. Doesn't Allah then deserve the greatest love?

Listen to Ibn al-Jawzi رَحِمَهُ ٱللَّهُ explain why we ought to love Allah. He wrote:

وكيف لا أحب من وهب لي ملذوذات حسي وعرفني ملذوذات علمي فإن التذاذي بالعلم وإدارك العلوم أولى من جميع اللذات الحسية فهو الذي علمني وخلق لي إدراكًا وهداني إلى ما أدركته إنه يتجلى لي في كل لحظة في مخلوق جديد أراه فيه بإتقان ذلك الصنع وحسن ذلك المصنوع فكل محبوباتي منه وعنه وبه الحسية والمعنوية وتسهيل سبل الإدراك به والمدركات منه وألذ من كل لذة عرفاني له فلولا تعليمه ما عرفته وكيف لا أحب من أنا به وبقائي منه وتدبيري بيده ورجوعي إليه وكل مستحسن محبوب هو صنعه وحسنه وعطف النفوس إليه فكذلك الكامل القدرة أحسن

من المقدور والعجيب الصنعة أكمل من المصنوع ومعنى الإدراك أحلى عرفانًا من المدرك ولو أننا رأينا نقشًا عجيبًا لاستغرقنا تعظيم النقاش وتهويل شأنه وظريف حكمته عن حب المنقوش وهذا مما تترقى إليه الأفكار الصافية إذا خرق نظرها الحسيات ونفذ إلى ما وراءها فحينئذ تقع محبة الخالق ضرورة وعلى قدر رؤية الصانع في المصنوع يقع الحب له فإن قوي أوجب قلقًا وشوقًا وإن مال بالعارف إلى مقام الهيبة أوجب خوفًا وإن انحرف به إلى تلمح الكرم أوجب رجاء قويًا ﴿قَدْ عَلِمَ كُلُّ أُنَاسٍ مَشْرَبَهُمْ﴾ [البقرة: ٦٠].

صيد الخاطر (ص٥٨-٥٩)

How do I not love the One who gave me joy through what I sense [i.e. the joy I receive through my senses], and gave me joy through what I know [i.e. the joy I receive from what I learn]? And the joy I receive from knowledge is greater than all physical joy. He is the one who taught me, gave me awareness, and guided me to what I comprehend. And I constantly see Him in every new creation [of His]. I see Him in the perfection and beauty of that creation. All that I love—physical and nonphysical—is from Him, by Him, and through Him. How I come to know [what I love] and [the existence of what I love] is from Him. And the best of all pleasures is knowing Him. If He did not teach me, I would not know Him. I exist because of Him, so how can I not love Him? My life is from Him, my affairs are in His Hand, my return is to Him, and He made every beautiful and lovable thing, beautified it, and turned people's hearts to it. Similarly, the One with Complete Capacity to create is superior to what is created, the Wondrous Maker is superior to what is made, and the realization of this meaning is sweeter than what we behold [i.e. realizing the Majesty of Allah that is imbedded in every creation is greater than the created thing itself]. If we were to see a marvelous engraving [i.e. a beautiful work of art], we would be consumed by the greatness of the engraver, their incredible ability, and the finesse of their wisdom over the admiration of the engraving. This is something that purified thought ascends to when it goes beyond the physical to what lies beyond it. At that moment, the love of the Creator undoubtedly occurs. Loving Him will be in proportion to seeing the Maker in what is made. When it is strong, it will lead to agitation and longing. If it moves one to the station of awe, it will lead to fear [of Allah]. And if it moves one to noticing [His] generosity, it will lead to strong hope. ﴿Each knew where to drink from﴾ [Al-Baqarah 60] [i.e. each have their path].

Sayd al-Khatir (pp. 58–59)

This is absolutely incredible! I cannot say more.

Allah loves beauty

Allah is Beautiful in Himself and Actions. And He loves beauty. But what type of beauty does Allah love? Expensive cars? Jewelry? Brand names? Fine art? Classical music? What matters to Allah is not the external beauty of faces and bodies but the inner beauty of *Iman* and character. The Prophet ﷺ said:

«إِنَّ اللهَ لَا يَنْظُرُ إِلَى صُوَرِكُمْ وَأَمْوَالِكُمْ وَلَكِنْ يَنْظُرُ إِلَى قُلُوبِكُمْ وَأَعْمَالِكُمْ.»

رواه مسلم (٢٥٦٤)

Allah does not look at your faces and wealth but looks at your hearts and deeds.

Reported by Muslim (2564)

Our images and body shapes are given, not earned, so why should something we had no hand in acquiring matter to Allah? Or if we had a hand in acquiring something, like money and slim bodies, it is not important enough to earn us favor with Allah. What matters is how much we purify our hearts and what good we do with our bodies. So, the beauty that Allah loves does not correspond to the different standards of beauty that humans have (e.g. fashion, music, and architecture) but the substantial beauty of the soul and everything that serves this end. And when external/material beauty is pursued to please Allah, it becomes something worthy of praise and admiration. Allah says:

يَٰبَنِيٓ ءَادَمَ خُذُواْ زِينَتَكُمۡ عِندَ كُلِّ مَسۡجِدٖ وَكُلُواْ وَٱشۡرَبُواْ وَلَا
تُسۡرِفُوٓاْۚ... ﴿٣١﴾

O children of Adam, take your adornment at every masjid (or when worshipping), and eat and drink and do no waste.

Al-A'raf (Q7:31)

Being adorned includes covering one's body (the *'awrah*) as well as getting cleaned up, dressing well, using siwak (or cleaning the mouth), and putting perfume on (for men only if outside the house). This is part of the respect that one gives to the worship of Allah, which, when done, will ennoble this worship in the eyes of the worshipper and everyone else who witnesses it. This is why it is also Sunnah to choose our best clothes for Friday and Eid Prayers. And it was a common practice of the Prophet ﷺ to dress well when receiving tribal delegates interested in Islam (al-Bukhari, 886). He did this for *da'wah*: to honor them as guests and to gain their respect, which hastened their acceptance of Islam. It is also recommended for a wife to adorn herself for her husband and for him to do the same for her. The bond of marriage between them saves them from committing sinful acts outside of marriage. Such beautification is desirable and loved by Allah. Highlighting the importance of pursuing external beauty in service of internal beauty in worship, Nafi' رَضِيَ ٱللَّهُ عَنْهُ recounted the following incident.

عن نافع رضي الله عنه قال: دَخَلَ عَلَيَّ ابْنُ عُمَرَ رضي الله عنهما
وَأَنَا أُصَلِّي فِي ثَوْبٍ وَاحِدٍ فَقَالَ لِي أَلَمْ تُكْسَ ثَوْبَيْنِ قُلْتُ بَلَى قَالَ

أَرَأَيْتَ لَوْ بَعَثْتُكَ إِلَى بَعْضِ أَهْلِ الْمَدِينَةِ أَكُنْتَ تَذْهَبُ فِي ثَوْبٍ وَاحِدٍ قُلْتُ لَا قَالَ فَاللهُ أَحَقُّ أَنْ تَتَجَمَّلَ لَهُ أَمِ النَّاسُ.

السنن الكبرى للبيهقي (٣٢٧٣) وصححه محققه إسلام منصور

Ibn Umar رَضِيَ اللَّهُ عَنْهُمَا stepped inside and saw me praying in one garment, so he asked me, "Were you not given two garments?" I said, "Yes." He asked, "If I were to send you to one of the people of Madinah, would you go like this?" I replied, "No." He then asked, "Is Allah more deserving of your beautification or the people?"

Al-Sunan al-Kubra by al-Bayhaqi (3273) and declared sahih by its editor

Though dressing in one piece covered the 'awrah and fulfilled the basic requirement of *Salah*, wearing a two-piece suit was the proper dress at the time. And Ibn Umar's رَضِيَ اللَّهُ عَنْهُمَا point was that if we dress up when we meet people, shouldn't we honor Allah more when we worship him? The more we respect a human, the more we care to look our best in front of them. And if we esteem Allah, we would want to look our best when we face Him in *Salah*. When we do that, *Salah* will become important in our eyes.

It is necessary to note, however, that not all beautification is acceptable and praiseworthy. Ibn al-Qayyim رَحِمَهُ اللَّهُ explained that beautification and adornment can be divided into three categories (*Al-Fawa'id*, pp. 270–271). The first is what Allah loves, is done for Allah, and supports what He loves, like the examples discussed above (e.g. dressing up for Friday and Eid prayers etc). Forbidden beautification is one done to support a sin (e.g. beautification that inflames desires and leads to fornication), showing off out of arrogance, when it wastes money, and when it becomes one's sole or primary concern in life. The third is an adornment that is free from both good and bad intentions and consequences, and this is permissible as long as it is not wasteful. The Prophet ﷺ summarized all this when he said:

«كُلوا واشرَبوا وتَصدَّقوا والبَسوا ما لم يخالِطْهُ إسرافٌ أو مَخيَلَةٌ.»

رواه أحمد (٦٦٩٥) وابن ماجه (٣٦٠٥) وحسنه الألباني (صحيح ابن ماجه ٣٦٠٥) والأرناؤوط

«Eat, drink, donate, and dress as long as you are not wasteful or arrogant.»

Reported by Ahmad (6695) and Ibn Majah (3605) and al-Arna'ut and al-Albani declared it hasan (*Sahih ibn Majah*, 3605)

Lofty and lowly matters

The *hadith* teaches both knowledge and action (معرفة وسلوك). When we recognize Allah as the Beautiful, the creator of beauty in this life and the next, we would want to extend this beauty to everything around us. With kind words, kind gestures, painting a smile on another's face, alleviating pain and hardship, eliminating injustice, with all of that and more, we add beauty to our lives and those around us. This is the beauty-oriented life of a Muslim. They worship the Beautiful and see the beauty of His actions every day of their life. Lofty and noble matters are an intrinsic part of this sense of beauty. It pervades or should pervade Muslim life, and flows from it to everyone and everything else. It encompasses everything noble and dignified, starting with the religious obligations and recommendations to good character and etiquette. In His revelation, Allah guides to the noblest of beliefs, practices, and manners. They do not elevate only in the next life but in this life too. Amid competing claims of nobility, refinement, and being culturally civilized, Allah's revelation acts as the compass of what is truly noble. The greater we hold on to what Allah loves, the higher we rise in His eyes and this world, despite the objections of those who do not know Allah well.

Part of nobility is to have lofty aspirations and goals, to give rather than receive, help rather than seek assistance, and praise and thank Allah rather than complain about our lives. Part of this nobility is that whenever there is a choice, we choose what is more pleasing to Him, what is more beautiful, what is more beneficial, what is more dignified even if we are the only ones doing it. Part of nobility is to see ourselves worthy of noble speech and deeds, unworthy of ignobility. Part of nobility is to adopt the good practices that others have (e.g. punctuality, discipline when driving and crossing the road, order, and patience in a queue) but not their misdeeds and disobedience. In sum, any dignified practice is pleasing to Allah, and it is pleasing to those who love Him.

No Muslim should be contented with undignified belief or practice. Therefore, one should avoid prohibitions and try to stay away from the disliked (*makruh*). If a word or an act is unbefitting the dignity of a Muslim, we should be the furthest from it, even if it happens to be common practice around us.

Allah is Generous

Allah's generosity is limitless. All that we have is from Him. He blesses us night and day. The Prophet ﷺ described His generosity saying:

«يَدُ اللَّهِ مَلأَى لَا تَغِيضُهَا نَفَقَةٌ سَحَّاءُ اللَّيْلَ وَالنَّهَارَ.»

رواه البخاري (٤٦٨٤) ومسلم (٩٩٣)

> The Hand of Allah is full; no spending decreases what is in it, continuously giving night and day.
>
> Reported by al-Bukhari (4684) and Muslim (993)

Our very life and consciousness are from Him. He is the only one Who truly gives; for everything that we receive, including what humans give us, happens because of Him. And He is the only one who invites people to ask Him.

وَقَالَ رَبُّكُمُ ٱدْعُونِيٓ أَسْتَجِبْ لَكُمْ... ﴿٦٠﴾

And your Rabb said, "Call upon Me and I shall answer you."

Ghafir (Q40:60)

As the *Hadith* of this chapter teaches, Allah's generosity even extends to those who have not asked yet. Karam and jud, mentioned in the *Hadith*, are two forms of generosity. The difference between them is that one happens after a request while the other without it (See *al-Kulliyat* by al-Kafawi p. 353). So, one type of generosity is to give upon request but not necessarily investigating people's needs and rushing to fulfill them. Another kind of generosity is fulfilling particular needs without being asked, but not necessarily being open to requests. Allah's generosity fully includes both: His door is always open to receive our prayers, and He also grants us without being asked. How many times did Allah bless us unexpectedly! How many times did He protect from evil that we were unaware of!

Part of His Generosity is that He becomes Angry when we neglect to ask Him. The Prophet ﷺ said:

«مَن لم يسألِ اللهَ يغضبْ عليهِ.»

رواه الترمذي (٣٣٧٣) وحسنه الألباني (صحيح الترمذي ٣٣٧٣)

Allah will be angry with those who do not ask Him.

Reported by al-Tirmidhi (3373) and al-Albani declared it hasan (*Sahih al-Tirmidhi*, 3373)

Why would this make Allah Angry? Because He is the Generous and loves to give. Because, as humans, we are in constant need. If we are not asking Allah, then we are asking and depending on someone else. This neglect is a sign of disconnect from our Creator, the One we truly need and should approach more than anyone else. Du'a is worship. If we are not engaged in this worship despite our need, then we are far away from Allah. This distance corrupts the heart and angers Allah.

Some of us ask Allah but start doubting His Generosity when the response is delayed or we do not receive what we want. Some, unfortunately, start accusing Allah. This is the misguided path of some of the People of the Book. Allah said:

وَقَالَتِ ٱلْيَهُودُ يَدُ ٱللَّهِ مَغْلُولَةٌ ۚ غُلَّتْ أَيْدِيهِمْ وَلُعِنُوا۟ بِمَا قَالُوا۟ ۘ بَلْ يَدَاهُ

﴿... مَبْسُوطَتَانِ يُنفِقُ كَيْفَ يَشَآءُ... ﴿٦٤﴾

And the Jews said, "The Hand of Allah is tied up [i.e. He is stingy]." Their hands are tied up and they are cursed because of what they said. Rather, both of His Hands are extended, giving as He wishes.

Al-Ma'idah (Q5:64)

They accused Allah of stinginess to explain why they have not received all that they wanted. But can we not see Allah's generosity in what He withholds as much as in what He gives? The Prophet ﷺ said:

«إِنَّ اللهَ لَيَحْمِي عَبْدَهُ الْمُؤْمِنَ مِنَ الدُّنْيَا وَهُوَ يُحِبُّهُ كَمَا تَحْمُونَ مَرِيضَكُمْ مِنَ الطَّعَامِ وَالشَّرَابِ تَخَافُونَهُ عَلَيْهِ.»

رواه أحمد (٢٣٦٢٢) والترمذي (٢٠٣٦) وصححه الألباني (صحيح الجامع ١٨١٤ وصحيح الترمذي ٢٠٣٦) وشعيب الأرناؤوط

«Indeed Allah protects His believing slave from the world, because He loves him, as you protect your sick from food and drink.»

Reported by Ahmad (23622) and al-Tirmidhi (2036) and al-Arna'ut and al-Albani declared it sahih (*Sahih al-Jami'*, 1814 and *Sahih al-Tirmidhi*, 2036)

(See *Hadith Eleven* in this book.)

Allah loves the generous

When we worship Allah through His Name, the Generous, we rush to ask Him, expecting the best from Him. And we never give up asking Him because we know that all the good of this world and the next is in His Hands. When we feel His Generosity overwhelming us, we become grateful, and we expect the best from Him all the time.

Part of this worship is for us to be generous too; generous because Allah loves it and generous because we want others to be blessed as Allah blessed us. Allah said:

...وَأَحْسِن كَمَآ أَحْسَنَ ٱللَّهُ إِلَيْكَ... ﴿٧٧﴾

And do good as Allah has been good to you.

Al-Qasas (Q28:77)

This generosity is with money, with time, with advice, with help, with a smile, with forgiveness, with patience, with well-wishes, and with making people's lives better whatever way we can. And if we ever feel like stopping, we should remember that what we are giving is a small part of what Allah gave us. As long as we stay generous, Allah will keep blessing us.

Thanking the blessings vs. displaying poverty

When Allah blesses, He loves to see the impact of this blessing. This display is not for ostentation or bragging but to thank Allah.

جاء إليه رجل وعليه ثوب دون فقال له رَسُولُ اللهِ ﷺ «ألك مال؟» قال: نعم. قال «من أي المال؟» قال: من كل المال قد أعطاني الله تعالى. قال «فإذا آتاك الله مالا فلير أثر نعمة الله عليك وكرامته.»

رواه النسائي (٥٢٣٩) والترمذي (٢٠٠٦) وصححه الألباني (صحيح النسائي ٥٣٢٩)

A man came to the Prophet ﷺ wearing cheap clothes, so he asked him, "Do you have money?" He replied, "Yes." He asked him, "What kind of money do you have?" He replied, "Allah gave me all kinds of wealth." So he answered and said, "If Allah gave you wealth, let the impact of Allah's blessing and honor be seen on you."

Reported by al-Nasa'i (5239) and al-Tirmidhi (2006) and al-Albani declared it sahih (*Sahih al-Nasa'i*, 5329)

Gratitude for blessings happens with the heart, tongue, and body. Ingratitude is the hiding of the blessings of Allah as if they do not exist. If the rich behave like they are poor, the healthy like they are sick, and the knowledgeable withhold their knowledge to look like they are ignorant, then the blessings of Allah will disappear. It will seem as if Allah blessed no one, leaving all to suffer. Moreover, when the blessings of Allah are hidden, those in need would not know where to go for help. Those who have will end up neglecting those who do not. But when one allows the blessings of Allah to be seen, people will recognize Allah's favors and Mercy, come to see that there is hope and be inspired to ask Allah for what they need. This is why Allah said in the Quran:

وَأَمَّا بِنِعْمَةِ رَبِّكَ فَحَدِّثْ ﴿١١﴾

And proclaim the blessings of your Rabb.
Al-Duha (Q93:11)

Showing the blessings of Allah should happen with moderation and with the good intention of thanking Him. When people see more of Allah's blessings, they will see His generosity and love Him for it. And more of the blessings of Allah will be shared: the rich will donate, the knowledgeable will teach, and the healthy will assist.

On the opposite end are those who purposely display poverty or pretend to be poor. What Allah hates is not for the poor to wear what they can afford but for one to wear the worst of what they have. What is wrong with this? It is wrong when it hides the blessings of Allah. And it is wrong when it is done as a complaint and a protest that Allah did not give. When one is constantly complaining with tongue and dress about their condition, they broadcast their dissatisfaction to the people and cover up the blessings of Allah that they have. This hopeless view spreads nihilism wherever it goes.

Some spread such desperation even though Allah blessed them. They are the ones who pretend not to have. They are rich, but whenever you see them, they are complaining about rising prices and the cost of living. They are healthy but always complaining about their health. They leave behind a trail of gloom and fear of the future. But when you meet the thankful, even though they have less, their positive attitude fills you with hope and recognition that Allah did bless, and He blessed us with so much. We do not need to share everything good in our lives with everyone: it is vital to be prudent and to share what is appropriate with those who will not abuse it. But let us proclaim the blessings of Allah and let us stop complaining. Allah blessed us with so much. Alhamdulillah.

HADITH THREE

الحديث
الحديث الثالث

Allah loves ease

سُئِلَ رَسُولُ اللهِ ﷺ أَيُّ الْأَدْيَانِ أَحَبُّ إِلَى اللهِ قَالَ «الْحَنِيفِيَّةُ السَّمْحَةُ.»

رواه أحمد (٢١٠٧) والطبراني في المعجم الكبير (١١٥٧٢) وحسنه الألباني (صحيح الجامع ١٦٠ وانظر الصحيحة ٨٨١)

The Prophet ﷺ was asked, "Which religion does Allah love the most?" He answered, «The monotheistic and easy one.»

Reported by Ahmad (2107) and al-Tabarani in al-Mu'jam al-Kabir (11572) and al-Albani declared it hasan (Sahih al-Jami', 160. See also al-Sahihah, 881)

Commentary

Religion and worship are founded on love. Tawhid and ease are the hallmarks of Islam, where the hearts turn to Allah alone with complete devotion.

Religion is built on love

Would you be surprised to hear that all that Allah does, He does out of love? And would it be surprising to learn that love is the foundation of religion? With the vilification of God and religion in the modern era, no one would blame you if this shocked you. This entire book is devoted to demonstrating how love is inseparable from Allah and Islam. So, let us examine those "surprising" statements.

Whatever Allah commands, He does because He loves it. This is plain and intuitive. Similarly, whatever Allah prohibits, He does so because it obstructs and stands in the way of what He loves. Here is an example. Allah said:

إِنَّمَا يُرِيدُ ٱلشَّيْطَٰنُ أَن يُوقِعَ بَيْنَكُمُ ٱلْعَدَٰوَةَ وَٱلْبَغْضَآءَ فِى ٱلْخَمْرِ
وَٱلْمَيْسِرِ وَيَصُدَّكُمْ عَن ذِكْرِ ٱللَّهِ وَعَنِ ٱلصَّلَوٰةِ ۖ فَهَلْ أَنتُم مُّنتَهُونَ ﴿٩١﴾

Shaytan only wants to incite hatred and animosity between you with alcohol and gambling and to stop you from remembering Allah and praying. So will you not give them up?

Al-Ma'idah (Q5:91)

The intention of Shaytan is the opposite of what Allah loves. Allah prohibited alcohol because, among other things, it stirs up enmity between people, impairs judgment, detracts from proximity to Allah (in *Salah*), and is physically harmful. Allah loves the opposite of what alcohol does: He loves harmony and love between people, mental clarity that allows sound judgment, proximity to Him, and protection of health. This is true for all commands and prohibitions: Allah wants us to do what He loves and avoid its opposite. Allah loves and commands honesty, justice, and kindness, and He hates and prohibits their opposites and anything that detracts from them.

Similarly, whatever Allah creates, He does so because He loves it or loves its consequences. When Allah brings something into existence, it is either entirely beneficial or more beneficial than harmful. An example of the first are the angels of Allah, while an example of the second is Shaytan. Though Allah hates the rebellion of Shaytan and the disobedience he promotes, Shaytan plays an essential role in the earthly test that produces the faith and sacrifice of the Prophets of Allah and their righteous followers. In other words, the excellence and purity of the people of Jannah is a consequence of their battle with Shaytan, and Allah loves the *Iman* of the righteous more than He hates the disbelief of Shaytan. Hence, Allah loved the existence of everything that He created, and that is why He brought it into existence. Since Allah hates what is purely or mostly harmful, He does not bring it into existence (see *Qa'idah fi al-Mahabbah* by Ibn Taymiyyah).

Love is also the motive behind all of our actions. Each step we take is to secure what we love, directly or indirectly. Whatever we hate, we hate because we love its opposite. Without love, we would not hate. Ibn Taymiyyah رَحِمَهُ ٱللَّهُ wrote:

فلا يوجد البغض إلا لمحبة

قاعدة في المحبة (ص٩)

Hate exists because of love.

Qa'idah fi al-Mahabbah (p. 9)

We love life, health, family, money, and we run away from their opposites: death, sickness, loneliness, and poverty. Love is the primary emotion, and hate is subsidiary to it: we hate only to attain, complete, and preserve what we love. So as it turns out, all movement in this universe—what Allah does and what we do—is based on love. Ibn Taymiyyah رَحِمَهُ ٱللَّهُ wrote:

أصل كل فعل وحركة في العالم من الحب...المحبة أصل كل أمر موجود.

قاعدة في المحبة (ص٧-٩)

The basis of every act and movement in the world is from love ... Love is the basis of everything in existence.

Qa'idah fi al-Mahabbah (pp. 7–9)

Imagine that you are living in a world of love! Whatever happens, or does not, is linked to Allah's love and bears its mark. It is blissful and comforting to feel that we are living in a world surrounded by love. If it rains, if it snows, if it is morning or evening, everything moves because Allah loves it, or it is leading us to His love. Even what we hate: Allah allows it because it leads to what He loves. If we see a wrong, we should change it, for Allah does not love evil. He loves our righteous reactions against evil. That is the wisdom behind the presence of evil. If there are things we cannot change and yet hate, our awareness of Allah's love rescues us. We know that Allah put it there because it leads to something wonderful. When something is out of our control, we let it flow and notice the beauty in it or that will come from it. We accept the Will of Allah because we love Him. When we see a world dominated by love, we are much more likely to act with love.

Religion and worship are also founded on love. Linguistically, both worship (*ibadah*) and religion (*din*) carry the meaning of submission, surrender, and humility. But it is not done out of subjugation and terror. Worship (*ibadah*) is defined as the utmost love that brings complete submission (*Jami' al-Masa'il* by Ibn Taymiyyah vol. 9, p. 177) (see also the *Introduction* and *Appendix I*). This means that both love and submission are the pillars of worshiping Allah. Loving Allah without listening to Him is obviously not worship. Listening to Him without love, like begrudgingly obeying a tyrannical king, is not worship. Submission to Allah must happen out of choice, and this choice is love (*Qa'idah fi al-Mahabbah* by Ibn Taymiyyah). People worship whatever they worship out of love. Allah said:

وَمِنَ ٱلنَّاسِ مَن يَتَّخِذُ مِن دُونِ ٱللَّهِ أَندَادًا يُحِبُّونَهُمْ كَحُبِّ ٱللَّهِ ۖ وَٱلَّذِينَ ءَامَنُوٓا۟ أَشَدُّ حُبًّا لِّلَّهِ ۗ... ﴿١٦٥﴾

And among people are those who adopt rivals besides Allah, loving them as they love Allah. But those who believe love Allah more.

Al-Baqarah (Q2:165)

They turn them into rivals and equals to Allah by loving them as much as they love Allah. This is Shirk in love (associating partners with Allah in love). Ibn al-Qayyim رَحِمَهُ ٱللَّهُ wrote commenting on this *ayah*:

أَصْلُ الشِّرْكِ بِاللَّهِ الإِشْرَاكُ به فِي الْمَحَبَّةِ

الداء والدواء لابن القيم(دار عالم الفوائد ص٤٣٩)

The basis of Shirk is associating others with Him in love.

Al-Da' wa al-Dawa' (Dar 'Alam al-Fawa'id, p. 439)

The foundation of all Shirk is loving another as much as Allah or more. And the foundation of Tawhid is loving Allah more than any other. As the *ayah* affirms, the believers love Allah more than the people of Shirk love His rivals. And how could anyone besides Allah be loved as much as He? Who has the qualities, perfection, and generosity to merit similar love? Who grants as many favors as He? Who helps in distress as He? Who attracts the hearts to Him as He does? This is why the believers could reach such heights in loving Him that no disbeliever could reach with false rivals.

Since loving Allah is the foundation of Tawhid, Allah loves it the most. And since Shirk detracts from this love, it is the most hated to Him. Ibn al-Qayyim رَحِمَهُ ٱللَّهُ remarked:

الشرك أبغض الأشياء إليه لأنه ينقص هذه المحبة ويجعلها بينه وبين من أشرك به

طريق الهجرتين (ص٥٢٣)

Shirk is what He hates most because it decreases this love and divides it between Him and the one whom they associate with Him.

Tariq al-Hijratayn (p. 532)

And because of that, the most beloved names to Allah are the ones that express Tawhid. The Prophet ﷺ said:

«أحبُّ الأسماءِ إلى اللهِ عبدُ اللهِ وعبدُ الرحمنِ.»

رواه أبو داود (٤٩٥٠) وصححه الألباني (صحيح أبي داود ٤٩٥٠)

The most beloved names to Allah are Abdullah and Abdurrahman.

Reported by Abu Dawud (4950) and al-Albani declared it sahih (*Sahih Abi Dawud*, 4950)

The basis of all religions, true or false, is love. No one prays, bows, prostrates, obeys, and sacrifices what is dear to them except to someone that they love and esteem, someone closer to their heart than any other. The core of the worship of Allah is for Him to be the most beloved and the greatest in the heart, with actions that reflect this love. This is the essence of Tawhid and Islam. All the Quran revolves around creating, strengthening, and preserving this love until it is greater than any other love (*Al-Da' wa al-Dawa'*, p. 464). Ibn al-Qayyim رَحِمَهُ ٱللَّهُ added:

والمقصود من الخلق والأمر إنما هو هذه المحبة وهى أول دعوة الرسل وآخر كلام العبد المؤمن الذى إذا مات عليه دخل الجنة اعترافه وإقراره بهذه المحبة وإفراد الرب تعالى بها فهو أول ما يدخل به فى الإسلام وآخر ما يخرج به من الدنيا إلى الله وجميع الأعمال كالأدوات والآلات لها وجميع المقامات وسائل إليها وأسباب لتحصيلها وتكميلها وتحصينها من الشوائب والعلل فهى قطب رحى السعادة وروح الإيمان وساق شجرة الإسلام

طريق الهجرتين لابن القيم (دار عالم الفوائد ص٦٤٣)

And the goal of creation and [Allah's] commands is the love [of Allah]. It is the beginning of the da'wah of the Messengers and the last statement of a believing slave [of Allah] who if he dies upon it, his admission and confession of this love and its sole dedication to Allah admit him into Jannah. It is the first thing that enters one into Islam, and the last thing one exits with from this world to meet Allah. And all actions are tools and means for it, and all stations [of Iman] are means and causes to attain it, complete it, and protect it from impurities

> and defects. It is the pillar of happiness, the soul of Iman, and the trunk of the tree of Islam.
>
> *Tariq al-Hijratayn* (p. 643)

Loving Allah is why He created us all, why He made this world. Allah said:

وَمَا خَلَقْتُ ٱلْجِنَّ وَٱلْإِنسَ إِلَّا لِيَعْبُدُونِ ٥٦

And I did not create the Jinn and humans except to worship Me.

Adh-Dhariyat (Q51:56)

Remember that worship (*ibadah*) is built on utmost love? Our creation and the creation of the universe we inhabit is our incredible opportunity to know Allah, freely choose Him over all others, and to love Him with every cell in our body. This is a transformative love that lifts one up to a heavenly state of being before they even die, where they witness the love of Allah every single day and in everything they see and do. And when they die, it is this love that opens the Gates of Jannah for them and propels them to the highest ranks.

Hanifiyyah

The word "hanif" linguistically signifies one who turns towards something and away from another (*Mufradat Alfadh al-Quran* and *'Umdat al-Huffadh*). This word is linked in the Quran to Ibrahim عَلَيْهِ ٱلسَّلَامُ who turned to Allah and away from all falsehood. This legacy of Ibrahim عَلَيْهِ ٱلسَّلَامُ is the pure religion that Allah loves and commands all to follow. It is the religion of Islam. Allah said:

قُلْ إِنَّنِي هَدَىٰنِي رَبِّيٓ إِلَىٰ صِرَٰطٍ مُّسْتَقِيمٍ دِينًا قِيَمًا مِّلَّةَ إِبْرَٰهِيمَ حَنِيفًا ۚ وَمَا كَانَ مِنَ ٱلْمُشْرِكِينَ ١٦١

Say, "Indeed, my Rabb has guided me to a straight path–a correct

religion—the way of Ibrahim, inclining toward truth. And he was not among those who associated others with Allah."
Al-An'am (Q6:161)

Tawhid cleanses the heart from all attachments except to Allah. It is based on the recognition that there is no real deity but Allah, that no one has any power except Allah, and that no one deserves to be worshipped but Him. It develops a special bond with Allah, where He is the most beloved. Ibn Taymiyyah رَحِمَهُ ٱللَّهُ wrote:

اللَّهُ فَطَرَ عِبَادَهُ عَلَى الْحَنِيفِيَّةِ مِلَّةِ إِبْرَاهِيم وَأَصْلُهَا مَحَبَّةُ اللَّهِ وَحْدَهُ

منهاج السنن النبوية لابن تيمية (ج٥ ص٤٠٣)

Allah created His slaves upon the Hanifiyyah, the religion of Ibrahim, and its foundation is loving Allah alone.

Minhaj al-Sunnah al-Nabawiyyah (vol. 5, p. 403)

When it comes to our relationship with Him, the religion that Allah loves is one that affirms His Oneness (in creation, in worship, and in His Names and Attributes) and supremacy, especially as the Supremely Beloved. This love made the sacrifices of Ibrahim عَلَيْهِ ٱلسَّلَامُ possible. No one would attempt to kill his only son unless he loved the One who commanded it more. When Allah saw this love in the heart of His beloved and his willingness to make this great sacrifice, Allah rescinded His command. The goal was not for a man to slaughter his son but for him to slaughter other loves in his heart until Allah's love was supreme. This is the Tawhid of Ibrahim عَلَيْهِ ٱلسَّلَامُ.

Allah loves Ease

In our practice of Islam and interactions with others, Allah loves and desires ease. Allah said:

...يُرِيدُ ٱللَّهُ بِكُمُ ٱلْيُسْرَ وَلَا يُرِيدُ بِكُمُ ٱلْعُسْرَ... ﴿١٨٥﴾

Allah desires ease for you, not hardship.
Al-Baqarah (Q2:185)

Allah described the mission of the Prophet ﷺ as:

...وَيَضَعُ عَنْهُمْ إِصْرَهُمْ وَٱلْأَغْلَٰلَ ٱلَّتِي كَانَتْ عَلَيْهِمْ... ﴿١٥٧﴾

And he relieves them of their burden and the shackles that were on them.
Al-A'raf (Q7:157)

The rebellion and disobedience of past nations brought difficulty to their religion. But the final message of Islam came to guide people to ease in all of their affairs and rescue humanity from burden. Highlighting this Islamic imperative, the Prophet ﷺ said:

«بُعِثتُ بالحنيفية السمحة.»

السلسلة الصحيحة (٢٩٢٤)

I was sent with the easy hanifiyyah.
Al-Silsilah al-Sahihah (2924)

There is ease and balance in Islamic laws and obligations, ease in repenting from sins, and ease in dealing with others. The following incident at the time of the Prophet ﷺ illustrates this:

بالَ أعْرابِيٌّ في المَسْجِدِ فثارَ إلَيْهِ النّاسُ لِيَقَعُوا به فقالَ لهمْ رَسولُ اللَّهِ ﷺ «دَعُوهُ وأَهْرِيقُوا على بَوْلِهِ ذَنُوبًا مِن ماءٍ أوْ سَجْلًا مِن ماءٍ فإنَّما بُعِثْتُمْ مُيَسِّرِينَ ولَمْ تُبْعَثُوا مُعَسِّرِينَ.»

رواه البخاري (٦١٢٨)

A bedouin urinated in the masjid, so people rushed to beat him. The Prophet ﷺ said to them, «Leave him [until he is done] and pour a bucket of water over his urine. You were sent to make things easy and were not sent to make things difficult.»
Reported by al-Bukhari (6128)

Religious ease and kindness attract the hearts to Allah and promote a pleasant practice of Islam, unlike hardship and cruelty. Allah loves those who inject ease into their interactions, especially in situations when most people do not. This includes teaching the ignorant and the foolish, responding to altercations, and financial dealings. The Prophet ﷺ said about commerce:

«إنَّ اللَّهَ يحبُّ سَمحَ البَيعِ سَمحَ الشِّراءِ سَمحَ القَضاءِ.»

رواه الترمذي(١٣١٩) وصححه الألباني (صحيح الترمذي ١٣١٩)

«Allah loves one who is affable when they sell, affable when they buy, and affable when repaying their debt.»

Reported by al-Tirmidhi (1319) and al-Albani declared it sahih (*Sahih al-Tirmidhi*, 1319)

People tend to be at their worst when there is money involved. But when one learns to love Allah more than wealth, they will be more forgiving in their interactions, knowing that bringing comfort to people is more pleasing to Allah. Since Allah loves ease, we should try to spread this ease in our daily dealings, inside and outside of our homes. Ease is found in applying the religion of Allah as it was revealed. We should always remember the following *ayah*:

...وَمَن يَتَّقِ ٱللَّهَ يَجْعَل لَّهُۥ مِنْ أَمْرِهِۦ يُسْرًا ۝٤

And the one who has taqwah of Allah, He will grant them ease in their affairs.

Al-Talaq (Q65:4)

If we follow what Allah loves and revealed, we would be choosing the best path in life. And when we bring ease to people's lives, so will Allah to ours.

Allah loves excellence

HADITH FOUR

الحديث الرابع

قال رسول الله ﷺ «إِنَّ اللهَ يُحِبُّ إذا عَمِلَ أَحَدُكُم عَمَلا أنْ يُتْقِنَهُ.»

رواه البيهقي في شعب الإيمان (٤٩٢٩) وحسنه الألباني (صحيح الجامع ١٨٨٠ وانظر الصحيحة ١١١٣)

The Prophet ﷺ said, «Allah loves that when one of you does something, that they perfect it.»

Reported by al-Bayhaqi in Shuʿab al-Iman (4929) and al-Albani declared it hasan (Sahih al-Jamiʿ, 1880 and al-Sahihah, 1113)

Commentary

Allah perfected and beautified creation out of mercy and love. One of the paths of attaining Allah's love is to perfect our deeds, the worldly and the otherworldly ones.

Allah loves

Sometimes, the magnitude of Allah's love escapes us. Though we frequently read about His love in the Quran and *Hadith*, we may fail to appreciate what it means entirely. Unfortunately, some feel that Allah is uncaring and distant. Perhaps due to how they were introduced to Allah or because of a struggle in their lives, they do not feel the love of Allah. Focus on sin and punishment can magnify to displace the other important side of Allah's Mercy and Love. Our inability to process and understand pain and suffering may also lead us to the wrong conclusions. It is vital that we have a deeper appreciation of who Allah is, especially His Love and Anger.

Allah is not a vengeful God who is waiting for the next sin to destroy us. This much should be clear. He is not a God who simply punishes, hurts, or complicates our lives. He is not a God who enjoys suffering, ignores prayers, or does not care about our pain. Allah said:

مَّا يَفْعَلُ ٱللَّهُ بِعَذَابِكُمْ إِن شَكَرْتُمْ وَءَامَنتُمْ ۚ وَكَانَ ٱللَّهُ شَاكِرًا عَلِيمًا ﴿١٤٧﴾

What would Allah do with your punishment if you are thankful and believe? Indeed, Allah is Thankful and Knowing.

An-Nisa (Q4:147)

If people were grateful and faithful, there would be no punishment in this world or the next. This is why the people of Jannah live in eternal bliss. Allah did not create humanity—including you—to punish you. As the *ayah* explains, what benefit does Allah receive from punishment and pain? What He wants is peace and happiness for all of His creation. Love was the cause of our creation and is its goal.

The fact that Allah loves means that He cares. It means that Allah knows us, understands our feelings, and understands our pain and fears. He created us and knows us better than anyone else. He is the closest to us. He is always with us. He sees us and hears us when no one else can. He is with our thoughts and our wishes when no one else can hear them. He truly knows us better than anyone else.

Allah's love means that Allah wants the best for us. This is why He repeatedly informed us in the Quran of how to get to Jannah. This is why He revealed a way of life that protects us from harm and leads us to happiness. Allah clearly outlined the path of happiness and warned us against the plots of Shaytan. He sent down book after book, and sent Messengers, some of whom died for the sake of delivering this message. Why would the One who had no beginning and has no end, the Almighty, bother with all of this if He simply did not care? Do we think the richest and strongest person on earth cares about us? We are nothing to them. Allah's greatness is unimaginable in comparison. Yet, He deeply cares.

The names of Allah testify to this. Allah is the All-Hearing and Seeing, He is the One who knows what is hidden deep inside our hearts. He is the Most-Forgiving, the One who repeatedly accepts repentance, and al-Rahman (One full of mercy). He is al-Wadud: the One who loves immensely and is loved immensely. And it is out of His love that He gave love to His creation. Allah said:

إِنَّ ٱلَّذِينَ ءَامَنُوا۟ وَعَمِلُوا۟ ٱلصَّٰلِحَٰتِ سَيَجْعَلُ لَهُمُ ٱلرَّحْمَٰنُ وُدًّا ﴿٩٦﴾

Those who believe and do good deeds, Allah will grant them love.

Maryam (Q19:96)

Al-Wadud will surround them with love, so that everyone loves them. This what He did with Musa عَلَيْهِ ٱلسَّلَامُ. Allah said:

...وَأَلْقَيْتُ عَلَيْكَ مَحَبَّةً مِّنِّي وَلِتُصْنَعَ عَلَىٰ عَيْنِيٓ ﴿٣٩﴾

And I bestowed upon you love from Me so that you will be brought up under My Eye.

Taha (Q20:39)

This means that anyone who saw Musa عَلَيْهِ ٱلسَّلَامُ, loved him immediately. This is how Allah protected and took care of this child. If Allah loves you, hearts cannot resist you. When Allah's love is around you, it pulls everyone to you. Imagine walking on this earth and feeling this love of Allah. Imagine how different this life would be if we start sharing this love with others.

It is true that Allah punishes and gets angry. This is part of balanced understanding of who Allah is, and we need this to guide our behavior. But some unduly focus on Allah's punishment and anger. But as Ibn Taymiyyah رَحِمَهُ ٱللَّهُ wrote:

ليس في أسماء الله الحسنى اسم يتضمن صفة الغضب والعذاب ولا في صفاته صفة تقتضي ذلك.

جامع المسائل (ج٨ ص٥٢)

> Among Allah's Most Excellent Names, there is no name [of His] that has the quality of anger and punishment, and there is no attribute among His attributes that entails this.
>
> *Jami' al-Masa'il* (vol. 8, p. 52)

What he meant was that though you will find among His names the Most Forgiving, the Most Patient, the One who rewards abundantly, and the Merciful, you will not find names such as the angry and the punisher. This is so because mercy, forgiveness, patience, and thankfulness are constant and dominant attributes of His. Anger and punishment happen only when there is a reason, and are thus not constant. They are subordinate to and are much less frequent than His Mercy and Forgiveness. Allah forgives much more than He punishes, and He is Merciful a lot more than He is angry. And if sins were to cease, Allah would not be angry at all. His Mercy, on the other hand, is uninterrupted, even with the most rebellious and ungrateful.

As for the name "the avenger" (al-muntaqim), reported in a *hadith* by al-Tirmidhi and frequently seen on wall-hanging-posters and tapestries of the Ninety-Nine Names of Allah, Ibn Taymiyyah رَحِمَهُ ٱللَّهُ wrote (p. 53)—agreeing with al-Tirmidhi رَحِمَهُ ٱللَّهُ—that the enumeration of the Names is weak, not an original part of the *hadith* but an addition from one of the narrators. In other words, the listing of all those names did not come from the Prophet ﷺ and he did not declare "the avenger" to be a name of Allah. Allah, indeed, has Ninety-Nine names, but the authentic *hadith* does not specify them. Vengeance is not a constant or dominant attribute of Allah.

But love is. And the nature of Allah's love is unique. We love—out of human weakness and need—expecting some benefit. It is Allah alone who loves without expecting or receiving any benefit from humanity (see also *Appendix I*). The difference between the two types of love should dismiss any anthropomorphic concerns over ascribing love to Allah. Some, imagining love only in human terms, reinterpret Allah's love to mean His pleasure and blessings. They imagine love as blushing cheeks, racing heartbeats, and troubled minds. But Allah's love is free from human deficiencies. Allah's love is real and befits His Majesty and Perfection. Allah's love is as unique as He is.

As we explore loving Allah in more depth, we should remember that we cannot approach Allah through love alone. Such would be a distorted relationship. Loving Allah as we do a spouse or a friend removes an integral part of worship: esteem. Esteem helps us remember the majesty of Allah and stay clear of His prohibitions. Love alone, without respect, turns Allah into an equal in a permissive relationship that fears no adverse consequences despite what it does. Such love is self-indulgent, a license to do what we desire, not what He wants. As much as this misguided love is corruptive when it exists among humans, it is extraordinarily corruptive between humans and Allah. Ibn al-Qayyim رَحِمَهُ ٱللَّهُ wrote:

أن المحبة المجردة لا توجب هذا الأثر ما لم تقترن بإجلال المحبوب وتعظيمه فإذا قارنها الإجلال والتعظيم أوجبت هذا الحياءَ والطاعة وإلا فالمحبة الخالية عنهما إنما توجب نوع أنس وانبساط وتذكر واشتياق ولهذا يتخلف عنها أثرها وموجبها ويفتش العبد قلبه فيرى نوع محبة لله ولكن لا تحمله على ترك معاصيه

وسبب ذلك تجردها عن الإجلال والتعظيم فما عمر القلب شيء كالمحبة المقترنة بإجلال الله وتعظيمه.

طريق الهجرتين (ص٢٧١-٢٧٢)

Love alone does not produce this effect [i.e. avoiding sin] unless it combines with esteeming the Beloved and glorifying Him. When it is combined with esteem and glorification, it necessarily produces shyness and obedience. Otherwise, love that is free from those two only leads to proximity, cheer, remembrance, and longing. And this is why it is not followed by its effect and consequence, and one searches their heart and sees in it some love for Allah but it does not move them to avoid sins. And the reason is that it is free from esteem and glorification. Nothing makes the heart thrive like love that is combined with esteeming Allah and glorifying Him.

Tariq al-Hijratayn (pp. 271–272)

If one only wants to love Allah, they will not be able to follow His commands. But if they love Him with respect and awe, then their relationship with Allah will be close, balanced, and productive.

Allah perfected creation

When you look at Allah's creation, you will find in it clear evidence of His Mercy and Wisdom. And you will also find clear signs of His love. Allah said:

﴿ ٱلَّذِيٓ أَحۡسَنَ كُلَّ شَيۡءٍ خَلَقَهُۥۖ... ٧ ﴾

The One who perfected everything He created.

As-Sajdah (Q32:7)

This is similar to the other *ayah*:

﴿ ...صُنۡعَ ٱللَّهِ ٱلَّذِيٓ أَتۡقَنَ كُلَّ شَيۡءٍۚ... ٨٨ ﴾

This is the creation of Allah who perfected everything.
An-Naml (Q27:88)

There is beauty, complexity, and balance in nature. Each creature is guided to what benefits it, given what it needs, and is part of an ecosystem that delicately sustains other creatures. This is clear evidence of Allah's care. And this care is a sure sign of His love. If it is hard to see this, consider the following. If you find a product made with a lot of care (e.g. woodwork or a painting), and this care is not out of compulsion or financial need, what do we typically assume about the motive behind the work? We assume that the maker loves their work and cares for the product, and this is why they took the time to create this beautiful piece. This is why the beauty we find around us is a sign of Allah's care and love.

The Ihsan of Allah in His creation has two dimensions to it: perfection and beauty. Both are seen in how everything is created for a purpose and is equipped to pursue this purpose. Consider the differences between land and sea animals, and within each group, and you will see that Allah varied their creation to fit their environment and function. Each fits perfectly in their environment as part of Allah's grand design. And each is beautiful in its own way. Ibn Taymiyyah رَحِمَهُ ٱللَّهُ wrote:

فعل الله كله حسن جميل.

مجموع الفتاوى (ج١١ ص٣٥١)

The actions of Allah are all good and beautiful.

Majmu' al-Fatawa (vol. 11, p. 351)

You can see beauty and care in everything that Allah created. Even when there is pain or harm, there is always a greater benefit than harm, in the short and long term. Since Allah's actions always lead to beauty, all of His actions are beautiful.

Allah's creation varies in its beauty. Some parts are more beautiful than others. But all are beautiful in the sense that Allah made them out of nothing, made them well, made them suited to their function, and made them serve a good end. Even when we notice a "flaw," we should remember that it is never devoid of beauty. It is truly a gift to live while sensing beauty in everything that surrounds us. Consider the following *hadith*.

تَبعَ النبيُّ صلّى اللهُ عليهِ وسلَّمَ رجلًا من ثقيفٍ حتى هرولَ في أَثَرِهِ حتى أخذَ بثوبِهِ فقال «ارفعْ إزارَكَ» فكشفَ الرجلُ عن رُكبتَيْهِ فقال: يا رسولَ اللهِ إني أَحنفُ وتصطكُّ ركبتايَ. فقال رسولُ اللهِ صلّى اللهُ عليهِ وسلَّمَ «كلُّ خلقِ اللهِ عزَّ وجلَّ حَسَنٌ» قال: ولم يُرَ ذلكَ الرجلُ إلا وإزارُهُ إلى أنصافِ ساقيه حتى ماتَ.

رواه أحمد (١٩٤٧٢) وصححه الألباني (السلسلة الصحيحة ١٤٤١) وشعيب الأرناؤوط

The Prophet ﷺ followed a man from [the tribe] of Thaqif until he ran after him and until he grabbed him by his clothes and said to him, «Lift up your lower garment.» The man uncovered his knees and said, "O Messenger of Allah, my legs are crooked, and my knees collide." The Messenger ﷺ said, «All the creation of Allah is beautiful.» The man continued to lift up his lower garment to the middle of his leg until he died.

Reported by Ahmad (19472) and and Shu'ayb al-Arna'ut and al-Albani declared it sahih (*al-Silsilah al-Sahihah*, 1441)

What the man saw as a flaw that had to be hidden, the Prophet ﷺ saw as a beautiful creation of Allah. It is beautiful because no one has the power to make something like this except Allah. These "flawed' legs still carried the man, still functioned the way Allah intended for them to work, and were witness to the Power and Wisdom of Allah who creates what He wants as He wants. When we discover the beauty in everything around us—the inherent beauty in everything that Allah makes—we become more grateful and content. When we see the beauty in everything around us, our life becomes more beautiful and tranquil. This should not drive us, however, to violate Allah's laws in the name of beauty. The fact that my body is beautiful should not push me to expose it and share it with everyone in the name of loving myself and being proud of who I am and how I look. Some beauty needs to be concealed or be off-limits, especially if it were to remain beautiful. A pristine area loses its beauty when many legs trample it. The Creator of all beauty is the One who knows what is truly beautiful and how it can stay beautiful.

Perfecting our actions

Worshipping Allah and knowing Him better through His Names and Attributes lead to adopting the noble and beautiful qualities in them. As we have seen, Allah is Beautiful and loves beauty. He is Forgiving and He loves those who forgive. And Allah perfected creation, and one path towards Allah's love is perfecting what we do. Ibn al-Qayyim رَحِمَهُ ٱللَّهُ explained that there is a link between Allah's love and His Names. He said:

وهذا شأن اسمائه الحسنى أحب خلقه اليه من اتصف بموجَبها وأبغضهم اليه من اتصف باضدادها.

عدة الصابرين (دار عالم الفوائد ص٥٤٤)

> And this is the case with His Most Excellent Names: the most beloved of His creation to Him are the ones who adopt their consequent qualities, and the ones whom He hates the most are those who adopt its opposite qualities.
>
> *'Uddat al-Sabirin* (p. 544)

For example, since Allah is Merciful, He loves the merciful and hates cruelty and those who choose to be cruel. Learning the Names and Attributes of Allah not only lets us know more about Allah but also guides us to what He loves.

Perfecting what we do means doing it well and in the most beautiful way, including the deeds of the Hereafter and deeds of this world. Perfecting the deeds of the Hereafter, like *Salah* and fasting, asks us to observe their conditions, times, pillars, recommended acts, and so on. In other words, to know how to do them and to value them enough to do them well. It also includes adding beauty to this performance: the beauty of sincerity, devotion, sensing the closeness of Allah while doing them, learning from them, not seeing them as a burden but an opportunity, asking Allah to accept them, not harming others while doing them, and being kind and considerate while performing them.

It is clear why perfecting the religious deeds will bring us the love of Allah. But what about our worldly deeds? Why would excelling in our engineering projects, academic papers and degrees, cleaning our homes, and any *halal* worldly task—why would this bring us Allah's love? Even how we queue in the grocery store, fix a sink, paint a house, cross the road, drive on the highway, and park our vehicles? When we perfect those deeds, we benefit others and remove pain and hardship; and Allah loves these who help others. When we are better parents, sons and daughters, teachers, students, researchers, lawyers, and architects, we improve people's lives. When we are better drivers and pedestrians, when we do not litter, and when we keep our homes, mosques, and cities clean, we will protect ourselves and others from harm.

The pursuit of excellence and beauty also spreads excellence and beauty. When we do what we do well, with kindness and a smile, we inspire others to do the same, and this spreads to improve the lives of everyone else they meet. Our entire society benefits as a result. We would also be sharing the blessings that Allah gave us: time, resources, and talents. This is how we thank Allah for His gifts: we use them to help everyone else.

The Islamic pursuit of excellence is different from the capitalist pursuit. While both are motivated by love, the first is driven by Allah's love whereas capitalism loves money and more of it. This is why the capitalist pursuit is not an act of Ihsan nor a true pursuit of excellence. Capitalism will lie and cheat, destroy everything in its path, and sacrifice human life and wellbeing for the sake of profit. Its achievements are an empty shell, and it will destroy what it builds in due time. Islam cultivates this life for the sake of the Hereafter. The Islamic pursuit is honest, comprehensive, merciful, and ethical. Capitalism is short sighted, cruel, empty, deceptive, and destructive. We, as individuals and nations, should be very cautious not to adopt the capitalist ethos. Our goal in life is not merely to be rich. We can be rich, but let us be rich with a conscience.

When we embark upon a task, we should remember that we have a choice. We can be careless and incompetent, and this will end up harming others, making society worse off, and earning us a sin. And society will be worse off because of us. Or, if we remember what Allah loves, we will approach it with diligence, dedication, and kindness. If we choose the first, we will make ourselves and everyone around us miserable. If we choose the second, we will be happy and Allah will love us. We cannot expect excellence from others if we are not trying to perfect what we do. And we cannot expect kindness if we are not kind.

HADITH FIVE

الحديث الخامس

Allah loves gentleness

قال رسول الله ﷺ «إِنَّ اللهَ يُحِبُّ الرِّفْقَ فِي الأَمْرِ كُلِّهِ.»

رواه البخاري (٦٠٩٣) ومسلم (٥٧٨٤) وفي رواية لمسلم (٦٧٦٦) «إِنَّ اللَّهَ رَفِيقٌ يُحِبُّ الرِّفْقَ وَيُعْطِي عَلَى الرِّفْقِ مَا لاَ يُعْطِي عَلَى الْعُنْفِ وَمَا لاَ يُعْطِي عَلَى مَا سِوَاهُ.»

The Prophet ﷺ said, «Allah loves gentleness in all matters.»

Reported by al-Bukhari (7027) and Muslim (174)

And in another narration by Muslim (6766), «Allah is Gentle and loves gentleness. And He grants through gentleness what He does not grant through harshness or anything else.»

Commentary

One of the common misconceptions about God is that He is harsh. This assessment extends to religion and the religious, conceiving of each as demanding, judgmental, and unmerciful. Yet, this is not the character of God we encounter in Islam, and it is not the feature of the religion of Islam that He revealed.

Allah is Gentle

One of the names of Allah, as the *hadith* attests, is the Gentle (Al-Rafiq). This Gentleness encompasses all of creation, as His

Mercy encompasses all. Allah has a myriad of Names that show His Care and Kindness for His creation. Another one is:

ٱللَّهُ لَطِيفٌۢ بِعِبَادِهِۦ... ﴿١٩﴾

Allah is Latif with His servants.

Ash-Shuraa (Q42:19)

Al-Latif combines the meaning of profound kindness and subtlety. Allah recognizes the most subtle of things (e.g. what is in the hearts and all secrets) and delivers His decrees in the subtlest and the gentlest of ways (e.g. relief and victory coming unexpectedly).

We observe the Gentleness of Allah in His creation and revelation. Allah answers the supplication of the distressed and removes their hardship. When everyone turns their backs on us, Allah never closes His door. When no one wants to listen to us, Allah is always there, ready to remove our pain and restore our happiness. When no one has the time to help or does not care enough to help, Allah engulfs us with His mercy and rescues us from distress. When we experience a drought, He sends down the rain, reviving the land and our hope. Allah said:

وَهُوَ ٱلَّذِي يُنَزِّلُ ٱلْغَيْثَ مِنۢ بَعْدِ مَا قَنَطُواْ وَيَنشُرُ رَحْمَتَهُۥۚ... ﴿٢٨﴾

And it is He who sends down the rain after they have lost hope and spreads His Mercy.

Ash-Shuraa (Q42:28)

Allah presented this as a living example of how He comes to our aid. He feeds us, quenches our thirst, and gives us shelter and security even when we disobey and upset Him. He multiplies the good we do by ten to seven hundred times and more, but sin is written as one and is erased once we repent. He created us for Heaven, prepared it for us, and sent Messengers and books to invite us to it. He keeps the door of repentance open until the last moment before our death.

We see evidence of Allah's Gentleness even in times of

hardship. It is because of hardship that we return to Allah and re-assess our lives. It is because of hardship that we start to notice and appreciate the rest of Allah's blessings. When we contemplate the extent of our difficulty, we realize that it could have been much worse, but Allah was Gentle. At the very moment of suffering, we feel Allah's proximity and care when we call on Him from our hearts. We then know—not theoretically but practically and emotionally—that He is always there, and His door is always open. Hardship itself carries in it signs of His Care and Love.

Some complain about Allah when they experience loss. They see in life's difficulties evidence of the Creator's harshness. But they forget that what they lost was a gift from Allah: they had it in the first place because Allah gave it to them. They forget that Allah's blessings are like a flood that never stops. At any point in time and even during dark times, we are enjoying innumerable blessings. In our distress and desperation, we tend to focus on the negative until it grows to occupy our entire world. But if we were to step back, we would see how minuscule it is compared to the blessings of Allah and what awaits us in the Hereafter.

Allah told us in His revelation that this life is a test. Anyone who has lived long enough—whether they believe in God or not—will attest to the difficulties of this life. But the question is, do these difficulties preclude Allah's Mercy and Gentleness? The fact is that they are part of it. Allah is Infinite. Knowing Allah well requires experiences that include these tests: having to choose between right and wrong and the consequences that follow. How would one begin to comprehend the extent of Allah's Forgiveness, Patience, and Mercy without sin and rebellion? How could we have a glimpse of the extent of His justice until we see how He treats those who oppose Him? How could we learn justice and forgiveness until we are faced with situations that demand them? This earthly journey is a gift from Allah. It allows us to grow, and it brings us closer to the Divine in ways that would not be possible otherwise.

Tests and hardship also mold us to be better humans. They

teach us the meaning of loss and suffering. As a result, we set out determined to help others because we understand their pain. These challenges teach us compassion, mercy, altruism, humility, and many other virtues. This is learning through practice. We may think that we understand patience, forgiveness, and sacrifice—to give but a few examples—but theoretical knowledge is quite different from practical experience. It is through practice that we test (and improve) our character and gain a fuller understanding of virtue.

Those with insight and wisdom will detect in hardship salvation from worldly intoxication and attachments. As long as things are going well in our lives, we will stray away from Allah, running after the trivial in this world. It is an intoxication mightier than any other intoxication—hard to resist. If we lack the will and wisdom to wake up voluntarily, Allah sends us a problem. And when we encounter a difficulty, we wake up: we pause to reassess our life and run back to Allah.

When we know that Allah is Gentle, we will start seeing reflections of His Gentleness in everything around us. We will love Him and expect nothing but the best from Him. The following is a moving story about how knowing Allah well makes a world of difference.

عَنْ حُمَيْدٍ قَالَ: كَانَ لِيَ ابْنُ أُخْتٍ مُرَهَّقٌ فَمَرِضَ فَأَرْسَلَتْ إِلَيَّ أُمُّهُ فَأَتَيْتُهَا فَإِذَا هِيَ عِنْدَ رَأْسِهِ تَبْكِي فَقَالَ يَا خَالِي مَا يُبْكِيهَا قُلْتُ مَا تَعْلَمُ مِنْكَ قَالَ أَلَيْسَ إِنَّمَا تَرْحَمُنِي قُلْتُ بَلَى قَالَ فَإِنَّ اللَّهَ أَرْحَمُ بِي مِنْهَا فَلَمَّا مَاتَ أَنْزَلْتُهُ الْقَبْرَ مَعَ غَيْرِي فَذَهَبْتُ أُسَوِّي لَبِنَهُ فَاطَّلَعْتُ فِي اللَّحْدِ فَإِذَا هُوَ مَدُّ بَصَرِي فَقُلْتُ لِصَاحِبِي رَأَيْتَ مَا رَأَيْتُ قَالَ نَعَمْ فَلْيُهْنِئْكَ ذَاكَ فَظَنَنْتُ أَنَّهُ بِالْكَلِمَةِ الَّتِي قَالَهَا.

رواه ابن أبي الدنيا في كتاب المحتضرين (ص٣٥)

Humayd reported saying: I had an ignorant nephew who got sick, so his mother sent for me and [when I came] she was next to his head crying. [My nephew] asked me, "Uncle, why is

> she crying?" I replied, "Because of your condition." He asked, "Is she not doing it out of mercy?" I replied, "Yes." He then said, "Allah is more Merciful to me than she is." So when he died, I and another man lowered him into his grave, and as I was about to start placing the bricks [to seal the side grave], I looked in the side grave, and it was spacious as far as the eye could see. So I asked my companion, "Do you see what I see?" He replied, "Yes. Be happy about it!" So I suppose this was because of that statement [the boy] uttered [before his death].
> *Kitab al-Muhtadirin* by Ibn Abi al-Dunya (p. 35)

He may have lived less than the ideal life, and may have done things that Allah hated. But what he had was a connection to Allah that refused to die or be diminished. He knew, nay he believed with all of his heart, that Allah is more merciful than his own mother. So, he met Allah with a heart full of faith and hope. And Allah wanted to honor him, and so He showed those two men a sign: a spacious grave indicative of Allah's pleasure. This is how Gentle and Loving Allah is. We just have to believe.

Islamic Law

Contrary to what some believe, Islamic law is not difficult and restrictive. If Allah is Gentle and loves gentleness, then the law He revealed will reflect this gentleness. We have seen in *Hadith Three* that Allah desires ease, not hardship. All the prohibitions in Islam are there to save and protect us, for everything that Allah prohibited is either harmful or leads to harm. And all that Allah obligated is necessary to establish a good and balanced life and edify us individually and collectively. All of Allah's commands and prohibitions are within the capacity of the average individual. And with all that, Islamic law has an internal mechanism for ease. In cases of necessity and incapacity, exemptions kick in to allow prohibitions that cannot be avoided and reduce or drop obligations that are hard to perform. Allah loves it when we take advantage of His allowances and exemptions. The Prophet ﷺ said:

«إِنَّ اللَّهَ يُحِبُّ أَنْ تُؤْتَى رُخَصُهُ كَمَا يَكْرَهُ أَنْ تُؤْتَى مَعْصِيَتُهُ.»

رواه أحمد (٥٩٧١) وصححه الألباني (صحيح الترغيب ١٠٥٩) وعند ابن حبان (٣٥٦٨) والبيهقي (٥٤١٥) (إِنَّ اللَّهَ يُحِبُّ أَنْ تُؤْتَى رُخَصُهُ كَمَا يحب أَنْ تُؤْتَى عزائمه) صححه الألباني (صحيح الترغيب ١٠٦٠)

«Allah loves that His exemptions be followed as He hates for what He prohibited to be committed.»

Reported by Ahmad and al-Albani declared it sahih (*Sahih al-Targhib*, 1059). And in another narration, «Allah loves for His exemptions to be followed as He loves for His commands to be followed.» Reported by Ibn Hibban (3568) and al-Bayhaqi (5415) and in *Sahih al-Targhib* (1060)

Why does Allah love that His exemptions be taken advantage of as He loves following His commands and avoiding His prohibitions? First, they are all from Allah, and the exemptions are His gift to us. He also loves ease, and He wants us to be comfortable in our practice of Islam. In addition, our consistency in worship and love for it will be adversely affected if the exemptions were not followed. When changing circumstances introduce new burdens, regular practice becomes too difficult to maintain. If this burden is not alleviated, practitioners will naturally come to a point where they cannot continue and will develop negative feelings towards Allah's command. So, in essence, the Law has to respond to people's needs to survive, and this is what the ease of exemptions does.

This, of course, should not be subject to whim or convenience. It should be a genuine effort to realize the Will of Allah and maintain a righteous balance between revelation and reality.

Allah loves gentleness

Allah is so Gentle that He commands gentleness between people and loves those who embrace it. When we embrace gentleness, it turns everything beautiful. The Prophet ﷺ said:

«إِنَّ الرِّفْقَ لَا يَكُونُ فِي شَيْءٍ إِلَّا زَانَهُ وَلَا يُنْزَعُ مِنْ شَيْءٍ إِلَّا شَانَهُ.»

رواه مسلم (٢٥٩٤)

Gentleness adorns anything that it is added to, and blemishes anything it is removed from.

Reported by Muslim (2594)

Gentleness is the secret ingredient that enhances and beautifies everything it touches. It is the quickest key to people's hearts. Teaching is far more effective with kindness, advice is more likely to be accepted, discussions are more fruitful, and relationships prosper. But when it is missing, our relationships suffer, our advice gets rejected, and our discussions turn into quarrels and fights. If we could only insert more gentleness into our words and actions, we and everyone around us would have better lives.

Gentleness is the quickest way to reach our objectives. Allah grants through it what would not be possible without it. Consider the following incident.

دَخَلَ رَهْطٌ مِنَ الْيَهُودِ عَلَى رَسُولِ اللَّهِ صَلَّى اللهُ عَلَيْهِ وَسَلَّمَ فَقَالُوا: السَّامُ عَلَيْكُمْ قَالَتْ عَائِشَةُ: فَفَهِمْتُهَا؛ فَقُلْتُ: وَعَلَيْكُمُ السَّامُ وَاللَّعْنَةُ، قَالَتْ: فَقَالَ رَسُولُ اللَّهِ صَلَّى اللهُ عَلَيْهِ وَسَلَّمَ «مَهْلًا يَا عَائِشَةُ إِنَّ اللَّهَ يُحِبُّ الرِّفْقَ فِي الْأَمْرِ كُلِّهِ» فَقُلْتُ: يَا رَسُولَ اللَّهِ أَوَلَمْ تَسْمَعْ مَا قَالُوا قَالَ رَسُولُ اللَّهِ صَلَّى اللهُ عَلَيْهِ وَسَلَّمَ «قَدْ قُلْتُ وَعَلَيْكُمْ.»

رواه البخاري (٦٠٢٤)

A group of Jews came to the Messenger ﷺ and said, "Assam [death] be upon you." 'A'ishah understood what they said and replied, "Death and curse be upon you." So the Messenger ﷺ said, «Be patient, O A'ishah. Allah loves gentleness in all matters.» She said, "O Messenger of Allah, did you not hear what they said?" The Messenger ﷺ replied, «I already said, "And upon you."»

Reported by al-Bukhari (6024)

And in another narration:

أَنَّ يَهُودَ أَتَوُا النَّبِيَّ صَلَّى اللهُ عَلَيْهِ وَسَلَّمَ فَقَالُوا: السَّامُ عَلَيْكُمْ. فَقَالَتْ عَائِشَةُ: عَلَيْكُمْ وَلَعَنَكُمُ اللَّهُ وَغَضِبَ اللَّهُ عَلَيْكُمْ، قَالَ «مَهْلًا يَا عَائِشَةُ عَلَيْكِ بِالرِّفْقِ وَإِيَّاكِ وَالعُنْفَ وَالفُحْشَ.» قَالَتْ: أَوَلَمْ تَسْمَعْ مَا قَالُوا؟ قَالَ «أَوَلَمْ تَسْمَعِي مَا قُلْتُ؟ رَدَدْتُ عَلَيْهِمْ فَيُسْتَجَابُ لِي فِيهِمْ وَلاَ يُسْتَجَابُ لَهُمْ فِيَّ.»

رواه البخاري (٦٠٣٠)

A group of Jews came to the Prophet ﷺ and said, "Assam [death] be upon you." A'ishah replied, "Upon you and may Allah curse you and be angry with you." The Messenger ﷺ said, «Be patient, O A'ishah. Be gentle and beware of harshness and coarseness.» She said, "Did you not hear what they said?" He said, «Did you not hear what I said to them? I replied to what they said. What I said to them will be accepted and what they said to me will not.»

Reported by al-Bukhari (6024)

'A'ishah رضي الله عنها had every right to be angry. After all, this is a verbal attack on the Prophet ﷺ, who is also her husband. But even in response to this blatant insult, the Prophet ﷺ did not condone harsh words or actions. His reply, "And upon you," was sufficient: if you had uttered virtue, then may that be for you; and if you chose foul language, that should return to you. This is justice. He handled their insults in the gentlest way so as not to antagonize them any further, not to give them an excuse to reject the truth, and for them to witness nobility and magnanimity firsthand. Perhaps this could change their hearts. Kindness is transformative. And if it does not convince them to embrace Islam, at least it stops further escalation of evil. He ﷺ did not have to overpower his opponent in every verbal exchange; he was confident in Allah's power that he could leave matters for Him to settle. Power is not in overpowering our opponents. He ﷺ said:

«لَيْسَ الشَّدِيدُ بِالصُّرَعَةِ إِنَّمَا الشَّدِيدُ الَّذِي يَمْلِكُ نَفْسَهُ عِنْدَ الْغَضَبِ.»

رواه البخاري (٦١١٤) ومسلم (٢٦٠٩)

«The powerful is not the one who overpowers people with his physical strength but the one who controls himself when angry.»

Reported by al-Bukhari (6114) and Muslim (2609)

What is even greater than withholding our anger is to receive insult with kindness, as he used to do ﷺ.

We, at times, seem to be lacking gentleness and kindness in our discussions and exchanges. Once we disagree with someone, we turn the issue into personal attacks and vendetta. We complicate the disagreement with harsh words, mockery, ad hominem attacks, belittling opponents, challenging motives and intentions, exaggerating mistakes, and backing the other into a corner. Our goal becomes winning at any cost and defeating the other by any means. But harsh words and insults are not the keys to a solution. The key, as the *hadith* affirms, is gentleness. It is through it that people feel respected enough to review their stance and arguments. Should this not be our goal? If we intend to reach a person's heart so they can change, we have to be gentle. Harshness will only push others to dig in their heels out of indignity and self-defense. This is why the Prophet ﷺ said:

«مَنْ يُحْرَمِ الرِّفْقَ يُحْرَمِ الْخَيْرَ.»

رواه مسلم (٢٥٩٢)

«Whoever is deprived of gentleness is deprived of good.»

Reported by Muslim (2592)

The harsh corrupt more than help, even if they happen to be preaching the truth. It is the gentle who change people and society, and it is they who earn people's love. Gentleness should find a permanent home in our households. Our family relations and interactions should be based on gentle words and acts, forgiveness, and support. The Prophet ﷺ said:

«إنَّ اللهَ إذا أحبَّ أهلَ بيتٍ أدخلَ عليهِمُ الرِّفقَ.»

صححه الألباني (صحيح الجامع ١٧٠٤)

«If Allah loves a household, He bestows gentleness upon them.»

Al-Albani declared it sahih (*Sahih al-Jami'*, 1704)

We want Allah to love us and to bless our homes. Kindness will do all that. Be gentle, and Allah will love you.

HADITH SIX

الحديث السادس

Allah loves harmony

قال رسول الله ﷺ «يا أبا أيّوب ألا أَدُلُّكَ على صدَقةٍ يُحِبُّها الله ورسوله تُصْلِحُ بينَ الناسِ إذا تَباغَضُوا وتفَاسَدوا.»

رواه الطبراني في المعجم الكبير (٣٩٢٢) وحسنه الألباني (صحيح الترغيب ٢٨٢٠)

The Prophet ﷺ said, «O Abu Ayyub, shall I not guide you to a charity that Allah and His Prophet love? Mend what is between people when they get angry and stop talking to each other.»

Reported by al-Tabarani in al-Mu'jam al-Kabir (3922) and al-Albani declared it hasan (Sahih al-Targhib, 2820)

Commentary

Allah loves it when we reconcile people. It is part of Allah's love for us and everything that benefits us.

Allah's love is the greatest

Allah loves and we love. But Allah's love is drastically different from ours. Our love is a reflection of human need. When we love, we expect a return on our love, a benefit of some sort. Allah, however, loves without gaining anything. Ibn al-Qayyim رَحِمَهُ ٱللَّهُ pointed to this difference when he wrote:

فَكُلُّ مَنْ تُحِبُّهُ مِنَ الْخَلْقِ وَيُحِبُّكَ إِنَّمَا يُرِيدُكَ لِنَفْسِهِ وَغَرَضِهِ مِنْكَ وَاللَّهُ سُبْحَانَهُ وَتَعَالَى يُرِيدُكَ لَك كَمَا فِي الْأَثَرِ الْإِلَهِيِّ «عَبْدِي كُلٌّ يُرِيدُكَ لِنَفْسِهِ وَأَنَا أُرِيدُكَ لَكَ» فَكَيْفَ لَا يَسْتَحِي الْعَبْدُ أَنْ يَكُونَ رَبُّهُ لَهُ بِهَذِهِ الْمَنْزِلَةِ وَهُوَ مُعْرِضٌ عَنْهُ مَشْغُولٌ بِحُبِّ غَيْرِهِ قَدِ اسْتَغْرَقَ قَلْبَهُ محبةُ سِوَاهُ وَأَيْضًا فَكُلُّ مَنْ تُعَامِلُهُ مِنَ الْخَلْقِ إِنْ لَمْ يَرْبَحْ عَلَيْكَ لَمْ يُعَامِلْكَ وَلَا بُدَّ لَهُ مِنْ نَوْعٍ مِنْ أَنْوَاعِ الرِّبْحِ وَالرَّبُّ تَعَالَى إِنَّمَا يُعَامِلُكَ لِتَرْبَحَ أَنْتَ عَلَيْهِ أَعْظَمَ الرِّبْحِ وَأَعْلَاهُ فَالدِّرْهَمُ بِعَشَرَةِ أَمْثَالِهِ إِلَى سَبْعِمِائَةِ ضِعْفٍ إِلَى أَضْعَافٍ كَثِيرَةٍ وَالسَّيِّئَةُ بِوَاحِدَةٍ وَهِيَ أَسْرَعُ شَيْءٍ مَحْوًا وَأَيْضًا هُوَ سُبْحَانَهُ خَلَقَكَ لِنَفْسِهِ وَخَلَقَ كُلَّ شَيْءٍ لَكَ فِي الدُّنْيَا وَالْآخِرَةِ فَمَنْ أَوْلَى مِنْهُ بِاسْتِفْرَاغِ الْوُسْعِ فِي مَحَبَّتِهِ وَبَذْلِ الْجُهْدِ فِي مَرْضَاتِهِ.

الداء والدواء (ص٥٣٦-٥٣٧)

Everyone in creation that you love and loves you wants you only for their own self [benefit] and their need from you, but Allah wants you for you[r benefit]. This is similar to the tradition where it is reported that Allah said, «My slave! All want you for their own selves [i.e. to benefit themselves], but I want you for you.» So how can one not be ashamed when this is what Allah is like for them, but they are turning their back on Him, busy loving another with a love that consumes all their heart. In addition, for everyone among creation that you deal with: if they do not profit from you, they will not interact with you. And they must receive some kind of profit. But the Rabb, the Highest, deals with you so that you receive the greatest and highest profit from Him: one dirham [spent] is multiplied ten times to seven hundred times to a lot more, but sin is recorded as one, and it is the fastest thing to erase. And He, glory be to Him, created you for Himself and created everything in this world

> and the Hereafter for you. So does anyone other than Him truly deserve maximum love and maximum effort in pleasing?
>
> *Al-Da' wa al-Dawa'* (pp. 536–537)

We benefit from whom and what we love, and this forms the basis of human love. This is not selfish or cynical but a reflection of our inherent nature (see *Appendix I*). We are dependent beings who are constantly looking to fulfill their needs and complete what is missing in their lives. We are poor by nature, and all of our movement is an effort to feed our needs. We need to eat and drink, and so we seek and love food. We need companionship and emotional support, so we marry and have friends. We cannot be independently happy, so we search for this happiness in wealth, shopping, travel, and entertainment. Allah pointed to the essential difference between Him and us when He said:

قُلْ أَغَيْرَ ٱللَّهِ أَتَّخِذُ وَلِيًّا فَاطِرِ ٱلسَّمَٰوَٰتِ وَٱلْأَرْضِ وَهُوَ يُطْعِمُ وَلَا يُطْعَمُ... ﴿١٤﴾

Say, "Shall I take for myself a wali other than Allah, the Creator of the heavens and the earth, who feeds but is not fed?"

Al-Anʿam (Q6:14)

Not needing food is the sign that He is the Self-Sufficient who does not need anyone or anything. Our dependence on food, however, points to our eternal dependence. We will always need someone else. This is why all human-to-human relationships are built on an exchange of benefits: I give but also receive. If I were to gain nothing from the other—whether physical or emotional rewards—no relationship will form or be sustained. This is true even for the noblest of human bonds. A mother derives emotional fulfillment/pleasure from her children and feels complete because of them. We receive emotional satisfaction from altruistic acts, grow as human beings, and reach our full potential. Allah offered Jannah as a reward for our good deeds because it is impossible for us to move without some benefit in return.

The love of Allah is markedly different. Allah receives no benefit at all from us; it is we who receive all the benefits. His commands and prohibitions are for our individual and communal happiness and wellbeing, and, on top of that, He rewards us. And His rewards are unlike anything a human can offer. He multiplies our good deeds beyond count, and an offense is quickly erased and forgotten when we ask for forgiveness. Unlike humans who hold grudges and refuse to forgive, Allah forgives and pardons sins as high as mountains in an instant. And He loves to forgive and take us back. The love of Allah, as Ibn al-Qayyim رَحِمَهُ ٱللَّٰهُ explained, is the best love we can ever attain because it expects no benefit in return. Many humans seek to profit at our own expense, never hesitating to harm us as long as they get what they want. Allah does not profit from us, does not hurt us with His commands, and takes care of all of our needs.

We need the love of Allah to heal us. We need the love of Allah to be able to give love. This life damages us in significant and profound ways. We look for love and acceptance, but are met with cruelty, deception, and selfishness. We take one blow after another until we are utterly exhausted. We lose trust in everything, and we start to lose hope. This world cannot assuage our fears and frustrations. It cannot satisfy our need for love. And if we keep looking for answers in the world, we will grow more desperate and cynical. It is only when we look beyond this world that we will find hope. The love of Allah transcends the limitations of this world and its pain. It is love on a whole new level, with the answer that will make us bigger than this world and its problems. The love of Allah can heal us.

Allah loves social goodwill

This is one of the realizations that help us know and love Allah more. What benefit does human harmony bring Allah? None at all. So, why does He love it? Because it is best for us. Since it helps us, Allah loves it and loves those who promote it.

There is ample evidence in the Quran and Sunnah of Allah's love for social amiability and goodwill. It is one of the main Islamic objective that underlies the Islamic message and guides its rulings.

To begin with, note the communal nature of many Islamic obligations. *Salah* takes place in mosques in congregation. The Friday prayer brings an even bigger crowd together. Fasting unites the entire Ummah in a single act of worship for a whole month. Hajj is the symbol of Muslim unity with an international gathering of the faithful. *Zakah* cements communal bonds when the rich care for the poor. If you think about it, these obligations could have been made private and individual: we each could have been left to choose the time of our fasting and Hajj, *Salah* could have been only commanded at home, and *Zakah* could not have even been obligated. But these acts of worship bring us out of our homes and countries and redirect aspects of our life so that we would socialize with other Muslims and worship with them. The congruence and synchronization of worship bring hearts together and create common realities and goals. One of the main goals of the Islamic revelation is to spread love and solidarity between people, a brotherhood and sisterhood that is nurtured by faith.

Allah commands the unity of the believers in the Quran and warns against division and infighting. For example, Allah said:

وَٱعْتَصِمُوا۟ بِحَبْلِ ٱللَّهِ جَمِيعًا وَلَا تَفَرَّقُوا۟ ۚ وَٱذْكُرُوا۟ نِعْمَتَ ٱللَّهِ عَلَيْكُمْ
إِذْ كُنتُمْ أَعْدَآءً فَأَلَّفَ بَيْنَ قُلُوبِكُمْ فَأَصْبَحْتُم بِنِعْمَتِهِۦٓ إِخْوَٰنًا وَكُنتُمْ
عَلَىٰ شَفَا حُفْرَةٍ مِّنَ ٱلنَّارِ فَأَنقَذَكُم مِّنْهَا ۗ كَذَٰلِكَ يُبَيِّنُ ٱللَّهُ لَكُمْ ءَايَٰتِهِۦ
لَعَلَّكُمْ تَهْتَدُونَ ١٠٣

Hold on all to the rope of Allah and do not divide. And remember the blessing of Allah upon you when you were enemies, and

He brought your hearts together, and you became through His blessing, brothers. And you were on the edge of a pit of the Fire, and He saved you from it. This is how Allah clarifies His ayahs to you so that you will be guided.
Ali 'Imran (Q3:103)

As the *ayah* explains, it was Islam that united the hearts of the first Muslims. It saved them from bloodshed and friction as it saved them from Hell. In fact, the two are connected. Islam removes the causes of friction and division, which happen to be the sins that Allah hates. And when the believers hold on to the rope of Allah—His revelation and obedience—they will be blessed with a love that unites their hearts. Islam cleanses our hearts, corrects our convictions, and rearranges our priorities. When we allow it to completely transform us and are born anew with *Iman*, we will abandon ignorant disagreements and embrace each other as brothers and sisters.

When the believers fight, Allah makes it an obligation on the Ummah to remove this discord and restore harmony. Allah said:

وَإِن طَآئِفَتَانِ مِنَ ٱلۡمُؤۡمِنِينَ ٱقۡتَتَلُواْ فَأَصۡلِحُواْ بَيۡنَهُمَاۖ فَإِنۢ بَغَتۡ
إِحۡدَىٰهُمَا عَلَى ٱلۡأُخۡرَىٰ فَقَٰتِلُواْ ٱلَّتِي تَبۡغِي حَتَّىٰ تَفِيٓءَ إِلَىٰٓ أَمۡرِ ٱللَّهِۚ
فَإِن فَآءَتۡ فَأَصۡلِحُواْ بَيۡنَهُمَا بِٱلۡعَدۡلِ وَأَقۡسِطُوٓاْۖ إِنَّ ٱللَّهَ يُحِبُّ
ٱلۡمُقۡسِطِينَ ٩

And if two parties of the believers fight, then reconcile them. But if one of them transgresses against the other, then fight the transgressor until it returns to the command of Allah. And if it returns, then reconcile them with justice and act justly. Indeed, Allah loves the just.
Al-Hujurat (Q49:9)

Discord is detrimental to the Hereafter and this world. It leads to countless minor and major sins and obstructs the performance of Islamic duties. Lying, deception, backbiting, suspicion, gossip, verbal insults, and physical conflicts are all the children of discord. And how could Muslims worship together or work together when they hate each other? This is why the Prophet ﷺ said:

«ألا أخبرُكم بأفضلِ من درجةِ الصيامِ والصلاةِ والصدقةِ؟» قالوا: بلى. قال «إصلاحُ ذاتِ البينِ وفسادُ ذاتِ البينِ الحالِقةُ.»

رواه أبو داود (٤٩١٩) والترمذي (٢٥٠٩) وصححه الألباني (صحيح أبي داود ٤٩١٩)

«Shall I not tell you about what is better than the rank of fasting, praying, and charity?» They said, "Yes." He said, «Mending relations. Spoiled relations is the shaver.»

Reported by Abu Dawud (4919) and al-Tirmidhi (2509) and declared sahih by al-Albani

Shaving the religion means removing it like a shaver removes hair; this is the terrible consequence of discord. An individual or community will slowly depart from Islam when they allow themselves to hate and attack each other unjustly. Just consider how we all behave. What do we do when we hate someone? We start backbiting them, suspecting them with no due cause, making fun of them just to feel better, and in time, we may be ready to hurt them. Those who mend relations save everyone from tremendous harm, and they restore love. This is why their rank is among the highest in Jannah, and this is why Allah loves them.

You and people

Now we may feel inspired and want to spread goodwill among people to reach the highest levels of Jannah. But our personal relationships need to be fixed first before we can fix other people's relationships. How we are with other people is part of the harmony we are commanded to spread. In fact, it is the basis of this harmony.

Eliminating discord from our own lives is the greater obligation. It takes precedence because it immediately affects us, and no one can fix it but us. It is not easy, I know. But we have to try, and we should ask Allah for support. Keep in mind the rewards of the Hereafter every time you think it is too difficult and you want to back out. No one is asking for or expecting perfection. With our best effort and dua, some of our relationships may remain tense and strained, and some may take a while before they recover. You do not have to be perfect before you set out to help others. But you should at least put effort into fixing your relations. When you do this, you will understand why it is important, how to go about softening people's hearts so they will reconcile, and Allah will grant you greater success in your mediation.

So, for the sake of Allah, for the sake of His love, make the first move. And be patient. The reward of Allah awaits you.

Mending relations

Reconciling people is a charity (*sadaqah*). Charity is something we give to help remove hardship and make someone's life better. Money, at times, can do this but not always. So, it is part of Allah's Mercy that He made good deeds a charity: a blessing for those of us who do not have money. We can assist by giving people advice, hope, and guiding them towards forgiveness. This should greatly inspire us to keep helping everyone in all possible ways. We will not be able to help everyone we meet with our wealth, but we can make their life better with kindness. Even a simple smile counts as charity! Is there anything easier than that? The Prophet ﷺ said:

«تبسُّمُكَ في وجهِ أخيكَ صدقةٌ.»

رواه الترمذي (١٩٥٦) وصححه الألباني (صحيح الترمذي ١٩٥٦)

You smiling in the face of your brother is a charity.

Reported by al-Tirmidhi (1956) and al-Albani declared it sahih (*Sahih al-Tirmidhi*, 1956)

One of the greatest charities that Allah loves is restoring love and peace to a relationship. When spouses are fighting and are on the brink of divorce, when the bonds between parents and their children are tested, when two dear friends have turned into bitter enemies, and when there is enmity and hatred between two Muslims rather than love, our intervention could save lives.

Loving Allah and what He loves means spreading love among His servants. The more people love each other, the more pleased Allah is. There is nothing dearer to a lover than the pleasure and happiness of their beloved. If we love Allah, we will try to make people love each other again. Spread love to receive Divine Love.

HADITH SEVEN

الحديث السابع

Allah loves the benefactors

قال رسول الله ﷺ «أَحَبُّ النَّاسِ إِلَى اللهِ تَعَالَى أَنْفَعُهُمْ لِلنَّاسِ وَأَحَبُّ الْأَعْمَالِ إِلَى اللهِ تَعَالَى سُرُورٌ تُدْخِلُهُ عَلَى مُسْلِمٍ أَوْ تَكْشِفُ عَنْهُ كُرْبَةً أَوْ تَقْضِي عَنْهُ دَيْنًا أَوْ تَطْرُدُ عَنْهُ جُوعًا وَلَأَنْ أَمْشِيَ مَعَ أَخِي فِي حَاجَةٍ أَحَبُّ إِلَيَّ مِنْ أَنْ أَعْتَكِفَ فِي هَذَا الْمَسْجِدِ - يَعْنِي مَسْجِدَ الْمَدِينَةِ شَهْرًا - وَمَنْ كَفَّ غَضَبَهُ سَتَرَ اللهُ عَوْرَتَهُ وَمَنْ كَظَمَ غَيْظَهُ وَلَوْ شَاءَ أَنْ يُمْضِيَهُ أَمْضَاهُ مَلَأَ اللهُ قَلْبَهُ رَجَاءً يَوْمَ الْقِيَامَةِ وَمَنْ مَشَى مَعَ أَخِيهِ فِي حَاجَةٍ حَتَّى يَتَهَيَّأَ لَهُ أَثْبَتَ اللهُ قَدَمَهُ يَوْمَ تَزُولُ الْأَقْدَامِ.»

رواه الطبراني في المعجم الكبير (١٣٦٤٦) وحسنه الألباني (السلسلة الصحيحة ٩٠٦)

The Prophet ﷺ said, «The most beloved of people to Allah are the most beneficial to people. And the most beloved deed to Allah is happiness you bring to a Muslim, or you remove their hardship, or you pay their debt, or chase away their hunger. And to walk with my brother to assist him in a need of his is more beloved to me than i'tikaf for a month in this Mosque, [meaning Madinah Mosque]. And if one holds back their anger, Allah will conceal their fault. And if one withholds their fury, which if they had wished to unleash it they would have been able to, Allah will fill their heart with hope on the Day of Resurrection. And if one walks with his brother to secure their need until they get it, Allah will confirm their feet on the Day when feet slip.»

Reported by al-Tabarani in al-Mu'jam al-Kabir (13646) and al-Albani declared it hasan (al-Silsilah al-Sahihah, 906)

Commentary

Allah the Beneficent

Allah gave us everything. Everything. Whatever we have, whatever we enjoy, whatever we love, Allah gave that to us. Allah said:

وَمَا بِكُم مِّن نِّعْمَةٍ فَمِنَ ٱللَّهِ... ﴿٥٣﴾

And whatever blessing you have is from Allah.
Al-Nahl (Q16:53)

Think about it. Every single thing you enjoy comes from Him. Who created beauty? Who blessed us with the ability to enjoy it? Who made humans able to love? To be loved? To feel joy? Who gave us imagination, hope, and tranquility? No one has this power but our Creator. Allah said:

ٱللَّهُ ٱلَّذِى خَلَقَ ٱلسَّمَٰوَٰتِ وَٱلْأَرْضَ وَأَنزَلَ مِنَ ٱلسَّمَآءِ مَآءً فَأَخْرَجَ بِهِۦ مِنَ ٱلثَّمَرَٰتِ رِزْقًا لَّكُمْ ۖ وَسَخَّرَ لَكُمُ ٱلْفُلْكَ لِتَجْرِىَ فِى ٱلْبَحْرِ بِأَمْرِهِۦ ۖ وَسَخَّرَ لَكُمُ ٱلْأَنْهَٰرَ ﴿٣٢﴾ وَسَخَّرَ لَكُمُ ٱلشَّمْسَ وَٱلْقَمَرَ دَآئِبَيْنِ ۖ وَسَخَّرَ لَكُمُ ٱلَّيْلَ وَٱلنَّهَارَ ﴿٣٣﴾ وَءَاتَىٰكُم مِّن كُلِّ مَا سَأَلْتُمُوهُ ۚ وَإِن تَعُدُّوا۟ نِعْمَتَ ٱللَّهِ لَا تُحْصُوهَآ ۗ إِنَّ ٱلْإِنسَٰنَ لَظَلُومٌ كَفَّارٌ ﴿٣٤﴾

It is Allah Who created the heavens and the earth and sent down rain from the sky and produced by it fruits as provision for you. And He subjected for you the ships to sail through the sea by His command and subjected for you the rivers. And He subjected for you the sun and the moon, continuously moving, and subjected for you the night and the day. And He gave you from all you asked of Him. And if you try to count the favors of Allah, you will not be able to count them. Indeed, humans are unjust and ungrateful.

Ibrahim (Q14:32-34)

Our inability to reckon the blessings of Allah is itself amazing. There are so many of them, every single minute, to be able to count. These are only the visible ones. We cannot even begin to comprehend the invisible favors of Allah. Abu al-Darda' رَضِيَ ٱللَّهُ عَنْهُ said:

قال أبو الدرداء رضي الله عنه:كم من نعمة لله تعالى في عرق ساكن؟

حياة السلف بين القول والعمل (ص٨٢٥)

How many blessings of Allah are there in a dormant vein?

Hayat al-Salaf bayna al-Qawl wa al-'Amal (p. 825)

He meant that every part of our body that is healthy is a blessing that goes unnoticed. We do not see the great things we have until we taste what it feels like to live without them. While we have them, we enjoy them but are blind to their value: we learned not to see them.

Whether Allah sends His blessings directly or indirectly, it is He who sent them. Humans can hire us, pay our salaries, give us advice, assist us in times of need, love us back, but it is Allah who made all this possible. He created goodwill in their hearts, put a smile on their face, and made their intervention possible and effective. It could not have happened without Him. Humans are only portals for the flow of blessings, not its cause. We should start to see Allah behind every act of kindness we receive, every beautiful thing in our lives, every blessing.

One of Allah's greatest gifts is consciousness. To be alive, to have feelings, to discover new things and grow as we learn—these are incredible gifts. Allah moved us from nothingness to awareness, and He allowed us to experience a full spectrum of emotions. He favored us with speech and the ability to reason. We can travel, we can smile, and we can eat. But above all, He favored us with His revelation: the blessing of guidance that illuminates our lives and saves us from doubt and misery. This revelation is rain to the parched soul and light to the dark heart. Without it, we sink to an animal-like existence. Allah said:

...لَهُمْ قُلُوبٌ لَّا يَفْقَهُونَ بِهَا وَلَهُمْ أَعْيُنٌ لَّا يُبْصِرُونَ بِهَا وَلَهُمْ ءَاذَانٌ لَّا يَسْمَعُونَ بِهَآ أُوْلَٰٓئِكَ كَٱلْأَنْعَٰمِ بَلْ هُمْ أَضَلُّ أُوْلَٰٓئِكَ هُمُ ٱلْغَٰفِلُونَ ﴿١٧٩﴾

They have hearts that they do not understand with, eyes that they do not see with, and ears that they do not hear with. They are like cattle. Indeed, they are even more astray. They are the heedless.

Al-A'raf (Q7:179)

Without Allah's revelation, our humanity is incomplete. With every piece of revelation we ignore, we lose a part of what makes us human, we lose a part of Allah's mercy. Without Allah's revelation, our existence loses its meaning, and we wander aimlessly without real goals. This is why Allah's revelation is an even greater gift than our own existence. In Surah al-Rahman where Allah reminds us of His favors, He begins with:

ٱلرَّحْمَٰنُ ﴿١﴾ عَلَّمَ ٱلْقُرْءَانَ ﴿٢﴾ خَلَقَ ٱلْإِنسَٰنَ ﴿٣﴾ عَلَّمَهُ ٱلْبَيَانَ ﴿٤﴾

Al-Rahman. He taught the Quran. He created humanity. He taught them to communicate.

Ar-Rahman (Q55:1-4)

It is out of His Mercy and Love that He sent us the Quran and sent us Muhammad ﷺ. It is out of His Mercy and Love that He created us and taught us what we know. It is out of His Mercy and Love that He keeps showering us with blessings every single day, even when we stray and disobey Him.

When we remember the favors of Allah, we will know Him better and love Him more. Sulayman al-Wasiti said:

قال أبو سُلَيْمَان الْوَاسِطِي: ذِكْرُ النِّعْمَةِ يُورِّثُ الْحُبَّ لِلَّهِ.

الشكر لابن أبي الدنيا (ص١١)

Remembering [or mentioning] the blessings brings on the love of Allah.

Al-Shukr by Ibn Abi al-Dunya (p. 11)

Humans are great at remembering, counting, and talking about all the wrong things in their lives. But we don't do the same with what is right. Focusing on the bad distorts reality by inflating loss, resentment, and fear until the blessings of Allah almost disappear. But if we remember and talk about Allah's favors, we will regain our balance: we will see more of Allah's blessings and realize that the bad is small in comparison. Then, Allah may grace us with the insight to see the blessings in our tests and the ability to turn each challenge into a blessing.

It is impossible for us to thank Allah adequately for all that He gives us. First, there is too much to thank Allah for, and a lot of it escapes our awareness. Second, we cannot sufficiently thank Allah for a single blessing of His, let alone all or most of them. Wahb ibn Munabbih said:

قَالَ وَهْبُ بْنُ مُنَبِّهٍ: عَبَدَ اللَّهُ عَابِدٌ خَمْسِينَ عَامًا فَأَوْحَى اللَّهُ إليه أَنِّي قَدْ غَفَرْتُ لَكَ قَالَ يَا رَبِّ وَمَا تَغْفِرُ لِي وَلَمْ أُذْنِبْ فَأَذِنَ لِعِرْقٍ فِي عُنُقِهِ فَضَرَبَ عَلَيْهِ فَلَمْ يَنَمْ وَلَمْ يُصَلِّ ثُمَّ سَكَنَ فَنَامَ فَأَتَاهُ مَلَكٌ فَشَكَا إِلَيْهِ فَقَالَ مَا لَقِيت مِنْ ضَرَبَانِ الْعِرْقِ فَقَالَ الْمَلَكُ إِنَّ رَبَّكَ يَقُولُ عِبَادَتُكَ خَمْسِينَ سَنَةً تَعْدِلُ سُكُونَ هَذَا الْعِرْقِ.

الشكر لابن أبي الدنيا (ص٥١)

A worshipper of Allah worshipped Him for fifty years, so Allah revealed to him that I have forgiven you. So he said, "O Rabb, forgive me what? I did not sin!" So Allah permitted a vein in his neck to throb, and he could not sleep or pray. Then the vein stopped throbbing, and he slept. An angel came to the man, and he complained to him and said, "How much did I

> suffer from a throbbing vein." So the angel said, "Your Rabb is saying that your worship for fifty years is equal to the quieting of that vein."
>
> *Al-Shukr* by Ibn Abi al-Dunya (p. 51)

Worship of fifty years is equal to the wellbeing of one vein! Can we ever dream of thanking Allah for a single blessing? We can only do our best, and Allah will forgive the rest. Third, thanking Allah is itself a blessing that needs to be thanked. So, the more we thank Him, the more He deserves to be thanked. We can only glorify and praise this Gracious Creator.

The greatest blessing to thank Allah for is the blessing of Islam and *taqwa*. Our minds tend to restrict His blessings to the material: money, health, and children. Though these are favors from Allah, the bigger and more lasting favor is religious guidance. We should view the Quran and Sunnah as blessings. We should count contentment with Allah and His decrees as a blessing. And we should consider following the straight path as a great blessing. We should truly thank Allah for it all. If we have these, then we indeed have everything.

Allah loves the beneficial

We saw in *Hadith Four* how we could come nearer to Allah by adopting the qualities of His Names and Attributes. Since Allah is the One who blesses all, He loves those who benefit others and alleviate their hardships. This *Hadith* teaches us that we can attain the love of Allah by helping those around us in whatever way possible.

This was how the Prophets of Allah lived. Allah described Prophet Jesus عَلَيْهِ السَّلَامُ as a source of constant blessings. Allah said:

وَجَعَلَنِي مُبَارَكًا أَيْنَ مَا كُنتُ... ﴿٣١﴾

And He made me [i.e. Jesus] a blessing wherever I may be.

Maryam (Q19:31)

Jesus عَلَيْهِ السَّلَامُ radiated benefits. No matter where he went and whom he met, his presence was a blessing, injecting benefit wherever He was. He taught the truth, made *du'a* for the afflicted, assisted the needy, commanded virtue and spoke out against evil, and was patient with his opponents. This was how all the Prophets of Allah عَلَيْهِمُ السَّلَامُ were. And this was how the Companions of the Prophet ﷺ were. The Prophet ﷺ once asked:

قَالَ رَسُولُ اللهِ صَلَّى اللهُ عَلَيْهِ وَسَلَّمَ «مَنْ أَصْبَحَ مِنْكُمُ الْيَوْمَ صَائِمًا؟» قَالَ أَبُو بَكْرٍ رَضِيَ اللهُ عَنْهُ: أَنَا. قَالَ «فَمَنْ تَبِعَ مِنْكُمُ الْيَوْمَ جَنَازَةً؟» قَالَ أَبُو بَكْرٍ رَضِيَ اللهُ عَنْهُ: أَنَا. قَالَ «فَمَنْ أَطْعَمَ مِنْكُمُ الْيَوْمَ مِسْكِينًا؟» قَالَ أَبُو بَكْرٍ رَضِيَ اللهُ عَنْهُ: أَنَا. قَالَ «فَمَنْ عَادَ مِنْكُمُ الْيَوْمَ مَرِيضًا؟» قَالَ أَبُو بَكْرٍ رَضِيَ اللهُ عَنْهُ: أَنَا. فَقَالَ رَسُولُ اللهِ صَلَّى اللهُ عَلَيْهِ وَسَلَّمَ: «مَا اجْتَمَعْنَ فِي امْرِئٍ، إِلَّا دَخَلَ الْجَنَّةَ.»

صحيح مسلم (١٠٢٨)

«Who fasted among you today?» Abu Bakr رَضِيَ اللَّهُ عَنْهُ replied, "I did." He asked, "Who among you followed a funeral today?" Abu Bakr رَضِيَ اللَّهُ عَنْهُ replied, "I did." He asked, "Who among you fed a poor person today?" Abu Bakr رَضِيَ اللَّهُ عَنْهُ replied, "I did." He asked, «Who among you visited a sick person today?» Abu Bakr رَضِيَ اللَّهُ عَنْهُ replied, "I did." So the Messenger of Allah ﷺ said, «Anyone in whom these good deeds are combined will enter Jannah.»

Reported by Muslim (1028)

What would prompt a person to do so much good in one day? Loving Allah and loving His servants is the answer. When one tastes the love of Allah, they would naturally gravitate towards what Allah loves. They will be looking for every opportunity to do what Allah loves. Every good deed is one step closer to Allah. Every good deed is more of Allah's love that we get to feel and enjoy. Every good deed is a gift that Allah sent us to get closer to Him. And when one feels love and compassion towards Allah's creation, they cannot sit back and not help. If we love the ones whom Allah loves, we cannot see them in pain and do nothing. Allah's beloveds are an extension of Allah's mercy and love, a conduit for His blessings, spreading goodness wherever they are, and searching for the opportunity to help. This person is from the people of Jannah.

If we desire to attain the love of Allah, we should care for Allah's creation. Allah made all this and it is dear to Him, so how will you take care of what is precious to Allah? This is where the righteous demonstrate their love for Allah. And for the seeker of righteousness, as Ibn Taymiyyah رَحِمَهُ ٱللَّهُ wrote:

مَن أحَبَّ أن يلحقَ بدرجةِ الأبرارِ ويتشبهَ بالأخيار فلينوِ في كل يوم تطلعُ فيه الشمس نفعَ الخلق.

الإيمان الأوسط لابن تيمية (ص٦٠٩)

> The one who loves to reach the rank of the pious and imitate the righteous should intend to benefit creation every single day.
>
> *Al-Iman al-Awsat* (p. 609)

That is, wake up each day with the intention of helping someone. Look for them and jump at the opportunity to help. It is a true gift when Allah sends someone your way and you happen to be the one who can help. It is a gift from Allah to you.

The greatest gift we can give is spreading Islam and Islamic knowledge. It is the best gift because it is beneficial in this life and the next. This was the mission of the Prophets of Allah and how they were the most helpful. Next comes bringing happiness to the life of a Muslim by removing their hardship. Some will need money, but others need reconciliation with loved ones, mediation to remove injustice, or advice. Finally, if we love Allah's creation, we will not hurt them. We will hold back our evil and rage for the sake of Allah. If we cannot help, at least we should not hurt.

Loving the servants of Allah means desiring the best for them, loving for them what we love for ourselves. If we were in hardship, would we not want someone to help? Well, this is what they need from you and me.

The comparison that the Prophet ﷺ made is fascinating. Many of us wish to travel and pray at the Prophet's Mosque in Madinah. Motivated by the great reward for praying there and by our love for him, we dream about it, save money for it, and are elated when it finally happens. Can you imagine how beautiful a month's stay in the Prophet's Mosque would be? But this is not possible for many of us. What is incredible is that something better than that is available to all of us. Helping people is better than staying at the Prophet's Mosque for a whole month! The merit and advantages of staying at the Prophet's Mosque are paramount. So it goes to show how much Allah loves it when we help people if it is better than worship for a whole month at that cherished Mosque.

Be kind as Allah was kind to you

Allah is very gracious to us. He secures our basic needs and gives beyond what we deserve, all without requesting anything in advance. He gave it all out of His generosity and love. Part of the gratitude we owe Him is sharing His gifts and spreading goodwill. Allah said:

...وَأَحْسِن كَمَآ أَحْسَنَ ٱللَّهُ إِلَيْكَ... ﴿٧٧﴾

And do good as Allah has done good to you.

Al-Qasas (Q28:77)

Sharing what we have only blesses it. We share some of our money when we pay *Zakah*, and the rest of the gifts of Allah have their *Zakah* too. If Allah taught you something, teach it. This is the *Zakah* of knowledge. The more that you teach, the more your understanding will grow and flourish. If you have a skill, share it. If you are healthy, help the sick. If you are a professional, use your position to make people's lives better. And as you share, remember that you are truly blessed: blessed to receive but also blessed to give. The gifts of Allah grow when we are generous with them.

HADITH EIGHT

الحديث الثامن

Allah loves forgiveness

قَالَتْ عائشة يَا رَسُولَ اللهِ أَرَأَيْتَ إِنْ وَافَقْتُ لَيْلَةَ الْقَدْرِ مَا أَدْعُو قَالَ ﷺ «تَقُولِينَ اللَّهُمَّ إِنَّكَ عَفُوٌّ تُحِبُّ الْعَفْوَ فَاعْفُ عَنِّي.»

رواه أحمد (٢٦٠٢١) والترمذي (٣٥١٣) وابن ماجة (٣٩٨٢) وصححه الألباني (صحيح سنن ابن ماجه ٣٨٥٠)

'A'ishah رضي الله عنها asked, "O Messenger of Allah, what should I supplicate if I happen to be in the Night of Qadr?" He ﷺ said, «You say, O Allah, You are Oft-pardoning, you love to pardon, so pardon me.»

Reported by Ahmad (26021), al-Tirmidhi (3513), and Ibn Majah (3982) and al-Albani declared it sahih (Sahih Sunah Ibn Majah, 3850)

Commentary

Allah loves to forgive and loves it when we forgive. Allah's forgiveness does not happen out of need, but out of love and mercy. And it demonstrates how much Allah cares about us and wants the best for us.

Allah is Oft-pardoning

Allah loves mercy, loves to forgive, and loves repentance and the repentant. Allah's Mercy is so vast that all other mercy in this universe is from it. His Mercy is so vast that it covers everything. Allah said:

...وَرَحْمَتِي وَسِعَتْ كُلَّ شَيْءٍ... ﴿١٥٦﴾

And My Mercy encompasses all.

Al-A'raf (Q7:156)

The angels closest to Allah—who carry His throne—know and testify to the extent of His Mercy when they say in the Quran:

...رَبَّنَا وَسِعْتَ كُلَّ شَيْءٍ رَّحْمَةً وَعِلْمًا... ﴿٧﴾

O our Rabb, You have encompassed all in mercy and knowledge.

Ghafir (Q40:7)

As Allah's Knowledge reaches all and nothing escapes it, so does His Mercy cover all. Even the non-believer who opposes Allah with words and deeds is a recipient of this mercy every single minute of the day. To illustrate the depth of Allah's mercy, the Prophet ﷺ said:

«إِنَّ اللَّهَ خَلَقَ يومَ خَلَقَ السَّمَواتِ والأَرْضَ مِئَةَ رَحْمَةٍ كُلُّ رَحْمَةٍ طِباقَ ما بيْنَ السَّماءِ والأَرْضِ فَجَعَلَ منها في الأَرْضِ رَحْمَةً فَبِها تَعْطِفُ الوالِدَةُ على وَلَدِها والْوَحْشُ والطَّيْرُ بَعْضُها على بَعْضٍ فَإِذا كانَ يَوْمُ القِيامَةِ أَكْمَلَها بِهذِه الرَّحْمَةِ.»

رواه مسلم (٢٧٥٣)

«When Allah created the heavens and the earth, He created one hundred mercies, each mercy fills what is between the sky and the earth. And He placed one of the mercies on earth, and it is through it that a mother is merciful with her child, and animals and birds are merciful with each other. And on the Day of Resurrection, He completes the ninety-nine with this mercy.»

Reported by Muslim (2753)

Imagine that all the mercy that we experience and has ever

existed on earth, in humans and animals, is part of this one percent of mercy that Allah created and sent to earth. And on the Last Day, this one mercy will join ninety-nine more to cover Allah's creation on that Day. Can you imagine how boundless mercy and forgiveness will be on the Day of Judgment? Now, compare these hundred created mercies to Allah's infinite Mercy, and you will understand that Allah's Mercy is beyond our comprehension. This is why the Prophet ﷺ said:

قَدِمَ على رَسُولِ اللهِ صَلّى اللَّهُ عليه وَسَلَّمَ بسَبْيٍ فَإِذا امْرَأَةٌ مِنَ السَّبْيِ تَبْتَغِي إذا وَجَدَتْ صَبِيًّا في السَّبْيِ أَخَذَتْهُ فألْصَقَتْهُ ببَطْنِها وَأَرْضَعَتْهُ فَقالَ لَنا رَسُولُ اللهِ صَلّى اللَّهُ عليه وَسَلَّمَ «أَتَرَوْنَ هذِه المَرْأَةَ طارِحَةً وَلَدَها في النّارِ؟» قُلْنا: لا واللَّهِ وَهي تَقْدِرُ على أَنْ لا تَطْرَحَهُ. فَقالَ رَسُولُ اللهِ صَلّى اللَّهُ عليه وَسَلَّمَ «لَلَّهُ أَرْحَمُ بعِبادِهِ مِن هذِه بوَلَدِها.»

رواه البخاري (٥٩٩٩) ومسلم (٢٧٥٤) واللفظ له

A group of captives was brought to the Prophet ﷺ and among them was a woman searching for someone. When she found a child among the captives, she took him, pressed him against her stomach, and suckled him. So the Messenger ﷺ asked, «Do you think this woman will throw her son in the fire?» We replied, "No, by Allah, as long as it is within her power not to throw him." So the Messenger ﷺ said, «Allah is more merciful with His servants than she with her child.»

Reported by al-Bukhari (5999) and Muslim (2754)

The captives—from one of the battles—had just arrived in Madinah when the Prophet ﷺ noticed this incident. The mother's extreme love and care for her child do not begin to compare with the Love and Mercy of Allah who created mercy in the hearts of all creation (see *Appendix I*).

Allah's Mercy precedes and overwhelms His Anger and punishment. The Messenger ﷺ said:

«إِنَّ اللَّهَ كَتَبَ كِتَابًا قَبْلَ أَنْ يَخْلُقَ الخَلْقَ إِنَّ رَحْمَتِي سَبَقَتْ غَضَبِي فَهو مَكْتُوبٌ عِنْدَهُ فَوْقَ العَرْشِ.»

رواه البخاري (٧٥٥٣) ومسلم (٢٧٥١)

«Allah wrote in a book before He created creation, "My Mercy supersedes My Anger," and it is written with Him above the Throne.»

Reported by al-Bukhari (7553) and Muslim (2751)

This declaration from Allah to His creation is a clear sign that Allah created them out of His Mercy, for His Mercy, and He will deal with them with mercy. Allah said:

وَلَوْ شَآءَ رَبُّكَ لَجَعَلَ ٱلنَّاسَ أُمَّةً وَٰحِدَةً ۖ وَلَا يَزَالُونَ مُخْتَلِفِينَ ﴿١١٨﴾ إِلَّا مَن رَّحِمَ رَبُّكَ ۚ وَلِذَٰلِكَ خَلَقَهُمْ ۗ... ﴿١١٩﴾

And if your Rabb wished, He would have made all people a single community. But they will continue to disagree, except for those whom Allah is merciful with. And it is for this that Allah created them.

Hud (Q11:118-119)

In Tafsir al-Tabari, one of the interpretations of the reason for creation (i.e. interpreting "And it is for this that Allah created them") is that Allah created them for His Mercy. This is what Ibn al-Qayyim رَحِمَهُ ٱللَّهُ confirmed when he wrote:

وَخَلَقَ الْخَلْقَ لِيَرْحَمَهُمْ لَا لِيُعَاقِبَهُمْ.

مختصر الصواعق المرسلة (ص٦٤٣)

And He created creation to show them mercy, not to punish them.

Mukhtasar al-Saqa'iq al-Mursalah (p. 643)

This is why Allah multiplies a good deed beyond count but records an evil deed as one, and it is easy to erase. And this is why Allah accepts repentance for all offenses, including shirk, and loves it more than we can ever imagine. The Prophet ﷺ said:

«لَلَّهُ أفْرَحُ بتَوْبَةِ عَبْدِهِ مِن رَجُلٍ نَزَلَ مَنْزِلًا وبِهِ مَهْلَكَةٌ ومعهُ راحِلَتُهُ عليها طَعامُهُ وشَرابُهُ فَوَضَعَ رَأْسَهُ فَنامَ نَوْمَةً فاسْتَيْقَظَ وقدْ ذَهَبَتْ راحِلَتُهُ حتّى إذا اشْتَدَّ عليه الحَرُّ والعَطَشُ أوْ ما شاءَ اللَّهُ قالَ أرْجِعُ إلى مَكانِي فَرَجَعَ فَنامَ نَوْمَةً ثُمَّ رَفَعَ رَأْسَهُ فإذا راحِلَتُهُ عِنْدَهُ.»

رواه البخاري (٦٣٠٨) ومسلم (٢٦٧٥)

«Allah is happier with the repentance of His servant than a man who camps in a desolate place with his mount and with his food and drink on it. He puts his head down and sleeps, and when he wakes up, he finds that his mount is gone. Then when he suffers from heat and thirst or whatever he suffers from [looking for it], he says, "I will go back to my place." He goes back and sleeps, and then when he raises his head, he finds his mount next to him.»

Reported by al-Bukhari (6308) and Muslim (2675)

This parable presents the ultimate human happiness. The man lost all hope of living and went back to await death. Then when he woke up, he found hope and his life restored through the return of his animal. If this is hard to relate to, think of someone who is diagnosed with a terminal illness. After resigning themselves to death, a visit to a second doctor reveals that it was a misdiagnosis, and they are completely healthy and disease-free. How happy will they be? If this happens to any of us, how happy will we be to have our life back? Allah is happier with our repentance than the greatest happiness a human can experience. Why is that? It is because Allah loves our wellbeing and happiness; He wants to forgive us and not punish us. As explained previously, the punisher and the avenger are not part of the names of Allah. But the Merciful and Most Forgiving are. This is so because Mercy and Forgiveness are constant and beloved attributes of His, while punishment is temporary and legislated for a reason. To clarify this point further, listen to this story narrated by Abdullah ibn Mas'ud رضي الله عنه. He said:

قال عبدِ اللهِ بنِ مسعودٍ رضي الله عنه إني لَأذكرُ أولَ رجلٍ قطعه رسولُ اللهِ صلَّى اللهُ عليهِ وسلَّمَ أُتِيَ بسارقٍ فأمر بقطعِه فكأنما أسِفَ وجهُ رسولِ اللهِ ﷺ فقالوا: يا رسولَ اللهِ كأنك كرهتَ قطعَه؟ قال «وما يمنعُني لا تكونوا أعوانًا للشيطان على أخيكم إنه لا ينبغي للإمامِ إذا انتهى إليه حدٌّ إلا أن يقيمَه إنَّ اللهَ عفُوٌّ يحبُّ العفوَ ﴿وَلْيَعْفُوا وَلْيَصْفَحُوا أَلَا تُحِبُّونَ أَنْ يَغْفِرَ اللهُ لَكُمْ وَاللهُ غَفُورٌ رَّحِيمٌ﴾»

رواه أحمد (٤١٦) والحاكم (٨١٥٥) وحسنه الألباني (السلسلة الصحيحة ١٦٣٨)

I remember the first man that the Messenger ﷺ cut [his hand]. He was brought a thief, so he ordered that [his hand] be cut. And the face of the Messenger ﷺ turned very sad, so they asked, "O Messenger of Allah, as if you hated that [his hand] be cut?" He replied, «Why not? Do not be helpers of Shaytan against your brother. The Imam must execute the prescribed punishment when an offense is brought to him. Indeed, Allah is Oft-pardoning, and He loves to pardon, [Allah said] ﴿And let them pardon and forgive. Do you not love for Allah to forgive you? And Allah is the Forgiving, the Merciful﴾ [Al-Nur (22)]»

Reported by Ahmad (416) and al-Hakim (8155) and al-Albani declared it hasan (*al-Silsilah al-Sahihah*, 1638)

The Prophet, ﷺ, could not but cut the hand of the thief after the matter was brought to him. He was the Imam (leader) who could not ignore the divine punishment for this crime. But he also wished that the people would have forgiven the man and that his hand would have been spared. It was clear from his reaction that he favored forgiveness and was not looking forward to punishing people. Allah ordained this punishment as a deterrent, and when executed, it protects society from plenty of harm. But it would be superior if the injured party could forgive and grant the offender another chance. Rushing towards punishment and revenge may carry in it harm that the

Prophet, ﷺ, called aiding the Shaytan against our brother. If the man was a repeat and unrepentant offender who terrorized people, then it would be better to punish him to reform him and stop his evil. Otherwise, forgiveness is the divine and legal goal, not punishment.

There is another incident that confirms this Islamic directive of forgiveness and mercy. When Ma'iz رضي الله عنه confessed adultery in front of the Prophet ﷺ, he had to do it four times. Each time, the Prophet ﷺ turned away from him and asked him to go back and repent. But Ma'iz wanted the punishment to purify him of that sin. Then the Prophet ﷺ asked him a series of questions aimed at verifying the offense, asking it each time to give him the chance to retract: "Perhaps you only looked? Perhaps you only kissed?" When Ma'iz insisted that he did commit adultery and asked to be purified, the Prophet ﷺ directed the Companions to take him and stone him. When the Companions started to stone him at the outskirts of Madinah, Ma'iz panicked and started to run away. One of the Companions caught up with him and finished him off. When news of what happened reached the Prophet ﷺ he said:

«هَلَّا تَرَكْتُمُوهُ لَعَلَّهُ يَتُوبُ فَيَتُوبَ اللهُ عَلَيْهِ.»

رواه أحمد (٢١٨٩٠) وحسنه الألباني (السلسلة الصحيحة ٣٤٦٠) وصححه الأرناؤوط

«Why did you not let him go? Perhaps he would repent and Allah would accept his repentance.»

Reported by Ahmad (21890) and al-Albani declared it hasan (*al-Silsilah al-Sahihah*, 3460) and al-Arna'ut declared it sahih

Then the Prophet ﷺ said to Hazzal—the one who advised Ma'iz to confess his guilt:

«وَاللهِ يَا هَزَّالُ لَوْ كُنْتَ سَتَرْتَهُ بِثَوْبِكَ كَانَ خَيْرًا مِمَّا صَنَعْتَ بِهِ.»

رواه أحمد (٢١٨٩٠) وحسنه الألباني (السلسلة الصحيحة ٣٤٦٠) وصححه الأرناؤوط

«By Allah, O Hazzal, if you had concealed him with your garment, it would have been better than what you did to him.»

Reported by Ahmad (21890) and al-Albani declared it hasan (*al-Silsilah al-Sahihah*, 3460) and al-Arna'ut declared it sahih

A frequent adulterer needs this punishment to stop him from causing so much harm to himself and the families he betrays. But since this was Ma'iz's first mistake and it was not public, it would have been better to allow him to repent in secret and ask Allah for forgiveness. Once the matter became public, there was no other option but to proceed with Allah's command. Despite this, the outcome was in favor of Ma'iz رَضِيَ ٱللَّهُ عَنْهُ. The Prophet ﷺ said about him:

«استغفروا لماعز بن مالك لقد تاب توبة لو قسمت بين أمة لوسعتهم.»

رواه مسلم (١٦٩٥)

«Ask forgiveness for Ma'iz son of Malik. He repented such a repentance that if it were to be distributed among a nation, it would have been enough for them.»

Reported by Muslim (1695)

Corporal punishments in Islam are curative restorations of balance, peace, and virtue for individuals and the community. They are the last remedy and not something to seek or rejoice in. Their aim is deterrence and purification, not revenge. And whenever forgiveness is possible and useful, it is always superior.

The same principle stands at the core of Jihad in Islam. When you examine the mission of the Prophet ﷺ, you will find that he spent most of his life preaching, not fighting. Permission for Jihad came at the heels of consistent attempts to eliminate Muslims. Without Jihad, the small Muslim community would have been completely wiped out. Jihad is there to repel the aggression of the nonbelievers and to remove the obstacles that stand between people and hearing the message of Islam. This is why when the Prophet ﷺ and the nonbelieving Makkans accepted the Truce of Hudaybiyah, people started flocking to Islam like never before. Jihad gave the Muslim community the chance to be heard. And when people listened to what Muslims had to say, they accepted Islam in droves. They did not accept it because of the sword, as some claim; the Treaty brought all hostilities to an end. They accepted it because Jihad pushed back the tyranny of the Makkans and opened their eyes to the truth (see *Qa'idah Mukhtasarah fi Qital al-Kuffar* by Ibn Taymiyyah). Ibn al-Qayyim رَحِمَهُ ٱللَّهُ wrote:

وَمَنْ تَأَمَّلَ سِيرَةَ النَّبِيِّ صَلَّى اللَّهُ عَلَيْهِ وَسَلَّمَ تَبَيَّنَ لَهُ أَنَّهُ لَمْ يُكْرِهْ أَحَدًا عَلَى دِينِهِ قَطُّ وَأَنَّهُ إِنَّمَا قَاتَلَ مَنْ قَاتَلَهُ وَأَمَّا مَنْ هَادَنَهُ فَلَمْ يُقَاتِلْهُ مَا دَامَ مُقِيمًا عَلَى هُدْنَتِهِ لَمْ يَنْقُضْ عَهْدَهُ.

هداية الحيارى (ص٢٣٨)

> And the one who examines the life of the Prophet ﷺ would find that he never compelled anyone to embrace his religion and that He only fought the ones who fought him. And he did not fight those who had a treaty with him as long as they adhered to it and did not break their covenant.
>
> *Hidayat al-Hayarah* (p. 238)

Islam does not crave conflict nor seek war. Allah said regarding some of the People of the Book:

...كُلَّمَآ أَوْقَدُوا۟ نَارًا لِّلْحَرْبِ أَطْفَأَهَا ٱللَّهُ... ﴿٦٤﴾

Every time they kindle the fire of war, Allah puts it out.

Al-Ma'idah (Q5:64)

Allah critically ascribed to them the desire to stir up conflict and declared that He spoils their plots and frustrates their efforts. Allah, the Most Merciful and Most Forgiving, does not love conflict and bloodshed. And this tells you that Islam is not inclined to war and conflict. But in the face of unrepentant and repeat offenders—just like corporal punishment—Jihad becomes a necessary response. Yet this response is only there to correct when all other efforts fail. For most of the history of Prophethood on earth, Allah forbade fighting for the Prophets and their followers. Jihad was allowed beginning with Musa عَلَيْهِ ٱلسَّلَامُ after the death of Pharaoh. The entirety or majority of the *da'wah* of the Prophets on earth was peaceful—exactly like Prophet Muhammad ﷺ—until it was no longer possible. Most of the Prophet's life and da'wah was in Makkah, and fighting was disallowed then. Fighting was the necessary exception, not the norm.

One of the puzzling questions some have trouble with is reconciling the Mercy of Allah with eternal punishment in Hell. If Allah is so Merciful, why would He punish people for eternity? Why would He create people whom He knows will end up in eternal punishment?

First, we have to believe that Allah's Wisdom, Justice, and Mercy transcend ours. If we believe in the Creator having perfect attributes, we cannot expect our minds to encompass the wisdom behind His acts. He does what He does for the most sublime of reasons, and His decisions are never devoid of mercy. So, if there is something we don't understand, we should refer the matter back to Him, believing that the mercy we feel is an infinitesimal fraction of the Mercy of Allah. In other words, we cannot be more merciful than the Merciful.

Second, the merciful impulses we have are often imbalanced by our human weakness and ignorance. Allah's Mercy, on the other hand, operates with His Wisdom and Justice. We may think that some divine punishment is harsh, but Allah knows what is best for the ones He created. We did not make this world and its people, and we do not understand it as Allah does. So, we cannot come between Allah and what He created, claiming to understand what is best for it and how its Creator should act. We should simply trust that in the Hereafter, Allah's Mercy and Justice will be evident to all.

Third, Ibn al-Qayyim رَحِمَهُ ٱللَّهُ presented an interesting argument about the eternality of punishment in Hell (see for example *Mukhtasar al-Sawa'iq al-Mursalah*, pp. 629–690). He argued that it runs contrary to Allah's Mercy and Wisdom to punish people forever. Blessing people and creation eternally is consistent with His Mercy, and Jannah and its bliss are eternal for this reason. But Hell, he argued, is not designed for infinite punishment, for there will come a day when its people will be purified enough of their crimes that they will get to leave. He based his argument on evidence from the Quran, *hadith*, sayings from the first and second generations, scholarly statements, and rational arguments. Though his is not the majority opinion among the scholarly community, Ibn al-Qayyim does present a compelling case for the impossibility of infinite punishment in Hell. Allah knows best.

Allah loves pardoning

Since Allah loves to forgive and pardon, He also loves for His servants to forgive and overlook the faults of others. This is a disposition that should spread far and wide in society. Since Allah loves forgiveness, we should practice what Allah loves so we can attain His love.

We forgive for two reasons: to be forgiven and out of mercy. Allah said in the Quran:

وَلَا يَأْتَلِ أُوْلُواْ ٱلْفَضْلِ مِنكُمْ وَٱلسَّعَةِ أَن يُؤْتُوٓاْ أُوْلِي ٱلْقُرْبَىٰ
وَٱلْمَسَٰكِينَ وَٱلْمُهَٰجِرِينَ فِي سَبِيلِ ٱللَّهِۖ وَلْيَعْفُواْ وَلْيَصْفَحُوٓاْۗ أَلَا تُحِبُّونَ
أَن يَغْفِرَ ٱللَّهُ لَكُمْۚ وَٱللَّهُ غَفُورٞ رَّحِيمٌ ٢٢

And let not the virtuous and wealthy among you swear not to give to their relatives, the poor, and the emigrants in the cause of Allah. And let them pardon and overlook. Would you not like Allah to forgive you? And Allah is Forgiving and Merciful.

An-Nur (Q24:22)

Allah exhorts the believers here to adopt an attitude of forgiveness if they want Allah to forgive them. How is it that we are desperate for Allah's mercy despite our terrible and numerous sins but refuse to forgive others for the smallest of offenses? The one whose heart is filled with Allah's love will find the space in it to forgive no matter what was done to them. This *ayah* was revealed because of what took place between Abu Bakr and his cousin Mistah رضي الله عنهما. Mistah repeated the accusations against our mother 'A'ishah رضي الله عنها. When Allah exonerated A'ishah رضي الله عنها from adultery and defended her honor in the Quran, Abu Bakr رضي الله عنه swore never to spend on Mistah رضي الله عنه again after what he had said. But despite his mistake, Mistah رضي الله عنه was a righteous man who had witnessed the battle of Badr. And he was a poor relative of Abu Bakr رضي الله عنه who relied on his support. Take a minute here and think about how much Allah cares. Allah revealed this *ayah* to remind Abu Bakr رضي الله عنه and all of us, that we should forgive if we truly are seeking Allah's forgiveness. The guilty man who repeated this terrible lie about your daughter and caused her and you so much distress still needs your help and forgiveness. If you find it in your heart to forgive, then Allah will forgive you. This is why Abu Bakr رضي الله عنه immediately said in response:

فَقَالَ أَبُو بَكْرٍ رضي الله عنه :بَلَى وَاللَّهِ إِنِّي لَأُحِبُّ أَنْ يَغْفِرَ اللَّهُ لِي فَرَجَعَ إِلَى مِسْطَحٍ الَّذِي كَانَ يُجْرِي عَلَيْهِ.

رواه البخاري (٢٦٦١)

"Indeed, by Allah, I love that Allah would forgive me." And he went back to spending on Mistah.

Reported by al-Bukhari (2661)

If a heart loves Allah, it will rush to what Allah loves as soon as it knows it. If a soul is worried about its sins, it rushes to forgive. Our sins before the Almighty are greater than any personal offense towards us. If forgiving others means that Allah will forgive us, then it benefits us the most when we forgive.

Many hesitate to forgive. They believe that forgiveness will bring them nothing in return, and the offender will walk away intact. But Allah said:

...فَمَنْ عَفَا وَأَصْلَحَ فَأَجْرُهُۥ عَلَى ٱللَّهِ... ﴿٤٠﴾

Whoever pardons and seeks islah, then their reward is with Allah.

Ash-Shuraa (Q42:40)

Whatever we think we will lose when we forgive is nothing but an illusion. How could we lose anything and Allah is promising that it is He who rewards and compensates. Can we ever imagine that our efforts to punish will yield a greater benefit than the promise of Allah? Never. The greatest victory is to receive Allah's reward. This belief transforms the believer into someone who expects their reward only from Allah into possessing the biggest and kindest heart. Ibn Othaymeen رَحِمَهُ ٱللَّهُ said:

وهو سبحانه يحب الذين يأخذون من الناس العفو بل أمر بذلك فقال: ﴿خذ العفو وأمر بالعرف﴾ قال العلماء: معنى العفو يعني خذ ما عفي من الناس يعني ما سهل منه خذه ولا تشد الحبل فخذ العفو واترك ما وراء ذلك وهذا من آداب القرآن أن الإنسان يكون واسع الصدر لبني آدم يأخذ العفو.

شرح رياض الصالحين (ج٥ ص٢٢٣)

And He, Glory be to Him, loves those who accept whatever people easily give, indeed He commanded it and said: ﴿Take what is easily given and command what is right.﴾ The scholars said, "The meaning of 'Afw is to take what people give easily," take it and do not pull with a rope [i.e. be rough and exhaustive]. So, accept the 'Afw and let go of the rest. This is of the manners of the Quran, for a human to have a big heart with the children of Adam and accepts 'Afw.

Sharh Riyad al-Salihin (vol. 5, p. 223)

Seeking *islah* in the *ayah* has two important meanings. The first is reconciling with the offender after we pardon them. Sometimes we pardon (i.e. not punish), but we remain angry and distant. Seeking *islah* is moving beyond this and patching things up with those whom we pardon. Restoration of normalcy and affection is the goal. What will help us achieve this level of forgiveness, in addition to seeking Allah's forgiveness, is developing compassion for others. The offender has gotten themselves in trouble with Allah, and they deserve our sympathy for that. Also, they may have committed their mistake out of human weakness, or there may have been mitigating circumstances (e.g. suffering or distress) that we were unaware of. Being merciful means sympathizing with the frailties of the offender. We forgive them because they did not know any better or were not strong enough to make the right choices. Rather than condemnation and ire, they need help and support. This is how we defeat Shaytan and not be his helpers against our brothers and sisters.

The second important meaning of *islah* is to improve and reform. And this is an important condition in forgiveness. When we forgive, we must ensure that our forgiveness will change the forgiven and not encourage them to commit more crimes. Some had become so seasoned in Allah's disobedience that only punishment will help them. In this case, forgiving them is not *islah* because they will not learn anything from it.

Asking Allah to pardon us

There are significant differences between how we forgive and how Allah forgives. For one, Allah forgives while having full power, but humans often forgive because they cannot avenge themselves. Many times, we forgive because we have no better alternative. But would we forgive if we had absolute power and feared none? We also forgive for the sake of some benefit we receive (e.g. good deeds and praise). Allah, however, forgives even though He fears no one, and He receives no benefit whatsoever. He forgives because He loves to forgive. And if He loves it, He loves that we ask Him for it.

On the best night of the year, forgiveness should be our main concern. When the Prophet's beloved, 'A'ishah رَضِيَ ٱللَّهُ عَنْهَا, asked him what she should say on Laylat al-Qadr, he gave her this short but important *du'a*. In it, we ask Allah by His great name "Al-'Afu" and by His love for forgiveness to pardon us. On that blessed night, forgiveness is the greatest gift we hope for. Of course, we can also ask for additional worldly and otherworldly bounties. But teaching her this *du'a* alone meant that this is our greatest request, our ultimate desire. The Prophet ﷺ loved Allah the most, and 'A'ishah رَضِيَ ٱللَّهُ عَنْهَا was the human he loved the most. When the human beloved wondered what she should ask the Divine Beloved, he connected his two loves with a supplication for forgiveness. And this is our connection to Allah. If we have distanced ourselves from Allah's love, forgiveness will bring us back to Him. So, ask Allah for it, and you will return to Him. You may have left. But Allah never left you.

HADITH NINE

الحديث التاسع

Allah loves noble manners

قَالَ رَسُولُ اللهِ ﷺ «أَحبُّ الناسِ إلى اللهِ أَحسنهم خلقًا.»

رواه ابن حبان (٤٨٦) وصححه الألباني (التعليقات الحسان ٤٨٦)

The Messenger ﷺ said, «The most beloved of people to Allah are the ones with the best character.»

Reported by Ibn Hibban (486) *and al-Albani declared it sahih* (*al-Ta'liqat al-Hisan*, 486)

Commentary

Allah has the best Qualities, and He loves those with the best qualities. Allah loves the best for humanity, and good character is the vehicle for spreading happiness and wellbeing. This is why the good-mannered are beloved to Allah.

The excellence of good character

We, as an Ummah, are going through a deficit of manners. We have strayed in many ways from Allah, and our character reflects it. It would not be possible for us to behave so poorly if we knew Allah well, loved Him, and channeled this love into practice. What is ironic, and deeply sad, is that Islam places a high premium on good character. The Prophet ﷺ said:

«إنما بُعِثْتُ لأُتَمِّمَ مكارمَ الأخلاق.»

رواه البخاري في الأدب المفرد (٢٧٣) وصححه الألباني (صحيح الأدب المفرد ٢٠٧)

«I was not sent but to complete honorable manners.»

Reported by al-Bukhari in *al-Adab al-Mufrad* (273) and al-Albani declared it sahih (*Sahih al-Adab al-Mufrad*, 207)

We know that the Prophet ﷺ reformed people's beliefs and practices with Aqidah and law, so his message carried more than the call for a noble character. So, what does this *hadith* mean? We have two possibilities. The first is that it is a hyperbole. There is such emphasis on developing good character in Islam that the Prophet ﷺ made it as if it was his only task. This is a common rhetorical device in the Arabic language, and it was used in other *hadiths*. The second possibility is that good character is much more than social behavior. It encompasses our relationship with Allah, the beliefs we hold, and how these beliefs influence the rest of our life. Aqidah and law are part of this transformative message since they elevate and guide human understanding and practice. Therefore, good character is an umbrella term for all good behavior, including worship and social conduct. In that sense, everything in Islam—including Aqidah and law—is about good character.

All this reflects the link between the worship of Allah and social relations. In the minds of many, unfortunately, the two are disconnected. We do not see how worshipping Allah (e.g. *Salah*, fasting, and *Zakah*) affects our mundane behavior, and so they operate separately. This is why we hear complaints about the religious being deficient in manners (e.g. rude, harsh, argumentative, and unpunctual). On the one hand, it is unfair to generalize and give the impression that everyone who is religious is flawed in character. The Ummah is indeed running a character-deficit, and the religious are a product of their society, carrying the same ills as everyone else. It is also true that the religious—because of their appearance—represent Islam and are scrutinized more. Thus, they must strive to enhance their character, especially since worship is supposed to lead to greater kindness and mercy. When we hear that excellence in character was central to the mission of the Prophet ﷺ, we understand that we are not truly following him until our manners improve. And this is not a trivial matter. The Prophet ﷺ said:

«إنَّ مِن أحبِّكم إليَّ وأقربِكُم منِّي مجلسًا يومَ القيامةِ أحاسنَكُم أخلاقًا وإنَّ مِن أبغضِكُم إليَّ وأبعدِكُم منِّي يومَ القيامةِ الثَّرثارونَ والمتشدِّقونَ والمتفَيهِقونَ.» قالوا: يا رسولَ اللَّهِ قد عِلمنا الثَّرثارينَ والمتشدِّقينَ فما المتفَيهقونَ؟ قالَ «المتَكَبِّرونَ.»

رواه الترمذي (٢٠١٨) وصححه الألباني (صحيح الترمذي ٢٠١٨)

«Of the most beloved and nearest in position to me on the Day of Judgment are those with the best character. And of the most hated to me and furthest from me on the Day of Judgment are the babblers, the blowhards, and the *mutafayhiqun*.» They said, "We know the babblers and the blowhards. But who are the *mutafayhiqun*?" He answered, «The arrogant.»

Reported by al-Tirmidhi (2018) and al-Albani declared it sahih (*Sahih al-Tirmidhi*, 2018)

The Prophet ﷺ was of great character, and it is natural for him to love those with similar beautiful traits. Acquiring and striving for good character is an act of worship in itself and it will bring one closest to the Prophet ﷺ on the Last Day. So, if we genuinely love him and want him to love us back, and if we want to be near him and enjoy his company, the path passes through moral excellence. What is frightening about bad character is that it earns one the dislike of Allah and the Prophet ﷺ. The three traits in the *hadith* are all about excessive, artificial, and arrogant speech. Pride, showing off, and putting others down are the motives. When one speaks and they pretend to know, twist their tongue to seem more eloquent, and exaggerate to elevate themselves, they are committing a sin that Allah and

His Prophet detest. If they had paid attention to their worship of Allah, it would have taught them humility, sincerity, and sensitivity not to hurt others. Worshipping Allah heals us and grants us calmer hearts, and this, in turn, leads to greater generosity. Competition for this world is the main cause of our quarrels. But if our worship lessens our attachment to this world, we will grow to be more courteous and forgiving. Bad character is a sign of internal conflict, deficiency, and corruption. This is why it distances one from Allah and His Messenger.

Good character, on the other hand, brings the love of Allah and people. It is in our nature to love those with beautiful character. Ali ibn Abi Talib رضي الله عنه said:

قال علي بن أبي طالب رضى الله عنه: من لانت كلمته وجبت محبته.

حياة السلف بين القول والعمل (ص٣٢١)

When one's words are kind, loving them becomes a necessity.

Hayat al-Salaf bayna al-Qawl wa al-'Amal (p. 321)

It is impossible not to love a kind person. The noble of character bring comfort and joy wherever they go. They assist others, suppress evil, and bring hope to desperate hearts. For all the good they bring to the people and the love they spread, Allah elevates them in Jannah. The Prophet ﷺ said:

«ما مِن شيءٍ يوضَعُ في الميزانِ أثقلُ من حُسنِ الخلقِ وإنَّ صاحبَ حُسنِ الخلقِ ليبلُغُ بِهِ درجةَ صاحبِ الصَّومِ والصَّلاةِ.»

رواه أبو داود (٤٧٩٩) والترمذي (٢٠٠٣) وصححه الألباني (صحيح الترمذي ٢٠٠٣)

«There is nothing heavier in the Scale than good character. Due to it, the one with good character reaches the level of the one with frequent praying and fasting.»

Reported by Abu Dawud (4799) and al-Tirmidhi (2003) and al-Albani declared it sahih (*Sahih al-Tirmidhi*, 2003)

It is an act of worship that lifts one all the way to the highest levels in Jannah. In fact, it is one of the main reasons people enter Heaven and Hell. The Prophet ﷺ said:

سُئِلَ رسولُ اللَّهِ صلَّى اللَّهُ علَيهِ وسلَّمَ عن أَكْثرِ ما يُدخلُ النَّاسَ الجنَّةَ فقالَ «تَقوى اللَّهِ وحُسنُ الخلُقِ» وسُئِلَ عن أَكْثرِ ما يُدخِلُ النَّاسَ النَّارَ قالَ «الفَمُ والفَرجُ.»

رواه الترمذي (٢٠٠٤) وحسنه الألباني (صحيح الترمذي ٢٠٠٤)

The Prophet ﷺ was asked about the thing that most admits people to Jannah, to which he replied, «The taqwa of Allah and good character.» And he was asked about the thing that most admits people to Hell, to which he replied, «The mouth and the private part.»

Reported by al-Tirmidhi (2004) and al-Albani declared it hasan (*Sahih al-Tirmidhi*, 2004)

If one relates to Allah with taqwa and to the people with nobility, they will be among the people of Jannah. But if they fail to restrain their mouth and private part—the basis of indecent and obnoxious behavior—they will enter Hell. This is why it is crucial to strive to attain the best manners and to ask Allah for it. Umm al-Darda' رضي الله عنها said:

عن أم الدرداء رضي الله عنها قالت: بات أبو الدرداء رضي الله عنه الليلة يصلي فجعل يبكي ويقول: اللهم أحسنت خلقي فأحسن خلقي، حتى أصبح فقلت: يا أبا الدرداء، ما كان دعاؤك منذ الليلة إلا في حسن الخلق؟ قال: يا أم الدرداء، إن العبد المسلم يحسن خلقه حتى يدخله حسن خلقه الجنة ويسوء خلقه حتى يدخله سوء خلقه النار.

حياة السلف بين القول والعمل (ص٣٢١)

Abu al-Darda' رضي الله عنه spent the night praying and crying and saying, "O Allah, You made my physical form beautiful, so make my character beautiful," until the morning. I said, "O Abu al-Darda', your entire du'a since the night was about good character!" He said, "O Umm al-Darda', a Muslim's character would be good until the beauty of their character admits them to Jannah. And their character would be bad until the ugliness of their character admits them to Hell."

Hayat al-Salaf bayna al-Qawl wa al-'Amal (p. 321)

When our manners change, our whole life will change. We will be more serene, we will have greater love for people and feel more of their love, and our hearts will feel closer to Allah. And we would be helping to rehabilitate the entire Ummah.

Why does Allah love good character?

Allah loves the happiness and wellbeing of His creation, and good character is the vehicle that spreads them. People, of course, help each other because they need each other. This need fuels the exchange of goods and services. But good manners move us to do more and to do it well. It moves us to give more than what we receive, to give even when we do not receive. It prompts us to fight selfishness, greed, and pride, and to strive to make others happy. When people receive the best, they will give back the best. This benevolence in time will uplift all of society, spreading love and comradery. And Allah loves this.

Good character is also a reflection of a life spent striving for Allah's sake. We all have to struggle to attain, maintain, and cultivate good traits. We do this despite the resistance of a weak and greedy self, against the temptations of this world and whispers of Shaytan, and despite the harsh and disappointing daily interactions. Yet, the one who stays steadfast, they do so because of Allah, even if they are alone. Nobility is not about who else is doing it. Many times, it requires resisting the pressure of the majority in society and never compromising your integrity. Good character is about pleasing Allah, every single day. And Allah loves those who strive to come closer to Him.

Finally, when good character is pursued for Allah's sake, it reflects an appreciation of Allah's Names and Attributes. Allah is Generous, Forgiving, Merciful, Concealer of mistakes, and

Kind. And He loves to see these qualities among His creation. This is why He commands them and rewards them. When we know this, Allah's Qualities will inspire us to adopt them on earth and come closer to Allah through them. If we want to get closer to the Merciful and to receive His Mercy, we should be merciful. If we wish to get closer to the Forgiving and receive His Forgiveness, we should be forgiving. If we want to get closer to the Generous, the Kind, and the Provider and to receive His blessings, we should adopt these qualities and help everyone. When we do, we should remember that Allah does not want any benefit back from His creation for the good that He gives them. Similarly, we should give without expectations of a human reward. Our reward comes only from Allah. These are the manners that propel to the highest levels of Jannah and win us the love of Allah.

Adopting good character

Naturally, we would want to adorn ourselves with the best qualities to receive Allah's love. Along this path, we will come to know what we possess and what we lack. Some of these qualities will be already in us (innate), and some will need to be acquired. The Messenger ﷺ said to Ashajj Abd al-Qays:

قَالَ رَسُولُ اللَّهِ صلى الله عليه وسلم لأَشَجِّ عبد القَيْسِ «إِنَّ فِيكَ خَلَّتَيْنِ يُحِبُّهُمَا اللَّهُ عَزَّ وَجَلَّ.» قُلْتُ: مَا هُمَا؟ قَالَ «الْحِلْمُ وَالْحَيَاءُ.» قُلْتُ: أَقَدِيمًا كَانَ فِيَّ أَمْ حَدِيثًا؟ قَالَ «بَلْ قَدِيمًا.» قُلْتُ: الْحَمْدُ لِلَّهِ الَّذِى جَبَلَنِي عَلَى خَلَّتَيْنِ يُحِبُّهُمَا.

رواه أحمد (١٨١٠٨) وابن ماجه (٤٣٢٨) وصححه الألباني (صحيح ابن ماجه ٤١٨٨). وعند مسلم (١٢٦) (الحِلْمُ والأناةُ) بدل (الْحِلْمُ وَالْحَيَاءُ)

«You have two qualities that Allah loves.» Ashajj Abd al-Qays asked, "What are they?" The Messenger ﷺ replied, «Deliberation and haya'.» I asked, "Did I have them for a long time, or are they new?" He ﷺ said, «You had them for a long time.» I said, "Praise and thanks be to Allah who created me with two qualities that He loves."

Reported by Ahmad (18108) and Ibn Majah (4328) and al-Albani declared it sahih (*Sahih Ibn Majah*, 4188). Muslim (126) narrated it as (Deliberation and patience) instead of (Deliberation and haya')

Each of us has a combination of good innate manners and others that we have adopted. Some are generous by nature, while others have to work on it. Some are patient, while others have anger problems. But even our innate good qualities need to be preserved, or else they will be disappear. And no matter what we already have, there is still more that we need to do. We are all on this lifelong path of pursuit and growth. On this path, we should take note of what Allah blessed us with and what we need to work on. We should preserve the gifts of Allah by thanking Him for our good qualities, attributing them to His Grace and not our virtue. We should further protect them by putting them into practice. As for what we lack, we begin by asking Allah for it. We need to read more about it, and we should try to adopt new habits gradually. We must not also forget the influence of good company in elevating character. Finally, let us remember that our goal is the pleasure of Allah, not human gratitude or recognition. With *du'a* and patience, we will change for the better insha-Allah.

Beautiful words and actions

This section presents some of the manners that Allah loves. The *hadiths* here can be thought of as suggested practical steps for change. These steps are gradual, making them the ideal starting point.

The Prophet ﷺ said:

«إنَّ اللَّهَ يحبُّ سَمْحَ البَيعِ سَمْحَ الشِّراءِ سَمْحَ القَضاءِ.»

رواه الترمذي (١٣١٩) وصححه الألباني (صحيح الترمذي ١٣١٩)

«Indeed, Allah loves one who is lenient when they sell, lenient when they buy, and lenient with repayment of debt.»

Reported by al-Tirmidhi (1319) and al-Albani declared it sahih (*Sahih al-Tirmidhi*, 1319)

This person is easygoing and forgiving when they sell, buy, repay debt, and recollect debt. Their words are sweet, respectful, and honest; and they are generous and humble in action. Some, on the other hand, cause harm when they intend to purchase: they haggle and lower the price until the seller loses money, they buy with the intent of returning what they bought after using it, or return the merchandise damaged and demand a full refund. Sellers err when they raise their prices so it harms consumers, when they monopolize the market to inflate prices, and when they sell defective goods. Both buyers and sellers stray away from Allah's love when they are rude and disrespectful to each other. The last part of the *hadith* is about debt. If it is due, the debtor should pay it on time if they have the money. If they do not, the creditor should sympathize with their hardship and and allow delay in repayment or forgive the debt (or some of it) if they are rich.

The Prophet ﷺ said:

«إنَّ من الغَيرةِ ما يُحبُّ اللهُ ومنها ما يُبْغِضُ اللهُ وإنَّ من الخُيلاءِ ما يُحبُّ اللهُ ومنها ما يُبغضُ اللهُ فأما الغَيرةُ التي يُحبُّها اللهُ فالغَيرةُ في الرِّيبةِ وأما الغَيرةُ التي يُبغضُ اللهُ فالغَيرةُ في غيرِ الرِّيبةِ وأما الخُيلاءُ التي يُحبُّها اللهُ فاخْتيالُ الرجلِ في القتالِ واختيالُه عند الصدقةِ وأما الخُيلاءُ التي يُبغضُ اللهُ فاختيالُ الرجلِ في البغيِ والفخرِ.»

رواه أبو داود (٢٦٥٩) والنسائي (٢٥٥٨) وحسنه الألباني (صحيح أبي داود ٢٦٥٩)

«There is jealousy that Allah loves and jealousy that Allah hates, and there is pride that Allah loves and pride that Allah hates. As for the jealousy that Allah loves, it is jealousy at the presence of something forbidden. As for the jealousy that Allah hates, it is jealousy without cause. And as for the pride that

Allah loves, it is a man's pride in battle and his pride when giving charity. And as for the pride that Allah hates, it is pride in aggression and boasting.»

Reported by Abu Dawud (2659) and al-Nasa'i (2558). Al-Albani declared it hasan (*Sahih Abi Dawud*, 2659)

Allah loves that we be jealous when there are grounds for jealousy, when something wrong is taking place. This jealousy stems the prohibited acts that Allah hates and saves families from breaking up, conflict, and much heartache. Jealousy without reason breeds suspicion, hostility, and destroys families, something that Allah hates. Pride in battle is for one to display their strength and talent to frighten and discourage the enemy. Pride in charity is to be happy that Allah enabled them to give, and to keep giving with enthusiasm and delight. The pride that Allah hates is one that leads to injustice and aggression, when one feels that they are better than others.

The Prophet ﷺ said:

«لا تحقرنّ من المعروفِ شيْئًا ولو أن تفرِغَ من دلوِكَ في إناءِ المستسقِي ولو أن تكلم أخاكَ ووجهكَ إليه منبسطٌ وإياكَ وتسبيلَ الإزارِ فإنه من الخيلاءِ والخُيلاءُ لا يُحبّها اللهُ عز وجلَ وإن امرُؤ سبكَ بما يعلمُ فيكَ فلاتسبّهُ بما تعلمُ فيهِ فإن أجرهُ لكَ ووبالهُ على من قالهُ.»

رواه أبو داود (٤٠٨٤) وصححه الألباني (السلسلة الصحيحة ١٣٥٢)

«Do not belittle any good deed, even if it is emptying from your bucket into the bucket of a seeker of water, and even if it is smiling while talking to your brother. And avoid making your clothes long, for this is from pride and Allah, glory be to Him, does not love pride. And if someone insults you using what they know about you, do not insult them back using what you know about them, for the reward of that exchange will be yours, and its sin will be on the one who said it.»

Reported by Abu Dawud (4084) and al-Albani declared it sahih (*al-Silsilah al-Sahihah*, 1352)

These are a series of seemingly small actions, but the Prophet ﷺ reminded us not to disregard any small act of righteousness. Small acts come together to form something big, and they become a habit that affects our behavior and major decisions. So, whenever there is an opportunity to do something good, seize it and do not think that it is insignificant. The first act mentioned in the *hadith* is any little assistance you can offer. The second is cheerfulness when talking to people. The third is specific for men: lifting their garments above their ankles to protect themselves from arrogance. The Prophet ﷺ said:

«إنَّ اللهَ لا يحبُّ المسبِلِينَ.»

رواه ابن ماجه (٢٨٩٢) وحسنه لغيره الألباني (صحيح الترغيب ٢٠٣٩)

«Indeed, Allah does not love those who wear long garments [i.e. below the ankles].»

Reported by Ibn Majah (2892) and al-Albani declared it hasan li-ghayrihi (*Sahih al-Targhib*, 2039)

It is such a small deed. But for those who love Allah, it is not small if Allah hates it. The last reminder is not to insult anyone. A Companion once asked the Prophet ﷺ for advice. The Prophet ﷺ told him:

«لا تَسبَّنَّ أحدًا» قالَ: فما سَببتُ بعدَهُ حُرًّا ولا عبدًا ولا بعيرًا ولا شاةً.

رواه أبو داود (٤٠٨٤) وصححه الألباني(السلسلة الصحيحة ١٣٥٢)

«Do not insult anyone.» The man said, "So, I did not insult

after him [giving me this advice] a freeman, a slave, a camel, or a sheep."

Reported by Abu Dawud (4084) and al-Albani declared it sahih (*al-Silsilah al-Sahihah*, 1352)

These are the manners of Islam! Even animals are safe from our harm and from our tongue. And if someone uses what they know about you to put you down, do not do the same to them. If you suppress your anger and frustration and remain calm, Allah will reward you for your lofty manners, and your accuser will carry the sin.

We need a strong motive to embrace better manners. And there is nothing stronger than the promises Allah made us. He will reward us immensely, and we will be among the select on the Last Day. I know it is hard to change. But if we really want the Hereafter, will try our best. And if you do, Allah will assist you.

HADITH TEN

الحديث العاشر

Allah loves the gentle hearts

قَالَ رَسُولُ اللَّهِ ﷺ «إِنَّ لِلَّهِ آنيةً من أَهْلِ الأرضِ وآنيةُ ربكم قُلوبُ عِبادِهِ الصَّالحينَ وأحبُّها إليهِ ألينُها وأرقُّها.»

رواه الطبراني في مسند الشاميين (٨٤٠) وجود إسناده العراقي في تخريج الإحياء وحسنه الهيثمي والألباني (السلسلة الصحيحة ١٦٩١)

The Messenger ﷺ said, «Allah has vessels from the people of earth, and the vessels of your Rabb are the hearts of His pious servants. And the most beloved to Him of these vessels are the softest and gentlest.»

Reported by al-Tabarani in Musnad al-Shamiyyin (840). Al-Iraqi declared its chain good in his study of the hadiths of al-Ihya. Al-Haythami and al-Albani declared the hadith hasan (al-Silsilah al-Sahihah, 1691)

Commentary

Soften your heart to receive Allah's love.

Allah's vessels

Our hearts are containers. And so, they will always carry something inside. They are filled with emotions, they retain knowledge, and they are constantly cogitating. They have the capacity to carry good as well as evil. Malik ibn Dinar رَضِيَ اللَّهُ عَنْهُ said:

قال مَالِكُ بْنُ دِينَارٍ: إِنَّ الأَبْرَارَ تَغْلِي قُلُوبُهُمْ بِأَعْمَالِ الْبِرِّ وَإِنَّ الْفُجَّارَ تَغْلِي قُلُوبُهُمْ بِأَعْمَالِ الْفُجُورِ وَاللَّهُ يَرَى هُمُومَكُمْ فَانْظُرُوا مَا هُمُومُكُمْ رَحِمَكُمُ اللَّهُ.

الهم والحزن لابن أبي الدنيا (ص٧٦)

The hearts of the pious are boiling with righteous deeds, while the hearts of the impious are boiling with sinful deeds. And Allah sees your concerns [inside your hearts], so consider what your concerns are, may Allah be merciful with you.

Al-Hamm wa al-Huzn by Ibn Abi al-Dunya (p. 76)

The hearts of the pious overflow with righteous thoughts and intents: they want to do so many good things that their hearts seem like they are overcrowded, boiling with good desires. The impious, on the other hand, are obsessed with sins. They chase after them with such craving that their hearts become agitated with sinful plans and desires, unable to sit still until they sin. But if Allah can see inside our hearts—something we often forget—we should protect our thoughts and desires as we do our deeds. All sins come from thoughts that we allowed to grow.

The hearts are the most essential vessels we have because they carry and preserve our beliefs and intents. They are also Allah's vessels, the place where Allah deposits what He loves. Allah sends His revelation to them, and they decide to believe and follow. They are where *Iman* and Taqwa settle, where the love of Allah resides. They are the core from which mercy and kindness flow. It is there that we decide to maintain our integrity and purity amid corruption and mistreatment. If your heart does not surrender, then you are never defeated.

To protect these vessels, we need to keep filling them with virtue and guard them against contamination. Ibn Mas'ud رَضِيَ اللَّهُ عَنْهُ said:

قَالَ عَبْدُ اللَّهِ بْنُ مَسْعُودٍ رضي الله عنه: إِنَّمَا هَذِهِ الْقُلُوبُ أَوْعِيَةٌ فَاشْغَلُوهَا بِالْقُرْآنِ وَلَا تَشْغَلُوهَا بِغَيْرِهِ.

مصنف ابن أبي شيبة (ج٧ ص١٠٦)

These hearts are but vessels. So occupy them with the Quran and do not occupy them with something other than it.

Al-Musannaf by Ibn Abi Shaybah (vol. 7, p. 106)

The condition of our hearts is simply a reflection of what we put into them, what we feed them, and what we allow to grow inside them.

Softest and gentlest

Not all hearts are alike. The traits of each heart determine what it can carry and do. Some hearts are big. When it is big, a heart will comprehend more, tolerate more, and give more. When a heart is small and tight, it will not accept much of the light of revelation inside it, it will be irritated with everything, and it will give very little to others (e.g. kindness, forgiveness, and help). Some of the People of the Book justified their rejection of Islam by saying:

وَقَالُوا۟ قُلُوبُنَا غُلْفٌۢ... ﴿٨٨﴾

And they said, "Our hearts are wrapped [against what you say]."

Al-Baqarah (Q2:88)

Allah explained in the rest of the *ayah* that it is their defiance that stands between them and *Iman*, not a real screen that hindered their understanding. Disbelief corrupts the heart, shrinks it, and hardens it. And it is the greatest obstacle to understanding the truth.

The feature that makes the heart beloved to Allah is softness and gentleness. In Arabic, there is a difference between the two words mentioned in the *Hadith*. When a heart is (رَقِيق), it is imagined as having a thin outer layer. The thinness of this layer allows outside influences to penetrate quickly, making this heart receptive and sensitive. The other word used to describe the heart is (لَيِّـن), a soft heart that is easily moved. The two words paint a picture of a heart that is wide open to the truth and follows it willingly.

How are the hearts that Allah loves open and soft? First and most importantly, they are open and soft with Allah's revelation. These hearts have not constructed barriers between them and Allah or allowed such construction. And because of how close they want to be to Allah, these hearts are ready to embrace what Allah says. Allah described the effect of the Quran on these hearts when He said:

ٱللَّهُ نَزَّلَ أَحۡسَنَ ٱلۡحَدِيثِ كِتَٰبٗا مُّتَشَٰبِهٗا مَّثَانِيَ تَقۡشَعِرُّ مِنۡهُ جُلُودُ
ٱلَّذِينَ يَخۡشَوۡنَ رَبَّهُمۡ ثُمَّ تَلِينُ جُلُودُهُمۡ وَقُلُوبُهُمۡ إِلَىٰ ذِكۡرِ ٱللَّهِۚ... ﴿٢٣﴾

Allah has sent down the best of speech: a consistent Book with repeated lessons. The skins of those who are in awe of their Rabb shiver because of it. Then their skins and their hearts soften at the mention of Allah.

Az-Zumar (Q39:23)

This is how sensitive and gentle the hearts of the believers are. And because they acquire this softness from the Quran—i.e. they allow the Word of Allah to change their hearts—they acquire sensitivity and softness when dealing with everyone and everything around them. This is the second meaning of the open and soft hearts: kindness and mercy towards creation.

We encountered in *Hadith Eight* the connection between knowledge and mercy when Allah said:

...رَبَّنَا وَسِعۡتَ كُلَّ شَيۡءٖ رَّحۡمَةٗ وَعِلۡمٗا... ﴿٧﴾

O our Rabb, you have encompassed all in mercy and knowledge.

Ghafir (Q40:7)

The *ayah* points to a direct connection between knowledge

and mercy: as the first increases, so does the second. Since Allah is the All-Knowledgeable, He is also the All-Merciful. As humans acquire more knowledge, they should also acquire more mercy. Knowledge devoid of mercy is destructive.

Why are knowledge and mercy connected? When our knowledge grows, three things happen. First, we know Allah to be The Merciful who loves compassion, kindness, and forgiveness. Our love of Allah and sincere desire to please Him will push us to adopt and promote these qualities. We realize that everything around us is Allah's creation, and we notice how much Allah is Merciful towards it. So, rather than go against Allah's wishes for His creation, we should be merciful as Allah is so incredibly Merciful. In other words, be to Allah's creation as He is to them and do not torment them. He did not create them for us to abuse them. This includes humans, animals, and the environment.

Mercy is proportional to *Iman*. When our *Iman* is strong, we are more likely to forgive others and seek our reward solely from Allah. But when our *Iman* is weak and our heart is hard, we will seek revenge on everyone around us, whether they deserve it or not.

Second, when our knowledge increases, we will unfailingly notice in Allah's revelation and law the heavy tilt towards mercy and kindness. The more that we learn, the more that Allah will remind us to forgive and be soft-hearted. We will also notice that there is latitude in Islamic law for legitimate differences of opinion, and so our hearts will expand to accommodate legal differences as our minds expand. We also realize that no matter how knowledgeable one is, they cannot escape their human nature and be infallible. Thus, we learn to excuse scholars for mistakes in religious pronouncements but continue to honor them even as we reject the error itself.

Third, as our knowledge increases, we will look at people through the lens of mercy as well as that of the Shari'ah. Ibn Taymiyyah رَحِمَهُ ٱللَّهُ spoke about these two viewpoints in *Al-Fatwa al-Hamawiyyah* (p. 555). When we view reality from the angle of Allah's commands and rights, we see why Allah threatened sinners with punishment. But when we look at the sinful as confused, in pain, hurting themselves with their choices, trapped by Shaytan, and with punishment awaiting them, we feel for them and try our best to help them. The sympathy we feel prompts us to forgive and reform, not punish and destroy. Our goal is not to send more people to Hell but to save all from Shaytan. This is why the more learned we become, the more merciful we should be. And if we find that our knowledge is not leading to increased mercy, then we are either learning the wrong thing or are learning the right thing wrongly.

The one who knew Allah the Best was the Prophet ﷺ, and this is why his heart was the softest and gentlest. As his heart was the depository of knowledge and wisdom, it was also the depository of mercy and kindness. Allah said about him in the Quran:

فَبِمَا رَحْمَةٍ مِّنَ ٱللَّهِ لِنتَ لَهُمْ ... ﴿١٥٩﴾

It is from Allah's Mercy that you were soft with them.

Ali 'Imran (Q3:159)

Allah, the Most Merciful, made the Prophet ﷺ merciful. This was why he attracted so many hearts to him. And as his love for Allah grew, his mercy grew as well. Loving Allah, the Most Merciful, made the Prophet ﷺ more merciful.

The Prophet ﷺ singled out the people of Yemen for soft-heartedness. He ﷺ praised them when he said:

«أَتَاكُمْ أَهْلُ الْيَمَنِ هُمْ أَرَقُّ أَفْئِدَةً وَأَلْيَنُ قُلُوبًا.»

رواه البخاري (٤٣٣٨) ومسلم (٥٢)

The people of Yemen have arrived. Their hearts are gentler and softer.

Reported by al-Bukhari (4338) and Muslim (52)

Possessing this heart is real virtue, not wealth and status. The latter brings temporary human esteem and praise. The former brings lasting love from Allah and the wise. The softer hearts receive the favors of Allah.

Allah the Merciful loves the merciful

Whatever Allah loves tells us something significant about Allah. Loving gentle and soft hearts tells us that Allah Himself is Gentle and Merciful. And it is out of His Gentleness that He exhorted us all to be gentle and merciful to each other. Take some time to ponder this. Allah is so Merciful with you that He commanded all those around you to treat you well. He receives nothing from this except your happiness. He rewards people when they take care of you, making these good deeds a path to Jannah. Your parents, your spouse, your children, your neighbors, and everyone who sees you are reminded to look after you for the sake of Allah. And if they do not, Allah will be angry with them. This should tell you how much Allah cares, and how much we should love Him.

The gentle hearts beat faster as soon as they hear Allah's Name and His *ayahs*. They are very close to Him, more attached to Him than they are to anyone else. They like what Allah likes, and are disturbed by what He hates. Their hearts move with a rhythm that repeats the Name of Allah, and can only find peace close to Him, like a child who can only be comforted by his mother. They have forgotten about the troubles of this world because their hearts have no space in them for that: Allah's love has chased away all these worries. Our Beloved will take care of us, their hearts repeat, so we will not worry. If I have Allah, I have everything.

As these hearts feel Allah's care for them, they also care for those around them. They pulse with compassion for all. They know that many people have hard lives, so they do not seek to make it harder. They offer excuses before condemnations, and forgiveness before vengeance. They can forgive because Allah loves forgiveness, offering the offender the chance to escape Hell. They forget about their selves for the Sake of their Beloved. If He is happy, they are delighted. He takes care of all of His creation, and we will take care of them too for His sake. What makes Him happy makes us happy.

If we want Allah's love, we have to soften our hearts and improve our character. The soft and gentle hearts receive the greatest gifts from Allah. He protects them and guides them. He grants them wisdom, serenity, and detachment from worldly concerns. He elevates them in this life and the next. They chose Allah, so Allah chooses them. And if you become Allah's chosen, do you need anyone else?

HADITH ELEVEN

الحديث الحادي عشر

Allah protects whom He loves

قَالَ رَسُولُ اللهِ ﷺ «إِنَّ اللهَ لَيَحْمِي عَبْدَهُ الْمُؤْمِنَ مِنَ الدُّنْيَا وَهُوَ يُحِبُّهُ كَمَا تَحْمُونَ مَرِيضَكُمْ مِنَ الطَّعَامِ وَالشَّرَابِ تَخَافُونَهُ عَلَيْهِ.»

رواه أحمد (٢٣٦٢٢) والترمذي (٢٠٣٦) وصححه الألباني (صحيح الجامع ١٨١٤ وصحيح الترمذي ٢٠٣٦) وشعيب الأرناؤوط

The Messenger ﷺ said, «Indeed Allah protects His believing servant from the world while loving him as you protect your sick from food and drink because you fear it for them.»

Reported by Ahmad (23622) and al-Tirmidhi (2036) and al-Albani declared it sahih (Sahih al-Jami‘, 1814 and Sahih al-Tirmidhi, 2036) and al-Arna‘ut

Commentary

We and the world

We all desire this world. We see its beauty, and our hearts long for it. This is natural. Allah placed us on earth with a firm desire for this world. Allah said:

زُيِّنَ لِلنَّاسِ حُبُّ ٱلشَّهَوَٰتِ مِنَ ٱلنِّسَآءِ وَٱلْبَنِينَ وَٱلْقَنَٰطِيرِ ٱلْمُقَنطَرَةِ

مِنَ ٱلذَّهَبِ وَٱلْفِضَّةِ وَٱلْخَيْلِ ٱلْمُسَوَّمَةِ وَٱلْأَنْعَٰمِ وَٱلْحَرْثِۗ ذَٰلِكَ مَتَٰعُ
ٱلْحَيَوٰةِ ٱلدُّنْيَاۖ وَٱللَّهُ عِندَهُۥ حُسْنُ ٱلْمَـَٔابِ ﴿١٤﴾

The love of attractive things is beautified for people—women, sons, piles of gold and silver, horses with fine markings, livestock, and farmland. These are the pleasures of this life, but Allah has the best place to return to.

Ali 'Imran (Q3:14)

Our love for these things is essential for the cultivation of earth and the continuation of life. But it is also our test. If our love for this world is measured, purposeful, and with Allah in mind, then it is permissible and useful. This is the beautification mentioned in the *ayah*, which Allah placed in our hearts. But our fascination with this world could grow to a level where it overtakes our lives. It then becomes our sole concern and sole happiness. When we reach this level of obsession and greed, the world becomes our sickness. This is the beautification of Shaytan who deceptively glamorizes the world to distract us, and then destroy us.

The Prophet ﷺ pointed to the insatiable appetite we have for the pleasures of this world when he said:

«لَوْ كانَ لِابْنِ آدَمَ وادٍ مِن ذَهَبٍ أَحَبَّ أنَّ له وادِيًا آخَرَ ولَنْ يَمْلأَ فاهُ إلَّا التُّرابُ.»

رواه البخاري (٦٤٣٩) ومسلم (١٠٤٨)

«If the child of Adam had a valley of gold, he would love another. And the only thing that fills his mouth is sand.»

Reported by al-Bukhari (6439) and Muslim (1048)

Ironically, the more we have, the more we want. We will never reach a point where we will say that we have enough. Hence, the only thing that will actually fill a human mouth is sand when they die. The one who approaches the world with greed and stinginess, and attains it from unlawful sources, will be as the *hadith* states:

«إِنَّهُ مَنْ يَأْخُذُهُ بِغَيْرِ حَقِّهِ [وفي رواية: مَنْ أَخَذَهُ بِإِشْرَافِ نَفْسٍ لَمْ يُبَارَكْ لَهُ فِيهِ] كَالَّذِي يَأْكُلُ وَلَا يَشْبَعُ.»

رواه البخاري (١٤٦٥) (١٤٧٢) ومسلم (١٠٣٥)

«The one who takes it [i.e. wealth] unlawfully (in another narration: The one who takes it greedily, it will not be blessed for them) will be like the one who eats but is never full.»

Reported by al-Bukhari (1465, 1472) and Muslim (1035)

Curiously, there is a strong parallel between our position on food and the world. Food is one of the main attractions on earth, and our attitude towards it encapsulates and represents our worldly attitudes. We love to eat, which is natural. But if we overeat, we will be sick. Moderation is the only healthy option. The Prophet ﷺ said:

«مَا مَلَأَ آدَمِيٌّ وِعَاءً شَرًّا مِنْ بَطْنٍ بِحَسْبِ ابْنِ آدَمَ أُكُلَاتٌ يُقِمْنَ صُلْبَهُ فَإِنْ كَانَ لَا مَحَالَةَ فَثُلُثٌ لِطَعَامِهِ وَثُلُثٌ لِشَرَابِهِ وَثُلُثٌ لِنَفَسِهِ.»

رواه الترمذي (٢٣٨٠) وصححه الألباني (صحيح الترمذي ٢٣٨٠)

«No human fills a container worse than a stomach. It is sufficient for the child of Adam to eat a few morsels that keep his back upright. But if he has to, then one-third for his food, one-third for his drink and one-third for his breathing.»

Reported by al-Tirmidhi (2380) and al-Albani declared it sahih (*Sahih al-Tirmidhi*, 2380)

This is exactly what our stance should be with the world. Take from it what you need and leave off the rest. If we have to, then take in moderation and leave space for other things in your heart and mind. But if you keep amassing worldly pleasures, the world will make you sick and eventually kill you, precisely like glutinous overeating.

Some perceive worldly fortunes as a sign that Allah loves

them and that they are special to Him. Nothing could be further from the truth. Allah said:

فَأَمَّا ٱلْإِنسَٰنُ إِذَا مَا ٱبْتَلَىٰهُ رَبُّهُۥ فَأَكْرَمَهُۥ وَنَعَّمَهُۥ فَيَقُولُ رَبِّىٓ أَكْرَمَنِ ﴿١٥﴾ وَأَمَّآ إِذَا مَا ٱبْتَلَىٰهُ فَقَدَرَ عَلَيْهِ رِزْقَهُۥ فَيَقُولُ رَبِّىٓ أَهَٰنَنِ ﴿١٦﴾ كَلَّا ... ﴿١٧﴾

As for the human, when their Rabb tests them by giving them honor and gifts, then they say, "My Rabb has honored me." But when He tests them by limiting their provision, they say, "My Rabb has humiliated me!" No!

Al-Fajr (Q89:15-17)

This is the response of many to what Allah gives them (or does not give). If they get what they want from this world, they are at peace, happy with their lives and Allah. They see this as a sign of honor, love, and special status. But as soon as they are denied something, their *Iman* collapses, and they turn against Allah. They equate wealth and health with Allah's love. Allah, unequivocally, declares this false thinking with the word "No" in the *ayah*. The Prophet ﷺ confirmed it when he said:

«إِنَّ اللهَ قَسَمَ بَيْنَكُمْ أَخْلَاقَكُمْ كَمَا قَسَمَ بَيْنَكُمْ أَرْزَاقَكُمْ وَإِنَّ اللهَ يُعْطِي الدُّنْيَا مَنْ يُحِبُّ وَمَنْ لَا يُحِبُّ وَلَا يُعْطِي الْإِيمَانَ إِلَّا مَنْ يُحِبُّ.»

رواه الحاكم (٩٥) وأحمد (٣٧٢٧) وصححه الألباني (السلسلة الصحيحة ٢٧١٤)

«Allah distributed your characters among you as He distributed your provisions. And Allah grants the world to those whom He loves and those whom He does not love. And He only grants Iman to those whom He loves.»

Reported by al-Hakim (95) and Ahmad (3727) and al-Albani declared it sahih (*al-Silsilah al-Sahihah*, 2714)

Our material status, health, and worldly success do not

correlate with Allah's love. If the world is not a sign of Allah's love, then why do we chase after it and neglect *Iman*, the sure sign of Allah's love?

Parables

We all can relate to the image in the *Hadith*. Someone dear to us becomes sick, and we naturally take care of them. Part of our responsibility then is to make sure that they eat the right food to recover. And if we know that certain foods and drinks will make them sicker, we will protect them from it until they are healthy again—even if they beg us for it. No matter how much they desire what harms them, we will do our best to protect them from it. In their sickly state, they may not be in a prime condition to make the best decisions.

The similarity of this scene to our worldly desires is striking. Many of us go after material gains with no consideration of what it may do to us. At times, we pant for it even though it is making us sick. We do not feel what it is doing to us, but others can see it. So, when Allah denies us something to save us, we complain about Him as we complain about a caretaker denying us the harmful food we crave. When we are physically sick, we are weak, impatient, shortsighted, and only see what we desire. Similarly, when we are sick with this world, we are weak, impatient, shortsighted, and only see what we desire. We complain when we are physically ill about being denied, and we complain when we are spiritually sick about the same thing.

Parables are important in helping us understand what lies beyond our senses. Allah created parallels and connections between what we perceive and what we do not. These similarities help us bridge gaps in our knowledge and understand one experience in light of another. This is what the parables in the Quran and Sunnah do, and they are extraordinarily important. If we do not understand how Allah could deny us what we like and yet still love us, just consider that you do the same thing with your children, sick family members, and even yourself. When you diet, either to lose weight or for health reasons, do you not deny yourself what you like to eat? And are you doing it because you hate yourself? Or are you doing it because you love yourself and are looking out for it? Do you stop your children from eating processed and sugary food because you hate them or love them? These observable and everyday experiences help us understand the hidden wisdom behind the actions of Allah. Pay close attention to the parables in the Quran and Sunnah. They can teach us a lot.

Allah protects those whom He loves

When we love someone, our love moves us to protect them, ensuring that no harm reaches them. Allah's love and protection are greater than anything humanly possible or conceivable. When one attains Allah's love, they will be under the umbrella of Allah's full protection, the All-Powerful and All-Wise. Allah said:

إِنَّ ٱللَّهَ يُدَٰفِعُ عَنِ ٱلَّذِينَ ءَامَنُوٓا۟ۗ... ﴿٣٨﴾

Allah defends the believers.

Al-Hajj (Q22:38)

Note that Allah took it upon Himself to do this. It is He who guards the believers and repels their enemies: humans or Jinn. He protects them from physical harm as well as defending their honor, reputation, and families. He also protects them from fitnah, doubts, and the whispers of Shaytan. He protects them from distractions that pull them away from Him. And if these distractions happen to be excess wealth or different worldly prizes, then Allah will protect them from it. He loves them, so He saves them, even if it is from something they like.

The difficult part for many is their inability to reconcile Allah's love with being denied what they desire. They rush to interpret their loss as divine hate or disregard. The reason for this hasty conclusion is our fixation—even mad obsession—with what we want, without any other consideration. We do not pay attention to how our cravings affect our Hereafter and the rest of our life.

Our obsession blinds us to the mercy that motivates the loss. If we pause to remember that loss emanates from Allah's love, we would be able to rise above our pain and see great favors in it. We would see each setback as a push forward from a loving Creator. Loss, then, disappears, and all that we receive becomes a favor from Allah.

At times, Allah is going to be the One who protects us from this world, while at other times, it is going to be us who must protect ourselves from it to reach Allah. Though the following narration is weak, it does represent the sacrifices that the Companions had to make. A sacrifice out of love.

نظر النبيُّ صلَّى اللهُ عليهِ وسلَّم إلى مصعبِ بنِ عميرٍ مقبلًا وعليه إهابُ كبشٍ قد تنطَّقَ به فقال النبيُّ صلَّى اللهُ عليهِ وسلَّم «انظروا إلى هذا الرجلِ الذي نوَّرَ اللهُ قلبَه لقد رأيتُه بين أبويْهِ يغذوانِه بأطيبِ الطعامِ والشرابِ ولقد رأيتُ عليه حُلّةً شَراها أو شُرَيتْ بمئةِ دِرهمٍ فدعاه حُبُّ اللهِ ورسولِه إلى ما تروْنَ.»

ضعيف الترغيب والترهيب (١٢٧٠)

> The Prophet ﷺ glanced at Mus'ab ibn 'Umayr as he was approaching, wearing untanned sheepskin that he tied around his waist with a rope, and said, «Look at this man whom Allah had filled his heart with light. I have seen him with his parents as they were providing him with the best of food and drink, and I have seen him wearing a suit that he bought, or it was bought for him, for two hundred dirhams. Then the love of Allah and His Messenger invited him to the state that you see.»
>
> *Da'if al-Targhib wa al-Tarhib* (1270)

We often do not appreciate or understand the extent of the sacrifice of the Companions. He left wealth and comfort and embraced real hardship for Allah's love. But does hardship remain as hardship if you are doing it for the Beloved?

Coming closer to Allah will sometimes require that we leave what we love for His sake. This is the real test of our love for

Him. Can we forego minor attachments for the Greatest Love? Allah said:

قُلْ إِن كُنتُمْ تُحِبُّونَ ٱللَّهَ فَٱتَّبِعُونِي يُحْبِبْكُمُ ٱللَّهُ وَيَغْفِرْ لَكُمْ ذُنُوبَكُمْ
وَٱللَّهُ غَفُورٌ رَّحِيمٌ ﴿٣١﴾ قُلْ أَطِيعُوا۟ ٱللَّهَ وَٱلرَّسُولَ فَإِن تَوَلَّوْا۟ فَإِنَّ ٱللَّهَ لَا
يُحِبُّ ٱلْكَٰفِرِينَ ﴿٣٢﴾

Say, "If you truly love Allah, then follow me and Allah will love you and forgive your sins. And Allah is Forgiving, Merciful." Say, "Obey Allah and His Messenger." But if they turn away, then Allah does not love the disbelievers.

Ali 'Imran (Q3:31-32)

These *ayahs* are the test of love. Each, and many indeed, claim that they love Allah. But what is the proof? Who is sincere and who is a poser? Allah told His Prophet ﷺ to inform anyone claiming to love Allah to follow the natural consequence of this love: listen to your Beloved. If you do, you will receive Allah's Love and Forgiveness. This is the real confirmation of love: leaving what we love for the sake of Allah. But if we don't, then it is a sign that our love is weak or non-existent. The reason the disbelievers refused the exclusive worship of Allah is that they did not love Him enough. They loved other than Him, and they obeyed and worshipped them. Tawhid is founded on love.

Favoring Allah over our desires is not easy. But when we do, we receive more of Allah's bounties than we could imagine. Consider the following *hadith*.

نَهى رسولُ اللهِ صلَّى اللهُ عليه وسلَّم عنِ الوِصالِ، قالوا: إنَّك تُواصِلُ! قال «إنَّكم لَستُم كهَيئَتي إنَّ اللهَ حِبِّي يُطعِمُني ويَسقِيْني.»

رواه أحمد (٧٥٤٨) وصححه الأرناؤوط وأحمد شاكر

The Prophet ﷺ forbade continuous fasting [i.e. without breaking

> the fast at night]. They said, "But you do it!" He replied, «You are not like me. Allah, My Beloved, gives me food and drink.»
>
> Reported by Ahmad (7548) and al-Arna'ut and Ahmad Shakir declared it sahih

The love the Prophet ﷺ had for Allah was so intense that he could stay without food and drink for days. This love gave him energy that sustained him as food would. If we need an example to understand this, consider how we tend to forget about eating and drinking when we do something we love. Joy chases away hunger and fatigue; it injects energy that is supplied by our love. And when we love Allah, the strength we receive is greater than anything else we have experienced.

The love of this world is the greatest competitor with the love of Allah. It is impossible for both of them to fully inhabit a heart (see *Hadith Seventeen*). We need to decrease one for the other to grow. Thu al-Nun عَلَيْهِ السَّلَام said:

> قَالَ ذُو النُّونِ عليه السلام: مِنْ عَلَامَاتِ الْمُحِبِّ لِلَّهِ تَرْكُ كُلِّ مَا شَغَلَ عَنِ اللَّهِ عَزَّ وَجَلَّ حَتَّى يَكُونَ الشُّغْلُ كُلُّهُ بِاللَّهِ وَحْدَهُ.
>
> الزهد الكبير للبيهقي (ص٧٨)
>
> One of the marks when someone loves Allah is to abandon all that distracts from Allah until one's preoccupation is Allah alone.
>
> *Al-Zuhd al-Kabir* by al-Bayhaqi (p. 78)

Our preoccupation is what we love. So, let us consider what is preoccupying us. And if we find that we need more of Allah's love in our hearts, we need to give more time to Him.

Let Allah protect you

We are all looking for safety in this life. We save money in case of emergencies, install alarms for protection, and wear seatbelts to guard against accidents. The unknown future, the danger that lies in it, brings us much anxiety. So, why not seek the best protection against the unknown? Is not Allah the Best Protector? Allah said:

...فَٱللَّهُ خَيۡرٌ حَٰفِظٗاۖ... ﴿٦٤﴾

Allah is the Best Protector.

Yusuf (Q12:64)

Allah protects those whom He loves. If you are under Allah's protection, no real harm will touch you. And if something you dislike happens, Allah will help you through it. If you have to leave something for Allah's sake, He will give you more than what you sacrificed. If He denies you something you like, He denies it to grant you something more exceptional. This is how Beautiful Allah is. He never abandons those who love Him.

HADITH TWELVE

الحديث الثاني عشر

Allah is the source of all love

قَالَ رَسُولُ اللَّهِ ﷺ «إِذَا أَحَبَّ اللَّهُ عَبْدًا نَادَى جِبْرِيلَ إِنَّ اللَّهَ يُحِبُّ فُلاَنًا فَأَحِبَّهُ فَيُحِبُّهُ جِبْرِيلُ فَيُنَادِى جِبْرِيلُ فِي أَهْلِ السَّمَاءِ إِنَّ اللَّهَ يُحِبُّ فُلاَنًا فَأَحِبُّوهُ فَيُحِبُّهُ أَهْلُ السَّمَاءِ ثُمَّ يُوضَعُ لَهُ الْقَبُولُ فِي أَهْلِ الأَرْضِ وَإِذَا أَبْغَضَ عَبْدًا دَعَا جِبْرِيلَ فَيَقُولُ إِنِّي أُبْغِضُ فُلاَنًا فَأَبْغِضْهُ قَالَ فَيُبْغِضُهُ جِبْرِيلُ ثُمَّ يُنَادِي فِي أَهْلِ السَّمَاءِ إِنَّ اللَّهَ يُبْغِضُ فُلاَنًا فَأَبْغِضُوهُ قَالَ فَيُبْغِضُونَهُ ثُمَّ تُوضَعُ لَهُ الْبَغْضَاءُ فِي الأَرْضِ.»

رواه البخاري (٣٢٠٩) ومسلم (٢٦٣٧) واللفظ لمسلم

The Messenger ﷺ said, «When Allah loves someone, He says to Jibril, "Allah loves so-and-so, so love them." So, Jibril loves them. Then, Jibril says to the inhabitants of the skies, "Allah loves so-and-so, so love them." So, the inhabitants of the skies love them. Then, acceptance is established for them on earth. And when Allah hates someone, He says to Jibril, "Allah hates so-and-so, so hate them." So, Jibril hates them. Then, Jibril says to the inhabitants of the skies, "Allah hates so-and-so, so hate them." So, the inhabitants of the skies hate them. Then, hate is established for them on earth.»

Reported by al-Bukhari (3209) and Muslim (2637)

Commentary

All love comes from Allah. If He loves you, everything else will.

Allah is the origin of all love

Love is the sublimest emotion there is. Sure, it can be misdirected and catastrophic at times, but when appropriate, there is nothing else like it, let alone above it. Most spend their lives looking for it. Many find it in a spouse, child, vocation, pet, or romantic stories and poetry. No matter where we locate it, we know it to be comforting, fulfilling, and inspiring. It is no exaggeration to say that it is the essence of life itself.

With all that, we seldom wonder at the source of all this love. A materialistic understanding of the universe cannot account for it, since matter possesses no emotions to give. Evolutionists claim emotions are about survival, but we know it to be something more profound than that. There must be a power greater than us all, and wiser and more compassionate to make love possible. It is something beyond matter. And this power—the Creator—must possess love. In fact, the Creator is the source of all love.

It is mind-boggling to try to wrap our brains around the fact that Allah is the source of all love. Ibn Abd al-Barr رَحِمَهُ ٱللَّهُ, the famous eleventh-century Andalusian scholar, affirmed:

الْوُدُّ وَالْمَحَبَّةُ بَيْنَ النَّاسِ اللَّهُ يَبْتَدِئُهَا وَيَبْسُطُهَا.

التسهيد لابن عبد البر (ج٢١ ص٢٣٨)

> Allah is the one who starts and spreads love and affection among people.
>
> *Al-Tamhid* (vol. 21, p. 238)

Allah creates and spreads all the love that we and everybody else experience. From the beginning of creation until the end of time. Humans, animals, and all living things. We learned in *Hadith Eight* that it is the same with mercy: Allah is behind it all, truly making Allah the All and Most-Merciful. This similarly makes Allah Al-Wadud: the One who loves more than any other, and is more deserving of love than any other.

Allah's love is the greatest of all love. The human love that we experience, both when we love and are loved, is but a small fraction of the love that Allah has for us. Just consider how human mercy is almost nothing compared to Allah's Mercy, and you will get how Allah's Love is far beyond our earthly experience. The following *hadith qudsi* provides us a glimpse of it. The Prophet ﷺ said:

«إِنْ تَقَرَّبَ إِلَيَّ بِشِبْرٍ تَقَرَّبْتُ إِلَيْهِ ذِراعًا وإِنْ تَقَرَّبَ إِلَيَّ ذِراعًا تَقَرَّبْتُ إِلَيْهِ باعًا وإِنْ أَتانِي يَمْشِي أَتَيْتُهُ هَرْوَلَةً.»

رواه البخاري (٧٤٠٥) ومسلم (٢٦٧٥)

«If [my servant] comes close to Me the distance of a handspan, I come close to them the distance of a cubit. And if they come close to Me the distance of a cubit, I come close to them the distance of two arm spans. And if they walk to Me, I will run to them.»

Reported by al-Bukhari (7405) and Muslim (2675)

What prompts the Lord of all, the Creator and King of everything, to respond to us in this way? To run to us when we walk to Him! This is love. This is mercy. We get from Our Beloved more than we get from any other lover. We find in His love the meaning of everything, and safety from all harm.

All earthly love leads to something else beyond it. It is a chain that does not end until we reach Allah (see *Appendix I*). When we love beautiful people and scenery, we are, in essence, searching for beauty. But where does beauty come from? We love people who are kind and generous because we are seeking nobility in character and actions. But who made it possible? We love the ones who help us and bring us benefit, not realizing that Allah is the real provider. We love pleasure that enhances our life, and we love companionship that chases away our loneliness. Yet, whenever we seek these things on earth, we find them incomplete and flawed. And they do not last. Earthly beauty fades. Earthly pleasures diminish with time. No one's character is complete and satisfactory all the time. And no companion lasts. It is in their nature to be incomplete. They can fulfill some of our needs, but a stubborn longing remains for more. We move to another love, another earthly possession, but we still cannot escape its incompleteness. People can give us something, but they cannot give everything. Earthly benefactors are deficient: they do not have all that we need, and they expect a benefit in return for their gift. We cannot chase away the desire for the perfect, the complete, the never-ending, and the love to surpass all love. This can only be Allah. He is Perfectly Beautiful. He is the Companion who never leaves or disappoints. He grants us permanent pleasure and safety. He gives us life and protects it. He always listens to us and comforts our hearts. He fulfills all of our needs. He loves us back even more than we love ourselves.

In essence, each love we have is us looking for Allah. All love leads back to Allah. Once our love reaches Him, we reach our destination. The journey is over. You do not need to tire anymore.

When Allah loves you, everything loves you

Love begins with Allah and spreads to His creation. Through the *Hadith* of the chapter, we become privy to how this takes place in the upper realms. When Allah loves someone, He announces it to Jibril عَلَيْهِ السَّلَامُ and asks him to love that person. Jibril عَلَيْهِ السَّلَامُ complies and delivers this message to the rest of the angels, who, in turn, love him/her. Finally, the people of earth turn towards that person with love and affection. Love on earth, many times, is an extension of love in the higher realms.

There are *ayahs* in the Quran that confirm the deep connection between Allah's love and the consequent love people experience. Allah said about Musa عَلَيْهِ السَّلَامُ:

...وَأَلْقَيْتُ عَلَيْكَ مَحَبَّةً مِّنِّي وَلِتُصْنَعَ عَلَىٰ عَيْنِيٓ ﴿٣٩﴾

And I endued you with love from Me, so that you may be brought up under My Eye.

Taha (Q20:39)

Allah loved Musa عَلَيْهِ ٱلسَّلَامُ and surrounded him with a love that attracted everyone's heart. Anyone who looked at infant Musa عَلَيْهِ ٱلسَّلَامُ loved him and could not harm him. Though he was alone, defenseless, and weak, the gift of love surrounding him broke all barriers and carried him all the way to Pharaoh's palace. He may have looked weak, but Allah's love gave him power that no one could resist. It made him more powerful than Pharaoh. Love achieves what force cannot.

In case one may think that this is exclusive to Musa and the Prophets عَلَيْهِمُ ٱلسَّلَامُ, Allah told us in the Quran:

إِنَّ ٱلَّذِينَ ءَامَنُوا۟ وَعَمِلُوا۟ ٱلصَّٰلِحَٰتِ سَيَجْعَلُ لَهُمُ ٱلرَّحْمَٰنُ وُدًّا ﴿٩٦﴾

The Merciful will bestow love to those who believe and do righteous deeds.

Maryam (Q19:96)

Mujahid, the famous second-generation exegete, wrote commenting on this *ayah*:

قال مجاهد: يُحِبُّهم ويُحَبِّبُهم إلى خَلْقِه.

تفسير الطبري

He loves them and makes people love them.

Tafsir al-Tabari

Those who have *Iman* and do good will receive Allah's love and the love of the people. This should be qualified, however, by remembering that even the Prophets of Allah عَلَيْهِمُ ٱلسَّلَامُ had enemies. So, when we say they will receive "the love of people," it means most people or the pious. The following *hadith* confirms that it is the pious.

مَرُّوا بجَنازَةٍ فأثْنَوْا عَلَيْها خَيْرًا فَقالَ النبيُّ ﷺ «وجَبَتْ» ثُمَّ مَرُّوا

بِأُخْرى فأَثْنَوْا عَلَيْها شَرًّا فَقالَ «وجَبَتْ» فَقالَ عُمَرُ بنُ الخَطّابِ رَضِيَ اللَّهُ عنْه: ما وجَبَتْ؟ قالَ «هذا أَثْنَيْتُمْ عليه خَيْرًا فَوَجَبَتْ له الجَنَّةُ وهذا أَثْنَيْتُمْ عليه شَرًّا فَوَجَبَتْ له النّارُ أَنتُمْ شُهَداءُ اللَّهِ في الأَرْضِ.»

رواه البخاري (٢٦٤٢) ومسلم (٩٤٩)

A funeral passed by [the Prophet ﷺ and the companions] and they praised the dead person, so the Prophet ﷺ said, «He received it.» Another funeral passed by, and they criticized the deceased person, so he said, «He received it.» Umar ibn al-Khattab رضي الله عنه asked, "What did you mean by 'He received it?'" He replied, «You praised this one, and he received Jannah, and you criticized this one, and he received Hell. You are the witnesses of Allah on earth.»

Reported by al-Bukhari (2642) and Muslim (949)

In another narration of this *hadith*, the Prophet ﷺ said:

«المؤمنونَ شهداءُ اللهِ في الأَرْضِ.»

أحكام الجنائز للألباني (ص٤٤)

«The believers are the witnesses of Allah on earth.»

Ahkam al-Jana'iz by al-Albani (p. 44)

The believers are the witnesses because they love what Allah loves, so their love reflects what is happening in the heavens. If the believers unite in praising or condemning someone, then it was Allah who joined their hearts. If the believers—or non-believers—love someone for the wrong reasons, in conflict with what Allah loves, their affection and testimony would not carry the same weight.

The reputation that one has on earth, specifically among the pious, matters. The Prophet ﷺ said:

«ما من عبدٍ إلّا ولهُ صِيتٌ في السماءِ فإنْ كان صِيتُهُ في السماءِ

حَسَنًا وُضِعَ في الأَرْضِ وإنْ كان صِيتُهُ في السماءِ سيِّئًا وُضِعَ في الأَرْضِ.»

رواه البزار في مسنده (٩٢٠٢) وصححه الألباني (صحيح الجامع ٥٧٣٢)

Everyone has a reputation in the heavens. If their reputation in the heavens was good, it would be sent to earth. And if their reputation in the heavens was bad, it would be sent to earth.

Reported by al-Bazzar in his *Musnad* (9202) and al-Albani declared it sahih (*Sahih al-Jami'*, 5732)

The best reputation belongs to the best, and the worst to the worst. The Prophet ﷺ said:

«خِيارُ أئِمَّتِكُمُ الَّذِينَ تُحِبُّونَهُمْ ويُحِبُّونَكُمْ، وتُصَلُّونَ عليهم ويُصَلُّونَ علَيْكُم، وشِرارُ أئِمَّتِكُمُ الَّذِينَ تُبْغِضُونَهُمْ ويُبْغِضُونَكُمْ، وتَلْعَنُونَهُمْ ويَلْعَنُونَكُمْ، قالوا: قُلْنا: يا رَسولَ اللهِ، أفَلا نُنابِذُهُمْ عِنْدَ ذلكَ؟ قالَ: لا، ما أقامُوا فِيكُمُ الصَّلاةَ.»

رواه مسلم (١٨٥٥)

«The best of your rulers are those whom you love and who love you back, and you pray for them and they for you. And the worst of your rulers are those whom you hate and who hate you back, and you pray against them and they against you.» They asked, "O Messenger of Allah, shall we not fight them then?" He replied, «No, as long as they establish Salah among you.»

Reported by Muslim (1855)

Muslims applied this principle and saw the connection between the feelings they had for someone and how much Allah loved them. Suhayl ibn Abi Salih said:

عَنْ سُهَيْلِ بْنِ أَبِي صَالِحٍ قَالَ: كُنَّا بِعَرَفَةَ فَمَرَّ عُمَرُ بْنُ عَبْدِ الْعَزِيزِ وَهُوَ عَلَى الْمَوْسِمِ فَقَامَ النَّاسُ يَنْظُرُونَ إِلَيْهِ فَقُلْتُ لِأَبِي: يَا أَبَتِ إِنِّي

أَرَى اللهَ يُحِبُّ عُمَرَ بْنَ عَبْدِ الْعَزِيزِ، قَالَ: وَمَا ذَاكَ؟ قُلْتُ: لِمَا لَهُ مِنَ الْحُبِّ فِي قُلُوبِ النَّاسِ.

رواه مسلم (٢٦٣٧)

We were in 'Arafah, and 'Umar ibn 'Abd al-'Aziz happened to pass by, and he was the Amir of Hajj. People stood up to catch a glimpse of him. I said to my father, "Father, I believe that Allah loves 'Umar ibn 'Abd al-'Aziz." He said, "Why?" I said, "Because of the love that people have for him in their hearts."

Reported by Muslim (2637)

'Umar ibn 'Abd al-'Aziz was pious and just, and people loved him for it. They loved him for the rights reasons, and Suhayl saw Allah's love reflected in it. This is available to us all. And it happens especially before our death. The Prophet ﷺ said:

«إذا أحبَّ اللهُ عَبدًا عسَّلَه،» قالوا: ما عسَّلَه يا رسولَ اللهِ؟ قال «يُوفِّقُ لهُ عملًا صالحًا بين يدَي أجلِه حتّى يرضى عنهُ جيرانُه» أو قال «...مَن حولَه.»

رواه الحاكم (١٢٥٨)وصححه الألباني (صحيح الترغيب ٣٣٥٨)

«If Allah loves someone, He sweetens them [literally, sweetens them with honey].» They asked, "What does sweeten them mean, O Messenger of Allah?" He replied, «He guides them to a righteous deed before their death so that their neighbors—or he said those around them—will be pleased with them.»

Reported by al-Hakim (1258) and al-Albani declared it sahih (*Sahih al-Targhib*, 3358)

If Allah loves them, they leave this earth with the sweetest (i.e. most pleasant) reputation. People love them, pray for them, and their name feels like honey on the tongue. They leave the most beautiful legacy behind. This is what love does.

It is such a comforting and overwhelming feeling to know that you can get everything to love you, to live in harmony with the universe because of the love of Lord of the universe. Electrons, like the planets in their orbits, move inside an atom out of love (i.e. Allah loves them to move, and so they do). The hearts of all living beings beat because of love. When you love Allah, you move because of the love of Allah and with it, like everything else in the universe, like the atoms of your body. This is harmony. This is true connection. Even the animals experience this connection. The Prophet ﷺ said:

«إِنَّ اللَّهَ وملائِكتَهُ وأَهلَ السَّماواتِ والأرضِ حتّى النَّملةَ في جُحرِها وحتّى الحوتَ ليصلُّونَ على معلِّمِ النّاسِ الخيرَ.»

رواه الترمذي (٢٦٨٥) وصححه الألباني (صحيح الترمذي ٢٦٨٥)

Indeed, Allah, His angels, the inhabitants of the heavens and earth, even the ant in its hole and the fish pray for the teacher of righteousness to people.

Reported by al-Tirmidhi (2685) and al-Albani declared it sahih (*Sahih al-Tirmidhi*, 2685)

The connection goes beyond our awareness, beyond our imagination. When Allah loves you, everything falls into place. All move with the same rhythm and goal.

When we understand this, it will free us from false-dependency on people. We are trying to please everyone all the time, worried about who likes us, who hates us, why they hate us, and how we can get them to like us. But if we remember that love begins with Allah and He determines its flow, we need only to please Him. The rest will follow. The Prophet ﷺ said:

«من التمس رِضا اللهِ بسخَطِ الناسِ رضِيَ اللهُ عنه وأرْضى عنه الناسَ ومن التَمس رضا الناسِ بسخَطِ اللهِ سخِط اللهُ عليه وأسخَط عليه الناسَ.»

رواه ابن حبان (٢٧٦) وصححه الألباني (التعليقات الحسان ٢٧٦)

«The one who seeks Allah's approval though it is upsetting to people, Allah will be pleased with them and will make people

> pleased with them. And the one who seeks people's approval though it is upsetting to Allah, Allah will be displeased with them and will make people displeased with them.»
>
> Reported by Ibn Hibban (276) and al-Albani declared it sahih (*Al-Ta'liqat al-Hisan*, 276)

Sometimes, there will be a conflict between what Allah loves and what people (or we) love. If we please Allah, then people will (eventually) be happy with us, and we will be happy with ourselves. But if we choose what people love (or what we love), people will (eventually) hate us, and we will start hating ourselves. It is easier to please one instead of many. Do not worry about who loves you, who hates you, or why they love so-and-so more than you. Do not worry about your earthly reputation and ignore your heavenly one. Love Allah and forget the rest. Love Allah, and He will fix the rest. This, of course, does not mean that we should stop caring about people's feelings, be rude, and disregard their rights. Allah hates this. We should do what Allah loves without alienating people or pushing them away from Allah. But if, despite our best efforts, they still oppose what Allah loves, then Allah's love is better than everything else.

How do you get Allah's love? As the rest of the book will demonstrate, we attain His love by doing what He loves. Receiving His love is the greatest achievement, and its deprivation is the greatest loss. When Allah spoke about the nonbelievers in the Quran, He would repeat that He did not love them. He did not say that He hated them; He always expressed it as the negation of love. This is significant. Though not loving something is hating it, putting it in the negative highlights the momentous deprivation when Allah's love is lost. Loving Allah is the goal of every living being, the comfort of every soul. When it is gone, everything else is gone. And when it is there, everything else is there. Set the love of Allah as your destination. Let everything else move you towards it.

HADITH THIRTEEN

الحديث الثالث عشر

Allah loves the faithful

قَالَ رَسُولُ اللهِ ﷺ «الْمُؤْمِنُ الْقَوِيُّ خَيْرٌ وَأَحَبُّ إِلَى اللهِ مِنَ الْمُؤْمِنِ الضَّعِيفِ وَفِي كُلٍّ خَيْرٌ احْرِصْ عَلَى مَا يَنْفَعُكَ وَاسْتَعِنْ بِاللهِ وَلَا تَعْجَزْ وَإِنْ أَصَابَكَ شَيْءٌ فَلَا تَقُلْ لَوْ أَنِّي فَعَلْتُ كَانَ كَذَا وَكَذَا وَلَكِنْ قُلْ قَدَرُ اللهِ وَمَا شَاءَ فَعَلَ فَإِنَّ لَوْ تَفْتَحُ عَمَلَ الشَّيْطَانِ.»

رواه مسلم (٢٦٦٤)

The Messenger ﷺ said, «The strong believer is better and more beloved to Allah than the weak believer, though there is good in both of them. Strive to attain what benefits you, seek assistance from Allah and do not be helpless. If a misfortune befalls you, do not say, "If I had done this, then this and that would have happened." But say, "Allah has decreed and He does what He wills," for "if I had" opens the door for Shaytan's work.»

Reported by Muslim (2664)

Commentary

Those with the strongest *Iman* have the strongest love for Allah. Allah loves them because of their patience and striving. They keep trying, they ask Allah for help, and they never give up. Their goal is the greatest love of all.

Strength: a blessing or a curse?

When we say that someone is strong, we are typically praising them. But is strength always a blessing? Who are the strong whom Allah loves?

Often, physical strength is a biological gift—i.e. people born naturally strong or with bigger bodies—and not a consequence of effort. On the other end, some are born physically weaker. Both of these states cannot be the reason why Allah loves some more or less. Indeed, physical strength can also be a product of training and hard work. But in itself, it is not an act of virtue. Many of those who frequent the gyms today are vain. They focus solely on their appearance, displaying their bodies for praise and recognition. Such display of strength and fitness, when not done for a good end, only feeds our ego and narcissism. We become more materialistic the more we invite people to look at our bodies, where our appearance decides our worth.

Allah, on the other hand, looks at our hearts and not our bodies. Our hearts define us, not our bodies. The Prophet ﷺ said:

«إِنَّ اللهَ لَا يَنْظُرُ إِلَى صُوَرِكُمْ وَأَمْوَالِكُمْ وَلَكِنْ يَنْظُرُ إِلَى قُلُوبِكُمْ وَأَعْمَالِكُمْ.»

رواه مسلم (٢٥٦٤)

«Allah does not look at your appearances and wealth, but He looks at your hearts and deeds.»

Reported by Muslim (2564)

Without the strength of *Iman* and character, physical strength leads to transgression and sin. This is why the Prophet ﷺ redefined strength by saying:

«لَيْسَ الشَّدِيدُ بِالصُّرَعَةِ إِنَّمَا الشَّدِيدُ الَّذِي يَمْلِكُ نَفْسَهُ عِنْدَ الْغَضَبِ.»

رواه البخاري (٦١١٤) ومسلم (٢٦٠٩)

«The strong is not the one who overpowers others physically but the one who controls themselves when angry.»

Reported by al-Bukhari (6114) and Muslim (2609)

Physical strength on its own is neither admirable nor condemnable. It is what we do with it that matters. When we pursue it for noble ends, it is praised and rewardable. Allah says:

وَأَعِدُّوا۟ لَهُم مَّا ٱسْتَطَعْتُم مِّن قُوَّةٍ... ٦٠

And prepare against them whatever you are able of power.

Al-Anfal (Q8:60)

If one intends to do good with their physical exercise (i.e. what is pleasing to Allah), their workout will be an act of worship. The pursuit of power is noble when the end is. And the same rule applies to all physical/material accomplishments. Fame for the sake of fame is egotistical. Academic degrees are not meant for bragging. Oratory skills in the service of falsehood are a curse. Poverty is better than wealth that leads away from Allah. Worldly accomplishments are corrupting when *Iman* is missing.

Iman enhances our life. This is not only true spiritually, but materially as well. Allah said:

وَيَـٰقَوْمِ ٱسْتَغْفِرُوا۟ رَبَّكُمْ ثُمَّ تُوبُوٓا۟ إِلَيْهِ يُرْسِلِ ٱلسَّمَآءَ عَلَيْكُم مِّدْرَارًا
وَيَزِدْكُمْ قُوَّةً إِلَىٰ قُوَّتِكُمْ وَلَا تَتَوَلَّوْا۟ مُجْرِمِينَ ٥٢

And O my people, ask forgiveness from your Rabb and repent to Him, and He will send rain abundantly upon you and add strength to your strength.

Hud (Q11:52)

Strength is boosted with *Iman*. How so? Obeying Allah blesses the body and brings about Allah's assistance and guidance. It could also be that when a soul is blessed with *Iman*, the body reaches more of its potential, and so it can do what it could not before.

Allah loves the strong believers

The strength praised in the *Hadith* is that of *Iman*. There are three pillars to this strength: knowledge, commitment, and worship.

Knowledge is the first step in the path of *Iman*. The more we know Allah and His revelation, the firmer our belief. We learn from Allah's revelation the wisdom behind His commands and actions, and the benefit and reward of worship. We also learn what Allah loves and hates, helping us to chart a course for our life and determine its goals. This knowledge protects us from doubt, teaches us how to repel the whispers of Shaytan, helps us conquer sin, and guides us back to Allah in repentance. If a Muslim desires the love of Allah, they must learn their religion. You cannot love what you do not know. This is especially important today because of the raging fire of temptations and doubts (fitnahs). A strong Muslim today must learn their religion in detail and in-depth.

Knowledge without commitment is fruitless. Allah sent down the message of Islam to be lived. This is the second natural step. When we recognize the truth and virtue of what Allah revealed, we will decide to follow it. The last step is the product of this commitment: the worship of Allah. This includes worshipping with sincerity, energy, and interest. It involves attempting to perfect our worship: on time and with the obligatory and recommended components. And it includes asking Allah for acceptance, consistency in worship, and guarding oneself against self-admiration. The strong believer is one who is strong in their love of Allah, strong in their physical worship, strong in avoiding sin, and strong in displaying the best of manners.

The Prophet ﷺ gave an example of the strength of *Iman* which Allah loves in the following *hadith*:

«ثَلَاثَةٌ يُحِبُّهُمُ اللهُ وَثَلَاثَةٌ يَشْنَؤُهُمُ اللهُ الرَّجُلُ يَلْقَى الْعَدُوَّ فِي الْفِئَةِ فَيَنْصِبُ لَهُمْ نَحْرَهُ حَتَّى يُقْتَلَ أَوْ يُفْتَحَ لِأَصْحَابِهِ وَالْقَوْمُ يُسَافِرُونَ

فَيَطُولُ سُرَاهُمْ حَتَّى يُحِبُّوا أَنْ يَمَسُّوا الْأَرْضَ فَيَنْزِلُونَ فَيَتَنَحَّى أَحَدُهُمْ فَيُصَلِّي حَتَّى يُوقِظَهُمْ لِرَحِيلِهِمْ وَالرَّجُلُ يكُونُ لَهُ الْجَارُ يُؤْذِيهِ جِوَارُهُ فَيَصْبِرُ عَلَى أَذَاهُ حَتَّى يُفَرِّقَ بَيْنَهُمَا مَوْتٌ أَوْ ظَعْنٌ وَالَّذِينَ يَشْنَؤُهُمُ اللهُ التَّاجِرُ الْحَلَّافُ وَالْبَخِيلُ الْمَنَّانُ وَالْفَقِيرُ الْمُخْتَالُ.»

رواه أحمد (٢١٣٤٠) وصححه الألباني (صحيح الجامع ٣٠٧٤) والأرناؤوط

«There are three people whom Allah loves and three whom He hates. [The first of the three whom He loves] is a man who faces the enemy with his company and stays steadfast until he is killed or his company is victorious. And travelers who journey long at night until they love to put their sides on the ground, so they camp but one of them steps aside to pray until he wakes them up for their departure. And the man who has a neighbor who annoys him, so he remains patient with his harm until death or relocation separates them. And the ones whom Allah hates are the often-swearing merchant, the stingy who reminds people of his favors, and the arrogant poor.»

Reported by Ahmad (21340) and al-Albani declared it sahih (*Sahih al-Jami'*, 3074) and al-Arna'ut

The first three are exceptionally brave and patient. They all demonstrate steadfastness despite difficulty. What allows one to sacrifice their life for the sake of Allah, standing alone even when others flee? Why would one stand praying at night, though extremely fatigued, while everyone else sleeps? How could you be so patient with an annoying neighbor, day after day? We cannot do any of these things if our *Iman* is weak.

The strong in *Iman* are strong in their love of Allah. They are strong in doing what Allah loves. They put the extra effort. They sacrifice. They want Allah more, so they do more. They want Allah more than anything else.

All of us get tired. All of us are busy. All of us lose our patience. All of us feel overwhelmed. The strength of *Iman* does not mean escaping human weakness and frustration to become an angelic figure. It means that we try to control our weaknesses and rise above them. We, at times, will fail. But we will always get up and try again, harder this time. It is a fresh start every single time, even if we fail a million times. We will push ourselves to learn. We will strive to apply. We will ask Allah for help. We will keep trying. We will learn from our mistakes. But we will never give up. The *Hadith* of the chapter provides the roadmap to strength (see next section).

There is a reinforcement loop between knowledge, commitment, and worship. When we engage in worship, we learn something new about that worship and ourselves. When we see the fruits of our worship, our commitment to it increases. *Iman* requires all of its three pillars to be strong, each feeding and enhancing the other. Love cannot be strong if there is no practice.

The roadmap to strength

After declaring that Allah loves those strong in *Iman*, the *Hadith* offers the steps needed to gain this strength and to gain Allah's love.

The first step is to "Strive to attain what benefits you." Though it should be a given that everyone naturally seeks what benefits them, our observation of humanity tells us otherwise. We sometimes do not know what is beneficial, and at other times we lack motivation and commitment. A straightforward remedy to the first problem is to trust Allah's judgment. If you are ever in doubt about what is beneficial, you will find it in what Allah loves. Allah only commanded what is good for us, and He prohibited what is harmful. In the area of the permissible acts, experience and science can tell us what to do and what to avoid (e.g. exercise and a balanced diet are good, lack of sleep and stress are bad).

If our problem is not ignorance, then we lack the will to follow the truth. It is when we say to ourselves: "I know that I am supposed to do this, but I do not have the energy to do it." Is there is a solution to this? Yes. It is to ponder the gravity of seeking Jannah and salvation from Hell. Like any prime real estate on earth, Jannah has a price. Everything of value requires sacrifice. We often do not feel like going to work or school, but we do. Why? We force ourselves because we know that we need the money and the degree, and the alternative is dire. We save to buy a house, and in the process, deny ourselves many luxuries. This tells us that we have the ability to sacrifice and persevere. Why is it possible to sacrifice for that cause? Because we understand how precious the outcome is. Will we not push ourselves to secure the best real estate in existence, Jannah? (P.S. If you find that you are too weak to internalize this, move to the "second step".)

When we have the knowledge and the will, we will be motivated to seek the beneficial everywhere it may be. Our goal each day will be to do as much good as possible before we leave this earth and meet Allah. If Allah opens a door of righteousness for us, we enter. We do not belittle any small act of piety because it leads to greater acts. Every good deed is possibly the step that puts us in Jannah. Every good deed is a gift from Allah, and we should accept His gifts. We approach each opportunity to do good with enthusiasm, remembering the great reward that it brings. Who knows if the chance will ever come back? We saw in *Hadith Seven* the example of Abu Bakr رَضِيَ ٱللَّهُ عَنْهُ who filled his day with righteousness (worship and the help of others). This is what seizing the day looks like. We will not be able to match the piety of Abu Bakr رَضِيَ ٱللَّهُ عَنْهُ but we can let it inspire us.

The second step is "Seek Allah's assistance and do not be helpless." Whenever we find ourselves unable to do something, we should never give up. Sometimes, circumstances stop us from reaching our goals: we lack the money, the time, or the opportunity. At other times, we are not motivated to do the right thing. For some, they have tried everything but were met only with frustration. No matter what the roadblock may be, the Prophet ﷺ asked us to cast despair aside. What is most important at this stage is not to surrender and lose hope. Instead, be sure that you can ask Allah for help and that He will assist you. He can remove any obstacle, inject you with energy, and make the seemingly impossible possible. He is the Lord of all, and He can change all. And if Allah decides to give you, no one can stand in your way.

This is something that we often forget. When we are facing some trouble, some of us are quick to retreat in disappointment and despair. We keep struggling with this failure, allowing it to undermine our trust in Allah and poisoning the rest of our life. We forget that we have access to the One with the greatest power to change everything. And if you rely on the Most Powerful, you will be unstoppable. This reliance (*tawakkul*) on Allah gives the believers eternal hope that nothing and no one can extinguish. It gives the believers physical strength and endurance beyond what they thought they were capable of. Listen to Allah when He said:

...إِن يَكُن مِّنكُمْ عِشْرُونَ صَٰبِرُونَ يَغْلِبُوا۟ مِا۟ئَتَيْنِ ۚ وَإِن يَكُن مِّنكُم مِّا۟ئَةٌ يَغْلِبُوٓا۟ أَلْفًا مِّنَ ٱلَّذِينَ كَفَرُوا۟... ﴿٦٥﴾

If there are twenty of you who are patient, they will overcome two hundred, and a hundred of you will overcome a thousand of the disbelievers.

Al-Anfal (Q8:65)

It is *Iman* and patience that gives the believers the advantage. It is a 1:10 ratio, but they are still more powerful because of *Iman*. If this is the power that Allah promised—mental, emotional, and physical—how can we ever think of ourselves as weak. How can we ever lose hope? We are weak if we do not call on Him to help us. We are weak if we surrender. We are weak if we depend on ourselves. But if Allah is with you, you are strong. No, you are the strongest by the will of Allah.

The third and final step in the *Hadith* is not regretting the past and moving forward. This is the trap that some of us are in at this moment. We look at a painful moment in the past and wonder "What if...?" This futile thinking brings a flood of sadness and regret. It saps us of energy and condemns us to anger, doubt, and hopelessness. It is a common trap of Shaytan. He tries to use any means to sadden us and cut our connection with Allah. The Prophet ﷺ explained that this thinking is harmful and useless. What happened had to happen because it was Allah's decree. No amount of planning or precaution could have changed the past. You could not have said anything or done anything to change it. If you believe this, then why trouble yourself with "If I only..."? This statement invites in the whispers of Shaytan and destroys our *Iman*. If you want your *Iman* to be strong, keep looking forward, and ignore the frustrations of the past. Yes, we can learn from our past, but we should never be hostages to it. Learn from it but fly above it. Your future is not going to be a replicate of your past. You are not the same person you were yesterday, so why would your tomorrow be a repeat of your past? Ask Allah to assist you, to change you, and you will be different, better. Trust Allah. Move forward. There is no reason for you to be weak anymore. He is with you if you are with Him.

Allah loves what benefits you

One of the many beautiful things about Allah is how much He cares about us. If something is good for us, He commands us to do it and rewards us when we do. And if it is harmful, He prohibits it and rewards us when we avoid it. All of Allah's revelation revolves around this goal: bringing what benefits us closer and protecting us from harm. Allah's revelation is there to make us happy.

Knowing this about Allah makes Him the joy of life itself, the truth that gives everything else meaning. Without Him, we would move aimlessly, live bitterly, and be emotionally unfulfilled no matter what we do. Allah rescues us with His revelation, a great mercy that supersedes the benefit of food and drink. When we approach the Quran and Sunnah as such, we will love Allah for everything He taught us and asked us to do. Every time we listen to Him, we will feel safe and loved. Every time we ignore His Wisdom, we feel lost and abandoned.

No one protects us from harm as Allah does. It begins with His revelation, but it does not end there. *Hadith Eleven* showed us how Allah protects us from worldly temptations. We run after them, and He gently removes them from our path. We cry for them and complain, like children crying for candy, and He patiently exposes us to different life experiences, so we mature and see how childish we were. He protects us from Shaytan and his whispers, from Jinn and their evil, and from humans who wish us harm. He protects us from accidents, sickness, and emotional pain. And when He allows some of this to happen, He allows it to protect us too, like medicine we take to reclaim our health. It is bitter, but it is effective. All natural medicine is from His Mercy. Anyone who helps us does so because of Him.

Some point to their pain and blame Allah. But we forget that each pain points to a blessing. We must have had something in order to lose it, and this possession was a blessing (e.g. if I lost money, I lost the money that Allah gave me). If Allah wanted your harm or hated you, why would He give you so much? He only took back some of what He gave you to bring you back to Him, to give you the greater reward of Jannah. Allah never mistreats anyone. He never harms you. He never leaves you alone. Be with Him, and you will find Him closer than your closest friend. All good flows from Him to you. From Him, all good is waiting for you.

HADITH FOURTEEN

الحديث الرابع عشر

Loving Allah and loving the world

قَالَ رَسُولُ اللهِ ﷺ «اللَّهُمَّ مَنْ آمَنَ بِكَ وَشَهِدَ أَنِّي رَسُولُكَ فَحَبِّبْ إِلَيْهِ لِقَاءَكَ وَسَهِّلْ عَلَيْهِ قَضَاءَكَ وَأَقْلِلْ لَهُ مِنَ الدُّنْيَا وَمَنْ لَمْ يُؤْمِنْ بِكَ وَلَمْ يَشْهَدْ أَنِّي رَسُولُكَ فَلَا تُحَبِّبْ إِلَيْهِ لِقَاءَكَ وَلَا تُسَهِّلْ عَلَيْهِ قَضَاءَكَ وَأَكْثِرْ لَهُ مِنَ الدُّنْيَا.»

رواه ابن حبان (٢٠٨) والطبراني في المعجم الكبير (٨٠٨) وصححه الألباني (السلسلة الصحيحة ١٣٣٨) وصحح إسناده شعيب الأرناؤوط في تحقيقه لابن حبان

The Messenger ﷺ said, «O Allah, whoever believes in You and testifies that I am Your Messenger, make meeting You beloved to them, ease Your decrees upon them, and give them less of this world. And whoever disbelieves in You and does not testify that I am Your Messenger, do not make meeting You beloved to them, do not ease Your decrees upon them, and give them more of this world.»

Reported by Ibn Hibban (208) and al-Tabarani in al-Mu'jam al-Kabir (808) and al-Albani declared it sahih (al-Silsilah al-Sahihah, 1338) and Shu'ayb al-Arna'ut

Commentary

Waiting to meet Allah, the greatest love, is the joy of the believer. Their hearts have migrated from worldly love to divine love, and they cannot wait to see Allah in the Hereafter.

Loving to meet Allah

This life is a journey. We move from one stage to another, from one place to another, from one day to another, and from one concern to another. We are constantly travelling, literally and figuratively. We travel in search of what we love, but we also long for what we leave behind. Travel as the Prophet ﷺ explained:

«السَّفَرُ قِطْعَةٌ مِنَ العَذابِ.»

رواه البخاري (١٨٠٤) ومسلم (١٩٢٧)

«Travel is a piece of torment.»

Reported by al-Bukhari (1804) and Muslim (1927)

Physical travel is difficult because it deprives one of food, drink, comfort, and family. There is no peace until one reaches their destination and return to their home. If this entire life is also a journey, it is also a piece of torment until we find a restful place and a loving embrace. We are constantly moving, looking for someone or something. But we are also seeking and moving towards Allah in all of our journeys. Allah informed us in the Quran that we are all moving towards meeting Him. He said:

وَٱتَّقُواْ ٱللَّهَ وَٱعۡلَمُوٓاْ أَنَّكُم مُّلَٰقُوهُۗ وَبَشِّرِ ٱلۡمُؤۡمِنِينَ ﴿٢٢٣﴾

And have Taqwa of Allah and know that you will meet Him. And give good news to the believers.

Al-Baqarah (Q2:223)

Meeting Allah brings lasting comfort and peace. This is the good news that the believers should hear. The One they love, whom they sacrificed for, and whom they were worshipping their whole life is waiting for them at the end of their journey. When they meet Him, all their pain will wash away. They will finally find complete and pure happiness. Ibn Mas'ud رَضِيَ ٱللَّهُ عَنْهُ said:

قَالَ عَبْدُ اللَّهِ بْنُ مَسْعُودٍ رضي الله عنه: لَيْسَ لِلْمُؤْمِنِ رَاحَةٌ دُونَ لِقَاءِ اللَّهِ عَزَّ وَجَلَّ وَمَنْ كَانَتْ رَاحَتُهُ فِي لِقَاءِ اللَّهِ فَكَأَنْ قَدْ.

الزهد لابن المبارك (ص٦)

The believer has no comfort until they meet Allah, glory be to Him. And the one whose comfort is in meeting Allah, comfort is close to them.

Al-Zuhd by Ibn al-Mubarak (p. 6)

There can be no true and lasting peace without Allah. Everything else is incomplete and impermanent. Every other destination is missing something. How can we enjoy what we know we are going to lose eventually? We strive so much to reach our goals only to be disappointed when we have them. Then, we go after something else. Yet, satisfaction eludes us. We think that this and that will make us happy, but they turn stale when they are in our hands. When will this end? When will we find comfort? Only Allah can satisfy the gap in our lives, only He can make us truly happy. Those who seek Allah will soon meet Him, and He will comfort them. They will finally meet the One that they loved and worshipped. They will get to meet the One they have sacrificed for, and He will receive them with love, forgiveness, and blessings. There is no greater reunion than this one. Therefore, Allah comforted the believers who cannot wait to see Him when He said:

مَن كَانَ يَرْجُواْ لِقَآءَ ٱللَّهِ فَإِنَّ أَجَلَ ٱللَّهِ لَأَتٍۚ وَهُوَ ٱلسَّمِيعُ ٱلْعَلِيمُ ۝٥

Whoever hopes to meet Allah, then Allah's appointed time is coming. And He is the All-Hearing, the All-Knowing.

Al-'Ankabut (Q29:5)

Can you wait to see your Beloved? The One who gave you everything? The One that you talk to all the time? The One who cares for you more than you care for yourself? This is the greatest wish of those who love Allah: to finally see Him, to finally find the peace of being close to Him, to attain His pleasure and fear nothing and no one anymore. This future reality brings them comfort in the face of every present difficulty. They remember their eventual departure to Allah, and every earthly pain appears small and fleeting. It will all go away, and Allah is the only One who remains.

We may be looking forward to seeing Allah, but is Allah looking forward to seeing us? Listen to this beautiful *hadith*. The Prophet ﷺ said:

«ما تَوَطَّنَ رجلٌ مسلمٌ المساجِدَ للصلاةِ والذكْرِ إلّا تَبَشْبَشَ اللهُ لَهُ من حينِ يَخرُجُ مِنْ بَيْتِهِ كما يتَبَشْبَشُ أهلُ الغائِبِ بغائِبِهِمْ إذا قدِمَ علَيْهم.»

رواه أحمد (٨٣٥٠) وابن ماجه (٨٠٠) وصححه الألباني (صحيح ابن ماجه ٦٥٩)

«Whenever a Muslim man settles in a mosque [i.e. attends it regularly until it becomes like a home for him] for Salah and dhikr, Allah will be happy with him from the time he leaves his home [heading for the mosque] like the family of an absentee is happy with him when he comes back.»

Reported by Ahmad (8350) and Ibn Majah (800) and al-Albani declared it sahih (*Sahih ibn Majah*, 659)

This is the happiness Allah feels for this daily meeting. (By the way, women have the same reward when they pray at home). Imagine Allah's joy when He meets us for the grandest meeting! Imagine our joy! Imagine the incredible bounties and wonders that we will see.

To put things in perspective, seeing Allah in Jannah is greater than all of its blessings and luxuries combined. The Prophet ﷺ said:

«إذا دَخَلَ أَهْلُ الجَنَّةِ الجَنَّةَ يقولُ اللَّهُ تَبارَكَ وتَعالى: تُرِيدُونَ شيئًا أَزِيدُكُمْ، فيَقولونَ: أَلَمْ تُبَيِّضْ وُجُوهَنا أَلَمْ تُدْخِلْنا الجَنَّةَ وتُنَجِّنا مِنَ

النَّارِ؟» قالَ «فَيَكْشِفُ الحِجابَ فَما أُعْطُوا شيئًا أحَبَّ إليهِم مِنَ النَّظَرِ إلى رَبِّهِمْ عزَّ وجلَّ.»

رواه مسلم (١٨١)

«When the people of Jannah enter it, Allah will say to them, "Do you want anything else from Me?" They will say, "Did You not brighten our faces, grant us Jannah, and save us from Hell?" So He removes the barrier, and nothing that they were given will be more beloved to them than looking at their Rabb.»

Reported by Muslim (181)

The greatest joy in Jannah is to gaze at the Face of Allah, glory be to Him. He is more Beautiful than everything, more Perfect than anything. The people of Jannah were seeking Him their entire lives, and now here He is. To finally get the chance to see Him is to finally see the One who is closer to you than your own soul. Their hearts were about to melt in this world waiting for this moment, and now they finally have their greatest wish. Jannah is blessed with being close to Allah. And the best of Jannah, al-Firdaws, is the nearest to Allah. The Prophet ﷺ said:

«إذا سَأَلْتُمُ اللَّهَ فَاسْأَلُوهُ الفِرْدَوْسَ فَإِنَّهُ أَوْسَطُ الجَنَّةِ وَأَعْلَى الجَنَّةِ فَوْقَهُ عَرْشُ الرَّحْمَنِ وَمِنْهُ تَفَجَّرُ أَنْهارُ الجَنَّةِ.»

رواه البخاري (٢٧٩٠)

«If you ask Allah, ask Him for al-Firdaws, for it is the best of Jannah, the highest Jannah, above it is the Throne of the Merciful, and the rivers of Jannah spring from it.»

Reported by al-Bukhari (2790)

The Throne of Allah is the ceiling of al-Firdaws, and above the Throne is Allah, the Highest. Al-Firdaws is the closest we can get to Allah, and no one can imagine the bliss of being this close to the Most Merciful.

All of us have someone that we are waiting to see, someone we cannot wait to see. For some, it is an absent or deceased family member. For some, unfortunately, it is a social media influencer, actor, dancer, or singer. No matter who they are, our desire to meet them is based on love. We want to be close to whom we love, to enjoy their company and to hear their words. Imagine the joy that an earthly union brings, the excitement and contentment you feel or have felt the last time you met a loved one. Now, imagine meeting Allah for the first time. Whatever joy meeting another human may bring, it is but a tiny fraction of the joy of meeting Allah. Seeing Allah is seeing perfect beauty, complete mercy and peace, overwhelming contentment, and knowledge that there is no pain or fear anymore. It is to be finally happy, wholly happy, with nothing to ever spoil this happiness. It is to know that all your work and sacrifice paid off, and now you can rest and enjoy His Presence, His direct Speech, His incredible Mercy, and His incredible Care. It is finally finding comfort after decades of looking. There is no suffering anymore, my friend. Now, you are home.

Lovers cannot wait to see their beloved. Those who love Allah actually miss Him. In fact, the Prophet ﷺ asked for such longing when he said:

«اللَّهُمَّ بِعِلْمِكَ الْغَيْبَ وَقُدْرَتِكَ عَلَى الْخَلْقِ أَحْيِنِي مَا عَلِمْتَ الْحَيَاةَ خَيْرًا لِي وَتَوَفَّنِي إِذَا عَلِمْتَ الْوَفَاةَ خَيْرًا لِي اللَّهُمَّ وَأَسْأَلُكَ خَشْيَتَكَ فِي الْغَيْبِ وَالشَّهَادَةِ وَأَسْأَلُكَ كَلِمَةَ الْحَقِّ فِي الرِّضَا وَالْغَضَبِ وَأَسْأَلُكَ الْقَصْدَ فِي الْفَقْرِ وَالْغِنَى وَأَسْأَلُكَ نَعِيمًا لَا يَنْفَدُ وَأَسْأَلُكَ قُرَّةَ عَيْنٍ لَا تَنْقَطِعُ وَأَسْأَلُكَ الرِّضَاءَ بَعْدَ الْقَضَاءِ وَأَسْأَلُكَ بَرْدَ الْعَيْشِ بَعْدَ الْمَوْتِ وَأَسْأَلُكَ لَذَّةَ النَّظَرِ إِلَى وَجْهِكَ وَالشَّوْقَ إِلَى لِقَائِكَ فِي غَيْرِ ضَرَّاءَ مُضِرَّةٍ وَلَا فِتْنَةٍ مُضِلَّةٍ اللَّهُمَّ زَيِّنَّا بِزِينَةِ الْإِيمَانِ وَاجْعَلْنَا هُدَاةً مُهْتَدِينَ.»

رواه أحمد (١٨٣٢٥) والنسائي (١٣٠٥) وصححه الألباني (صحيح النسائي ١٣٠٥)

«O Allah, by Your knowledge of the unseen and Your power over creation, let me live as long as You know that living is good for me, and let me die when You know that death is better for me. O Allah, let me fear You in secret and in public. I ask You to make me true in speech in times of pleasure and anger. And I ask You for moderation during poverty and wealth. And I ask You for everlasting delight and joy that will never cease. I ask You to make me pleased with what You decreed and for a comfortable life after death. I ask You for the pleasure of looking upon Your Face and for longing to meet You without a calamity that brings harm or a trial that causes misguidance. O Allah, beautify us with the adornment of Iman and make us guides and rightly guided.»

Reported by Ahmad (18325) and al-Nasa'i (1305) and al-Albani declared it sahih (*Sahih al-Nasa'i*, 1305)

This *du'a* asks Allah to grant us such love of Him that we will wait with anticipation for that moment when we get to see and talk to Him. Allah then becomes the greatest joy we have in our life, the greatest goal. Everything else shrinks and disappears. Waiting to meet Allah becomes the greatest delight in this world, just as anticipating meeting a loved one fills us with happiness. Only joy is left when you know that you will soon meet Allah. Pain and hardship disappear.

Loving to meet Allah intensifies just before death. The following important *hadith* clarifies the matter superbly. The Prophet ﷺ said:

«مَن أحَبَّ لِقاءَ اللَّهِ أحَبَّ اللَّهُ لِقاءَهُ ومَن كَرِهَ لِقاءَ اللَّهِ كَرِهَ اللَّهُ لِقاءَهُ.» قالَتْ عائِشَةُ أوْ بَعْضُ أزْواجِهِ: إنّا لَنَكْرَهُ المَوْتَ. قالَ «ليسَ ذاكِ ولَكِنَّ المُؤْمِنَ إذا حَضَرَهُ المَوْتُ بُشِّرَ برِضْوانِ اللَّهِ وكَرامَتِهِ فليسَ شيءٌ أحَبَّ إلَيْهِ ممّا أمامَهُ فأحَبَّ لِقاءَ اللَّهِ وأَحَبَّ اللَّهُ لِقاءَهُ وإنَّ الكافِرَ إذا حُضِرَ بُشِّرَ بعَذابِ اللَّهِ وعُقُوبَتِهِ فليسَ شيءٌ أكْرَهَ إلَيْهِ ممّا أمامَهُ كَرِهَ لِقاءَ اللَّهِ وكَرِهَ اللَّهُ لِقاءَهُ.»

رواه البخاري (٦٥٠٧) ومسلم (٢٦٨٤)

«Whoever loves to meet Allah, Allah loves to meet him. And whoever hates to meet Allah, Allah hates to meet him.» 'A'ishah or one of his wives said, "We hate death." He said, «Not that. Rather, when the believer is about to die, they will be given the glad news of the pleasure of Allah and His reward, so nothing will be more beloved to them than what lies ahead. They love to meet Allah and Allah loves to meet them. And when the disbeliever is about to die, they will be give the news of the punishment of Allah and His torment, so nothing will be more hated to them than what lies ahead. They hate to meet Allah and Allah hates to meet them.»

Reported by al-Bukhari (6507) and Muslim (2684)

We have a natural aversion to death. 'A'ishah رَضِيَ اللَّهُ عَنْهَا wondered how our hatred of death can be reconciled with loving to meet Allah. The Prophet ﷺ explained that this hatred of death disappears once one receives news of the great honor and mercy awaiting them. It is incredible to know that this scary moment in one's life—where one is leaving all familiar things behind and facing ultimate uncertainty—can turn into such a peaceful and pleasurable moment. The joy of meeting Allah turns everything bitter sweet.

As some welcome death because of their love of Allah, others wish for it to escape their worldly troubles. The Prophet ﷺ said:

«لا تَقُومُ السَّاعَةُ حتى يَمُرَّ الرجلُ بِقبرِ الرجلِ فيقولُ: يا لَيْتَنِي مكانَهُ، ما بِهِ حُبُّ لِقَاءِ اللهِ.»

رواه أحمد (١٠٨٦٦٦) وصححه الألباني (السلسلة الصحيحة ٥٧٨) والأرناؤوط

«The Hour shall not take place until a man would pass by another's grave and say, "I wish I were in his place," not out of love to meet Allah.»

Reported by Ahmad (108666) and al-Albani declared it sahih (*al-Silsilah al-Sahihah*, 578) and al-Arna'ut

The wisher in the *hadith* desires death because of all the difficulties that will mount before the Day of Judgment. The *hadith* also points to some who anxiously await death because they love to meet Allah. There are some, however, who wish to remain in this world to earn more good deeds in preparation for meeting Allah. Mu'adh ibn Jabal رَضِيَ اللَّهُ عَنْهُ said before his death:

مَرْحَبًا بِالْمَوْتِ مَرْحَبًا زَائِرًا مُغَيَّبًا حَبِيبًا جَاءَ عَلَى فَاقَةٍ اللَّهُمَّ إِنِّي قَدْ كُنْتُ أَخَافُكَ فَأَنَا الْيَوْمَ أَرْجُوكَ اللَّهُمَّ إِنْ كُنْتَ تَعْلَمُ أَنِّي لَمْ أَكُنْ أُحِبُّ الدُّنْيَا وَطُولَ الْبَقَاءِ فِيهَا لِكَرْيِ الْأَنْهَارِ وَلَا لِغَرْسِ الشَّجَرِ وَلَكِنْ لِظَمَأِ الْهَوَاجِرِ وَمُكَابَدَةِ السَّاعَاتِ وَمُزَاحَمَةِ الْعُلَمَاءِ بِالرُّكَبِ عِنْدَ حِلَقِ الذِّكْرِ

الزهد لأحمد بن حنبل (ص١٤٨)

> Welcome death, welcome a beloved and hidden visitor that came when needed [or came while I am poor of good deeds]. O Allah, I used to fear You, but today I hope from You. O Allah, You know that I did not love the world and a lengthy stay in it to dig rivers or plant trees but for the thirst of hot afternoons [when fasting], bearing the burden of [praying for] hours [at night], and crowding the scholars with the knees in circles of remembrance.
>
> *Al-Zuhd* by Ahmad ibn Hanbal (p. 148)

Mu'adh رَضِيَ اللَّهُ عَنْهُ loved the worship of Allah in this world because it brought him closer to Allah. But which is better? Is it better to long for death because it will bring us to Allah or desire life because it allows us to worship Allah more and know Him better? The answer is that it is best to go with what Allah decrees and loves. The *hadith* quoted above—reported by Ahmad (18325) and al-Nasa'i (1305)—surrenders the matter to Allah. If Allah knows that continued living is better for us and He extends our lives, then this is what we should love because Allah loves it. And if Allah knows that there is no good left in our lives and brings about our death, then this is best for us. Try to train yourself to accept and love what Allah loves. If you do, your life will be happier and simpler.

Ease of Allah's decree and less of this world

The Prophet ﷺ in the *Hadith* prayed to Allah to ease His decrees for the believers. It is *Iman* and the love of Allah that bring about this ease. No matter the hardship and difficulty, the believers can be patient because they know where it came from and what it is leading to. If we understand that Allah decrees every hardship, we will absorb it better. If we know that every hardship is leading back to Allah—with forgiveness and rewards for our patience and compensations for our loss—we can rise above it. Our *Iman* will soften the blow of every hardship. Our love of Allah keeps us focused on the Hereafter, not on the necessary vicissitudes of life. 'Amir ibn Qays said:

قال عَامِرِ بْنِ عَبْدِ قَيْسٍ: أَحْبَبْتُ اللهَ عَزَّ وَجَلَّ حُبًّا سَهَّلَ عَلَيَّ كُلَّ مُصِيبَةٍ وَرَضَّانِي فِي كُلِّ قَضِيَّةٍ فَمَا أُبَالِي مَعَ حِبِّي إِيَّاهُ مَا أَصْبَحْتُ عَلَيْهِ وَمَا أَمْسَيْتُ.

حلية الأولياء (ج٢ ص٨٩)

I loved Allah such a love that eased for me every ordeal and made me content in all affairs, so I do not care while loving Him in what condition I may be in the morning or at night.

Hilyat al-Awliya' (vol. 2, p. 89)

Loving Allah is the greatest aid in overcoming life's problems. If His love dominates the heart, it diminishes worldly problems until they go away.

كان نبيُّ اللهِ صلَّى اللهُ عليه وسلم إذا جلس يجلسُ إليه نَفَرٌ من أصحابِه وفيهم رجلٌ له ابنٌ صغيرٌ يَأْتِيهِ من خَلْفِ ظهرِه فيُقْعِدُه بين يَدَيْهِ فقال له النبيُّ صلَّى اللهُ عليه وسلَّم «تُحِبُّه؟» فقال: يا رسولَ اللهِ أَحَبَّكَ اللهُ كما أُحِبُّه، فهلَكَ فامتنَعَ الرجلُ أن يَحْضُرَ الحَلْقَةَ لِذِكْرِ ابنِه فحَزِنَ عليه ففقده النبيُّ صلَّى اللهُ عليه وسلَّم فقال «ما لِي لا أَرَى فلانًا؟» فقالوا: يا رسولَ اللهِ بُنَيُّه الذي رَأَيْتَه

هَلَك، فلَقِيَهُ النبيُّ صلَّى اللهُ عليه وسلَّم فسأله عن بُنَيِّهِ فأخبره بأنه هَلَك فعَزَّاه عليه ثم قال «يا فلانُ أَيُّما كان أَحَبُّ إليكَ أن تَمَتَّعَ به عُمُرَك أولا تأتي غدًا إلى بابٍ من أبوابِ الجنةِ إلا وَجَدْتَه قد سبقك إليه يَفْتَحُه لك» قال: يا نبيَّ اللهِ بل يسبقُني إلى بابِ الجنةِ فيفتحُها إليَّ لَهُوَ أَحبُّ إلَيَّ، قال «فذاك لك» فقال رجلٌ من الأنصارِ: يا رسولَ اللهِ جعلني اللهُ فداءَك أله خاصةٌ أو لِكُلِّنا؟ قال «بل لِكُلِّكم.»

رواه النسائي (١٨٧٠) وصححه الألباني (صحيح الترغيب ٢٠٠٧)

When the Prophet ﷺ would sit, a group of his Companions would sit with him. Among them was a man who had a young boy. This boy would approach his father [while he was sitting with the Prophet] from behind, and he would carry him and put him on his lap. The Prophet ﷺ once asked him, «Do you love him?» He replied, "O Messenger of Allah, may Allah love you as much as I love him." Then the boy died, and the man was sad over him and he stopped coming to the circle [of the Prophet] because it reminded him of his son. The Prophet ﷺ noticed his absence and said, «How come I do not see so-and-so?» They replied, "O Messenger of Allah, the young boy you saw had died." The Prophet ﷺ met the man and asked him about his young boy. He told him that he was dead, so he consoled him. And then he said, «O so-and-so, which would be more beloved to you: that you enjoy him [alive] for the rest of your life or that you would not come tomorrow to any gate of the gates of Jannah except to find that he has proceeded you to it to open it for you?» He replied, "O Prophet of Allah, that he proceeds me to the gate of Jannah to open it for me is more beloved to me." He said, «This will be for you.» A man from the Ansar asked, "O Messenger of Allah, may Allah accept me as a ransom for you, is this for him specifically or for all of us?" He replied, «No, for all of you.»

Reported by al-Nasa'i (1870) and al-Albani declared it sahih (*Sahih al-Targhib*, 2007)

This is an emotionally charged *hadith*. The father deeply loved his young boy. You get a feeling for it when he said, "May Allah love you as much as I love him." His love was deep and immense. And you can see it too in his inability to attend the circle of the Prophet ﷺ. It was not easy for the Companions to stay away from the Prophet and miss his comforting words. But he did because the pain was deep, and the gathering would only renew his sadness. He would remember there all the times his son would run to him, and he would hug him while on his lap and continue to listen to the Prophet's teachings. The Prophet's consoling words, however, successfully mitigated that loss. It informed the man that he was given more than what he had lost, that he will see his son again, and enjoy his company for eternity in Jannah. This reality helps us all cope with life's uncertainty. Whatever happens here is impermanent: no pain or sadness lasts. It must come to an end. And when it does, Jannah will be waiting for the virtuous.

His love for Allah and His Prophet helped him overcome his loss. If his heart were only filled with love for his son, his death would have devastated him. But he also loved Allah and trusted Him. You can never lose hope when you love Him. You can move on because your gaze is fixed on Him. You know that if you reach Him, you will have everything you ever wanted. So, as long as you are seeking Him, no loss is real anymore. He is s substitute for everything, but nothing is a substitute for Him.

Our hearts are the arenas where different loves compete. One love is always on top, superior to all others. If our hearts are slaves to the world, it is difficult for them to attain the love of Allah. The world intoxicates as alcohol does. How could a heart that is always drunk on this world aspire to love Allah?

The first remedy to minimizing the influence of this world is to seek only the *halal*, avoiding the clear *haram* and the ambiguous. The second step is to limit our intake of this world: avoid excess, waste, and unnecessary luxury. If we do not, our hearts will always be obsessed, worried about losing what we have or getting more of it. The *du'a* of the Prophet ﷺ for the believers to receive smaller portions of this world is a protection from fitnah. The temptation of this world decreases when we limit our access to it. This way, the heart will be freer and healthier. There are, of course, those who can be rich and yet very loving of Allah. They do not allow their wealth to enter their hearts, for this space is reserved only for Allah and what He loves.

Since the nonbeliever does not love Allah, they lack the divine love that can alleviate all hardship. The decrees of Allah will naturally be more difficult for them: they see no benefit in hardship and cannot lean on Allah to make things better. They are also rabid lovers of this world, willing to do anything to retain it. For these reasons—stemming from their stubborn rejection of faith—the Prophet ﷺ made *du'a* against them. But this *du'a* could also help them. If they cannot deal with life's problems despite having so much of this world, perhaps they will reconsider and seek a different path. Maybe they will rethink what they love and why they love it; maybe they will understand that it is not bringing them answers. Perhaps they will seek Allah because they cannot find any peace without Him.

The greatest joy in life is to live waiting to meet Allah. There is nothing else like it. As children, we could hardly wait for Eid with all its lights, presents, food, family visits, and pure fun. Meeting Allah is the real Eid. The real joy. But this Eid requires worship before it, just like Ramadan and Hajj before our Eids. Allah said:

...فَمَن كَانَ يَرْجُوا۟ لِقَآءَ رَبِّهِۦ فَلْيَعْمَلْ عَمَلًا صَـٰلِحًا وَلَا يُشْرِكْ بِعِبَادَةِ
رَبِّهِۦٓ أَحَدًۢا ﴿١١٠﴾

So whoever hopes to meet their Rabb, let them do righteous deeds
and not associate anyone in the worship of their Rabb.
Al-Kahf (Q18:110)

If you are looking forward to meeting Allah, get ready for it. Get excited about it with every *Salah*, fasting, and charity you give. And if it seems like the wait is taking too long, know that you can come closer to Allah in this world. Allah said:

...وَٱسْجُدْ وَٱقْتَرِب ۩ ﴿١٩﴾

And prostrate and come closer.
Al-'Alaq (Q96:19)

You can keep coming closer to Allah in your prostration. Those who are close to Him here will be close to Him up there.

HADITH FIFTEEN

الحديث الخامس عشر

Allah does not punish His beloveds

مَرَّ النَّبِيُّ ﷺ بِأُنَاسٍ مِنْ أَصْحَابِهِ وَصَبِيٌّ بَيْنَ ظَهْرَانَيِ الطَّرِيقِ فَلَمَّا رَأَتْ أُمُّهُ الدَّوَابَّ خَشِيَتْ عَلَى ابْنِهَا أَنْ يُوطَأَ فَسَعَتْ وَالِهَةً فَقَالَتْ: ابْنِي ابْنِي، فَاحْتَمَلَتِ ابْنَهَا فَقَالَ الْقَوْمُ: يَا نَبِيَّ اللهِ مَا كَانَتْ هَذِهِ لِتُلْقِيَ ابْنَهَا فِي النَّارِ، فَقَالَ رَسُولُ اللهِ صَلَّى اللهُ عَلَيْهِ وَسَلَّمَ «لَا وَاللهِ لَا يُلْقِي اللهُ حَبِيبَهُ فِي النَّارِ.»

رواه أحمد (١٢٠١٨) والحاكم (٧٣٤٧) وصححه الألباني (السلسلة الصحيحة ٢٤٠٧)

The Prophet ﷺ passed by some of his companions and there happened to be a boy on the road. When his mother saw the riding animals, she feared that her son would be trampled on and so she rushed to him, distressed, saying, "My son, my son," and she carried him away. The people said, "O Prophet of Allah, she would never throw her son in a fire," and the Prophet ﷺ said, "No by Allah, Allah does not throw His beloved in the Fire."

Reported by Ahmad (12018) and al-Hakim (7347) and al-Albani declared it sahih (al-Silsilah al-Sahihah, 2407)

Commentary

Allah's Love for us is greater than any other love, and His Mercy is astounding. Love should be the inspiration and goal of our worship. It is what saves us in this life and in the Hereafter.

Love is the destination

There are many things that we want to achieve in our life. These goals vary from the great and noble to the trivial and even the harmful. Each goal and achievement reflects our understanding of life and what we consider to be important. It is these goals—especially the sublime ones—that give our lives meaning and direction.

Among all these goals, there is no worldly accomplishment greater than the love of Allah. It subsumes all greatness, all success, and all content. It is the soul of all worship and its greatest goal. It is the foundation and pinnacle of Islam. Al-Ghazali رَحِمَهُ ٱللَّهُ wrote:

> فإن المحبة لله هي الغاية القصوى من المقامات والذروة العليا من الدرجات فما بعد إدراك المحبة مقام إلا وهو ثمرة من ثمارها وتابع من توابعها كالشوق والأنس والرضا وأخواتها ولا قبل المحبة مقام إلا وهو مقدمة من مقدماتها كالتوبة والصبر والزهد وغيرها.
>
> إحياء علوم الدين (ج٤ ص٣١٦)
>
> The love of Allah is the ultimate end of all the stations and the highest level of all degrees. There is no station after that of love except that it is one of its fruits and subsidiaries, such as longing, feeling happy with keeping Allah's company, contentment, and the rest. And there is no station before love except that it is one of the introductions that lead to it, such as repentance, patience, disinclination from the world, and others.
>
> *Ihya' 'Ulum al-Din* (vol. 4, p. 316)

Our relationship with Allah should be based on love. Yes,

we should also fear Allah and hope from Him. But love is the basis and the most important part. Ibn al-Qayyim رَحِمَهُ ٱللَّٰهُ wrote:

الْقَلْبُ فِي سَيْرِهِ إِلَى اللَّهِ عَزَّ وَجَلَّ بِمَنْزِلَةِ الطَّائِرِ فَالْمَحَبَّةُ رَأْسُهُ وَالْخَوْفُ وَالرَّجَاءُ جَنَاحَاهُ فَمَتَى سَلِمَ الرَّأْسُ وَالْجَنَاحَانِ فَالطَّائِرُ جَيِّدُ الطَّيَرَانِ وَمَتَى قُطِعَ الرَّأْسُ مَاتَ الطَّائِرُ وَمَتَى فُقِدَ الْجَنَاحَانِ فَهُوَ عُرْضَةٌ لِكُلِّ صَائِدٍ وَكَاسِرٍ.

مدارج السالكين (ج١ ص٥١٣)

The heart's journey to Allah is like a bird. Love is its head, and hope and fear are its wings. If the head and wings are sound, the bird can fly well. But if the head is severed, the bird dies. And if the wings are missing, it will be an easy target for every hunter and predator.

Madarij al-Salikin (vol. 1, p. 513)

Iman and practice need all three. Some suggested, according to Ibn al-Qayyim رَحِمَهُ ٱللَّٰهُ, that fear needs to be more dominant when we are healthy, while hope takes precedence over fear right before our death. Others recommended a balance between hope and fear and said:

أَكْمَلُ الْأَحْوَالِ اعْتِدَالُ الرَّجَاءِ وَالْخَوْفِ وَغَلَبَةُ الْحُبِّ فَالْمَحَبَّةُ هِيَ الْمَرْكَبُ وَالرَّجَاءُ حَادٍ وَالْخَوْفُ سَائِقٌ وَاللَّهُ الْمُوَصِّلُ بِمَنِّهِ وَكَرَمِهِ.

مدارج السالكين (ج١ ص٥١٣)

The best state is a balance between hope and fear and the dominance of love. Love is the mount, hope is the caller, fear is the driver, and Allah is the one who helps to reach with His bounty and generosity.

Madarij al-Salikin (vol. 1, p. 513)

The analogy is that of travel. Love is the main component—hence the dominance of love. Love is the vehicle you ride to reach Allah. Hope is at the front, calling you to Allah and motivating you to keep going. Fear is the driver who keeps you focused, firmly restraining your impulses so you could arrive on time. All our lives, we have learned about fearing Allah and hoping from Him. But we have not learned to love Him. And it is an essential part of *Iman*.

If our love of Allah is not strong yet, strengthening it should be the purpose of our worship, the primary goal of our life. Weakness in this love is behind our sins and unhappiness. Sin happens because we love something or someone more than Allah. When the love of Allah grows, it will displace sin from our hearts. And the power that sin has over us will diminish and disappear. Sadness will leave us too. Allah's love offers hope and compensation that rescues every soul from the darkness of loss and uncertainty. If you love Allah, you trust Him. If you trust Him, you know that you do not need to worry. You can find peace in Allah's love.

Claim of love vs. reality

It is easy to claim the love of Allah. Many do. But who truly loves Allah? And whom does Allah love? Some of the People of the Book claimed the love of Allah at the time of the Prophet ﷺ. In response to this, Allah said:

وَقَالَتِ ٱلْيَهُودُ وَٱلنَّصَٰرَىٰ نَحْنُ أَبْنَٰٓؤُا۟ ٱللَّهِ وَأَحِبَّٰٓؤُهُۥ ۚ قُلْ فَلِمَ يُعَذِّبُكُم
بِذُنُوبِكُم ۖ... ﴿١٨﴾

And the Jews and the Christians say, "We are the children of Allah and His loved ones." Say, "Then why does He punish you for your sins?"

Al-Ma'idah (Q5:18)

That is, if you love Allah and He loves you, if you are indeed Allah's children (i.e. His chosen ones), then why do you disobey Him? Why does He punish you? Ibn al-Qayyim رَحِمَهُ ٱللَّهُ explained how their lives belied their claim when he wrote:

التعذيب بالذنب ثمرة الغضب المنافي للمحبة. فلو كانت المحبة

قائمة كما زعموا لم يكن هناك ذنوب يستوجبون عليها العذاب من المسخ قردة وخنازير وتسلط أعدائهم عليهم يستبيحونهم يستعبدونهم ويخربون متعبداتهم ويسبون ذراريهم فالمحب لا يفعل هذا بحبيبه ولا الأب بابنه ومعلوم أن الرحمن الرحيم لا يفعل هذا بأمة إلا بعد فرط إجرامها وعتوها على الله واستكبارها عن طاعته وعبادته وذلك ينافي كونهم أحبابه فلو أحبوه لما ارتكبوا من غضبه وسخطه ما أوجب لهم ذلك ولو أحبهم لأدبهم ولم يعذبهم فالتأديب شيء والتعذيب شيء والتأديب يراد به التهذيب والرحمة والإصلاح والتعذيب للعقوبة والجزاء على القبائح فهذا لون وهذا لون.

بدائع الفوائد (ص١٥٧٠)

Punishment for sins is a consequence of anger, which is the opposite of love. If there was love as they claimed [between them and Allah], there would be no sin that they would deserve punishment for, such as transformation into monkeys and pigs and the dominance of their enemies over them where they violate their rights, enslave them, demolish their temples, and seize their children. The beloved does not do this with the one that he loves, and a father does not do this with his son. It is well known that al-Rahman al-Rahim does not do this [i.e. punishment] to a nation except after their excessive crimes and rebellion against Allah and their arrogant refusal to obey and worship Him. And this [state of sinful rebellion] contradicts them being His loved ones. If they loved Him, they would not have committed acts that bring about His anger. And if He loved them, He would have disciplined them and not punished them, for discipline is different from punishment. Discipline is for correction, reform, and mercy, while punishment is for retribution and repayment for evil deeds. This is different from that.

Bada'i' al-Fawa'id (p. 1570)

Many claim to love Allah, but not all claims are true. Some state—and actually believe—that Allah loves them, and they continue to live their lives under this assumption. But what validates this claim? How do you know? Loving Allah means loving what Allah loves and listening to Him. If one continuously disobeys Him and opposes His Will, they must reexamine their assumption of love.

The second point Ibn al-Qayyim رَحِمَهُ ٱللَّهُ made reassures the afflicted. When tested, some develop the feeling that Allah hates them, and this—they believe—is the cause of their suffering. We equate hardship with divine hatred and punishment. But bad things do not happen to you because Allah hates you. They happen because Allah loves you. I want you to remember this; it is one of the most important realizations in life. The Prophet ﷺ confirmed this critical point when he said:

«إنَّ اللهَ إذا أحبَّ قومًا ابتَلاهم.»

رواه الترمذي (٢٣٩٦) وحسنه الألباني (صحيح الترمذي ٢٣٩٦)

«When Allah loves a people, He tests them.»

Reported by al-Tirmidhi (2396) and al-Albani declared it hasan (*Sahih al-Tirmidhi*, 2396)

Ibn al-Qayyim رَحِمَهُ ٱللَّهُ explained that rebellious criminals are the ones who receive punishment, which is different from discipline. (Another point I want you to hold on to and never forget is the difference between punishment and discipline. You can help many people with this gem.) What Allah intends with discipline is to remind His servants that they need to change, to cleanse them of sin. Discipline is not a sign of hate but care. Do we hate our children when we discipline them? Is not our love for them, that we desire the best for them, the motive behind it? When Allah wants the best for us, He tests us to distance us from sin and temptation. The Prophet ﷺ said:

«إِذَا سَبَقَتْ لِلْعَبْدِ مِنَ اللهِ مَنْزِلَةٌ لَمْ يَبْلُغْهَا عَمَلًا ابْتَلَاهُ فِي جَسَدِهِ

أَوْ فِي مَالِهِ أَوْ فِي وَلَدِهِ ثُمَّ صَبَّرَهُ حَتَّى يَنَالَ الْمَنْزِلَةَ الَّتِي سَبَقَتْ لَهُ مِنَ اللهِ عَزَّ وَجَلَّ.»

رواه أبو داود (٣٠٩٠) وصححه الألباني (صحيح أبي داود ٣٠٩٠)

«If one already has a station with Allah that their deeds will not help them reach, Allah afflicts them in their body or wealth or children and then grants them patience so they can attain the station that they have with Allah.»

Reported by Abu Dawud (3090) and al-Albani declared it sahih (*Sahih Abi Dawud*, 3090)

Affliction is the elevator that takes us up to he highest levels in Jannah. This beautiful *hadith* tells us that Allah sends down patience with affliction so we can withstand it. Some worry about what the future holds and whether they can be patient with loss. But there is no need to worry. If today you do not have the strength and patience to deal with a particular loss, you will have it later. If something bad happens, Allah will give you the power you need to survive it. Meanwhile, work on increasing your *Iman* and know that Allah will always send you the best. And if there is an affliction, He will be by your side.

Tests are a sign of Allah's care and love, and they are also an opportunity to move closer to Allah and correct our life. This is, after all, why they are there. It is conceited to take these tests as signs of religious perfection. Tests are there because there are sins in our lives: we need to keep changing, learning, and growing. When bad things happen, they are a message that we should inspect our lives and remove disobedience from it.

Love saves

Love makes our worship easier and purposeful. It helps us connect to Allah on a personal and more profound level. It helps us get much closer to Him because we know who He is, what He loves, and what we mean to Him. The Prophet ﷺ wanted us to know Allah better through the parable of a mother. In another version of the *Hadith*:

قَدِمَ على رَسُولِ اللهِ صَلّى اللّهُ عليه وَسَلَّمَ بِسَبْيٍ فَإِذا امْرَأَةٌ مِنَ السَّبْيِ تَبْتَغِي إذا وَجَدَتْ صَبِيًّا فِي السَّبْيِ أَخَذَتْهُ فَأَلْصَقَتْهُ بِبَطْنِها وَأَرْضَعَتْهُ فَقالَ لَنا رَسُولُ اللهِ صَلّى اللّهُ عليه وَسَلَّمَ «أَتَرَوْنَ هذِه المَرْأَةَ طارِحَةً وَلَدَها فِي النّارِ؟» قُلْنا: لا واللّهِ وَهِيَ تَقْدِرُ على أَنْ لا تَطْرَحَهُ، فَقالَ رَسُولُ اللهِ صَلّى اللّهُ عليه وَسَلَّمَ «لَلّهُ أَرْحَمُ بِعِبادِهِ مِن هذِه بِوَلَدِها.»

رواه البخاري (٥٩٩٩) ومسلم (٢٧٥٤) واللفظ له

A group of captives was brought to the Prophet ﷺ and among them was a woman searching [for someone]. When she found a child among the captives, she took him, pressed him against her stomach, and suckled him. The Messenger ﷺ asked, «Do you think this woman will throw her son in a fire?» We replied, "No, by Allah, as long as it is within her power not to throw him." So the Messenger ﷺ said, «Allah is more merciful with His servants than she with her child.»

Reported by al-Bukhari (5999) and Muslim (2754)

This version complements the *Hadith* of the chapter. It was the Prophet ﷺ who drew the Companions' attention to the incident to deliver a message. He wanted to teach them that Allah is more merciful than the greatest mercy they can witness on earth. And he wanted them to know that it is the love of Allah that saves from Hell. Allah does not punish whom He loves. Ibn al-Qayyim رحمه الله wrote:

وسُئِلَ بعضُ العلماء أينَ تَجِدُ في القرآن أنَّ الحَبيبَ لا يُعذِّبُ حبيبَه فقال في قوله تعالى ﴿وَقَالَتِ الْيَهُودُ وَالنَّصَارَى نَحْنُ أَبْنَاءُ اللَّهِ وَأَحِبَّاؤُهُ قُلْ فَلِمَ يُعَذِّبُكُمْ﴾

روضة المحبين (ص٤١٦)

> A scholar was asked, "Where do you find in the Quran that a lover does not punish his beloved?" He replied, "In Allah's saying: ﴾And the Jews and the Christians say, 'We are the children of Allah and His loved ones.' Say, 'Then why does He punish you?'﴿
>
> *Rawdat al-Muhibbin* (p. 416)

If you love Allah, Allah will love you. And if He loves you, He will never punish you.

Love is the essence of our connection with Allah, and the greatest incentive to do His Will. When our *Iman* is weak, fear of Hell may be the best motivator (or desire for Jannah, for some). But there is a difference between worship that is simply done out of fear and one where the love of Allah is dominant. Allah's love brings joy to worship. Love moves you to do more because you want to. Love chases away hardship and boredom from worship: one starts to find their happiness and comfort in it. We must learn to love Allah and teach it to our children. We must see our Islam as the pursuit of the love of Allah, a love that subsumes all other loves and ends all suffering and loneliness. It is a love that sweetens hardship and rescues heart and soul from despair and apathy. If our relationship with Allah has become dull and weak, we can revive it with love. Look for love in the Quran and Sunnah. Look for it in moments of worship done in solitude. Look for it in your *du'a*. Look for it in your prostrations (*sujud*). Ask Allah for it. Do not leave this earth without tasting the greatest love there is. The love of Allah will save you in the Hereafter. And the love of Allah can save you here.

Allah is the Kindest

It is so endearing to know how Close and Kind Allah is to us. Imagine that the Lord of all, the One who has neither beginning nor end, the one who is Greater than all great things, loves you! Who are we to deserve that? With all of our flaws and sins, yet He loves us? We are insignificant specks in this universe, yet we matter to Him? And He wants to elevate us to the highest levels of Jannah, so we are near Him forever? Consider how Gentle Allah is with us in the following *hadith*. The Prophet ﷺ said that Allah said:

«مَا تَرَدَّدْتُ عَنْ شَيْءٍ أَنَا فَاعِلُهُ تَرَدُّدِي عَنْ نَفْسِ الْمُؤْمِنِ يَكْرَهُ الْمَوْتَ وَأَنَا أَكْرَهُ مَسَاءَتَهُ.»

رواه البخاري (٦٥٠٢)

«I do not hesitate about something I do as I hesitate about [taking] the soul of the believer: he hates death, and I hate to upset him.»

Reported by al-Bukhari (6502)

This is not human hesitation. We hesitate because we are unsure of an outcome or cannot decide which one of the different options is best. But Allah knows everything. His Hesitation, glory be to Him, is as the *hadith* explains: He does not want to hurt us, but we have to die to move to the next life. His Hesitation is two conflicting wills, but He knows which one is best. Now, think about it. This is Allah's greatest hesitation. His greatest one! And who causes it? You! This is how much you matter. When He loves you, this is how much He loves you: He takes care of your feelings, and He hates your pain. It is a tragedy that we have this much love waiting for us, yet we do not know about it or care. It is a tragedy to leave this life without it. It is the greatest joy in life, the highest achievement, and yet few are seeking it. Allah is waiting for you. So, what is holding you back? Say Bismillah and start your journey to Him.

HADITH SIXTEEN

الحديث السادس عشر

Read the Quran to love Allah

قَالَ رَسُولُ اللهِ ﷺ «من سرَّه أن يحبَّ اللهَ ورسولَه فلْيقرأْ في المصحفِ.»

رواه أبو نعيم في حلية الأولياء (ج٧ ص٢٠٩) والبيهقي في شعب الإيمان (٢٠٢٧) وحسنه الألباني (السلسلة الصحيحة ٢٣٤٢)

The Messenger ﷺ said, «The one who would like to love Allah and His Messenger should read the mushaf [i.e. the Quran].»

Reported by Aby Nu'aym in Hilyat al-Awliya' (vol. 7, p. 209) and al-Bayhaqi in Shu'ab al-Iman (2027) and al-Albani declared it hasan (al-Silsilah al-Sahihah, 2342).

Commentary

Allah is the best in teaching us about love, and His book is the best guide to it. Read the Quran and understand it if you want to experience Allah's love.

What pleases you?

What is it that you like? What makes you happy? I mean really happy. Our happiness says a lot about us. Beyond what we claim to be, what we tell ourselves and people, our happiness reveals what is close to our hearts. The cuisine we like, for instance, says a lot about us. It is an amalgamation of the culture of our birthplace, parents' eating habits, experience in life, travels, nostalgia, convictions, how we relax, and what we hope to be. If we like a specific sports team but not another, we do so because of very personal reasons. This team may belong to a region we like, it may tell a story we identify with (e.g. the underdog who wins big despite the odds or the invincible champion who always comes on top), it may give us a sense of belonging, or provide us with an escape more satisfying than reality. Shopping does not only reveal our taste but also how much we value wealth, love ourselves, care for others, what we deem central in life, and our entire worldview (e.g. are we capitalists or anti-capitalists, idealists or materialists). If something brings joy to our souls, it is because it is important to us.

Allah teaches us in the Quran that we have multiple sources of happiness. Allah said:

قُلْ بِفَضْلِ ٱللَّهِ وَبِرَحْمَتِهِۦ فَبِذَٰلِكَ فَلْيَفْرَحُوا۟ هُوَ خَيْرٌ مِّمَّا يَجْمَعُونَ ﴿٥٨﴾

Say, "In the bounty of Allah and in His Mercy, let them rejoice. It is better than what they amass."

Yunus (Q10:58)

In the books of Tafsir, the bounty of Allah and His mercy are explained as Islam, the Quran, and religious guidance. And what we amass are worldly gains. The following incident, recorded in explanation of this *ayah*, highlights the difference between the two sources of pleasure.

لَمّا قَدِمَ خَراجُ العِراقِ إلى عُمَرَ خَرَجَ عُمَرُ ومَوْلًى لَهُ فَجَعَلَ عُمَرُ يَعُدُّ الإبِلَ فَإذا هو أكْثَرُ مِن ذَلِكَ فَجَعَلَ عُمَرُ يَقُولُ الحَمْدُ لِلَّهِ ويَقُولُ مَوْلاهُ يا أمِيرَ المُؤْمِنِينَ هَذا واللَّهِ مِن فَضْلِ اللَّهِ ورَحْمَتِهِ فَقالَ عُمَرُ كَذَبْتَ لَيْسَ هَذا هو يقول الله {بِفَضْلِ اللَّهِ وبِرَحْمَتِهِ فَبِذَلِكَ فَلْيَفْرَحُوا هو خَيْرٌ مِمّا يَجْمَعُونَ} وهَذا مِمّا تَجْمَعُونَ

تفسير ابن أبي حاتم

When the land tax of Iraq reached Umar رَضِيَ اللَّهُ عَنْهُ, he and his

servant came out [to receive it]. Umar رَضِيَ ٱللَّهُ عَنْهُ started counting the camels, and they were bountiful, so Umar رَضِيَ ٱللَّهُ عَنْهُ praised and thanked Allah. His servant said, "O Emir of the Faithful, this is by Allah from the bounty of Allah and His mercy." Umar رَضِيَ ٱللَّهُ عَنْهُ replied, "You are wrong! This is not it. Allah said, ﴿In the bounty of Allah and in His Mercy, let them rejoice. It is better than what they amass.﴾ And this is from what you amass."
Tafsir Ibn Abi Hatim

There is worldly and otherworldly happiness. The other-worldly joy, Allah reminds us, is the real deal while the worldly one is a sad imitation. Religious gifts last and deliver us to Jannah. This world, however, perishes and is mixed with pain and anguish. Despite the vast difference between the two worlds and what each promise, we are happiest with this world. Allah said:

...وَفَرِحُوا۟ بِٱلْحَيَوٰةِ ٱلدُّنْيَا وَمَا ٱلْحَيَوٰةُ ٱلدُّنْيَا فِى ٱلْـَٔاخِرَةِ إِلَّا مَتَـٰعٌ ﴿٢٦﴾

And they rejoice in the worldly life, yet compared to the Hereafter, the worldly life is but a brief enjoyment.
Ar-Ra'd (Q13:26)

This honestly describes how most of us live. We are happiest when we receive more of this world, even though we know it is destined to end one day. The problem is not that this world makes us happy. The problem is that we do not love the Hereafter. Religious gifts do not make us happy. Or, if they do, they do not make us as happy as this world does. We are ecstatic when we get a perfect score on an exam, graduate, land our dream job, get married, and have children. We feel content when we buy a new car or move into a big house, and we are on cloud nine when we receive a bonus or our investments pay off. It is natural to be happy with all these things, for they are blessings from Allah. And as long as we are thankful, close to Allah, and are using these gifts in ways that please Him, they are indeed blessings. But we do not get the same joy and contentment from religious blessings, even though they matter more. Reading and memorizing new chapters from the Quran, praying on time, frequenting the masjid, praying the night prayer, giving charity, fasting Mondays and Thursdays, engaging in *dhikr* of Allah—we do not appreciate these as we do worldly success. We do not appreciate religious achievements, even though they should make us happier. Listen carefully to the real value of piety.

خَرَجَ رَسولُ اللهِ صلى الله عليه وسلم وَنَحْنُ في الصُّفَّةِ فَقالَ «أَيُّكُمْ يُحِبُّ أَنْ يَغْدُوَ كُلَّ يَومٍ إلى بُطْحانَ أَوْ إلى العَقِيقِ فَيَأْتِيَ منه بناقَتَيْنِ كَوْماوَيْنِ في غيرِ إثْمٍ وَلا قَطْعِ رَحِمٍ؟» فَقُلْنا: يا رَسولَ اللهِ نُحِبُّ ذلكَ، قالَ «أَفلا يَغْدُو أَحَدُكُمْ إلى المَسْجِدِ فَيَعْلَمُ أَوْ يَقْرَأُ آيَتَيْنِ مِن كِتابِ اللهِ عَزَّ وَجَلَّ خَيْرٌ له مِن ناقَتَيْنِ وَثَلاثٌ خَيْرٌ له مِن ثَلاثٍ وَأَرْبَعٌ خَيْرٌ له مِن أَرْبَعٍ وَمِنْ أَعْدادِهِنَّ مِنَ الإبِلِ.»

رواه مسلم (٨٠٣)

The Messenger of Allah ﷺ came out when we were in al-Suffah and said, «Which of you would like to leave every morning to Buthan or al-'Aqiq and bring back two large camels without being guilty of sin or severing the ties of kinship?» We said, "O Messenger of Allah, we would like to do it." He said, «Does not one of you go out in the morning to the mosque and teach or recite two ayahs from the Book of Allah, glory be to Him? This is better for him than two camels, and three ayahs are better for him than three camels, and four ayahs are better for him than four camels, and [any number of ayahs is better than] their number in camels.»

Reported by Muslim (803)

Imagine the joy we feel if we were to come back home one day with a new car, ten thousand dollars, or tickets to a dream vacation in an exotic destination. Do we feel similar joy when we finish reading the Quran, fast the month of Ramadan, or receive Sahih al-Bukhari as a gift? Should we not feel immensely fortunate when we are religiously blessed? Why do we not?

If our happiness is always tied to this world, then the world is what matters to us. It dominates our happiness because it dominates our hearts. When Allah's pleasure and nearness become important, religious blessings will bring us joy. How do we make it important, you ask? Bring more of Islam into your life. And ask Allah for a heart that transcends the transient.

The Word of Allah

The Prophet ﷺ taught us how to love for Allah. It is one of the best voluntary deeds to bring us closer to Allah. 'Abdullah ibn 'Umar رَضِيَ اللَّهُ عَنْهُمَا said:

قَالَ عَبْدُ اللَّهِ بْنُ عُمَرَ رضي الله عنهما: لَوْ بَاتَ رَجُلٌ يُنْفِقُ دِينَارًا دِينَارًا وَدِرْهَمًا دِرْهَمًا وَيَحْمِلُ عَلَى الْجِيَادِ فِي سَبِيلِ اللَّهِ وَبَاتَ رَجُلٌ يَتْلُو كِتَابَ اللَّهِ حَتَّى يُصْبِحَ مُتَقَبَّلًا مِنْهُ وَبِتُّ أَتْلُو كِتَابَ اللَّهِ حَتَّى أُصْبِحَ مُتَقَبَّلًا مِنِّي لَمْ أُحِبَّ أَنَّ لِي عَمَلَهُ بِعَمَلِي.

مصنف ابن أبي شيبة (ج٦ ص١٣٥)

If a man spent the night spending one dinar after another and one dirham after another, and equipping horses to fight in the cause of Allah, and a man spent the night reciting the book of Allah until the morning and it was accepted from him, and I spent the night reciting the book of Allah until the morning and it was accepted from me, I would not love to have his deeds instead of mine.

Musannaf Ibn Abi Shaybah (vol. 6, p. 135)

Spending for the sake of Allah is highly meritorious, and Allah calls for it in many places in the Quran. It is one of the effective ways to combat love of money, materialism, and to care more about the Hereafter. What 'Abdullah ibn 'Umar رَضِيَ اللَّهُ عَنْهُمَا was attempting to say was that reading the Quran, available to rich and poor alike, matches the best of deeds. And especially if one is too attached to money to be able to spend it, reading the Quran will transform their heart to become more pious and generous.

If your love for Allah is weak, rush to the Quran and start your journey of love. Why does the Quran have this effect? Khabbab ibn al-Aratt رَضِيَ ٱللَّهُ عَنْهُ answered:

قَالَ خَبَّابُ بْنُ الْأَرَتِّ: إِنِ اسْتَطَعْتَ أَنْ تَقَرَّبَ إِلَى اللَّهِ فَإِنَّكَ لَا تَقَرَّبُ إِلَيْهِ بِشَيْءٍ أَحَبَّ إِلَيْهِ مِنْ كَلَامِهِ.

مصنف ابن أبي شيبة (٣٠٠٩٨)

> If you want to draw nearer to Allah, you will not get closer to Him with something more beloved to Him than His Speech.
>
> *Musannaf Ibn Abi Shaybah* (30098)

The Quran is Allah talking about Himself to us. He reveals Himself in it. And the best description of who Allah is comes from Allah. You encounter in the Quran the Mercy and Forgiveness of Allah, and the rest of His Beautiful Attributes. You understand His Majesty and Power, why He created us, and how He promised to take care of us. You see in it that Allah will always take care of His people, will always protect and guide them. He tells you there that He listens and answers your prayers, for He is closer to you than you are. You learn in it that if you rely on Him, you need no one else. And if He forgives you, you will be happy forever in Jannah. You learn that nothing is eternal but Him, so you cannot trust and turn but to Him. Nothing lasts but Him, so He is the goal, and He is the end. The Quran gives you purpose, and it is Allah.

The other thing that the Quran does is cleanse our hearts to allow us to receive the gifts of Allah. It warns us about the deception of the world so we can open our eyes to see the truth. It tells us about Jannah—our home—so we long for it. It gives us solutions to our problems, insights into our own selves, and wisdom to deal with people. It elevates us above this life so we can be bigger than our problems and limitations. It is our faithful companion. Our solace. Our weapon. Our medicine. Our everything.

The Quran is Allah talking to us. Are we listening?

The Book of Love

This may be the first time that you have heard that the Quran is the Book of Love. You may not have thought about the Quran in this way. But the *Hadith* of this chapter leaves no doubt. If you are seeking love, head to the Quran. The Quran will teach you the meaning of love and nurture it until it blossoms in your heart. If Allah is best in showing us what love means, there is no better book than the Quran to explain it. It is no exaggeration then to call the Quran "The Book of Love."

Some may object that the Quran cannot be such a book while mentioning Hell, punishment, and Allah's Anger with the disobedient. Love is forgiving and all-embracing, while the Quran has a harsh and stern tone. According to this argument, it seems more like a book of discipline than a book of love.

To that we ask, what is divine love? How do we know what loving Allah is, and what is appropriate and inappropriate in that love? Do we love Allah like a father, a friend, or a spouse? These objections conceive of love in human terms, as romantic attachments, and require Allah's love to conform to these molds. Allah's love is unique, unlike any other relationship we have. And it is Allah who sets the proper parameters of this love. This is why as we read the Quran and ponder it, we discover Allah in all of His Majesty and Splendor. And when you experience this, you will love Him. You will love Him as the Great Creator of all. You will not love Him like you love other humans. Allah's love is mixed with awe and reverence. It recognizes our complete dependence on Him. It is not love between equals. It is not romantic affection that unites the lovers to become one. Allah's love is in a league of its own. And the mention of Hell and punishment in the Quran only highlights how precious this love is, where some could have had it but lost it because of their disobedience. Loving Allah is not carte blanche to act as we wish or to imagine Allah as we want to. Such conceptions of the divine only feed our ego. When we conceive of Allah as approving of whoever we are and whatever we do, we change Him to fit our needs instead of changing ourselves to earn His pleasure. The love of Allah is there to elevate and edify us, not to demote the divine to the human plane. If we want to love Allah on our terms, we would be loving ourselves, creating a fantasy that does not exist. But if we are going to love Allah on His terms, we should be willing to listen to Him to understand who He is, who we are, and how to love Him.

If the Quran sounds stern in some places, it is a firmness that prunes human excesses and weakness, edifying to allow the experience of loving Allah. Love is a path. And this path requires the purification of its seeker to be ready to receive and appreciate the love of Allah. Excessive focus on love before one is prepared for it is pointless: the self cannot appreciate it and follow it. This is so because it has not walked the path of sacrifice and humility. If one's greatest love is themselves and the world, how can they love Allah? Should they not detach from the world in order to love Allah? This is what the laws of Allah and the threat of His punishment are there to do. Humans, in general, respond to rules and threats more than they do to love. This is why we regulate our societies with penalties, not love. But Allah knows that when we respond to His laws, we would be ready to love Him. Change and sacrifice are needed to discover the love of Allah. For some, the love of Allah is an excuse to escape change, imagining a God who is always happy with what they like.

The Prophets of Allah grew in their love of Allah with every test and ordeal, with every renewed commitment to Allah, every time they sacrificed for His sake and saw His favors. As we shall see, the intensity of the love of Allah grows when we walk the path of piety. Before that, it is incomprehensible and misapplied. An academic novice cannot understand advanced work in their field. But as they advance in knowledge, they will. Similarly, the love of Allah is clear and present in the Quran.

It is behind each *ayah*. It is the consequence of each *ayah*. It is what you feel when you follow it, a plant that sprouts when the land is tilled.

The Path of Love

Since the worship of Allah is founded on love, and since the Quran is the Book of Love, we can confidently affirm that Islam is the Path of Love. It is a path that has Allah at its end: on it, one journeys to Allah with Allah's help. The first stage of this path will seem difficult. It is the stage where we are weaned off the world and selfishness and reborn into something new. Every birth comes with some difficulty, and every weaning requires patience. It is the stage where we learn to seek Allah rather than the self, to be willing to give up some of what we love for His sake. It is the stage to understand that we need to rely on Allah, not our strength, and to put more of our trust in Him. The more we shed what we love for His sake, the more we realize how much we need Him, the more that His love will grow inside us.

Cultivating our love for Allah takes time and effort. This love will increase when we take care of it and decrease if we neglect it. This is why the Prophet ﷺ directed us to the Quran if we wanted to nurture this love. The more we read and understand (understanding is vital), the more we will love Allah. But if we stop, our love for Allah will shrivel. This love is precious, and—like every precious love—needs to be protected. You will feel it grow with the passage of every day of worship, with every righteous act that emanates from the heart. It takes time, but you will get there. It takes sacrifice, but it is worth it.

Allah loves it when we remember Him. And there are specific phrases that He loves. The Prophet ﷺ said:

«كَلِمَتانِ خَفِيفَتانِ على اللِّسانِ ثَقِيلَتانِ في المِيزانِ حَبِيبَتانِ إلى الرَّحْمَنِ سُبْحانَ اللَّهِ وبِحَمْدِهِ سُبْحانَ اللَّهِ العَظِيمِ.»

رواه البخاري (٦٦٨٢) ومسلم (٢٦٩٤)

> «Two sentences are light on the tongue but heavy in the Scale and beloved to al-Rahman: *Subhana Allahi wa bi hamdihi* and *Sabhana Allahi al-'Adhim* [Glory be to Allah and praise be to Him, and Glory be to Allah the Greatest].»
>
> Reported by al-Bukhari (6682) and Muslim (2694)

Together with the Quran, this and similar *dhikr* can bring us much closer to Allah. And it does not take much to start. We just need to move our tongues with Allah's praise and glorification. Imagine! Few words and you can fill the Scale.

HADITH SEVENTEEN

الحديث السابع عشر

Love the world less, and Allah will love you more

أَتَى النَّبِيَّ ﷺ رَجُلٌ فَقَالَ: يَا رَسُولَ اللهِ دُلَّنِي عَلَى عَمَلٍ إِذَا أَنَا عَمِلْتُهُ أَحَبَّنِي اللهُ وَأَحَبَّنِي النَّاسُ، فَقَالَ رَسُولُ اللهِ ﷺ «ازْهَدْ فِي الدُّنْيَا يُحِبَّكَ اللهُ وَازْهَدْ فِيمَا فِي أَيْدِي النَّاسِ يُحِبُّكَ النَّاسُ.»

رواه ابن ماجه (٤١٠٢) وصححه الألباني (السلسلة الصحيحة ٩٤٤)

A man came to the Prophet ﷺ and said, "Guide me to a thing that if I do, Allah will love me and people will love me." The Prophet ﷺ said, «Abstain from the world and Allah will love you, and abstain from people's possessions and they will love you.»

Reported by Ibn Majah (4102) and al-Albani declared it sahih (al-Silsilah al-Sahihah, 944)

Commentary

Loving Allah and loving the world are opposites. If we are seeking Allah's love, we need to learn to detach from the world.

Loving Allah vs. loving the world

Few on earth today are searching for Allah's love. Most of us are intoxicated with this world. We are so obsessed with material success and riches that this world has become the center of our existence. It defines our worth—individually and collectively—and is the basis of our happiness. The successful country is the rich country, regardless of how unethical and immoral it is. This is how we assess ourselves and each other. It is no exaggeration to say that we allowed the world to enslave our hearts and bodies.

When the Companion in the *Hadith* wondered how he could attain the love of Allah and people, the answer to both was to stay away from this world. It turns out that worldly avarice undermines divine and human love. Why?

The heart is where various loves reside, each competing to be the supreme love. We can accept this request (giving it attention and energy) or reject it (focusing on a greater love). Some loves are also contradictory, forcing us to choose one rather than another (e.g. we love to be rich, which requires hard work and worry, but we also love leisure; we cannot have both). The love and pursuit of this world are in direct competition with the love of Allah. Allah said:

...تُرِيدُونَ عَرَضَ ٱلدُّنْيَا وَٱللَّهُ يُرِيدُ ٱلْـَٔاخِرَةَ... ﴿٦٧﴾

You desire the transient goods of this world, but Allah desires the Hereafter.

Al-Anfal (Q8:67)

Loving this world glues you to it, whereas Allah wants to elevate you above it and move your heart to the Hereafter. Attachment to this world is attachment to money, long life, and sensual pleasures. These enslave the heart. If left untreated, it becomes self-obsessed and materialistic. Then, when Allah asks us to be selfless and sacrifice, to prepare for the Hereafter, we disobey because the world is all that we want. Allah said:

يَـٰٓأَيُّهَا ٱلَّذِينَ ءَامَنُوا۟ مَا لَكُمْ إِذَا قِيلَ لَكُمُ ٱنفِرُوا۟ فِى سَبِيلِ ٱللَّهِ ٱثَّاقَلْتُمْ
إِلَى ٱلْأَرْضِ ۚ أَرَضِيتُم بِٱلْحَيَوٰةِ ٱلدُّنْيَا مِنَ ٱلْـَٔاخِرَةِ ۚ فَمَا مَتَـٰعُ ٱلْحَيَوٰةِ

ٱلدُّنْيَا فِي ٱلْـَٔاخِرَةِ إِلَّا قَلِيلٌ ﴿٣٨﴾

O you who have Iman, why is it that when you are told to go forth in the cause of Allah, you adhere firmly to the ground? Do you prefer the worldly life to the Hereafter? But the enjoyment of the worldly life is little when compared to the Hereafter.

At-Tawbah (Q9:38)

Allah pointed out in the *ayah* the reason why some were slow to respond to His commands, clinging to their comfort and pleasures. If we prefer this world, we will not jeopardize it. Yet, Allah's pleasure is in sacrificing this life for His sake. The Prophet ﷺ said:

«مَنْ أحبَّ دُنْياهُ أَضَرَّ بِآخِرَتِه ومَنْ أحبَّ آخِرَتَهُ أَضَرَّ بِدُنْياهُ فآثِرُوا ما يَبْقى على ما يَفْنى.»

رواه أحمد (١٩٦٩٧) وابن حبان (٧٠٩) وصححه الألباني (صحيح الموارد ٢٠٩٣)

«The one who loves their world will harm their hereafter, and the one who loves their hereafter will harm their world. So, give preference to what lasts over what perishes.»

Reported by Ahmad (19697) and Ibn Hibban (709) and al-Albani declared it sahih (*Sahih al-Mawarid*, 2093)

We are going to choose what we love most. If one's love for this world is greater, they will favor it over the Hereafter. They will make choices and live a life that prioritizes worldly satisfaction. But this will come at the expense of their *Iman*. The one who loves the Hereafter will sacrifice (some of) their worldly success for the sake of the Hereafter. Why is the Hereafter at odds with the world?

Allah created the Hereafter as the destination and this world as the means to it. This world, however, also acts as a temptation that derails people from Allah. This is our test. The world is extremely attractive, deceptively making promises that it cannot keep. It promises happiness, long life, health, and wealth. Its attractions are so intense that they overtake the heart. And so, we end up doing everything and anything for its sake. Shaytan understands this and exploits our weakness. He traps us with these worldly temptations to pull us away from Allah. Malik ibn Dinar said:

قال مَالِكُ بْنُ دِينَارٍ: حُبُّ الدُّنْيَا رَأْسُ كُلِّ خَطِيئَةٍ.

الزهد لابن أبي الدنيا (ص٢١٢)

Loving this world is the root cause of all sin.

Al-Zuhd by Ibn Abi al-Dunya (p. 212)

Every sin has the love of the world behind it. We sin because we love money, power, fame, praise, sex, and food. Had we loved Allah more, we would not put anything or anyone before Him. Every sinner at the moment of sin loves this world more than Allah. They put what they love, their desire, ahead of what Allah loves. Had the love of Allah been strong and present, we would not disobey. This is why turning away from this world is key to pleasing Allah.

Abstaining from the world does not mean abandoning it completely. This, after all, was not the Sunnah of the Prophet ﷺ. He married, had children, owned property, liked certain types of food, and dressed well on special occasions (Eid, Friday Prayer, and when receiving delegates). All this is permissible, and in fact, an act of worship with the right intention. We cannot do without the blessings of Allah. Abstaining from the world (Zuhd) does not mean hating everything in it. The best definition of Zuhd comes from Abu Sulayman al-Darani who said:

قال ابو سليمان الداراني: الزُّهْدُ فِي تَرْكِ مَا يَشْغَلُكَ عَنِ اللَّهِ.

حلية الأولياء (ج٩ ص٢٥٨)

Zuhd is leaving off what takes you away from Allah.

Hilyat al-Awliya' (vol. 9, p. 258)

Ibn Taymiyyah رَحِمَهُ ٱللَّهُ said something similar:

الزهد الْمَشْرُوع هُوَ ترك الرَّغْبَة فِيمَا لَا ينفع فِي الدَّار الْآخِرَة.

التحفة العراقية (ص٤٤)

Legitimate Zuhd is staying away from what does not benefit in the Hereafter.

Al-Tuhfah al-Iraqiyyah (p. 44)

So, if something does not help you in the Hereafter, Zuhd would ask you to leave it, or take less of it so it does not distract you.

Some misunderstood Zuhd to mean starving themselves, intentional bachelorism and childlessness, deliberate poverty, shabbiness, homelessness, solitude, vagrancy, and never smiling. This has become entrenched in some circles despite its stark contradiction to the Sunnah and life of the Prophet ﷺ. The Prophetic Zuhd is to take what you need from this world for the sake of the Hereafter and leave the rest. The desire to be intimate with the opposite sex is natural, and marriage should be its conclusion. The problem is not in this desire but in channeling it into the *haram* or putting our human love before Allah. Proper Zuhd is not suppressing or denying this desire but *halal* unions that protect from sin and bring comfort and love. Money earned to support our needs and our dependents is a good deed. The problem is when material greed opens the gates of sin. Intentional poverty, however, is not the Prophetic solution. There is a healthier middle way.

So, what is the Zuhd that the Prophet ﷺ recommended? To answer this question, we can divide this world into three parts:

The first is the harmful part. This is *haram* and must be avoided. The desire for fame and praise, illicit affairs, superiority (Kibr), and unlawful money are examples. Zuhd here is necessary. All who avoid these prohibitions receive the love of Allah. This is the first level of Zuhd and it is obligatory.

The second part of what exists in this world is the beneficial, like religiously meritorious acts and the *halal*. These must be adopted. This includes the religious obligations and recommendations, marriage to stay away from fornication, earning *halal* income to avoid the *haram*, making enough money to be self-reliant and not dependent on others, eating and drinking to stay alive and healthy, and so on. There is no Zuhd in this category.

The third is the permissible that we do not need. Overeating, luxurious cars and homes, shopping for what we do not need, and overspending on brands and vacations are a few instances of this category. Zuhd here is recommended. Ibn Taymiyyah رَحِمَهُ ٱللَّهُ wrote:

قال ابن تيمية رحمه الله: الزهد الْمَشْرُوع هُوَ ترك الرَّغْبَة فِيمَا لَا ينفع فِي الدَّار الْآخِرَة وَهُوَ فضول الْمُبَاح الَّتِي لَا يستعان بهَا على طَاعَة الله.

التحفة العراقية (ص٤٤)

> Legitimate Zuhd is staying away from what does not benefit in the Hereafter, which is the extra halal that does not aid in the obedience of Allah.
>
> *Al-Tufah al-Iraqiyyah* (p. 44)

Indulgence in the permissible is a distraction. It pulls us away from more significant work, and it slowly increases our love for this world and dependence on it. If one desires to be wealthy, they will spend their time collecting money, taking care of it, and then worrying about it. This will significantly limit the time they can give to Allah. In time, their love for their wealth grows stronger, and they will not hesitate to step into *haram*. The same goes for obsessions with clothes, bags, shoes, cars, professional sports, gaming, movies, TV, and music: they pull the heart away from Allah. If one desires fame, they cannot work for the Hereafter. Working for Allah means desiring no human reward or recognition, only His pleasure. Zuhd helps us keep our love for the world in check, small enough not to hinder our journey to Allah. This includes Zuhd in what we choose to look at. Allah said:

وَلَا تَمُدَّنَّ عَيْنَيْكَ إِلَىٰ مَا مَتَّعْنَا بِهِۦٓ أَزْوَٰجًا مِّنْهُمْ زَهْرَةَ ٱلْحَيَوٰةِ ٱلدُّنْيَا لِنَفْتِنَهُمْ فِيهِ ۚ وَرِزْقُ رَبِّكَ خَيْرٌ وَأَبْقَىٰ ﴿١٣١﴾

And do not gaze at what We have given some of them to enjoy from the beauty of the worldly life as a test for them. The provision of your Rabb is better and more lasting.

Taha (Q20:131)

The *ayah* directed the Prophet ﷺ to keep his eyes away from the finer things in life so as not to distract his heart. When the heart sees temporal beauty, it craves it. And when it craves it, it forgets the Hereafter. This is why it is important to counter these sights and impulses with the phrase of the Prophet ﷺ:

«إنما الخير خير الآخرة.»

رواه أحمد (١٣٦٤٦) وصححه الألباني (السلسلة الصحيحة ٢١٤٦)

«True goodness is the goodness of the Hereafter.»

Reported by Ahmad (13646) and al-Albani declared it sahih (*al-Silsilah al-Sahihah*, 2146)

He said this ﷺ during the Battle of the Trenches, a time of great hardship. The Muslims were exhausted, frightened, and had little food. When he ﷺ saw their hard work in digging the trench, he uttered this phrase. And when he was brought barley bread to eat with some rancid fat, he repeated it. Whether we see hardship or get a glimpse of something expensive, remember that all of it will perish. What remains, the only real thing, is the Hereafter.

As there is Zuhd in sight, there is also Zuhd in thought. What we fantasize about and allow ourselves to admire soon turns into a pursuit that competes with what Allah loves. Zuhd in the world is to believe that everything in it is temporary. It is to use this world for the sake of Allah, not to be attached to it, and to take what you need from it and leave the rest.

If we are struggling to love Allah as we should, it is because we have not emptied our hearts of other loves. How could we love Allah more if we have immense love and attachment to this world? The two cannot coexist. If we want to love Allah, we have to make space for Him in our hearts. This is why Zuhd in this world is the door to the love of Allah.

The world vs. people's love

Abstaining from the world happens to also be the key to people's hearts. Humans are naturally attracted to this world. For most, it is the greatest love in their lives. The main reason behind conflicts and tension on earth is competition over the world. This is how deep and disturbing this love is. So, if people suspect that you want what they have, they will hate and fear you. If you try to wrestle what they have out of their hands, they will fight you. But if you are disinterested in what they possess, they will feel safe around you. If you do not need them, they will like you. And if they need you without you needing anything in return, they will love you.

قال أعرابي لأهل البصرة: من سيد أهل هذه القرية؟ قالوا: الحسن، قال: بم سادهم؟ قالوا: احتاج الناس إلى علمه واستغنى هو عن دنياهم.

جامع العلوم والحكم (ج٢ ص٢٠٦)

A Bedouin asked the people of Basrah, "Who is the dignitary of this city?" They replied, "Al-Hasan [al-Basri]." He asked, "How did he attain this?" They replied, "People needed his knowledge, and he did not need their wealth."

Jami' al-'Ulum wa al-Hikam (vol. 2, p. 206)

One of the recommendations of the Prophet ﷺ was to refrain from asking people for anything as long as we can afford to (*Sahih Muslim*, 1043). We should remember this advice and practice this *adab*. If you can do things yourself, do not ask for help. Try to be as self-sufficient as possible. If you succeed, more people will love you. This will also protect you from becoming subservient to anyone except Allah.

Only the believers can practice the first element of Zuhd: abstaining from the world for the sake of Allah. The second element, Zuhd in what people possess, is a piece of advice that even non-Muslims can follow. It will bring everyone worldly happiness, even if they are non-believers. We all love those who help us and ask for nothing in return. Yet, any joy this brings will be incomplete. It is missing the more important element of Allah's love. Seeking and receiving the love of Allah is far more satisfying than anything people can give. Therefore, the focus of self-help books on improving our earthly experience alone will always remain incomplete. No self-help plan is truly successful until it redirects us to Allah. He is the One who brings lasting, deep, and meaningful happiness.

Seeking love

What is noteworthy about the Companion in the *Hadith* is that he was seeking love. He wanted Allah and the people to love him. His noble desire left us with this valuable Prophetic advice. It is quite remarkable to think in those terms, to ask yourself: "What can I do so Allah would love me?" Many live their lives without ever thinking about this, or expressing the slightest interest in it. They wonder how they can make others love them but not Allah. How can I win her/his heart? How can I make my boss like me? How can I make friends? How can I get more likes on social media? We ask all these questions but not the fundamental one: how do I get Allah to love me? He is the beginning and end of all love, yet we are distracted with inferior passions. We forget that winning His love is winning everything, and losing it is losing everything. This Companion should inspire us. We should spend less time worrying about people liking us and focus on the One who matters.

It is not wrong to seek human respect and love. If it were, the Prophet ﷺ would have advised his Companion not to seek it. His answer indicated that the inquiry was legitimate. Seeking human love is permissible and even desirable as long as it is not the primary pursuit and concern. It should always be secondary to Allah's love and pleasure. Why? Because at times, there will be a conflict between the two. And when there is, Allah's pleasure and love should come first. The Prophet ﷺ said:

«من أرْضى اللهَ بِسَخَطِ الناسِ رَضِيَ اللهُ عنه وأَرْضى عنه الناسَ ومن أرْضى الناسَ بسَخَطِ اللهِ عادَ حامِدُهُ مِنَ الناسِ له ذامًّا.»

صححه الألباني (شرح الطحاوية ٢٦٨)

«If one pleases Allah despite people's anger, Allah will be happy with him and will make people happy with him. And if one pleases people despite Allah's anger, his human praisers will become his condemners.»

Al-Albani declared it sahih (*Sharh al-Tahawiyyah*, p. 268)

There can be no love without Allah. Period. If Allah is unhappy, the rest of creation will be so, sooner or later. Seeking human love is simply a subset of seeking divine love. This is why human approval should always remain secondary. Allah's love is far too precious to be compromised for the sake of anyone or anything else.

Life would be so beautiful if we spend it seeking divine and human love. If our goal is to increase love, we will see and receive more of it. This would be a beautiful thing. And it will be even more beautiful in the Hereafter.

PART TWO

Loving His Prophet

HADITH EIGHTEEN

الحديث الثامن عشر

Iman is loving the Prophet

قَالَ رَسُولُ اللهِ ﷺ «لاَ يُؤْمِنُ أَحَدُكُمْ حَتَّى أَكُونَ أَحَبَّ إِلَيْهِ مِنْ وَالِدِهِ وَوَلَدِهِ وَالنَّاسِ أَجْمَعِينَ.»

رواه البخاري (١٥) ومسلم (٧٠)

The Messenger ﷺ said, «One of you does not believe until I am more beloved to them than their parents, children, and all people.»

Reported by al-Bukhari (15) and Muslim (70)

Commentary

Loving the Prophet is part of loving Allah. When we understand who he was and what he did, we will naturally love him more than any other human. And the more we love and follow him, the more Allah will love us.

Everyone has a prophet

This may seem odd at first glance. How could everyone, even those who do not believe in God, still have a prophet? If one believes in nothing, they cannot possibly believe in prophets! The assertion made here is not that they believe in a divine power that spoke to someone (i.e. a prophet). The assertion, for all intents and purposes, is that they must treat someone as a prophet. Allow me to explain.

There are two dimensions to a Prophet: the supernatural and the worldly. On the supernatural end, Allah communicates with them and sends them with His messages. On the worldly end, people admire them, listen to them, and model their lives after them. They tell us how to live, and explain the world to us. We accept what they say because they speak on behalf of Allah, and so we give them our complete love and obedience. Therefore, whenever we treat a human as such, we treat them as a Prophet. We may not believe that they are connected to the divine, but we give them the love and respect reserved for those who are.

The Prophets in the past were Ibrahim (Abraham), Musa (Moses), Isa (Jesus), and Muhammad ﷺ. Today, we have rappers, rock stars, actors, social media influencers, and supermodels. We follow their every move, and their news fills our minds and airwaves. We dress as they do, talk as they do, and believe what they believe. They tell us what is important in life, and we follow it. They tell us how to live, and we accept it. We admire them so much that they have become our role models. We love them so much that we do not contradict them.

Some of us treat scientists in similar ways. When some reject God, they end up believing in science as the absolute truth. They accept everything scientists say, and *only* what they say, as if they are the bearers of all truth. They substitute the authority of Allah's Prophets with the authority of scientists. They reject Allah as absolute but confer this attribute to science. In reality, having a God and a Prophet is inescapable. If our God is not Allah, it is someone else. If our Prophet is not Muhammad ﷺ, we will find another. Everyone must adopt a prophet in their life.

This is one main reason why some of us find it hard to love and hence follow Muhammad ﷺ as a Prophet. We are emotionally unavailable. We already have someone that we follow and love. We already have someone to tell us how to live. And so when we hear that Muhammad ﷺ said this and did that, we are not interested. We say we are committed to the statement "Muhammad is the Messenger and Prophet of Allah," but do not understand what it means. We say that he is our Prophet but follow someone else. We say that he is our Prophet but love someone else. The question then is, is he still our Prophet?

The other main reason why we do not love Muhammad ﷺ is that we do not know him well enough. We do not realize how much he impacts our lives.

Why love him?

To begin with, because Allah loves him. Anyone who truly loves Allah will feel compelled to love what Allah loves. They cannot help it. Their love of Allah would be so overwhelming that they would be looking for what Allah loves in order to love it. And when we know that Allah loves this man so much, more than any other, we will cherish him as Allah cherishes him. Ibn Rajab رَحِمَهُ ٱللَّهُ wrote:

> محبة النبي صَلَّى اللهُ عَلَيْهِ وَسَلَّمَ من أصول الإيمان وهي مقارنة لمحبة الله عز وجل وقد قرنها الله بها وتوعد من قدم عليها شيء من الأمور المحبوبة طبعا من الأقارب والأموال والأوطان وغير ذلك فقال تعالى ﴿قُلْ إِن كَانَ آبَاؤُكُمْ وَأَبْنَآؤُكُمْ وَإِخْوَانُكُمْ وَأَزْوَاجُكُمْ وَعَشِيرَتُكُمْ وَأَمْوَالٌ اقْتَرَفْتُمُوهَا وَتِجَارَةٌ تَخْشَوْنَ كَسَادَهَا وَمَسَاكِنُ تَرْضَوْنَهَا أَحَبَّ إِلَيْكُم مِّنَ اللهِ وَرَسُولِهِ وَجِهَادٍ فِي سَبِيلِهِ فَتَرَبَّصُواْ حَتَّى يَأْتِيَ اللهُ بِأَمْرِهِ﴾ [التوبة: ٢٤].
>
> فتح الباري (ج ١ ص٤٨)

Loving the Prophet ﷺ is of the foundations of Iman, and it is linked to loving Allah, Glory be to Him. Allah coupled his love with His love, and He warned those who put ahead of it any natural love of relatives, wealth, hometowns, and anything else by saying, ﴾Say, "If your parents, children, siblings, spouses, your family, the wealth you collected, the business you fear its decline, and homes you cherish are more beloved to you than

> Allah, His Messenger, and Jihad in His sake, then wait until Allah brings about His punishment.﴿ [Al-Tawbah 24]
>
> *Fath al-Bari* (vol. 1, p. 48)

We naturally love many things in this world, and it is not wrong to love them. But here Allah is instructing us that this natural love should never stand in the way of loving Allah. The measure of a true believer is that if they see a conflict between what they love and what Allah and His Prophet love, they will choose the latter. Anything else reflects weakness in Allah's love, weakness in *Iman*.

Muhammad, ﷺ, is the most beloved to Allah. This says much about who he was. His love for Allah was unparalleled. It increased with every struggle he went through. Time after time, he faced tests and challenges and, guided by Allah's love, he triumphed. He was not patient with all of these troubles because of any worldly gain. In worldly terms, he lost a lot and gained little. But in the scales of the Hereafter, he won it all. He lost family, dear friends, wealth, hometown, safety, and peace of mind. He was attacked physically and verbally, went hungry, and saw his followers go hungry and suffer. But he never gave up despite all the rejection and opposition. He sat patiently to teach an illiterate nation for twenty-three years. And what did he get in return from this world? He lived humbly. He would go hungry with his family for many days, and all that he owned went to charity after his death. Others in his position would do everything in their power to be rich and make their family rich. He was not interested in all that. He loved Allah's so much that this world held no sway on him.

He was a man of impeccable character. Allah, Himself, praised this when he said:

وَإِنَّكَ لَعَلَىٰ خُلُقٍ عَظِيمٍ ﴿٤﴾

And you are of outstanding character.

Al-Qalam (Q68:4)

Take a moment to soak in the fact that Allah praised this man for his manners. What does this say about him? The fact that he was able to attract so many to Allah and change their lives so drastically is a testament to who he was. He turned enemies into brothers and sisters, the ignorant into the most learned and pious, and the weak and oppressed into a strong nation that stood up for justice. His companions loved him more than they loved themselves.

كُنَّا مَعَ النَّبِيِّ صَلَّى اللهُ عَلَيْهِ وَسَلَّمَ وَهوَ آخِذٌ بِيَدِ عُمَرَ بْنِ الْخَطَّابِ فَقالَ لَهُ عُمَرُ يَا رَسُولَ اللَّهِ لأَنْتَ أَحَبُّ إِلَيَّ مِنْ كُلِّ شَيْءٍ إِلَّا مِنْ نَفْسِي، فَقالَ النَّبِيُّ صَلَّى اللهُ عَلَيْهِ وَسَلَّمَ «لَا وَالَّذِي نَفْسِي بِيَدِهِ حَتَّى أَكُونَ أَحَبَّ إِلَيْكَ مِنْ نَفْسِكَ.» فَقالَ لَهُ عُمَرُ: فَإِنَّهُ الآنَ وَاللَّهِ لأَنْتَ أَحَبُّ إِلَيَّ مِنْ نَفْسِي، فَقالَ النَّبِيُّ صَلَّى اللهُ عَلَيْهِ وَسَلَّم «الآنَ يَا عُمَرُ.»

رواه البخاري (٦٦٣٢)

We were with the Prophet ﷺ while he was holding the hand of 'Umar ibn al-Khattab. 'Umar said to him, "O Messenger of Allah, you are more beloved to me than everyone else except myself." So, the Prophet ﷺ said, «No, by the One who has my soul in His Hand, not until I am more beloved to you than yourself.» 'Umar replied, "Then now, by Allah, you are more beloved to me than myself." So, the Prophet ﷺ said, «Now, O 'Umar.»

Al-Bukhari (6632)

This is the highest level of love for the Prophet ﷺ, a recommended station. 'Umar's *Iman* was so firm that a moment's reflection gave him the fuel he needed to elevate the Prophet ﷺ above himself. What came to his mind to allow him to advance to this exceptional level?

Maybe he thought about what the Prophet ﷺ means to every Muslim. We know everything about Allah through him. He guided us to every benefit and warned us about every harm.

He illuminated for us the path to Jannah, and taught us how to live the best life on earth. We need him more than we need any other human. We may be unaware of how much we rely on him every day, but he is closer to you than your family. You need him more than you need them. What you believe, how you worship, how and what you eat, how and whom to marry, how to raise your children, how to solve your problems, how you sleep, how you wake up—all this and more comes from him. His impact is greater than any other. Your name, where you were born, your favorite food, how you were raised, your spouse, and the future of your children is connected to the spread of Islam, which he started. If you want to get closer to Allah, you need him to tell you how. If something terrible happens, you need him for you understand why it happened, how to be patient with it, and how you can turn it into a blessing. If we have *Iman*, we are connected to him every minute of each day. This is why you need him more than your parents and children. This is why he should mean more to you than all of them put together.

It may seem hard to believe that we could love him ﷺ more than our children, spouses, and parents, for they are the ones we love the most on in life. It is permissible and natural to love the forenamed people, who represent different types and categories of love. Abu al-Zinad, one of the commentators of *Sahih al-Bukhari*, explained:

قال أبو الزناد: هذا من جوامع الكلم الذى أوتيه صلى الله عليه وسلم لأنه قد جمع فى هذه الألفاظ اليسيرة معانى كثيرة لأن أقسام المحبة ثلاثة محبة إجلال وعظمة كمحبة الوالد ومحبة شفقة ورحمة كمحبة الولد ومحبة استحسان ومشاكلة كمحبة سائر الناس فحصر صنوف المحبة.

شرح ابن بطال على البخاري (ج١ ص٦٥)

This [Hadith] is from the eloquent and comprehensive speech that he was given ﷺ because he distilled in these few words many meanings. [This is so] because love is of three kinds: love

> based on esteem and veneration, like loving a parent; love based on mercy and care, like loving a child; and love based on admiration and similarities, like loving everyone else. So, he encompassed all types of love.
>
> *Sharh Ibn Battal* (vol. 1, p. 65)

Our attachment to people is worldly. But our love for Muhammad ﷺ is religious. When religion becomes more meaningful to us than this world, our love for him will transcend anything worldly. But we should also love him for worldly reasons. When we follow his guidance, we avoid worldly harms and gain the most from this world. Do you not love the one who reconciles you and your spouse, children, or parents? The Prophet ﷺ taught this to us and recommended it. Do you not love the one who protects you from financial loss and guides to financial success? You will find this guidance in his teachings about *halal* and *haram*. Do you not love the one who counsels you when you are down and gives you hope again? The one who protects you from social harm? The one who teaches you the meaning of life and tranquility in a chaotic world? His Sunnah has all of that. And he gave it to you for free.

Our love for him will soar when we realize how much the people around him loved him. This is an example:

جَاءَ رَجُلٌ إِلَى النَّبِيِّ صَلَّى اللهُ عَلَيْهِ وَسَلَّمَ فَقَالَ: يَا رَسُولَ اللهِ وَاللهِ إِنَّكَ لَأَحَبُّ إِلَيَّ مِنْ نَفْسِي وَإِنَّكَ لَأَحَبُّ إِلَيَّ مِنْ أَهْلِي وَأَحَبُّ إِلَيَّ مِنْ وَلَدِي وَإِنِّي لَأَكُونُ فِي الْبَيْتِ فَأَذْكُرُكَ فَمَا أَصْبِرُ حَتَّى آتِيَكَ فَأَنْظُرُ إِلَيْكَ وَإِذَا ذَكَرْتُ مَوْتِي وَمَوْتَكَ عَرَفْتُ أَنَّكَ إِذَا دَخَلْتَ الْجَنَّةَ رُفِعْتَ مَعَ النَّبِيِّينَ وَإِنِّي إِذَا دَخَلْتُ الْجَنَّةَ خَشِيتُ أَنْ لَا أَرَاكَ، فَلَمْ يَرُدَّ عَلَيْهِ النَّبِيُّ صَلَّى اللهُ عَلَيْهِ وَسَلَّمَ حَتَّى نَزَلَ جِبْرِيلُ بِهَذِهِ الْآيَةِ ﴿وَمَنْ يُطِعِ اللهَ وَالرَّسُولَ فَأُولَئِكَ مَعَ الَّذِينَ أَنْعَمَ اللهُ عَلَيْهِمْ مِنَ النَّبِيِّينَ وَالصِّدِّيقِينَ﴾ [النساء ٦٩]

رواه الطبراني في المعجم الأوسط (٤٧٧) وحسنه الألباني (السلسلة الصحيحة ٢٩٣٣)

A man came to the Prophet ﷺ and said, "O Messenger of Allah, I love you more than myself, I love you more than my family, and I love you more than my children. While I am at home, I remember you and I cannot wait to come and see you. And when I think about my death and yours, I realize that when you enter Jannah, you will be raised with the Prophets. But if I enter Jannah, I fear that I may not see you." So, the Prophet ﷺ did not reply until Jibril came down with this ayah, ﴿And whoever obeys Allah and the Messenger will be with those whom Allah blessed: the Prophets and Siddiqs.﴾ [Al-Nisa' 69]

Reported by al-Tabarani an al-Awsat (477) and al-Albani declared it hasan (al-Silsilah al-Sahihah 2933)

We will encounter this *hadith* again (see *Hadith Thirty-Four*). But for now, appreciate the love this man had for him. He could not stand to stay away from him.

'Ali ibn Abi Talib رضي الله عنه was asked:

وَسُئِلَ عَلِيُّ بْنُ أَبِي طالب رضي الله عنه: كيف كان حُبُّكُمْ لِرَسُولِ اللَّهِ صَلَّى اللَّهُ عَلَيْهِ وَسَلَّمَ؟ قَالَ: كَانَ وَاللَّهِ أَحَبَّ إِلَيْنَا مِنْ أَمْوَالِنَا وَأَوْلَادِنَا وَآبَائِنَا وَأُمَّهَاتِنَا وَمِنَ الْمَاءِ الْبَارِدِ عَلَى الظَّمَإِ.

الشفا للقاضي عياض (ج٢ ص٥١-٥٢)

"How much did you love the Messenger ﷺ?" He replied, "By Allah, we loved him more than our money, our children, our fathers, our mothers, and more than cold water when thirsty."

Al-Shifa by Qadi 'Iyad (vol. 2, pp. 51–52)

Their love for him rose above all the natural love they had for themselves and their family.

وَرُوِيَ عَنْ أَبِي بَكْرٍ رَضِيَ اللَّهُ عَنْهُ أَنَّهُ قَالَ لِلنَّبِيِّ صَلَّى اللَّهُ عَلَيْهِ وَسَلَّمَ وَالَّذِي بَعَثَكَ بِالْحَقِّ لَإِسْلَامُ أَبِي طَالِبٍ كَانَ أَقَرَّ لِعَيْنِي مِنْ إسلامه يَعْنِي أَبَاهُ أَبَا قُحَافَةَ وَذَلِكَ أَنَّ إِسْلَامَ أَبِي طَالِبٍ كَانَ أَقَرَّ لِعَيْنِكَ وَنَحْوَهُ عَنْ عمر بن الخطاب قال للعباس أن تسلم أحب

إلي أَنْ يُسْلِمَ الْخَطَّابُ لِأَنَّ ذَلِكَ أَحَبُّ إِلَى رسول الله صلى الله عليه وسلم.

الشفا للقاضي عياض (ج٢ ص٥٠-٥١)

It was reported from Abu Bakr ﵁ that he said to the Prophet ﷺ, "I swear by the One who sent you with the truth, Abu Talib's acceptance of Islam is more pleasing to me than his acceptance of Islam—referring to Abu Bakr's father, Abu Quhafah—because Abu Talib's acceptance of Islam is more pleasing to you." Something similar was reported from 'Umar when he said to al-'Abbas, "Your acceptance of Islam is more beloved to me than al-Khattab's acceptance of Islam ['Umar's father] because this is more beloved to the Messenger ﷺ."

Al-Shifa by Qadi 'Iyad (vol. 2, pp. 50–51)

They loved everything about him. Anas ﵁ said:

عن أنس رضي الله عنه قال: لقد رأيت رسول الله صلى الله عليه وسلم والحلاق يحلقه وأطاف به أصحابه فما يريدون أن تقع شعرة إلا في يد رجل.

رواه مسلم (٢٣٢٥)

I saw the Messenger ﷺ while the barber was cutting his hair, and his companions had surrounded him, desiring that not a hair would fall except in the hand of one of them.

Reported by Muslim (2325)

His hair and body were special, for there was barakah (blessing) in them. But it is also a demonstration of love, attachment, and respect. 'Amr ibn al-'Aas ﵁ confirmed this love and respect when he said on his death bed:

قال عَمْرو بْنَ الْعَاصِ رضي الله عنه وَهُوَ فِي سِيَاقَةِ الْمَوْتِ: مَا كَانَ أَحَدٌ أَحَبَّ إِلَيَّ مِنْ رَسُولِ اللهِ صَلَّى اللهُ عَلَيْهِ وَسَلَّمَ وَلَا أَجَلَّ فِي

عَيْنِي مِنْهُ وَمَا كُنْتُ أُطِيقُ أَنْ أَمْلَأَ عَيْنَيَّ مِنْهُ إِجْلَالًا لَهُ وَلَوْ سُئِلْتُ أَنْ أَصِفَهُ مَا أَطَقْتُ لِأَنِّي لَمْ أَكُنْ أَمْلَأُ عَيْنَيَّ مِنْهُ.

رواه مسلم (١٩٢)

I did not love anyone more than the Messenger ﷺ and I respected no one more than him. I could not continue to gaze at him out of respect for him. If I were asked to describe him, I would not be able to because I never fully gazed at him.

Reported by Muslim (192)

This esteem and love are amazing. If the Prophet ﷺ were in front of our eyes now, we would not take our eyes off of him. But those Companions were something else, and their love and reverence are unmatched. But it does mean that later generations do not have their portion of this love. This story from Malik رَحِمَهُ ٱللَّٰهُ demonstrates his deep connection to the Prophet, even though he never saw him.

كَانَ مَالِكٌ إِذَا ذُكِرَ النَّبِيُّ صَلَّى اللَّهُ عَلَيْهِ وَسَلَّمَ يَتَغَيَّرُ لَوْنُهُ وَيَنْحَنِي حَتَّى يَصْعُبَ ذَلِكَ عَلَى جُلَسَائِهِ فَقِيلَ لَهُ يَوْمًا فِي ذَلِكَ فَقَالَ لَوْ رَأَيْتُمْ مَا رَأَيْتُ لَمَا أَنْكَرْتُمْ عَلَيَّ مَا تَرَوْنَ وَلَقَدْ كُنْتُ أَرَى مُحَمَّدَ بْنَ الْمُنْكَدِرِ وَكَانَ سَيِّدَ الْقُرَّاءِ لَا نَكَادُ نَسْأَلُهُ عَنْ حَدِيثٍ أَبَدًا إِلَّا يَبْكِي حَتَّى نَرْحَمَهُ

الشفا للقاضي عياض (ج٢ ص٩٣-٩٤)

When the Prophet ﷺ was mentioned, Malik's face color would change and he would bend and lean forward until those sitting with him would be distressed for him. He once was advised against it, and he said, "If you had seen what I had seen, you would not criticize what you saw me doing. I used to see Muhammad ibn al-Munkadir, who was the scholar of scholars, cry whenever we asked him about a hadith until we felt sorry for him."

Al-Shifa by Qadi 'Iyad (vol. 2, pp. 93–94)

They loved him so much that they missed him. And because they missed him, they would cry when they would hear his name.

How to love him?

It is one thing to understand the Prophet's love in theory and another to experience it. We may understand that we should love him, but how do we start?

We have to first understand that our hearts are never empty vessels. They are always full. And at any moment, someone/something occupies the central position in it. Increasing our love for the Prophet ﷺ will gradually take the place of other dominant loves in our hearts. His love slowly grows to top other loves. How do we increase our love for him?

The first step is to follow him. Ibn Rajab رَحِمَهُ ٱللَّهُ wrote:

إنما تتم المحبة بالطاعة كما قال تعالى: ﴿قُلْ إِن كُنتُمْ تُحِبُّونَ اللهَ فَاتَّبِعُونِي يُحْبِبْكُمُ اللهُ﴾ [آل عمران: ٣١]

فتح الباري (ج١ ص٤٩)

Love can only be complete through obedience, as Allah said, ﴾Say: 'If you love Allah, then follow me and Allah will love you.﴿ [Ali Imran 31]

Fath al-Bari (vol. 1, p. 49)

The more we follow Muhammad ﷺ, the more that we will appreciate and savor his teachings. When we start to live like him, his stature will grow in our hearts. The more we lean on him for guidance and wisdom, the less we will seek it from others. The more we allow his Sunnah to saturate our lives, in small and significant matters, the lesser we will imitate and admire other paths. On the road to Allah, there is no small and insignificant Sunnah. Every small act from him is a treasure that builds up love for him, a small step towards the love of Allah. In time, he will become very dear to us.

The second step is to learn more about him and his teachings. One of the greatest obstacles to loving the Prophet ﷺ is ignorance: we hardly know him and his Sunnah. Yes, we know bits and pieces from here and there, superficial knowledge without depth or breadth. We possess no coherent picture of who the man was and what he taught. The remedy is to pick up his biography and a *hadith* book and learn in person why he is so special. As you read, relate what you learn to your reality. Ponder how what you are reading may affect you and change your life. In other words, feel its relevance.

The third step is to ask Allah to grant us the love of the Prophet ﷺ. Religious gifts are the most precious of gifts. And if we are used to asking Allah for worldly favors, we should be more eager and persistent in our religious requests. The Prophet ﷺ deserves all this love, and we deserve to love him. If we love him, his love will take us to Jannah. If we love him, Allah will love us. When we remember him, Allah remembers us. The Prophet ﷺ said:

«مَنْ صَلَّى عَلَيَّ وَاحِدَةً صَلَّى الله عَلَيْهِ عَشْرًا.»

رواه مسلم (٤٠٨)

> «The one who says salah once for me, Allah will say salah ten times for them.»
>
> Reported by Muslim (408)

Repeating salah and salam for the Prophet ﷺ brings us closer to him and closer to Allah. The more we remember him, the more we will love him. Try to assign yourself a daily portion of this remembrance, especially on Fridays. It may be the key that opens the beautiful gates of loving the Prophet ﷺ.

Obligatory and recommended love

Like loving Allah, loving the Prophet ﷺ has a basic obligatory level and a higher recommended level.

The obligatory love for the Prophet ﷺ is to observe the religious obligations and avoid the prohibitions. It is to love him enough to listen to him. It is to believe that he is the best teacher and guide, and that his Sunnah is the only way to Allah. It is to be happy and satisfied with him as a Prophet of Allah: he delivered the truth from Allah and showed us how to reach Jannah. Part of this obligatory level is to love him more than all other humans. The *Hadith* negates the *Iman* of those who love other people more than him. This negation of *Iman* is a negation of its completeness and strength, not a denial of its existence altogether. One would still be a Muslim if they loved the Prophet less than a family member. Every Muslim, no matter how weak their *Iman* may be, loves the Prophet ﷺ. It is just that their *Iman* is weak, and so their love for him is weak. If we were to strengthen our *Iman*, we would realize how much we need him and how much Allah loves him, and we will love him too.

Obedience and compliance determine who you love most. Whose desire and request will you follow? If a dear family member asked for something that would upset the Prophet ﷺ, would you do it? If we follow the Prophet, then it is a mark that we love him more. If we follow some other advice and guidance, it is because our heart is there and not with him.

Loving the Prophet ﷺ is primarily a religious love, while loving our family is a natural love. When they clash, it is common to put our families first if our religious commitment is weak. The strong of faith will resist worldly pressure because they understand that their best interest is in following Allah, not other humans. This is how religious love starts taking precedence over natural love. When we love the Prophet religiously, and know him better, our religious love will guide us to develop natural love for him. You will see examples of what this entails as you keep reading.

The recommended level of love is to perform the recommended acts in addition to the obligations. When our love for him grows, it will move us to imitate him even when it is not a must. The simple fact that he did it, and that this act brings us closer to Allah, is more than enough to convince us to adopt it. Every such act is an opportunity to be closer to him, and closer to Allah. Who would want to miss this opportunity?

Included in the recommended level of love is to love him

more than we love ourselves, as the *hadith* of 'Umar illustrates. This is not easy, but it is not impossible. It will take time, effort, and a lot of *du'a*. Maybe you will be one of those who get there.

What does it mean to love him?

To love him is to want to be like him. In matters small and big, he is the role model. There is no small or insignificant Sunnah anymore. All of his acts are valuable. All of his advice is dear. His choices are better than ours, and his guidance is the best guidance. If someone contradicts him, we ignore him. If his Sunnah is attacked, we defend it. If we cannot be close to him physically, we stay close to what he used to do as if he is right next to us. If I want to hear his voice, I open a book of *hadith* and read. If I want to feel his presence, I practice one Sunnah of his. If I want to talk to him, I say *salah* and *salam* upon him, and he will receive it. The Messenger ﷺ said:

«إنَّ للَّهِ ملائِكةً سيّاحينَ في الأرضِ يُبلِّغوني من أُمَّتي السَّلامَ.»

رواه النسائي (١٢٨٢) وصححه الألباني (صحيح الترغيب (١٦٦٤)

Allah has angels who travel the earth conveying to me the salam of my Ummah.

Reported by al-Nasa'i and al-Albani declared it sahih (*Sahih al-Targhib*, 1664)

Imagine an angel carrying your salam to the Prophet ﷺ. And he will know you by name. The Prophet ﷺ said:

«أكثِروا الصَّلاةَ عليَّ فإنَّ اللهَ وكَّلَ بي مَلَكًا عندَ قبري فإذا صلّى عليَّ رجلٌ مِن أُمَّتي قال لي ذلكَ الملَكُ: يا محمَّدُ إنَّ فلانَ ابنَ فلانٍ صلّى عليكَ السّاعةَ.»

رواه الديلمي في مسند الفردوس وحسنه الألباني (صحيح الجامع ١٢٠٧)

«Increase your salah for me, for Allah has appointed me an angel at my grave. Whenever one of my Ummah makes a salah for me, this angel will say to me, "O Muhammad, so-and-so son of so-and-so made salah for you now."»

Reported by al-Daylami in *Musnad al-Firdaws* and al-Albani declared it hasan (*Sahih al-Jami'*, 1207)

Loving him will naturally compel us to want to see him. And not merely to want to see him, but to ache so much for it that we would sacrifice anything dear to us to get a glimpse of him. The Prophet ﷺ said:

«مِنْ أَشَدِّ أُمَّتِي لِي حُبًّا ناسٌ يَكونُونَ بَعْدِي يَوَدُّ أَحَدُهُمْ لو رَآنِي بأَهْلِهِ ومالِهِ.»

رواه مسلم (٢٨٣٢)

«Of the people who love me the most in my Ummah are ones who will come after me. One of them would love to see me even if it were to cost them their family and wealth.»

Reported by Muslim (2832)

This is how much they love him. They would be willing to give up their families and wealth just to see him. They would be ready to migrate to him (*hijrah*) as the first generation migrated to him and sacrificed everything for it. If they cannot physically migrate to him, they migrate to his Sunnah. They migrate with their hearts to him. Note that he was describing people who will come after him, like you and I. And it could very well be someone like you and I.

Many today only dream of meeting celebrities (athletes, rappers, actors, etc). They would travel, stand in line for hours, and pay hundreds of dollars just to be close to them. And if they cannot, they would dream about such an encounter and imitate the mannerisms and style of their idol to feel closer to them. Those who love the Prophet ﷺ are willing to do much more to see him. They do not fawn over celebrities because their hearts are full and content. What would you be willing to give up to be close to Muhammad ﷺ?

HADITH NINETEEN

الحديث التاسع عشر

Be kind for the Prophet to love you

كُنَّا عِنْدَ رَسُولِ اللّٰهِ ﷺ فَدَعَا بِطَهُورٍ فَغَمَسَ يَدَهُ فِيهِ ثُمَّ تَوَضَّأَ فَتَتَبَّعْنَاهُ فَحَسَوْنَاهُ فَقَالَ رَسُولُ اللّٰهِ صَلَّى اللّٰهُ عَلَيْهِ وَسَلَّمَ «مَا حَمَلَكُمْ عَلَى مَا صَنَعْتُمْ؟» قُلْنَا: حُبُّ اللّٰهِ وَرَسُولِهِ، قَالَ «فَإِنْ أَحْبَبْتُمْ أَنْ يُحِبَّكُمُ اللّٰهُ وَرَسُولُهُ فَأَدُّوا إِذَا ائْتُمِنْتُمْ وَاصْدُقُوا إِذَا حَدَّثْتُمْ وَأَحْسِنُوا جِوَارَ مَنْ جَاوَرَكُمْ.»

رواه الطبراني في الأوسط (٦٥١٧) وحسنه الألباني (صحيح الجامع ١٤٠٩)

We were with the Messenger ﷺ and he asked for Wudu' water, then he put his hands in it and made Wudu'. We collected his Wudu' water and drank it. The Messenger ﷺ asked us, «What moved you to do this?» We said, "The love of Allah and His Messenger." He ﷺ replied, «If you would love for Allah and His Messenger to love you, then fulfill if you are entrusted, be honest when you speak, and be good to your neighbors.»

Reported by al-Tabarani in al-Awsat (6517) and al-Albani declared it hasan (Sahih al-Jami', 1409)

Commentary

Loving Allah and His Prophet is the best motivation for worship. And if we want Allah and His Prophet to love us, we should live and spread the love that they gave to us.

Why did they love him so much?

The amount of love the Companions had for the Prophet ﷺ is mind-boggling. This says a lot about them and him. Listen to the following *hadith*.

كانَ رَسولُ اللهِ صلى الله عليه وسلم إذا صَلّى الغَداةَ جاءَ خَدَمُ المَدِينَةِ بآنِيَتِهِمْ فِيها الماءُ فَما يُؤْتى بإناءٍ إلّا غَمَسَ يَدَهُ فِيها فَرُبَّما جاؤُوهُ في الغَداةِ البارِدَةِ فَيَغْمِسُ يَدَهُ فِيها.

رواه مسلم (٢٣٢٤)

> When the Messenger ﷺ would finish Fajr Prayer, the servants of Madinah would bring their vessels with water in them. Whenever they brought a vessel, he would dip his hand in it. At times, they came on cold mornings and he dipped his hand in them.
>
> Reported by Muslim (2324)

It was their habit to bless their water with his hands ﷺ. And he, in return, always obliged their requests, even if it was inconvenient and cold. This gives us a glimpse of why they loved him so much: he was very close to them and very merciful. Despite all ordeals and challenges, he continued to smile and comfort. He genuinely cared for them, and they could see that. He found the time to help, and was big-hearted and patient. He did not seek any worldly return, and they could see that too. They also realized the value of what he gave, and how much they owed him. How do you repay someone who brings you closer to Allah? Who teaches you how to live again? To be happy now and to be happy forever in the next life? And on top of all of that, it is so easy to love him. He always receives you with a smile.

He is the humblest person you have ever seen, yet you know deep inside he has endless wisdom. The world offered itself to him, and he gave it all away. He lived on this earth but did not belong to it. His heart was with his Creator. You cannot be too comfortable here, he would say, for we are about to leave. Your real home is waiting for you, do not worry about this life. When you were with him, you felt as if you flew to the heavens and were seated next to the angels. When you left him, you could not wait to come back and see him again. How can you not love someone who reminds you of Allah every time you see him? Who takes your troubles and worries away just by looking at you? Who always makes you feel better because he reminds you that Allah is near? We cannot fully understand today how life-changing it was to be around him. Their love for him was deep and intense, this we know. And his love for them created wonderful human beings that are the best of humanity. We do not have the opportunity today to be around him as they did, to hear his comforting words, and be blessed with his company. But just like the *Hadith* teaches (more on this shortly), we have his words and wisdom. If we cannot be with him physically, we can be with his Sunnah. And with that, he will be around us. With that, we will love him, and he will love us. And in the Hereafter, we will physically be with him. This is what loving Muhammad ﷺ offers you.

It is worth noting that seeking blessings from someone's body is exclusive to the blessed body of the Prophet ﷺ. No similar practice was extended to the Companions, including the best four: Abu Bakr, 'Umar, 'Othman, and 'Ali رَضِيَ اللَّهُ عَنْهُمْ. They are the best of the best of Allah's *awliya'* (*walis*). If we were permitted to extend this practice to someone else, these four would be the most deserving. Since no Companion treated them in this fashion, it should be clear that no *wali* after them—who will always be inferior to them—deserves this unique treatment.

It is also worth noting that the blessings from the body of the Prophet ﷺ come from Allah. He is the only One who has the power to bless and cure. So, if someone touched the body of the Prophet ﷺ and was blessed, it was Allah who blessed him. Allah deposited the blessing in the Prophet's body, and He transfers it to others if He wishes.

The right expression of love

The Prophet ﷺ gently redirected his Companions to a fuller and more lasting expression of their love. And with that, he was teaching us a valuable lesson about love. Not all expressions of love are appropriate, even though the love itself may be. This is religiously important, but it is also true everywhere else. If you love someone—a spouse or a child for instance—you have to translate this love into meaningful and beneficial acts. Otherwise, you could end up hurting them. We may love someone but fail to relay this love to them. We need to understand them to know what they need, what they expect, and what they appreciate.

This is true in our worship of Allah too. There are two conditions for the acceptance of a religious good deed: the intention must be pure (*Ikhlas*), and Allah must love the act. The way we know that Allah loves it is if He legislated it. For instance, when *Salah* is insincere, it is invalid. And a sincere intention inappropriately pursued is invalid too. For example, prostrating in front of the Prophet ﷺ (or his grave now) because we love him is inappropriate, even though the motive behind it is love. The following *hadith* illustrates this well.

كَانَ أَهْلُ بَيْتٍ مِنَ الْأَنْصَارِ لَهُمْ جَمَلٌ يَسْنُونَ عَلَيْهِ وَإِنَّ الْجَمَلَ اسْتُصْعِبَ عَلَيْهِمْ فَمَنَعَهُمْ ظَهْرَهُ وَإِنَّ الْأَنْصَارَ جَاءُوا إِلَى رَسُولِ اللهِ صَلَّى اللهُ عَلَيْهِ وَسَلَّمَ فَقَالُوا: إِنَّهُ كَانَ لَنَا جَمَلٌ نُسْنِي عَلَيْهِ وَإِنَّهُ اسْتُصْعِبَ عَلَيْنَا وَمَنَعَنَا ظَهْرَهُ وَقَدْ عَطِشَ الزَّرْعُ وَالنَّخْلُ، فَقَالَ رَسُولُ اللهِ صَلَّى اللهُ عَلَيْهِ وَسَلَّمَ لِأَصْحَابِهِ «قُومُوا» فَقَامُوا فَدَخَلَ الْحَائِطَ وَالْجَمَل فِي نَاحِيَةٍ فَمَشَى النَّبِيُّ صَلَّى اللهُ عَلَيْهِ وَسَلَّمَ نَحْوَهُ فَقَالَتِ الْأَنْصَارُ: يَا نَبِيَّ اللهِ إِنَّهُ قَدْ صَارَ مِثْلَ الْكَلْبِ الْكَلِبِ وَإِنَّا نَخَافُ

عَلَيْكَ صَوْلَتَهُ، فَقَالَ «لَيْسَ عَلَيَّ مِنْهُ بَأْسٌ» فَلَمَّا نَظَرَ الْجَمَلُ إِلَى
رَسُولِ اللهِ صَلَّى اللهُ عَلَيْهِ وَسَلَّمَ أَقْبَلَ نَحْوَهُ حَتَّى خَرَّ سَاجِدًا بَيْنَ
يَدَيْهِ وَأَخَذَ رَسُولُ اللهِ صَلَّى اللهُ عَلَيْهِ وَسَلَّمَ بِنَاصِيَتِهِ أَذَلَّ مَا كَانَتْ
قَطُّ حَتَّى أَدْخَلَهُ فِي الْعَمَلِ فَقَالَ لَهُ أَصْحَابُهُ: يَا نَبِيَّ اللهِ هَذِهِ بَهِيمَةٌ
لَا تَعْقِلُ تَسْجُدُ لَكَ وَنَحْنُ نَعْقِلُ فَنَحْن أَحَقُّ أَنْ نَسْجُدَ لَكَ، قَالَ
«لَا يَصْلُحُ لِبَشَرٍ أَنْ يَسْجُدَ لِبَشَرٍ.»

رواه أحمد (١٢٦١٤) وصححه الألباني (صحيح الترغيب ١٩٣٦)

There was a household from the Ansar who had a camel that they used to transport water on, and it became stubborn and refused to carry anything on its back. So these Ansar came to the Messenger ﷺ and said, "We have a camel that we used to transport water on, and it became stubborn and refuses to carry anything on its back, and the crops and trees are parched." So the Messenger ﷺ said to his Companions, «Let us go.» So they left, and he entered the garden, and the camel was in a corner, so the Prophet ﷺ walked towards it. The Ansar said, "O Prophet of Allah, he is like a rabid dog, and we fear that he will harm you." He ﷺ said, «He will not harm me.» When the camel saw the Messenger ﷺ, he walked to him and prostrated in front of him. The Messenger ﷺ held the camel's forehead—it was the most docile that he ever was—and guided him to work. His Companions said to him, "O Prophet of Allah, this is an unintelligent animal that prostrates to you, and we are intelligent beings, so it is more of a right upon us to prostrate to you." He said, "No human should prostrate to another human."

Reported by Ahmad (12614) and al-Albani declared it sahih (*Sahih al-Targhib*, 1936)

The Prophet ﷺ knew that his Companions suggested prostration out of love, but he disallowed it. No matter how intense our emotions may be, there has to be a check to help us avoid the extremes of love. Knowing very well love's inclination to move to the extreme, he ﷺ said:

«لا تُطْرُونِي كما أَطْرَتِ النَّصارى ابْنَ مَرْيَمَ فإنَّما أَنا عَبْدُهُ فَقُولوا عبدُ اللَّهِ وَرَسُولُهُ.»

رواه البخاري (٣٤٤٥)

«Do not exaggerate in praising me as the Christians exaggerated in praising the Son of Mary, for I am only His slave. So say, "The slave of Allah and His Messenger."»

Reported by al-Bukhari (3445)

Some love the Prophet ﷺ, yet contradict his wishes and exaggerate his praise. True love would ask us not to go against his teachings. We cannot attribute anything to him unless it is authentic and reliable, or else we would be helping to spread lies about him. Calling Jesus عَلَيْهِ السَّلَامُ the son of God is not love. Love is to respect the thing he gave his life for, and that is the message of Tawhid. If we go against Muhammad ﷺ in the name of love, we would be disrespecting him and upsetting the One who sent him. And the Prophet would not be happy with us if he were to see that. What made him happiest was our piety and love for Allah. If we love him, we should follow his message precisely as his Companions did. We cannot change it in the name of love and expect him to love us.

Worshipping out of love

Multiple motivations spur our worship. We may worship out of fear, where we are disturbed by our sins and their potential punishment. Seeking Allah's forgiveness and escaping from Hell would be the motivation for our worship. We may also pray out of hope. Attracted to all that Allah promised us in Jannah, we worship Him to win His Mercy and the beauty of eternal life in Paradise. Both of these approaches are legitimate and needed. We need hope and fear in our relationship with Allah to balance our excesses. When we are overconfident with our piety and lax with Allah's prohibitions, an injection of fear is a healthy corrective to restore the balance. This is why Allah talked about Hell at length in the Quran. Most people, even in worldly affairs, respond to fear of punishment more than enticement of reward. But as potent as fear is as a motivator, it is not the only one. At other times, hope is what will excite us to worship Allah. This is also why Allah motivated us the Quran with the mention of Jannah and its splendor. Yet, there is a third motivator that is often overlooked. It is love. When one worships Allah out of love, they do so because Allah deserves it, out of gratitude for His bounties, and with the desire to be close to Him. Heaven and Hell are not the prominent motivators here, but Allah Himself is—even though the worshipper still desires Heaven and escape from Hell. The three approaches—love, hope, and fear—are complementary, not contradictory. All three are needed. Otherwise, the outcome will be a great imbalance in *Iman* and worship. Makhul, the famous Tabi'i, said:

قال مكحول الدمشقي: من عبد الله بالخوف فهو حروري ومن عبده بالرجاء فهو مرجىء ومن عبده بالمحبة فهو زنديق ومن عبده بالخوف والرجاء والمحبة فهو موحد.

إحياء علوم الدين (ج٤ ص١٦٦)

The one who worships Allah with fear [alone] is from the Khawarij. The one who worships Allah with hope [alone] is from the Murji'ah. The one who worships Allah with love [alone] is a heretic. The one who worships Allah with fear, hope, and love is on Tawhid.

Ihya' 'Ulum al-Din (vol. 4, p. 166)

If one worships Allah exclusively with fear, they will grow hopeless, grim, and harsh. When the Khawarij put undue emphasis on the fear of Allah, they excommunicated anyone who disagreed with them or committed a major sin from Islam. They were infamous for slaughtering other Muslims. On the other extreme, worshippers with hope alone tend to disregard the religious law, believing in guaranteed salvation. Surprisingly, worshipping with love alone is the most severe offense among the three. The first victim will be the laws of Islam, which will be disregarded based on a misguided sense of Allah's overwhelming love. If Allah loves no matter what, the laws lose their meaning. The second and more devastating lapse is their relationship with Allah. Unchecked, love grows deformed and ends up compromising the Majesty of Allah. Thus the heresy Makhul warned against. When some express the desire to be one with the Creator or deny any duality of existence (i.e. they and the Creator have always been one), you hear in their statements how imbalanced love can corrupt Tawhid. This is why Ibn Taymiyyah رَحِمَهُ ٱللَّهُ wrote:

قال ابن تيمية: وَيُوجَدُ فِي مُدَّعِي الْمَحَبَّةِ مِنْ مُخَالَفَةِ الشَّرِيعَةِ مَا لَا يُوجَدُ فِي أَهْلِ الْخَشْيَةِ... وَكَانَ الْمَشَايِخُ الْمُصَنِّفُونَ فِي السُّنَّةِ يَذْكُرُونَ فِي عَقَائِدِهِمْ مُجَانَبَةَ مَنْ يُكْثِرُ دَعْوَى الْمَحَبَّةِ وَالْخَوْضِ فِيهَا مِنْ غَيْرِ خَشْيَةٍ لِمَا فِي ذَلِكَ مِنْ الْفَسَادِ.

مجموع الفتاوى (ج١٠ ص٨١-٨٢)

> There is more opposition to the Shari'ah among those who claim the love [of Allah] than the people of the fear [of Allah]...And the scholars who authored the books of Sunnah [i.e. Aqidah] used to note in their creeds the avoidance of the one who excessively claims the love of Allah and talks about it without fear, for there is much corruption in that.
>
> *Majmu' al-Fatawa* (vol. 10, p. 81–82)

The three ingredients together (fear, hope, and love) produce the Prophetic balance that moves us closer to Allah without compromising the purity of Islam.

At times, fear may be our dominant motivator. It could also be hope. Or it could be love. The Prophet ﷺ pointed in the *Hadith* to worship out of love. He made the love of Allah and His Messenger the motive for what he asked them to do. In the Quran, Allah made love the first feature of those whom He chose when He said:

يَٰٓأَيُّهَا ٱلَّذِينَ ءَامَنُواْ مَن يَرْتَدَّ مِنكُمْ عَن دِينِهِۦ فَسَوْفَ يَأْتِي ٱللَّهُ بِقَوْمٍ يُحِبُّهُمْ وَيُحِبُّونَهُۥٓ... ﴿٥٤﴾

O believers, if any of you abandons your religion, Allah will replace you with people whom He loves and who love Him.
Al-Ma'idah (Q5:54)

Love is the premise of our worship of Allah and its goal. It is the strongest motive to worship Him. There is no denying that fear and hope are indispensable components of our relationship with Allah. But love towers above them as a motive. The following from Wahb ibn Munabbih, the Tabi'i, conveys the potency of the love of Allah.

سَمِعُوا وَهْبَ بْنَ مُنَبِّهٍ يَقُولُ: قَالَ حَكِيمٌ مِنَ الْحُكَمَاءِ إِنِّي لَأَسْتَحْيِي مِنْ رَبِّي عَزَّ وَجَلَّ أَنْ أَعْبُدَهُ رَجَاءَ ثَوَابِ الْجَنَّةِ فَأَكُونَ كَالْأَجِيرِ إِنْ أُعْطِيَ أَجْرًا عَمِلَ وَإِلَّا لَمْ يَعْمَلْ وَإِنِّي لَأَسْتَحْيِي مِنْ رَبِّي عَزَّ وَجَلَّ أَنْ أَعْبُدَهُ مَخَافَةَ النَّارِ فَأَكُونَ كَعَبْدِ السُّوءِ إِنْ رَهِبَ عَمِلَ وَإِنْ لَمْ يَرْهَبْ لَمْ يَعْمَلْ وَلَكِنِّي أَعْبُدُهُ كَمَا هُوَ لَهُ أَهْلٌ) وَقَالَ عُمَرُ عَنْ وَهْبِ بْنِ مُنَبِّهٍ: (وَلَكِنْ يَسْتَخْرِجُ مِنِّي حُبُّ رَبِّي عَزَّ وَجَلَّ مَا لَمْ يَسْتَخْرِجْ مِنِّي غَيْرُهُ.

الزهد لابن المبارك (باب تعظيم ذكر الله) بإسناد صحيح إلى وهب ابن منبه (ص٢٤٦)

They heard Wahb ibn Munabbih say, "A wise man once said 'I feel embarrassed of my Rabb—Glory be to Him—to worship Him hoping for Heaven as a reward like a wageworker: he works if he is given his wage, but if not, he does not. And I feel embarrassed of my Rabb—Glory be to Him—to worship Him out of fear of Hell like a bad slave: if he is afraid he works but if he is not, he does not. But I worship Him because He deserves it.'" 'Umar reports from Wahb ibn Munabbih that he said, "But the love of my Rabb—Glory be to Him—extracts from me what nothing else extracts."

Al-Zuhd by Ibn al-Mubarak with an authentic chain to Wahb ibn Munabbih (p. 246)

Some are more motivated by fear, some by hope, and some by love. Each one of us moves between the three and relies on them as our *Iman* fluctuates and our needs change. For Wahb ibn Munabbih, love brought the best out of him, a more intense and devoted worship than out of hope and fear.

If love does not yield devoted worship, it is not true love but merely a claim and a wish. Allah said:

قُلْ إِن كُنتُمْ تُحِبُّونَ ٱللَّهَ فَٱتَّبِعُونِي يُحْبِبْكُمُ ٱللَّهُ وَيَغْفِرْ لَكُمْ ذُنُوبَكُمْ... ﴿٣١﴾

Say, "If you love Allah, then follow me and Allah will love you and forgive your sins."

Ali 'Imran (Q3:31)

The proof of one's love of Allah is obeying and worshipping Him. If one desires the love of Allah without good deeds, they are indulging in fantasy. Worship is essential in watering the tree of love, or it will dry out and die. The Prophet ﷺ loved Allah the most and worshipped Him the most; he did not stop His worship in the name of love.

There is a point in Wahb ibn Munabbih's saying that merits further elaboration. His statement should not be mistaken to mean that desiring Heaven and fearing Hell is to be discouraged. This has been—and continues to be—a grave misunderstanding in some circles. Such an approach goes against the Quran and Sunnah. If it were true, why would Allah speak at length about Jannah and what awaits us in it? Then He said about Jannah:

...وَفِي ذَٰلِكَ فَلْيَتَنَافَسِ ٱلْمُتَنَٰفِسُونَ ﴿٢٦﴾

So for this let the competitors compete.
Al-Mutaffifin (Q83:26)

Why would Allah warn us about Hell with such detail if not to do our best to run away from it? If we believe that we are not working to win Heaven and escape Hell, all these *ayahs* become irrelevant for us when we read the Quran. All the *du'a* of the Prophet ﷺ for Jannah and against entry to Hell stop making sense. What Wahb ibn Munabbih noted was different. He was pointing to a state of worship where we are focused on ourselves and not Allah's worthiness of worship. Someone at this stage will attain salvation, but they are missing the joy of worshipping Allah out of love, out of gratitude, and out of the desire to be near Him. Heaven and Hell move this person to be righteous, but they do not consider that Allah deserves this worship for who He is. Were they to worship Him out of love, they will get Heaven and safety from Hell. The following from Ibn al-Qayyim رَحِمَهُ ٱللَّهُ explains this.

وَأَمَّا قَوْلُهُ وَلَا تَشُوبُ إِجَابَتَكَ بِعِوَضٍ أَيْ تَكُونُ إِجَابَتُكَ لِدَاعِي الْحَقِّ خَالِصَةً إِجَابَةَ مَحَبَّةٍ وَرَغْبَةٍ وَطَلَبٍ لِلْمَحْبُوبِ ذَاتِهِ غَيْرَ مَشُوبَةٍ بِطَلَبِ غَيْرِهِ مِنَ الْحُظُوظِ وَالْأَعْوَاضِ فَإِنَّهُ مَتَى حَصَلَ لَكَ حَصَلَ لَكَ كُلُّ عِوَضٍ وَكُلُّ حَظٍّ بِهِ وَكُلُّ قَسَمٍ كَمَا فِي الْأَثَرِ الْإِلَهِيِّ (ابْنَ آدَمَ اطْلُبْنِي تَجِدْنِي فَإِنْ وَجَدْتَنِي وَجَدْتَ كُلَّ شَيْءٍ وَإِنْ فُتُّكَ فَاتَكَ كُلُّ شَيْءٍ وَأَنَا أَحَبُّ إِلَيْكَ مِنْ كُلِّ شَيْءٍ) فَمَنْ أَعْرَضَ عَنْ طَلَبِ مَا سِوَى اللَّهِ وَلَمْ يَشُبْ طَلَبَهُ لَهُ بِعِوَضٍ بَلْ كَانَ حُبًّا لَهُ وَإِرَادَةً خَالِصَةً لِوَجْهِهِ فَهُوَ فِي الْحَقِيقَةِ الَّذِي يَفُوزُ بِالْأَعْوَاضِ وَالْأَقْسَامِ وَالْحُظُوظِ كُلِّهَا فَإِنَّهُ لَمَّا لَمْ يَجْعَلْهَا غَايَةَ طَلَبِهِ تَوَفَّرَتْ عَلَيْهِ فِي حُصُولِهَا وَهُوَ مَحْمُودٌ مَشْكُورٌ مُقَرَّبٌ وَلَوْ كَانَتْ هِيَ مَطْلُوبَةً لَنَقَصَتْ عَلَيْهِ بِحَسَبِ اشْتِغَالِهِ بِطَلَبِهَا وَإِرَادَتِهَا عَنْ طَلَبِ الرَّبِّ تَعَالَى لِذَاتِهِ وَإِرَادَتِهِ فَهَذَا قَلْبُهُ مُمْتَلِئٌ بِهَا وَالْحَاصِلُ لَهُ مِنْهَا نَزْرٌ يَسِيرٌ وَالْعَارِفُ لَيْسَ قَلْبُهُ

مُتَعَلِّقًا بِهَا وَقَدْ حَصَلَتْ لَهُ كُلُّهَا فَالزُّهْدُ فِيهَا لَا يُفِيتُكُهَا بَلْ هُوَ عَيْنُ حُصُولِهَا وَالزُّهْدُ فِي اللَّهِ هُوَ الَّذِي يُفِيتُكَهُ وَيُفِيتُكَ الْحُظُوظَ.

مدارج السالكين (ج ٢ ص٣٣٢)

As for [Al-Harawi's] statement, "And do not taint your compliance with compensation," it means that your pursuit of the truth should be pure, compliance out of love, desire, and seeking the Beloved Himself, not tainted with seeking another prize and compensation. For once you have Him, you will have every compensation, every prize, and all portions. As it was mentioned that Allah said, "O child of Adam, seek me and you shall find me. And when you find me, you shall find everything. But if you lose me, you shall lose everything. And I am dearer to you than everything [An Israelite tradition]." So, he who does not seek anyone but Allah and does not taint his pursuit with other compensations, but makes it out of love for Him and sincerely seeks His Face, it is he who wins all compensations, portions, and prizes. Since he did not make these [compensations] his goal, they became his while also being worthy of praise, thanks, and he was brought closer to Allah. But if these were his goal, he will have less of them in so much as he is distracted by them from seeking Allah for Himself and wanting Him. This person's heart is occupied with them but only gets very little of them, but the heart of the knowledgeable is not attached to them, and he wins them all. So, turning away from them does not make you lose them but is, in fact, how you get them. But turning away from Allah is the thing that makes you lose Him and all winnings.

Madarij al-Salikin (vol. 2, p. 332)

Worshipping Allah out of love does not contradict seeking Heaven but elevates it to the next level. Heaven can be sought and enjoyed for all the created beauty that is in it—food, drink, indescribable sights—and this is praiseworthy. Allah highlighted it in the Quran because it is a legitimate goal. But the greatest joy in Heaven is seeing Allah and talking to Him. This is the greatest beauty of Jannah. And so when our *Iman* is strong, we aspire for the latter. And when we are weaker, we focus on all the beauty Allah prepared in Heaven. This energizes us again to march towards Allah and seek Him out of love for Him.

The nature of worship and the satisfaction we receive from it vary based on the motivation. Let us listen again to Ibn al-Qayyim رَحِمَهُ ٱللَّهُ

لَا يَسُوقُ نَفْسَهُ إِلَى اللَّهِ كَرْهًا كَالْأَجِيرِ الْمُسَخَّرِ الْمُكَلَّفِ بَلْ تَكُونُ دَوَاعِي قَلْبِهِ وَجَوَاذِبُهُ مُنْسَاقَةً إِلَى اللَّهِ طَوْعًا وَمَحَبَّةً وَإِيثَارًا كَجَرَيَانِ الْمَاءِ فِي مُنْحَدَرِهِ وَهَذِهِ حَالُ الْمُحِبِّينَ الصَّادِقِينَ فَإِنَّ عِبَادَتَهُمْ طَوْعًا وَمَحَبَّةً وَرِضًا فَفِيهَا قُرَّةُ عُيُونِهِمْ وَسُرُورُ قُلُوبِهِمْ وَلَذَّةُ أَرْوَاحِهِمْ كَمَا قَالَ النَّبِيُّ صَلَّى اللَّهُ عَلَيْهِ وَسَلَّمَ وَجُعِلَتْ قُرَّةُ عَيْنِي فِي الصَّلَاةِ وَكَانَ يَقُولُ يَا بِلَالُ أَرِحْنَا بِالصَّلَاةِ فَقُرَّةُ عَيْنِ الْمُحِبِّ وَلَذَّتُهُ وَنَعِيمُ رُوحِهِ فِي طَاعَةِ مَحْبُوبِهِ بِخِلَافِ الْمُطِيعِ كَرْهًا الْمُتَحَمِّلِ لِلْخِدْمَةِ ثِقَلًا وَفِي قَوْلِهِ ذُلُّ الْإِكْرَاهِ لَطِيفَةٌ وَهِيَ أَنَّ الْمُطِيعَ كَرْهًا يَرَى أَنَّهُ لَوْلَا ذُلُّ قَهْرِهِ وَعُقُوبَةُ سَيِّدِهِ لَهُ لَمَا أَطَاعَهُ فَهُوَ يَتَحَمَّلُ طَاعَتَهُ كَالْمُكْرَهِ الَّذِي قَدْ أَذَلَّهُ مُكْرِهُهُ وَقَاهِرُهُ بِخِلَافِ الْمُحِبِّ الَّذِي يُعِدُّ طَاعَةَ مَحْبُوبِهِ قُوتًا وَنَعِيمًا وَلَذَّةً وَسُرُورًا فَهَذَا لَيْسَ الْحَامِلُ لَهُ ذُلَّ الْإِكْرَاهِ.

مدارج السالكين (ج٢ ص١٠١-١٠٢)

He should not move himself unwillingly to Allah like a forced laborer, but what attracts and pulls his heart should be willingly and lovingly compliant like water running down a slope. This is the condition of true lovers: their worship is voluntary, out of love and content. In it, they find their eyes' contentment, their hearts' happiness, and the joy of their souls, as the Prophet ﷺ said, «And the contentment of my eye was put in Salah.» And he used to say, «O Bilal, bring us comfort with it.» The contentment of the eyes of the lover, their delight, and the bliss of their soul is in obeying their beloved, unlike one who obeys begrudgingly and serves like carrying a weight. As for [al-Harawi's] statement, "the humiliation of compulsion," there is a hidden benefit, which is that the one who obeys begrudgingly believes that were it not for him having to submit to being overpowered and were it not for the punishment of their master, he would not obey him. So, he tolerates his obedience like one who is compelled and had been subdued by the one who forced him and overpowered him. This is unlike the lover who considers obeying his beloved to be nourishing, a blessing, a delight, and happiness. For this one, his motive is not the humiliation of compulsion.

Madarij al-Salikin (vol. 2, p. 101–102)

When one worships out of love, they find joy in their worship. They want to do more of it, and they cannot wait for it. It gives them more than anything in the world can. The Prophet ﷺ found absolute joy in his *Salah*. He enjoyed it because it comforted him. When one worships consistently out of fear alone, it may create a burden that takes away the beauty of worship. There is a difference between one who drags themselves to worship, bored and tired, and one who happily runs to it. We need love to motivate us, to extract the best out of us.

When the love of Allah is the inspiration, all our worship will seem insufficient. Thu al-Nun said:

قَالَ ذو النُّونِ: مَنْ أَحَبَّ اللَّهَ اسْتَقَلَّ كُلَّ عَمَلٍ يَعْمَلُهُ.

الزهد الكبير (ص٧٨)

The one who loves Allah sees all their deeds as insignificant.

Al-Zuhd al-Kabir (p. 78)

When we worship out of love, we will know that all our worship falls short of what Allah deserves. How can we repay and thank Allah for all His blessings when we cannot even count them? Even our gratitude is a blessing from Allah that needs to be thanked, so how can we ever thank Him? How can we worship Allah in ways that befit His Perfection? Our worship is plagued with imperfection: we forget, we daydream, and we sin. Yet even if we were to worship like the angels, it would not be enough. Salman al-Farisi رَضِيَ اللَّهُ عَنْهُ explained that the angels will say on the Day of Judgment:

> سبحانَكَ ما عَبَدْناكَ حقَّ عِبادَتِكَ.
>
> السلسلة الصحيحة (٩٤١)
>
> Glory be to You, we did not worship You as You deserved to be worshipped.
>
> *Al-Silsilah al-Sahihah* (941)

Worship out of love saves us from feeling entitled, feeling like we have done so much and deserve something in return. It saves us from paying undue attention to our actions, and helps us to focus instead on the One we are worshipping. When we do that, He will give us all that we need and more.

How to get His love

The Prophet ﷺ revealed to us in this *Hadith* what to do to gain the love of Allah and His Messenger. And in the following *hadiths* in this book, he will tell us more. But we need to understand why he said what he said.

The Companions in the *Hadith* expressed their love through seeking physical proximity and blessings from the Prophet ﷺ. And this, as we explained before, was legitimate. But it is also limited. It was not available to the Companions when they were not near him, and not available to us and them after his death. The Prophet ﷺ sought to move them to something bigger and more lasting: from bodily blessing to the blessings of his teachings, and from receiving to giving. It is as if he was saying to them: if you want love, spread love. If you want love, be it. If you want love, then practice it after my death.

When we are honest when we speak, kind when we act, and trustworthy, we exemplify the message of Muhammad ﷺ. This is why he came and sacrificed, for us to embrace Islam and spread it, for us to change and help others to change. He will be happy when we become a mercy to others as he was a mercy to all. The circle of love that he started must expand. This will happen when we embrace the truth and act on it. The Prophet ﷺ was telling them that the message of Islam is not about one man—no matter how great he was—and not about a specific time and place—no matter how blessed it was. It is about a belief that transforms lives and changes the world. This is how we reach the love of Allah and His Messenger.

HADITH TWENTY

الحديث العشرون

Love through suffering

أَتَى رَجُلٌ النَّبِيَّ ﷺ فَقَالَ: وَاللهِ يَا رَسُولَ اللهِ إِنِّي لَأُحِبُّكَ، فَقَالَ لَهُ رَسُولُ اللهِ ﷺ «إِنَّ الْبَلَايَا أَسْرَعُ إِلَى مَنْ يُحِبُّنِي مِنَ السَّيْلِ إِلَى منتهاه.»

رواه ابن حبان (٢٩٢٢) وحسنه الألباني (السلسلة الصحيحة ١٥٨٦)

A man came to the Prophet ﷺ and said, "O Prophet of Allah, by Allah I love you." So the Messenger ﷺ said to him, «Affliction runs faster towards those who love me than a stream running down to its mouth [i.e. bottom end].»

Reported by Ibn Hibban (2922) and al-Albani declared it hasan (Al-Silsilah al-Sahihah, 1586)

Commentary

Tests are part of the experience of *Iman*. But they carry with them many gifts.

The price of commitment

Did this *Hadith* scare you? Hearing that hardship will be seeking you if you love the Prophet ﷺ may be causing you to rethink what you read so far. Should I keep my distance from him to be safe? But is this an option? Not to love him? So, what do I do with this *Hadith*?

Let us examine another narration of this *Hadith* to understand it better.

قَالَ رَجُلٌ لِلنَّبِيِّ صَلَّى اللَّهُ عَلَيْهِ وَسَلَّمَ: يَا رَسُولَ اللهِ وَاللَّهِ إِنِّي لَأُحِبُّكَ فَقَالَ لَهُ «انْظُرْ مَاذَا تَقُولُ» قَالَ: وَاللهِ إِنِّي لَأُحِبُّكَ ثَلَاثَ مَرَّاتٍ، فَقَالَ «إِنْ كُنْتَ تُحِبُّنِي فَأَعِدَّ لِلْفَقْرِ تِجْفَافًا فَإِنَّ الفَقْرَ أَسْرَعُ إِلَى مَنْ يُحِبُّنِي مِنَ السَّيْلِ إِلَى مُنْتَهَاهُ.»

رواه الترمذي (٢٣٥٠) وصححه الألباني (السلسلة الصحيحة ٢٨٢٧، ٢٨٢٨)

A man once said to the Prophet ﷺ, "O Prophet of Allah, by Allah I love you." He ﷺ said to him, «Consider what you are saying.» He replied, "By Allah I love you," repeating it three times. He ﷺ then said to him, «If you love me, put on protection from poverty. Indeed, poverty runs faster towards those who love me than a stream running down to its mouth [i.e. bottom end].»

Reported by al-Tirmidhi (2350) and al-Albani declared it sahih (*Al-Silsilah al-Sahihah*, 2827, 2828)

The man came to proclaim His love for the Prophet ﷺ, something we will come to see, in another *hadith*, is highly recommended. The Prophet ﷺ asked him to stop and reconsider what he had said. This is a grand claim. And it has consequences. So, if you are swearing by Allah that you love him, are you sure? And do you know what that means?

Loving the Prophet ﷺ is not like loving anyone else. It is born out of loving Allah, the Highest. Loving the trivial in this life does not put plenty of demands on us. You may love a movie, fried chicken, or a pair of shoes, but none of these things is serious enough to demand something from you. If you say that you love another human—spouse or your child—this love will ask you for things in return. You cannot love your child and spouse and neglect them. Your love will require you to change your priorities and put your family, at times, ahead of yourself.

If you say you are passionate about a serious cause—environmentalism, saving endangered animals, or economic equality—then the weight of this cause will demand your activism. Or if not activism, then life choices that reflect your proclaimed passion. You cannot be an environmentalist and not recycle, in support of animal wellbeing but use toxic chemicals, or for economic equality but support greedy conglomerates. If you are passionate about any of these causes, it will change your life (e.g. you will not use plastic, you will not eat animals raised or killed inhumanly, and maybe you will not purchase a new iPhone). In other words, there is a price to pay for this love. And the more serious you are about this love, the heavier the price. But it will be worth it if you believed in the cause.

Now, there is nothing more important and more serious than Allah and His Messenger. They dwarf all other causes and subsume them. This is the greatest thing you could ever care about. So naturally, it will completely change your life if you are serious about it. And naturally, this will have a price. Just consider how the message of Islam altered the life of the Prophet ﷺ. It changed it completely. He could have chosen to ignore it and stay home with his loving wife and kids, but Allah was too important to let go of. And so, he lost his home, lost his job and money, put himself and family in danger, fled to a new land, and began a life of struggle that lasted for twenty-three years. Yes, it culminated in victory, but he did not know if he would live to see that day. He knew that he had a message, and it needed everything from him. And he gave it all he had. Look at the lives of the Companions, and you will see the price they paid for loving Allah and His Messenger. It turned their lives upside down. They lost family and friends. It changed how they slept and ate, whom they married and where they lived. It did not leave a single detail in their life unaltered. This is a message that changes everything if taken seriously.

And so, when this man proclaimed his love for the Prophet ﷺ, he asked him to pause and consider if he was serious. This is a monumental claim and a high honor. And so when the man came back to affirm it three times, each time swearing by Allah, the Prophet ﷺ told him what this love entails. The test is not always poverty—some Companions were pious and wealthy—but there is always a test.

Now, someone may think that it easier for them to stay away from this love, to protect themselves from pain and hardship. In response to that, you should read what Ibn al-Qayyim رَحِمَهُ ٱللَّهُ wrote:

قال تعالى: ﴿ألم أَحَسِبَ النَّاسُ أَنْ يُتْرَكُوا أَنْ يَقُولُوا آمَنَّا وَهُمْ لا يُفْتَنُونَ وَلَقَدْ فَتَنَّا الَّذِينَ مِنْ قَبْلِهِمْ فَلَيَعْلَمَنَّ اللَّهُ الَّذِينَ صَدَقُوا وَلَيَعْلَمَنَّ الْكَاذِبِينَ أَمْ حَسِبَ الَّذِينَ يَعْمَلُونَ السَّيِّئَاتِ أَنْ يَسْبِقُونَا سَاءَ مَا يَحْكُمُونَ مَنْ كَانَ يَرْجُو لِقَاءَ اللَّهِ فَإِنَّ أَجَلَ اللَّهِ لَآتٍ وَهُوَ السَّمِيعُ الْعَلِيمُ وَمَنْ جَاهَدَ فَإِنَّمَا يُجَاهِدُ لِنَفْسِهِ إِنَّ اللَّهَ لَغَنِيٌّ عَنِ الْعَالَمِينَ﴾ فذكر سبحانه في هذه السورة أنه لا بد أن يمتحن خلقه ويفتنهم ليتبين الصادق من الكاذب والمؤمن من الكافر ومن يشكره ويعبده ممن يكفره ويعرض عنه ويعبد غيره وذكر أحوال الممتحنين في العاجل والآجل وذكر أئمة الممتحنين في الدنيا وهم الرسل وأتباعهم وعاقبة أمرهم وما صاروا إليه وافتتح السورة بالإنكار على من يحسب أنه يتخلص من الامتحان والفتنة في هذه الدار إذا دعى إلى الإيمان وأن حكمته سبحانه وشأنه في خلقه يأبى ذلك وأخبر عن سر هذه الفتنة والمحنة وهو تبيين الصادق من الكاذب والمؤمن من الكافر وهو سبحانه كان يعلم ذلك قبل وقوعه ولكن اقتضى عدله وحمده أنه لا يجزي العباد بمجرد علمه فيهم بل بمعلومه إذا وجد وتحقق والفتنة هي التي أظهرته وأخرجته إلى الوجود فحينئذ حسن وقوع الجزاء عليه ثم أنكر سبحانه على من لم يلتزم الإيمان به ومتابعة رسله خوف الفتنة والمحنة التي يمتحن بها رسله وأتباعهم ظنه وحسبانه أنه بإعراضه عن الإيمان

وتصديق رسله يتخلص من الفتنة والمحنة فإن بين يديه من الفتنة والمحنة والعذاب أعظم وأشق مما فر عنه فإن المكلفين بعد إرسال الرسل إليهم بين أمرين إما أن يقول أحدهم آمنت وإما أن لا يقول بل يستمر على السيئات فمن قال آمنا امتحنه الرب تعالى وابتلاه ليتحقق بالامتحان صحة إيمانه وثباته عليه وأنه ليس بإيمان عافية ورخاء فقط بل إيمان ثابت في حالتي النعماء والبلاء ومن لم يؤمن فلا يحسب أنه يعجز ربه تعالى ويفوته بل هو في قبضته وناصيته بيده فله من البلاء أعظم مما ابتلى به من قال آمنت فمن آمن به وبرسله فلا بد أن يبتلى من أعدائه وأعداء رسله بما يؤلمه ويشق عليه ومن لم يؤمن به وبرسله فلا بد أن يعاقبه فيحصل له من الألم والمشقة أضعاف ألم المؤمنين فلا بد من حصول الألم لكل نفس مؤمنة أو كافرة لكن المؤمن يحصل له الألم في الدنيا ابتداءا ثم ينقطع ويعقبه أعظم اللذة والكافر يحصل له اللذة والسرور ابتداء ثم ينقطع ويعقبه أعظم الألم والمشقة وهكذا حال الذين يتبعون الشهوات فيلتذون بها ابتداء ثم تعقبها الآلام بحسب ما نالوه منها والذين يصبرون عنها يتألمون بفقدها ابتداء ثم يعقب ذلك الألم من اللذة والسرور بحسب ما صبروا عنه وتركوه منها فالألم واللذة أمر ضروري لكل إنسان لكن الفرق بين العاجل المنقطع اليسير والآجل الدائم العظيم ولهذا كان خاصة العقل النظر في العواقب والغايات فمن ظن أنه يتخلص من الألم بحيث لا يصيبه البتة فظنه أكذب الحديث.

شفاء العليل (ص٢٤٥)

Allah the Most High said, ﴿Alif Lam Mim. Do people think that they will be left to say, "We believe" without being tested? We certainly tested those before them. And Allah will make evident the ones who are truthful and the liars. Or do the evildoers think that they can escape us? How mistaken is their judgment. Whoever hopes to meet Allah, then Allah's appointed time is sure to come; He is the All-Hearing, the All-Knowing. And whoever strives only strives for themselves. Allah does not need His creation﴿ [Al-'Ankabut 1–6]. Allah mentioned in this Surah that He must test His creation and expose them to fitnah to distinguish the honest from the liar, and the believer from the disbeliever, and the one who thanks and worships Him from the one who denies Him, turns away from Him, and worships another. And He mentioned the condition of those who are tested in the short and the long terms. And He mentioned the chiefs of those who are tested in this world—the Messengers and their followers—and the consequence of their situation and what happened to them. And He began the Surah with chastising the one who thinks that they can escape test and fitnah in this world when they are asked to believe, and that His Wisdom and how He deals with His creation goes against this [i.e. running away from Iman does not protect you from hardship]. And he explained the secret behind this fitnah and test, which is distinguishing the honest from the liar and the believer from the disbeliever, which he knew beforehand but His Justice and His Excellence dictated that He would not treat creation according to what He knows they will do but [according to] the physical manifestation of His Knowledge as it happens. It is fitnah that made it visible and brought it out into existence [i.e. only when they are tested, do they believe or disbelieve]. And then, the recompense is suitable [but not before that when no one obeyed or disobeyed]. Then He, Glory be to Him, criticized the one who does not believe in Him and does not follow His Messengers out of fear of fitnah and hardship which Allah tests His Messengers and their followers with, thinking that by turning away from Iman and belief in the Messengers that they can escape from fitnah and hardship, for in front of them lies greater fitnah, hardship, and torment than the ones they ran away from. After the Messengers are sent, people have two options: either they believe or reject and continue to sin. The one who says that they believe, Allah tests them and afflicts them so the test would verify the soundness of their Iman and their adherence to it and show that it is not an Iman of ease and luxury but an Iman that is stable in both states of blessings and hardship. And the one who does not believe, they should not think that they can escape their Rabb and outrun Him; no, they are in His Grip and their forehead is in His Hand. They will have greater hardship than the one that tested the believer. The one who believes in Him and His Messengers has to be tested by Allah's enemies and the enemies of His Messengers with what hurts them and is hard on them. And the one who does not believe in Him and His Messengers, Allah must punish them, and so they will receive pain and hardship that is many times more the pain of the believers. Every soul, believing or nonbelieving, must experience pain. But the believer experiences pain in this world in the beginning, then it stops and is followed by the greatest joy. And the nonbeliever receive joy and happiness in the beginning, then it stops and is followed by the greatest pain and hardship. And it is the same for those who follow sinful desires: they enjoy it in the beginning and then it is followed by plenty of pain in proportion to what they gained from it. But those who patiently stay away from sinful temptations, they hurt in the beginning because they do not have it, but this pain is followed by joy and happiness in proportion to what they patiently stayed away from and abstained from. So, pain and joy are necessary for each human. But the difference is between the hastened that is little and ending, and the postponed that is lasting and great. And that is why the nature of the mind is to consider the consequences and ends [and not be fooled by immediate appearances]. So, whoever thinks that they can escape pain so it never touches them, then their thinking is the falsest of thinking.

Shifa' al-'Alil (p. 245)

If this was a little long and hard to understand, please allow me to encapsulate. If one thinks that they can escape hardship by avoiding *Iman*, think again. The hardship in *Iman* is temporary and small. The greater and more lasting hardship is in opposing Allah. Allah decreed that anyone who loves Allah and decides to obey Him will be afflicted. There is a purpose to this affliction: it tests the reality of their *Iman*. Is it an *Iman* of conviction or convenience, an *Iman* that withstands pressure or collapses under it? And if one passes this test, they will emerge with their love for Allah stronger than ever, and their *Iman* as the dearest thing they have in this life. Then Allah will remove their pain and grant them the pleasure of this life and the greatest pleasure of the Hereafter. Note as proof how the Prophet ﷺ and his Companions were tested in the beginning, and because they were strong, Allah granted them His love and worldly victory. They won the honor of this life and the honor of the Hereafter. On the other end, if someone disobeys Allah to escape hardship, let them know that they chose hardship itself. They will have some fun and joy in the start, but what they chose carries in it the seeds of pain. Sooner or later, these seeds will grow and bring severe hardship and regret. And the hardship of those who defy Allah is much greater and much longer than any hardship Allah's beloveds experience. Plus, those who love Allah begin to see hardship as a gift.

Gifts from the Beloved

Everything that comes from Allah is a gift. It is all good. This may be hard to believe at times, especially when the calamity is big and we feel like we are hopelessly drowning in it. But our assessment of any calamity and hardship is flawed and incomplete if we look at it in isolation. Who sent this calamity? What is its purpose? Do I have to endure it alone, or can someone help? Once you note those three—the sender, the reason, and the assistance—your perception of pain and suffering will begin to change.

If hardship is random, we cannot assign any rational purpose to it. If it comes from one who wishes you harm, then it is meant to hurt us. But if it comes from the All-Wise and All-Merciful, then it must be good. Even if it is coated with pain, the essence of hardship is love. If this is hard to see, listen to the following *hadith*. Abu Sa'id al-Khudri رَضِيَ ٱللَّهُ عَنْهُ said:

قال أبو سعيد الخدري رضي الله عنه دخلتُ على النَّبيِّ ﷺ وَهوَ يوعَكُ فوضعتُ يدي عليهِ فوجدتُ حرَّهُ بينَ يديَّ فوقَ اللِّحافِ فقلتُ: يا رسولَ اللَّهِ ما أشدَّها عليكَ! قالَ «إنّا كذلِكَ يضعَّفُ لَنا البلاءُ ويضعَّفُ لَنا الأجْرُ» قلتُ: يا رسولَ اللَّهِ أيُّ النّاسِ أشدُّ بلاءً؟ قالَ «الأنبياءُ» قلتُ: يا رسولَ اللَّهِ ثُمَّ مَن؟ قالَ «ثُمَّ الصّالِحونَ إن كانَ أحدُهُم ليُبتَلى بالفَقرِ حتّى ما يجدُ أحدُهُم إلّا العَباءَةَ يَحويها وإن كانَ أحدُهُم ليفرَحُ بالبلاءِ كما يفرَحُ أحدُكُم بالرَّخاءِ.»

رواه ابن ماجه (٤٠٢٤) وصححه الألباني (السلسلة الصحيحة ١٤٤)

I visited the Prophet ﷺ when he was sick, and I placed my hand on him and felt his fever with my hand from above the blanket. I said, "O Messenger of Allah, how hard it is for you!" He ﷺ said, «We [the Prophets] are like that. Affliction is multiplied for us, and so is the reward.» I said, "O Messenger of Allah, which people are most tested?" He ﷺ said, «The Prophets.» I said, "O Messenger of Allah, then whom?" He ﷺ said, «Then the righteous. Some were tested with poverty until they could not find anything except a cloak to put around themselves. Some would rejoice at calamity as one of you would rejoice at ease.»

Reported by Ibn Majah and al-Albani declared it sahih (*al-Silsilah al-Sahihah*, 144)

The Prophets and the righteous have the severest tests. This is not because Allah hates them. As the next *hadith* states:

«مَنْ يُرِدِ اللهُ بِهِ خَيْرًا يُصِبْ مِنْهُ.»

رواه البخاري (٥٦٤٥)

«If Allah desires good for someone, He afflicts them.»

Reported by al-Bukhari (5645)

The test could be so severe that some of the Prophets would own nothing of this world except one piece of clothing to cover their naked bodies, all this while being the best people on earth. The Prophet ﷺ would receive double the sickness an average man would, and his fever was so high that it could be felt from on top of a blanket. What is astonishing is not the severity of the test. What is truly amazing is their patience despite these tests. And what is beyond amazing is that they used to be happy with hardship as the rest of us would be happy with ease. This could only be because they saw the good in the hardship Allah sent, a good that supersedes reveling in ease.

We have seen previously (*Hadith Fifteen*) some of the benefits of hardship. The greatest of these benefits is its purification of the heart to prepare it for Allah's love. Hardship breaks our worldly attachments, one by one. We love money, and so we lose it. We love health, and we lose it. We love youth, and we lose it. We love others, and we lose them. We feel secure and comfortable in this world, and it demonstrates how incredibly unstable and unreliable it is. It keeps changing so drastically from underneath our feet. These detachments are difficult because our attachments are strong. But the heart cannot be free to love Allah when it is a slave to all of these other distractions. We cannot consume healthy food when are bellies are full of junk. So hardship descends like a fast: it empties our hearts of dependence and moves us towards Allah. Ease does the opposite: it feeds our worldly attachments and moves us further away from Allah.

In our hardship, when we find that we can turn to no other but Allah, we discover what He means to us. Our pain compels us to pray for relief. And in prayer, we find something greater than what we were seeking: we discover Allah. We find that being close to Him is all that we need. We thought that we needed the world because we did not know Him. But once we experience the joy of talking to Him, trusting Him, and relying on Him, we know that there is nothing in this world that begins to compare to Him. And so, our pleading for more of this world transforms into an intimate time with Allah, a rediscovery of the joy of *Iman* and the beautiful promise of the Hereafter. This all comes because of hardship. For the Prophets of Allah, more difficulty meant more love and fewer distractions. This is what made them happy when they were afflicted. No human loves pain and loss. But the reality and consequence of each are beautiful. This is why Allah reserved the hardest for His Prophets and the pious. It is only through our pain that we are elevated, that we get to discover who we are and what Allah means to us. Hardship is a gift from Allah who loves you. We do not pray for difficulties because we do not know if we are ready to receive it. No, let Allah choose this for us. But when He does, see that He is gifting you something special. Al-Fudayl ibn 'Iyad said:

لاَ يَبْلُغُ العَبْدُ حَقِيْقَةَ الإِيْمَانِ حَتَّى يَعُدَّ البَلاَءَ نِعمَةً وَالرَّخَاءَ مُصِيبَةً وَحَتَّى لاَ يُحِبَّ أَنْ يُحْمَدَ عَلَى عِبَادَةِ اللهِ.

سير أعلام النبلاء (ج٨ ص٤٣٤)

One does not attain the reality of Iman until they view hardship as a blessing, ease as an affliction, and until they do not love to receive praise for worshipping Allah.

Siyar 'A'lam al-Nubala' (vol. 8, p. 434)

Iman has the power to alter our perception of the world and our experience of it. Rather than seeing any test as a setback, see it as an opportunity, a message of love from the One who wants the best for you. And know that He gave it to you, and promised to help you overcome it. You are not alone. Allah is always with you. Feel His Mercy in everything that He sends you.

What is the protection?

The Prophet ﷺ advised those who love Him to shield themselves from upcoming tests. This protection resembles wearing armor in preparation for battle, as the Arabic word (*tijfaf*) suggests. So now, we know that the tests are coming. How do we get ready?

We protect ourselves by strengthening our *Iman*, and practicing patience and Zuhd. These will deflect the pain and save our faith from doubt and despair. When we voluntarily lessen our worldly attachments, tests will not devastate us because we are free. When we have learned to rely on Allah, we will not be crushed under pressure because we know where to go. When we increase our love of Allah now, it will enlighten our life when darkness knocks on our doors. Our love will always lead us back to Him, no matter how strong the test. This is why the Prophet ﷺ prayed for Allah's love. This is what you will see in the next *hadith*.

HADITH TWENTY ONE

الحديث الواحد والعشرون

Praying for love

احْتُبِسَ عَنَّا رَسُولُ اللهِ ﷺ ذَاتَ غَدَاةٍ مِنْ صَلاَةِ الصُّبْحِ حَتَّى كِدْنَا نَتَرَاءَى عَيْنَ الشَّمْسِ فَخَرَجَ سَرِيعًا فَثُوِّبَ بِالصَّلاَةِ فَصَلَّى رَسُولُ اللهِ ﷺ وَتَجَوَّزَ فِي صَلاَتِهِ فَلَمَّا سَلَّمَ دَعَا بِصَوْتِهِ فَقَالَ لَنَا «عَلَى مَصَافِّكُمْ كَمَا أَنْتُمْ» ثُمَّ انْفَتَلَ إِلَيْنَا فَقَالَ «أَمَا إِنِّي سَأُحَدِّثُكُمْ مَا حَبَسَنِي عَنْكُمُ الغَدَاةَ أَنِّي قُمْتُ مِنَ اللَّيْلِ فَتَوَضَّأْتُ فَصَلَّيْتُ مَا قُدِّرَ لِي فَنَعَسْتُ فِي صَلاَتِي فَاسْتَثْقَلْتُ فَإِذَا أَنَا بِرَبِّي تَبَارَكَ وَتَعَالَى فِي أَحْسَنِ صُورَةٍ فَقَالَ: يَا مُحَمَّدُ قُلْتُ: لَبَّيْكَ رَبِّ، قَالَ: فِيمَ يَخْتَصِمُ الْمَلأُ الأَعْلَى؟ قُلْتُ: لاَ أَدْرِي رَبِّ، قَالَ: يَا مُحَمَّدُ فِيمَ يَخْتَصِمُ الْمَلأُ الأَعْلَى؟ قُلْتُ: لاَ أَدْرِي رَبِّ، قَالَ: يَا مُحَمَّدُ فِيمَ يَخْتَصِمُ الْمَلأُ الأَعْلَى؟ قُلْتُ: لاَ أَدْرِي يا رَبِّ، فَرَأَيْتُهُ وَضَعَ كَفَّهُ بَيْنَ كَتِفَيَّ حَتَّى وَجَدْتُ بَرْدَ أَنَامِلِهِ بَيْنَ ثَدْيَيَّ فَتَجَلَّى لِي كُلُّ شَيْءٍ وَعَرَفْتُ، فَقَالَ: يَا مُحَمَّدُ قُلْتُ: لَبَّيْكَ رَبِّ، قَالَ: فِيمَ يَخْتَصِمُ الْمَلأُ الأَعْلَى؟ قُلْتُ: فِي الكَفَّارَاتِ، قَالَ: مَا هُنَّ قُلْتُ: مَشْيُ الأَقْدَامِ إِلَى الجَمَاعَاتِ وَالجُلُوسُ فِي الْمَسَاجِدِ بَعْدَ الصَّلَوَاتِ وَإِسْبَاغُ الوُضُوءِ فِي الْمَكْرُوهَاتِ، قَالَ: وَمَا الدَّرَجَاتُ؟ قُلْتُ: إِطْعَامُ الطَّعَامِ وَلِينُ الكَلاَمِ وَالصَّلاَةُ بِاللَّيْلِ وَالنَّاسُ نِيَامٌ، قَالَ: سَلْ، قُلْتُ: اللَّهُمَّ إِنِّي أَسْأَلُكَ فِعْلَ الخَيْرَاتِ وَتَرْكَ الْمُنْكَرَاتِ وَحُبَّ الْمَسَاكِينِ وَأَنْ تَغْفِرَ لِي وَتَرْحَمَنِي وَإِذَا أَرَدْتَ فِتْنَةً فِي قَوْمٍ

فَتَوَفَّنِي غَيْرَ مَفْتُونٍ وَأَسْأَلُكَ حُبَّكَ وَحُبَّ مَنْ يُحِبُّكَ وَحُبَّ عَمَلٍ يُقَرِّبُ إِلَى حُبِّكَ»
قَالَ رَسُولُ اللهِ ﷺ «إِنَّهَا حَقٌّ فَادْرُسُوهَا ثُمَّ تَعَلَّمُوهَا.»

رواه أحمد (٢٢١٠٩) والترمذي (٣٢٣٥) وصححه الألباني (السلسلة الصحيحة ٣١٦٩)

The Messenger of Allah ﷺ was delayed one morning from coming to us for Morning Prayer, until we were about to see the sunrise. Then he came out quickly, the Iqamah was called, and the Messenger of Allah ﷺ prayed a short Salah. When he finished the Salah with the Salam, he called with his voice saying to us, «Stay in your rows as you are.» Then he turned to us and said, «I am going to narrate to you what kept me from you this morning. I got up during the night, I performed Wudu' and prayed what was destined for me to pray, and I got sleepy during my Salah and fell asleep. Then I saw my Rabb, Blessed and Most High, in the best appearance. He said, "O Muhammad!" I said, "Here I am, my Rabb!" He said, "What are the angels arguing about?" I said, "I do not know, Rabb." He said, "What are the angels arguing about?" I said, "I do not know, Rabb." He said, "What are the angels arguing about?" I said, "I do not know, Rabb." So I saw Him place His Palm between my shoulders, and I felt the coolness of His Fingertips between my breasts. Then everything became clear to me and I knew. So He said, "O Muhammad!" I said, "Here I am, my Rabb!" He said, "What are the angels arguing about?" I said, "In the acts that atone." He said, "And what are they?" I said, "Walking to congregational prayers, sitting in the mosques after Salah, and completing Wudu' despite difficulties." He said, "And what are the acts that elevate?" I said, "Feeding others, speaking leniently, and Salah at night while people are asleep." He said, "Ask." I said, "O Allah, I ask you to help me do good deeds, avoid evil deeds, love the poor, and that You forgive me and have mercy on me. And if You want to tempt a people, take my soul untempted. And I ask You that You love me, that whomever You love loves me [or I ask You that I love You, that I love whomever

You love], and that I love the deeds that bring one nearer to Your Love.» The Messenger of Allah ﷺ said, «Indeed this is true, so learn it to understand it.»

Reported by Ahmad (22109) and al-Tirmidhi (3235) and al-Albani declared it sahih (al-Silsilah al-Sahihah, 3169)

Commentary

Praying for Allah's love, and for what He loves, is one of the greatest things we can ask for and receive. Such a gift will illuminate our life and teach us whom to love, what to love, and what to avoid.

The great vision

This was a tremendous dream. There is so much in it that behooves us to understand the advice of our Prophet ﷺ and try to follow it. Ibn Rajab رَحِمَهُ ٱللَّهُ wrote a short book explaining this *Hadith* (اختيار الأولى في شرح حديث اختصام الملأ الأعلى), and yet there is even more that can be added. I will highlight a few of its gems:

1. This was a dream, and the dreams of the Prophets are true. Since their dreams are protected from error (*'Ismah*), this is one of the ways that Allah reveals the truth to them. We, on the other hand, do not have the same privilege, so we have to check our dreams against the Quran and Sunnah. These two are our protection from error.
2. Note what the angels were arguing about. Allah described them in the *Hadith* as "the Upper Crowd," signifying their nobility and high station. This may refer to all angels or specifically to the highest among the angels. So, when they discuss a matter, you know it is important. And what are they concerned with? It is not politics. It is not fashion. It is not sports. These things may be important or fun to talk about, but they are not the most important

and beneficial. I write this because some among us, once you start talking about the very things the angels were talking about, tune you out because the topic is too dull. But when you bring up movies, games, shopping, and the likes, their eyes light up, and you become interesting again. The believers need to remember this. If they accuse you of being "boring," remember that the angels of Allah do not discuss trivial matters. If you find yourself alone and discouraged, remember the noble angels of Allah and try to be like them. If you stay close to them in this life, you will be with them in the Hereafter. As for the "interesting" people who think that religion is "boring," make *du'a* for them. And do not let them tempt you away from what Allah revealed. On the Day of Judgment, only one topic will matter. And it is what the angels are talking about. The rest will vanish into memory.

3. The Prophet ﷺ saw this dream as he was praying at night. And there is a connection between Allah's favors and night prayer. We have seen previously and will see later in the book, that getting closer to Allah takes effort and sacrifice. This is what distinguishes those who truly love Allah from those who simply claim to love Him. When one draws nearer to Allah, they will see more and more of His favors. It is not necessary or important to see dreams. The greatest favor is the joy and peace He gifts. The greatest favor is Allah's love and Jannah. But it all has a price. Love will only grow if you nurture it. The Prophet ﷺ continued to worship to keep getting closer and closer to Allah, and this is our path as well. If we want Allah to love us, we have to do what His beloved ﷺ did. Do something extra today to bring you closer to Allah, simply out of loving Him and thanking Him. Make it a habit. Let it be a daily, weekly, or monthly thing. In time, you will be able to build on it. It will take you to a new exciting place in your life.
4. The actions that atone and those that elevate may seem

very ordinary: everyone knows about them. In other words, no mystery was revealed here. Or was it?

Many may expect from such a dream something that nobody else knows: secret worship or supplication that changes everything instantaneously and drastically. But this was not the case. We are drawn to mystery and salivate at the thought of hidden and privileged knowledge. But Islam is not a mystery. This cannot be stressed enough. Islam is not a mystery. The path to Allah is as clear as day. And this *Hadith* is evidence. When the highest circle of angels were discussing what forgives sins and raises people in Jannah, they were talking about these "ordinary" things that all of us know. But the very fact that they spoke about them makes them extraordinary. And maybe this is part of the message of the *Hadith*. Because these acts are common knowledge, we stop valuing them. Though we all know about them, we seldom do them. And here lies the real mystery: extremely precious acts that few appreciate, like precious metal that people mistake for sand, but turns out to be more expensive than gold. If we are seeking mystery and privileged knowledge, look at what the Prophet ﷺ taught, but few are following. Look at what we made into dull acts but are highly meritorious, and inject life into them. Wudu', congregational prayers, spending time at the masjid, feeding the hungry, kind speech, and night prayer are all within reach. They are so close and yet seem so far. The real privilege is to be among the few who do them.

He asked for love

He could have asked for anything. And it is instructive to think about it. If we had this chance, what would we ask for? I do not mean rehearsed answers of what we are supposed to ask. I mean the truth. If I had this opportunity, what is the first thing I would ask for?

The most beloved to Allah, Muhammad ﷺ, asked for love. It is the most comprehensive thing one can get. We should memorize this *du'a* and make it our own. But before love, he asked for five things.

He asked Allah to help him do good, avoid evil, for forgiveness, protection from fitnah, and good company. You can think of these five as the love recipe, the ingredients to reach the love of Allah. See, Allah's love is the pinnacle of Islam, the highest fruit. We can wish for it, claim to have it, assure ourselves that somehow someday we will get it, or believe that we already have it. But reality could be something else. Unless the ingredients of love are present, love will remain a fantasy (even in human relationships). The Prophet ﷺ was teaching us that you need to soar to reach it. You need to be ready to love Allah and receive His love. For that, you need the five ingredients.

Doing good is the path that will take us to Allah. But this path remains incomplete until we avoid evil. Doing what Allah loves requires avoiding what He hates. If not, we will not find our way to Allah or be severely delayed. The journey must also avoid fitnah, which steals us away from Allah. Fitnah confuses, and will lead us to believe that we are on the right path when we are not. And since we are going to make mistakes along the way, we need Allah's forgiveness and mercy to protect us from the consequence of sin. Finally, we need good company on our journey. They help us when we are weak, and remind us when we forget. So, the Prophet ﷺ asked for loving the poor (or the humble, according to another interpretation). He chose the poor for at least two reasons. The first is that loving them will happen for the sake of Allah, since they have no worldly attractions that pull us to them. If we keep their company, it will be because of Allah. The second reason is that they are more likely to be humble, closer to Allah, and least distracted by this world. Their company will not tempt us—like the rich may with their wealth—but remind us of what is important in this life.

With these five ingredients, we would be ready for the next and most important phase: the love of Allah. This is not to say that we will not experience any love for and from Allah before that. Rather, the full experience and joy of Allah's love are founded on a bed of obedience and sacrifice. Before that, it is faint and experienced sporadically.

When he ﷺ turned to love, he asked for Allah's love, the love of those who love Allah, and the love of deeds that Allah loves. The first request is simultaneously about loving Allah and receiving His love. The latter is more precious than the former. Ibn Kathir رَحِمَهُ ٱللَّهُ wrote:

لَيْسَ الشَّأْنُ أَنْ تُحِبَّ إِنَّمَا الشَّأْنُ أَنْ تُحَبَّ.

تفسير ابن كثير (ج٢ ص٣٢)

What is significant is not that you love, but that you be loved.

Tafsir Ibn Kathir (vol. 2, p. 32)

Allah's love for us is the happiness of this life and the next. It is the culmination of all our work, the fruit of all our sacrifices. We reach this love by loving Allah and drawing closer and closer to Him each day. When we come close enough, Allah will love us a love that will change our lives. You will read more about that in the last *hadith* in this book.

The second and third love requests teach us, among other things, that not all love is good. We may love someone who hates Allah, who stands between us and Him. Or we may love something that corrupts our life and distances us from Allah. This would be a disaster. We would be in love with something that is going to destroy us. We may think that we cannot live without it, yet it is making us sick and miserable. We must ask Allah to protect our hearts from harmful love, to grant us a love that He loves. The Companion Abdullah ibn Yazid al-Khatmiyy رَضِيَ ٱللَّهُ عَنْهُ said:

عَنْ عَبْدِ اللَّهِ بْنِ يَزِيدَ الْخَطْمِيِّ رضي الله عنه أَنَّهُ كَانَ يَقُولُ: اللَّهُمَّ ارْزُقْنِي حُبَّكَ وَحُبَّ مَنْ يَنْفَعُنِي حُبُّهُ عِنْدَكَ اللَّهُمَّ وَارْزُقْنِي مَا أُحِبُّ وَاجْعَلْهُ قُوَّةً لِي فِيمَا تُحِبُّ وَمَا زَوَيْتَ عَنِّي مِمَّا أُحِبُّ فَاجْعَلْهُ لِي فَرَاغًا فِيمَا تُحِبُّ.

مصنف ابن أبي شيبة (٢٩٥٩٢)

> O Allah, grant me Your Love and the love of whomever their love is beneficial for me with You. O Allah, and grant me what I love and let it strengthen me to do what You love. And whatever I love but You kept away from me, let it be a disengagement [i.e. free time] to be used in what You love.
>
> *Musannaf ibn Abi Shaybah* (29592)

Sometimes we love what harms us, and sometimes we hate what is good for us (more on this later in the book). What we love may become a burden. It could distract us from greater loves. For that, we have to be careful with what we allow into our hearts. Abdullah ibn Yazid asked for a love that Allah would be pleased with. If he were to love someone, he prayed that this love would bring him closer to Allah, not the opposite. And if he were to love something, it would feed into the love of Allah, not undermine it.

Allah may decide that some of what we love is not going to be ours. This is a tough one: to love someone or something but not have it. This is when a lot of us break down. We start believing that since Allah does not grant us what we want, He does not care about us. But Abdullah ibn Yazid's *du'a* reminded us that compared to Allah's love, every worldly love is small. If we do not get what we want, Allah can fill that space. If we do not get what we want, the gap it leaves can be filled with what Allah loves. This may be the very reason why Allah did not give it to us: it was going to take us away from Him. Allah deprives us to give us, takes away the tawdry to replace it with the valuable. He protects us from this world to bring us closer to Him.

If we love Allah, we will love for His sake. We will look at everything around us differently. We would not love for personal reasons only. Our ephemeral feelings and social conventions would not trap us. There is a deeper reality that transcends our limited experience, transcends the trivial and popular. Our hearts would have the benefit of Allah's love to discover what is good and what is not. Loving for Allah's sake is transcendent and noble. It extends love to everything in this universe and brings it all back to the Most Beloved, Allah.

PART THREE

Loving His Creation

HADITH TWENTY TWO

الحديث الثاني والعشرون

Love others as you love yourself

قَالَ رَسُولُ اللَّهِ ﷺ «وَالَّذِي نَفْسِي بِيَدِهِ لَا يُؤْمِنُ أحدكم حَتَّى يُحِبَّ لِأَخِيهِ مَا يُحِبُّ لِنَفْسِهِ مِنَ الْخَيْرِ.»

رواه أحمد (١٣١٤٦) والبخاري (١٣) ومسلم (٤٥) واللفظ لأحمد

The Messenger ﷺ said, «I swear by the One in Whose Hand is my soul, one of you does not believe until they love good for their brother as they love it for themselves.»

Reported by Ahmad (13146), al-Bukhari (13), and Muslim (45). The wording is that of Ahmad.

Commentary

Iman moves us to love others and want the best for them. The absence of this love is a sign of a weak *Iman* and a soul obsessed with the world.

Iman is incomplete without love

We cannot live without love. It is impossible to exist without experiencing this emotion. Even the most selfish of humans love themselves. As the most basic and primary motivation, all human effort relies on it. We have seen that love is the religious beginning and end. Worshipping Allah is based on loving Him, and the goal of this worship is to gain His love. The purpose of all Islamic injunctions is to make Allah the ultimate love in our hearts. What this *Hadith* adds is that our *Iman* is incomplete until we love other humans.

It is easy to understand why. If one truly loves Allah, they will naturally love what He loves. We do this all the time with other loves. If you have a spouse, child, or parent that you love dearly, you will be drawn to the things they love simply because they love it. You may not be personally interested in your child's favorite toy or your spouse's favorite food, but if you were apart for a while and saw what they liked, it will put a big smile on your face. You will be drawn to it and feel a flood of emotions overtaking you. Your love for them flows to what they love. It is the same with Allah's love except that the love of Allah is the greatest and most intense of all loves. If we truly love Him, what He loves will be the dearest thing to us.

We can unpack this a little more. When you think about it, you will come to realize that Allah created this world because—as discussed previously—He loved for it to exist. Every single second, Allah cares for it and its inhabitants: He feeds, protects, and guides all to what benefits them. And anyone who loves Allah should care for it too. Something that Allah made and is taking care of should be precious to us. Our love for Allah flows to it. So, how can we go against our Beloved and destroy what He loves? Those who pollute the earth, hurt animals, and abuse people are straying far away from Allah's love, for Allah did not put His creation on earth to be harmed. Allah did not create them for us to abuse and torment. If you see humans, especially the believers, as precious to Allah, it will be easy to extend the love we have for Allah to them. Even a sinner will elicit compassion in us as one of Allah's special creation. One of the pious men from the early generations said:

قَالَ بَعْضُ الصَّالِحِينَ مِنَ السَّلَفِ: أَهْلُ الْمَحَبَّةِ لِلَّهِ نَظَرُوا بِنُورِ اللَّهِ

وَعَطَفُوا عَلَى أَهْلِ مَعَاصِي اللَّهِ مَقَتُوا أَعْمَالَهُمْ وَعَطَفُوا عَلَيْهِمْ لِيُزِيلُوهُمْ بِالْمَوَاعِظِ عَنْ فِعَالِهِمْ وَأَشْفَقُوا عَلَى أَبْدَانِهِمْ مِنَ النَّارِ.

جامع العلوم والحكم (ج١ ص٣٠٨)

Those who love Allah see with the aid of Allah's light and have compassion for the sinners. They hate their actions but care about them so they can rescue them from their deeds with reminders, and they fear for their bodies to be put in Hell.

Jami' al-'Ulum wa al-Hikam (vol. 1, p. 308)

This is why the Prophet ﷺ used to agonize over people refusing Islam. Allah had to remind him in the Quran on more than one occasion not to be disturbed by their rejection: his role is only to convey and Allah guides. But he cared. And caring for someone is based on love for them and their wellbeing. So, we should love and care for all creation in so far as Allah is the One behind it. Yes, humans can act in ways to reduce this love. And the believers ultimately follow Allah's wishes and not their own. If Allah declared that He hates an act or a person, who are they to oppose Him? Our will follows His, and our love is all for Him. The mistake that some Muslims made historically is to equate everything Allah created and allowed with what He loves. So, they used to look at some common sins in society and fail to fight them, thinking that they are there because Allah must like it. But Allah creates and allows at times what He hates because of a greater good that it brings, and our task is to hate sin and combat it. We love in every person the fact that Allah made them and cares for them, and we love in them the potential to be pleasing to Him. Every sinner and disbeliever has this potential, and it does us no good if they suffer in Hell. We hate to see them sad or in pain, and we want to protect them from all harm. This is loving for everyone what we love for ourselves. And it is there because of our Creator.

Love is incomplete without Iman

Iman needs love. But does love need *Iman*? Love is a neutral force, neither good nor bad. As we saw previously, everything moves in this world because of love, even crimes are committed out of love: love of self, love of money, or illicit love. What *Iman* does is protect love from misdirection and exaggeration. *Iman* tells us what to love, what not to love, and the proper limits of our emotions. But *Iman* does something else that is very significant: it elevates love to heights unreachable without it.

The *Hadith* of this chapter is evidence of it. It declares loving others a religious duty. The Prophet ﷺ said:

«لِلْمُسْلِمِ عَلَى الْمُسْلِمِ مِنَ الْمَعْرُوفِ سِتٌّ يُسَلِّمُ عَلَيْهِ إِذَا لَقِيَهُ وَيُشَمِّتُهُ إِذَا عَطَسَ وَيَعُودُهُ إِذَا مَرِضَ وَيُجِيبُهُ إِذَا دَعَاهُ وَيَشْهَدُهُ إِذَا تُوُفِّيَ وَيُحِبُّ لَهُ مَا يُحِبُّ لِنَفْسِهِ وَيَنْصَحُ لَهُ بِالْغَيْبِ.»

رواه أحمد (٦٧٣) وحسنه لغيره شعيب الأرناؤوط

> «A Muslim owes another Muslim six acts of virtue: greets them with Salam when they meet, says *Yarhamuka Allah* when they sneeze, visits them when they are sick, accepts their invitation, attends their funeral, loves for them what they love for themselves, and desires the best for them in their absence.»
>
> Reported by Ahmad (673) and Shu'ayb al-Arna'ut declared it hasan li-ghayrihi

It is not simply loving them but loving for them what we love for ourselves. When any believer hears this, they know that their *Iman*, which is their highest priority, is deficient without love. It becomes their greatest motivation to strive to love. Love becomes their mission, an act of worship that they do for Allah's sake, regardless of how others reciprocate. They continue to nurture it—despite difficulty—as they nurture any act of worship, knowing that it takes them closer to Allah.

Loving for others what we love for ourselves is an obligation. Its absence is a sin, and it weakens *Iman*. The one who lacks it has not reached *Iman*'s reality, its heights, and its fullness, and this is what was negated in the *Hadith*. The weaker this love is, the weaker their *Iman* is. This sheds light on a common contradiction. Some love Allah and are constant in their worship but are not kind to others. Conversely, some are great socially but neglect their worship. Both possess weak *Iman*. Loving Allah means worshipping Him, and loving what Allah loves means treating others as we treat ourselves. It is insufficient to emphasize one side and ignore the other. My *Salah*, *Zakah*, and fasting should increase the love I have for Allah and move me to share this love. And I cannot claim to be a good person without the worship that Allah loves the most. If there is an imbalance, then my love of Allah itself is weak. Or at least misinformed.

How can we love the same for others?

Is it possible to love for someone else what I love for myself? The love we have for ourselves is the strongest and most intense love we experience. We are the center of our existence, constantly obsessed with our needs and wants. And this life is rife with competition over limited resources. How can I compete in school or the job market and yet wish the same good fortune for my competitors? Is my success not someone else's failure? So, is it still possible?

It would be impossible if this level of love was the first thing we ask of ourselves. Love is the pinnacle of *Iman*. Anyone who did not cultivate their love for Allah and did not strive to purify their soul cannot put this *Hadith* to practice. The first thing one has to do is combat envy, greed, and hatred in their heart. Selfishness (excessive self-love) is in us all and feeds the rest of our bad traits. Because of it, we seek more than what we need, hate it when others are blessed, and commit *haram* to be on top. It is a severe attachment to this world and the self, and one suffering under this affliction cannot fathom loving the best for others. No, a process of self-purification must come first, where the love of Allah gradually displaces the love of this world and selfishness. When one loves Allah and knows Him well, it would be easier for them to share this world. Allah becomes their goal, not this world. The Prophet ﷺ said:

«أَحِبَّ للناسِ ما تُحِبُّ لنفسك تكنْ مؤمنًا و أَحسِنْ مجاورةَ مَن جاوَرَك تكنْ مُسلمًا.»

صححه الألباني (صحيح الجامع ٤٥٨٠)

«Love for people what you love for yourself, and you will be a believer. And be a good neighbor, and you will be a Muslim.»

Al-Albani declared it sahih (*Sahih al-Jami'*, 4580)

When they hear this *hadith*, they know that their Islam and *Iman* are contingent on how they feel towards others and behave with them. So, seeking this love is not a luxury but a necessity of *Iman*. When we have this love, we will understand that Allah is the Bestower, and it is insolent to question His judgment out of envy. He knows to whom He gives and why. Jealousy is a shortsighted objection to Allah's decision, a sentiment of mistrust. If I love Allah, I believe that He gives me what is best for me and gives others what is best for them. If I love Allah, I trust His judgment more than mine. And why should I harbor greed? Chasing after the world is like running after a mirage. None of it lasts. But if I allow myself to love Allah, His love will save me from my worldly obsessions. If I have Allah, worldly glitter will not impress me. Why should it tempt me if I know it is going to perish? If I have Allah, I have it all. But if I never taste Allah's love because I was obsessed with this world, my life would be wasted. Have we been breaking our backs chasing a mirage?

The *Hadith* is not asking us to put others ahead of ourselves. It is asking that we wish them the good that we want for ourselves. If I am blessed, I wish everyone to receive similar blessings. And if another is blessed, I feel joy for their good fortune and ask Allah to bless me too. I love the best for them because Allah loves it. I care about their wellbeing because Allah cares about them. If I see them as Allah's creation, I cannot wish harm to what Allah created. I am happy for their happiness, and I am saddened by their sadness.

The bitter feelings that competition generates (e.g. envy, sadness) are an illusion. If I know that Allah's gifts are limitless, there is room for us all to be blessed. And if someone has what I do not, I know that Allah gave me (or will give me) what they do not have. But if I think of others as members of my family, where we support each other, there will be no need for competition. This takes a good deal of wisdom and worldly detachment. Above all, it needs the love of Allah to eliminate our negative impulses. When I know that Allah loves the believers and wants the best for them, I will not go against His wishes. I will love for them what He does and consider their pain mine. And if I suffer any worldly loss, I will not allow it to make me bitter. I will take my grief to Allah and ask Him to mend my heart. I do not need any help from anyone else. I will ask Him to grant me from His favors and fill my heart with content. Someone's misfortune cannot conceivably make me feel better. This world is too trivial to fight over. Someone's happiness does not diminish mine, and I gain nothing from their sadness.

If we achieve this, we can climb higher to putting others before ourselves. Allah described the Ansar in the Quran as:

...وَلَا يَجِدُونَ فِي صُدُورِهِمْ حَاجَةً مِّمَّآ أُوتُوا۟ وَيُؤْثِرُونَ عَلَىٰٓ أَنفُسِهِمْ وَلَوْ
كَانَ بِهِمْ خَصَاصَةٌۚ وَمَن يُوقَ شُحَّ نَفْسِهِۦ فَأُو۟لَـٰٓئِكَ هُمُ ٱلْمُفْلِحُونَ ﴿٩﴾

And they harbor no desire in their hearts for what has been given to the Muhajirin. They prefer them over themselves, even if they were in need. And those who are saved from their souls' greed are the successful.

Al-Hashr (Q59:9)

This is a recommended state where we put others before ourselves. It can only happen when the love of this world has left the heart, and the love of Allah and the Hereafter has taken its place. At that point, the coming and going of the world are irrelevant. What is relevant is the pleasure of Allah, even at the cost of losing this world.

If all this seems like fiction or extremely far-fetched, it is not. Start putting this *Hadith* to practice, and you will slowly change. You will start to understand the beauty and peace that loving the best for others gives. And you would never want to return to the torment of envy, hatred, and unending greed. As you practice, you will love Allah more. And as your love increases, your practice will flourish too.

There remains one point to discuss before moving forward: is "loving for their brother" in the *Hadith* a reference to Muslims only, or does it cover non-Muslims as well? In other words, is the *Hadith* obligating that we love for non-Muslims what we love for ourselves? Some scholars restrict the brotherhood in the *Hadith* to Muslims (religious brotherhood), while others expand it to mean all humans (human brotherhood). Scholars who support the second interpretation cite evidence like the alternate narration of the *Hadith* reported in Muslim that states:

«...حتى يحب لجاره ما يحب لنفسه.»

في رواية لمسلم (٤٥)

«...until they love for their neighbor what they love for themselves.»

Reported by Muslim (45)

They explained that "neighbor" is inclusive of non-Muslims. In another *hadith*, the Prophet ﷺ said:

«لَا يُؤْمِنُ أَحَدُكُمْ حَتَّى يُحِبَّ لِلنَّاسِ مَا يُحِبُّ لِنَفْسِهِ وَحَتَّى يُحِبَّ الْمَرْءَ لَا يُحِبُّهُ إِلَّا لِلَّهِ.»

رواه أحمد (١٣٨٧٥) وقال شعيب الأرناؤوط إسناده صحيح على شرط الشيخين

«One of you does not believe until they love for people what they love for themselves, and until they love someone only for Allah.»

Reported by Ahmad (13875) and Shu'ayb al-Arna'ut declared its chain sahih

Again, "people" is inclusive of Muslims and non-Muslims. Even if we were to say that the *Hadith* is specific to Muslims, this does not exclude loving the best for non-Muslims (see *Appendix III* for more).

The effects of this love

It would be a different world if we all followed the *Hadith*. We would trust each other.

كان محمد بن واسع يبيع حمارا له بسوق مرو فقال له رجل: يا أبا عبد الله أترضاه لي؟ قال: لو رضيته لم أبعه.

تاريخ دمشق (ج٥٦ ص١٦٦)

Muhammad ibn Wasi' was selling his donkey in the market in Merv. A man asked him, "O Abu Abdillah, would you be satisfied with this donkey for me?" He replied, "If I were satisfied with it, I would not sell it."

Tarikh Dimashq (vol. 56, p. 166)

He did not lie nor hide the truth. If it is not good enough for me, it is not good enough for my brother/sister. We will not lie to others because we would not like it if they lied to us. Allah is the Witness and Provider, and honesty is not going to make us poor; deception will.

If we followed the *Hadith*, we would also worry about others and not only ourselves. We would treat people well and protect them from what we hate. The Prophet ﷺ said:

«انظر ما تحبُّ من الناسِ أن يأتوهُ إليك فافعلْهُ بهم وما كرهتَ أن يأتوهُ إليك فذَرْهُم منه.»

صححه الألباني (السلسلة الصحيحة ٣٥٠٨)

«Consider what you love that people would do to you, and do so to them. And consider what you hate that they would do to you, and do not do so to them.»

Albani declared it sahih (*al-Silsilah al-Sahihah*, 3508)

If we followed the *hadith*, we would help those in need without any expectation or reward. We would excuse others when they make mistakes, and conceal their faults to allow them to repent. We would help people overcome their weaknesses and be happy when they prosper. If we receive a good fortune, we will want all to have the same. And if we encounter a misfortune, we pray that Allah protects all from it. Our hearts would be gentle, moved by the suffering of others. We spring to help as we would like others to be quick in helping us. We would not look for self-glory or recognition, but the mere benefit and happiness of others. We would know that the real reward for what we do is with Allah, not with people. Whatever people give will vanish. So, we only seek Him and are only happy with Him. People's fascination with the world seems childish to us. We would compete for the life to come because worldly concerns seem petty. We would become selfless because we feel the nearness of Allah. And it brings us immense satisfaction and contentment. Listen to Ibn 'Abbas رَضِيَ اللَّهُ عَنْهُمَا express this when he said:

قَالَ ابْنُ عَبَّاسٍ رضي الله عنهما: إِنِّي لَأَمُرُّ عَلَى الْآيَةِ مِنْ كِتَابِ اللَّهِ فَأَوَدُّ أَنَّ النَّاسَ كُلَّهُمْ يَعْلَمُونَ مِنْهَا مَا أَعْلَمُ.

جامع العلوم والحكم (ج١ ص٣١٠)

When I read an ayah from the Book of Allah, I wish that all people knew what I know about it.

Jami' al-'Ulum wa al-Hikam (vol. 1, p. 308)

There is no pursuit of glory or need for recognition. There is no selfish need to know more than others. It is a pure desire for all to learn and be blessed. Al-Shafi'i رَحِمَهُ اللَّهُ expressed the same ideals when he said:

قَالَ الشَّافِعِيُّ: وَدِدْتُ أَنَّ النَّاسَ تَعَلَّمُوا هَذَا الْعِلْمَ وَلَمْ يُنْسَبْ إِلَيَّ مِنْهُ شَيْءٌ.

جامع العلوم والحكم (ج١ ص٣١٠)

I wish that all people would learn this knowledge of mine and none of it would be attributed to me.

Jami' al-'Ulum wa al-Hikam (vol. 1, p. 308)

Imagine reaching the stage where you have this invaluable knowledge, for which you could be super famous, and desire none of the fame? All you wish for is the betterment of people. His was a selfless and generous soul, a soul that desired the best for others and expected nothing from them. Such a soul can help others because it is not in need anymore. It has been filled with Allah's love and His gifts, so there is no room in it for people's gifts. It gives because it only sees Allah's favors, and nothing less than that impresses it. Consider this generous spirit:

كَانَ عُتْبَةُ الْغُلَامُ إِذَا أَرَادَ أَنْ يُفْطِرَ يَقُولُ لِبَعْضِ إِخْوَانِهِ الْمُطَّلِعِينَ عَلَى أَمْرِهِ وَأَعْمَالِهِ: أَخْرِجْ إِلَيَّ مَاءً أَوْ تَمَرَاتٍ أُفْطِرُ عَلَيْهَا لِيَكُونَ لَكَ أَجْرٌ مِثْلُ أَجْرِي.

جامع العلوم والحكم (ج١ ص٣١٠)

When 'Utbah al-Ghulam wanted to break his fast, he would say to some of his brothers who were privy to his affairs, "Give me some water or dates to break my fast on so that you will have a reward similar to mine."

Jami' al-'Ulum wa al-Hikam (vol. 1, p. 308)

What an inspiring generosity. He loved for others to have what he had, so he shared the reward of his fast. When you bring a blessing to your brother, Allah blesses you too. There is no need for us to compete. The more we give, the more Allah will give us back.

When we become more religious, our love for Allah will grow. And when we feel more of Allah's love, we have to spread more of it. You cannot have *Iman* without spreading love.

HADITH TWENTY THREE

الحديث الثالث والعشرون

You will not enter Jannah until you spread love

قَالَ رَسُولُ اللهِ ﷺ «والَّذِي نَفْسِي بِيَدِهِ لَا تَدْخُلُوا الْجَنَّةَ حَتَّى تُؤْمِنُوا وَلَا تُؤْمِنُوا حَتَّى تَحَابُّوا أَفَلَا أَدُلُّكُمْ عَلَى شَيْءٍ إِذَا فَعَلْتُمُوهُ تَحَابَبْتُمْ أَفْشُوا السَّلَامَ بَيْنَكُمْ.»

رواه مسلم (٥٤)

The Messenger ﷺ said, «By the One in Whose Hand is my soul, you will not enter Jannah until you believe, and you will not believe until you love each other. Shall I not tell you about a thing which if you do, you will love each other? Spread Salam among yourselves.»

Reported by Muslim (54)

Commentary

Allah created us to love and be loved. He made the spreading of love a good deed that takes us to Jannah, and Salam is one of the best ways to do that. We must love each other in order to please Allah.

No love, no Jannah

Reread the *Hadith*. I mean it! Reread it, please. We probably have heard it countless times, but we do not appreciate what it is saying. Is it not saying that you cannot enter Jannah without love? If we cannot enter Jannah without *Iman*, and cannot have *Iman* without love, then we cannot enter Jannah without love. It is essential to let this sink in to dissipate any suspicion about how necessary love is in Islam. If we notice a love gap among Muslims, it is not because Islam lacks love. It is because Muslims forgot about it.

I hope it has become a truism by now that Islam and love are inseparable. Without loving Allah and His Prophet, one cannot be a Muslim. Every Muslim, no matter how sinful they may be, enjoys a minimum of this love, and it saves them from Hell eventually. Those with strong faith possess a more profound love that saves from Hell altogether. The vigor of our *Iman* depends on the love of Allah and His Prophet. And the opposite is absolutely true: weakness in religious certitude and practice stems from weaker love. Reviving our *Iman* rests on reviving our love for Allah and His Prophet.

But we cannot stop there. Our *Iman* will remain deficient, jeopardizing our entry to Jannah, until we love each other. The possibilities are that we may lose the higher positions in Jannah, be delayed entry to it, or pass through Hell first if this love is missing. The absence of this love is no trivial matter. This is how essential it is.

"Why?" you may ask. I am glad you did. First, it points to a weakness in the love of Allah itself. It is a failure to love what Allah loves. If Allah's love is strong, it will surely extend to what Allah loves. The Prophet ﷺ said:

«إِنَّ أَوْثَقَ عُرَى الإسلامِ أَنْ تُحِبَّ في اللهِ وتُبغِضَ في اللهِ.»

رواه أحمد (١٨٥٢٤) حسنه الألباني لغيره (صحيح الترغيب ٣٠٣٠)

«The firmest of the knots [i.e. obligations] of Islam is for you love for the sake of Allah and to hate for the sake of Allah.»

Reported by Ahmad (18524) and al-Albani declared it hasan li-ghayrihi (*Sahih al-Targhib*, 3030)

In another *hadith*, he ﷺ said:

«مَنْ أَحَبَّ لِلَّهِ وَأَبْغَضَ لِلَّهِ وَأَعْطَى لِلَّهِ وَمَنَعَ لِلَّهِ فَقَدِ اسْتَكْمَلَ الْإِيمَانَ.»

رواه أبو داود (٤٦٨١) وصححه الألباني (السلسلة الصحيحة ٣٨٠)

«The one who loves for Allah's sake, hates for Allah's sake, gives for Allah's sake, and withholds for Allah's sake has completed [their] Iman.»

Reported by Abu Dawud (4681) and al-Albani declared it sahih (*al-Silsilah al-Sahihah*, 380)

Love and hate are the internal movements of the heart. And giving and withholding are its external movements, founded on the internal ones. When one moves internally and externally for Allah's sake, not simply for personal preferences and gain, they have reached the summit of *Iman*. Some who read this and similar *hadiths* may think that it promotes hate. But it does the opposite: it restricts it. Rather than leaving the door open for us to hate whatever and whomever we feel like, it restricts it to what the All-Wise hates. And rather than allow us the freedom to mistreat whatever and whomever we hate, it asks us to observe Allah's rules. Plus, if we do not hate for Allah's sake, we will hate for another reason (nationalism, wealth, color, ethnicity, political affiliations, and personal conflicts). No one escapes this. And this type of hate is blind, excessive, and merciless. But our discussion here is not about hate. We discuss it further in *Appendix II*. So, let us go back to love.

Failing to love each other points to weakness in loving Allah. This is the first reason why it is a serious concern. The second is that the absence of this love damages Allah's revealed laws, society, and our character. Allah made us social beings, needful of each other. This human dependency requires congregation, and for that to work, we need laws. One of the essential roles of Shari'ah is to regulate and guide human congregation and protect it from harm. This is accomplished by attaching social etiquette to the pleasure of Allah and loving each other to the love of Allah. If we abandon this love, we will surrender to hate and selfishness. Consequently, the laws of Allah will be violated, and society will deteriorate. When we care about no one but ourselves, we will treat everyone as a means to our ends. We will abuse our neighbors' rights whenever we can get away with it. If this is how society runs, it will miserably collapse, and chaos will follow.

Our morality will collapse too. When we love each other, our socialization improves our character. When we interact with others, we learn to be patient, empathic, forgiving, and selfless. We cannot learn patience if there is no one around us to test our patience, right? Allah said:

...وَجَعَلْنَا بَعْضَكُمْ لِبَعْضٍ فِتْنَةً أَتَصْبِرُونَ... ﴿٢٠﴾

And We made some of you a test for others, so will you be patient?

Al-Furqan (Q25:20)

Failure to love each other is a failure to live by Allah's laws, as well as a failure to grow as Allah intended for us. It goes against the purpose of creation.

We can glean from the *Hadith* that Allah created us to teach us love. Think about it for a minute. Allah commanded us all to have *Iman*, put us together on earth, and made loving each other an essential requisite for *Iman*. This is a love that we are supposed to cultivate as we grow, learn what He revealed, and socialize. All the worldly challenges we meet, and the difficulties that proximity to other humans generate, are designed to mold us into beings that transcend their shortcomings. We start our journey ignorant and selfish, but we learn from Him that we have to change. Social interaction, which is difficult at times, is the obstacle course that allows love to grow in practice after it was learned in theory. This is how we graduate in love. It is why Allah made us.

Allah declared that He created us to Worship Him when He said:

وَمَا خَلَقْتُ ٱلْجِنَّ وَٱلْإِنسَ إِلَّا لِيَعْبُدُونِ ۝٥٦

And I did not create humans and the Jinn except to worship Me.
Adh-Dhariyat (Q51:56)

This worship is to know Allah and love Him. Mujahid, the famous Tabi'i, explained Shirk as loving other than Allah (see the *Introduction*). Hence, the essence and intent of worship are to establish Tawhid, which is the love of Allah. Allah's commands guide us to the love of Allah and each other. This is why Allah made us: to love Allah and to love each other. Allah created you for love.

Spreading love

The *Hadith* makes it abundantly clear that we are to spread Salam to spread love. The profound implication is that spreading love is dear to Allah. Any act that promotes love between the believers is recommended, and any act that diminishes it is prohibited. In fact, we can say that this is a major theme and an intent of the Shari'ah that guides its individual commands. If you look at why many things are prohibited (e.g. alcohol, gambling, fornication, backbiting, and gossiping), you will see that they promote hatred and friction. On the other end, what is pleasing to Allah (e.g. charity, forgiveness, and congregational worship) cements social connections and boosts love. Remember *Hadith* Seven where the Prophet ﷺ said:

«أَحَبُّ النَّاسِ إِلَى اللهِ تَعَالَى أَنْفَعُهُمْ لِلنَّاسِ وَأَحَبُّ الْأَعْمَالِ إِلَى اللهِ تَعَالَى سُرُورٌ تُدْخِلُهُ عَلَى مُسْلِمٍ أَوْ تَكَشِفُ عَنْهُ كُرْبَةً أَوْ تَقْضِي عَنْهُ دَيْنًا أَوْ تَطْرُدُ عَنْهُ جُوعًا وَلَأَنْ أَمْشِيَ مَعَ أَخِي فِي حَاجَةٍ أَحَبُّ إِلَيَّ مِنْ أَنْ أَعْتَكِفَ فِي هَذَا الْمَسْجِدِ - يَعْنِي مَسْجِدَ الْمَدِينَةِ شَهْرًا - وَمَنْ كَفَّ غَضَبَهُ سَتَرَ اللهُ عَوْرَتَهُ وَمَنْ كَظَمَ غَيْظَهُ وَلَوْ شَاءَ أَنْ

يُمْضِيَهُ أَمْضَاهُ مَلأَ اللهُ قَلْبَهُ رَجَاءً يَوْمَ الْقِيَامَةِ وَمَنْ مَشَى مَعَ أَخِيهِ فِي حَاجَةٍ حَتَّى يَتَهَيَّأَ لَهُ أَثْبَتَ اللهُ قَدَمَهُ يَوْمَ تَزُولُ الأَقْدَامِ.»

رواه الطبراني في المعجم الكبير (١٣٦٤٦) وحسنه الألباني (السلسلة الصحيحة ٩٠٦)

«The most beloved of people to Allah are the most beneficial to people. And the most beloved deed to Allah is happiness you bring to a Muslim, or you remove their hardship, or you pay their debt, or chase away their hunger. And to walk with my brother to assist him in a need of his is more beloved to me than *i'tikaf* for a month in this Mosque, meaning Madinah Mosque. And if one holds back their anger, Allah will conceal their faults. And if one withholds their fury, and if they had wished to unleash it, they would have been able to, Allah will fill their heart with hope on the Day of Resurrection. And if one walks with his brother to secure their need until they get it, Allah will make firm their feet on the Day when feet slip.»

Reported by al-Tabarani in *al-Mu'jam al-Kabir* (13646) and al-Albani declared it hasan (*al-Silsilah al-Sahihah*, 906)

Anything that brings happiness to people is beloved to Allah (as long as it is *halal*, of course). The mission of the believer who is seeking Allah's love would be to look for and adopt all the acts that spread love. Conversely, they also should avoid all the acts that spread hate. One simply has to look at what Allah revealed—that which He loves and that which He hates—to have a complete to-do-list of how they can nurture love in themselves and among Muslims. The Prophet ﷺ highlighted Salam because of its potency in spreading love. But the journey only starts here. Good manners are an essential component of showing love and receiving it: being courteous, honest, forgiving, empathic, and humble. Today, people jump into conflicts at the first sign of a disagreement. They mock and ridicule, expose mistakes, refuse to forgive, are happy at other's misfortune, and willfully harm others for their own benefit or amusement. Look at all the political dissension and rancor or all the racial tension and bitterness. Or look at how we lose our sanity on social media and try to tear each other apart. Muslims are supposed to suppress evil and decrease it whenever they find it, not inflame it. They are supposed to use every opportunity to plant the seeds of harmony between people. The Muslim inclination is to extend the love they have for Allah to others, and not to export the hatred and bitterness of Shaytan to humanity.

The excellence of Salam

There is something unique about Salam. It is not like any other greeting. This is why it is such a loss when we fail to spread it. We need to understand what it means to appreciate it. The Prophet ﷺ said:

«السلامُ اسمٌ من أسماءِ اللهِ وضَعَهُ اللهُ في الأرضِ فأفْشُوهُ بينكم فإنَّ الرجلَ المسلمَ إذا مَرَّ بقومٍ فسلَّمَ عليهم فردُّوا عليه كان لهُ عليهم فضلُ درجةٍ بتذكيرِهِ إيّاهُمُ السلامَ فإنْ لمْ يرُدُّوا عليه رَدَّ عليه مَنْ هوَ خيرٌ مِنهمْ وأطْيبُ.»

رواه البخاري في الأدب المفرد (١٠٣٩) والطبراني في المعجم الكبير (١٠٣٩١) وصححه الألباني (صحيح الجامع ٣٦٩٧)

«Al-Salam is a Name of the Names of Allah that He placed on earth, so spread it among yourselves. For if a Muslim passes by a group of people and greets them with Salam and they reply, he would have an extra degree [of virtue] over them because he reminded them of Salam. And if they do not reply, those who are better and purer than them will reply [i.e. the Angels].»

Reported by al-Bukhari in *al-Adab al-Mufrad* (1039) and al-Tabarani in *al-Mu'jam al-Kabir* (10391) and al-Albani declared it sahih (*Sahih al-Jami'*, 3697)

Al-Salam is one of the Names of Allah, which means the One free from any deficiency and shortcoming; He is perfect, complete, and eternal. When we say Salam, we are invoking the protection and blessing of Allah's Name for that person. It is as if we are saying, may Allah's Name surround you, protect you, guide you, and bless you. It is also a declaration on the part of the greeter that people are safe from his harm. And if people are safe from your harm, they can only expect the best from you. Whenever you greet with Salam, you are sharing Allah's Name with another Muslim, and promising that you will not hurt them. Tell me, what other greeting comes close to this? This is why some of the People of the Book were envious of this greeting as the Prophet ﷺ explained (see Ibn Majah, 856). They knew its value. They knew its worth better than many of us know it today.

Salam is a unique dynamo of love. First, it brings Allah's Name to each encounter. And He brings love. Allah said in the Quran:

وَأَلَّفَ بَيْنَ قُلُوبِهِمْ ۚ لَوْ أَنفَقْتَ مَا فِي ٱلْأَرْضِ جَمِيعًا مَّآ أَلَّفْتَ بَيْنَ
قُلُوبِهِمْ وَلَٰكِنَّ ٱللَّهَ أَلَّفَ بَيْنَهُمْ ۚ... ﴿٦٣﴾

And Allah brought their hearts together. If you were to spend all that is on earth, you would not be able to bring their hearts together, but Allah did.

Al-Anfal (Q8:63)

This *ayah* is significant, very significant. The love that Allah gives is unlike any other in its intensity, longevity, and healing. Allah alone can fix certain rifts. This *ayah* explains that no amount of money or human effort could have brought the hearts of the early Muslims together. The differences were too significant, and their history was too complicated. But when they surrendered their hearts to Allah, Allah filled their souls with such love to melt away all the impurities of the past. This should be an important lesson for all who are trying to fix their societies: you will not be able to mend the hearts and chase away the divisions of Shaytan until you bring the love of Allah in. If you do, the hearts will come together. If you do not, your success, at best, will be partial and short-lived.

Second, Salam spreads love because it spreads righteousness.

Beginning others with Salam requires *Iman* and humbleness, especially when done according to the Sunnah. A *hadith* states:

سَأَلَ رجل النبيَّ ﷺ: أيُّ الإسْلامِ خَيْرٌ؟ قالَ «تُطْعِمُ الطَّعامَ وتَقْرَأُ السَّلامَ على مَن عَرَفْتَ ومَن لَمْ تَعْرِفْ.»

رواه البخاري (١٢)

A man asked the Prophet ﷺ, "What Islamic acts are best?" He replied, «Feeding [those in need] and greeting whom you know and whom you do not with Salam.»

Reported by al-Bukhari (12)

Greeting only those whom we know is a sign of the impendence of the Day of Judgment, generally considered a sign of decline. He ﷺ said:

«بين يَدَي الساعةِ تسليمُ الخاصةِ.»

رواه البخاري في الأدب المفرد (١٠٤٩) وصححه الألباني (الأدب المفرد ١٠٤٩)

«Just before the Hour is Salam between acquaintances only.»

Reported by al-Bukhari in *al-Adab al-Mufrad* (1049) and al-Albani declared it sahih (*Sahih al-Adab al-Mufrad*, 805)

This is what we do now, right? But to greet everyone with Salam, even whom you do not know, is a sign of *Iman*. Why else would you do it? There is no connection between you two except that of Islam, and you do not expect anything from them. And to keep doing it even when others fail to reply is another sign of *Iman*. For there is no room for bitterness when you are trying to spread love. If they reject your greeting, the love of Allah and your love for them will chase any negative feelings away. And you resume because the love of Allah keeps refueling you. Every time you say it, it brings you closer to Him, and for that, you can take anything that may come at you. Salam is also humility in practice, where we learn not to elevate ourselves above others. Motivated by your love for them, you keep trying to bring them the gift of Salam in order to get them closer to Allah.

Third, Salam is kind words and smiles that you share with all. We are all in desperate need of kindness these days. Since spreading Salam is spreading love, it should be done with love. When you say it, remember what you are trying to spread and what you are gaining from Allah. Spread this Sunnah with kindness and a smile. Imagine a stranger receiving this gift from you for nothing but being a Muslim. And imagine yourself receiving this gift from strangers who want nothing in return for their kind words and smiles but to make you happy. You would love this person even if you were never to see them again. This is how love spreads.

The Companions understood the importance of this worship and practiced it with intent. Here is the example of Abu Bakr رَضِيَ ٱللَّهُ عَنْهُ:

عنِ الأغَرِّ - أغرِّ مُزَيْنَةَ - رضي الله عنه قال: كانَ رسولُ الله صَلَّى اللهُ عَلَيْهِ وَسَلَّمَ أمرَ لي بجَرِيبٍ مِنْ تَمرٍ عند رجلٍ مِنَ الأنْصارِ فمَطَلني بِهِ فكلَّمتُ فيه رسولَ الله صَلَّى اللهُ عَلَيْهِ وَسَلَّمَ فقال «أُغْدُ يا أبا بكْرٍ فخُذْ له تَمْرَهُ» فوَعدني أبو بكرٍ المسْجِدَ إذا صَلَّيْنا الصُّبْحَ فوجَدْتُه حيثُ وَعدني فانْطلَقْنا فكُلَّما رأى أبو بكرٍ رجُلاً مِنْ بعيدٍ سلَّم عليه فقالَ أبو بَكْرٍ رضي الله عنه أمَا ترى ما يصيبُ القومُ عليكَ مِنَ الفَضلِ لا يَسْبِقْكَ إلى السلامِ أحَدٌ فكنَّا إذا طَلَعَ الرجُلُ مِنْ بعيدٍ بادَرْناهُ بالسلام قَبْلَ أنْ يُسلِّمَ علينا.

رواه الطبراني في المعجم الكبير (٨٨٠) وحسنه الألباني (صحيح الترغيب ٢٧٠٢)

Al-Agharr رَضِيَ ٱللَّهُ عَنْهُ said, "The Messenger ﷺ earmarked some dates for me with a man from the Ansar, but the man delayed handing them to me. So, I spoke to the Messenger ﷺ about it and he said, «O Abu Bakr, head out in the morning and get him his dates.» Abu Bakr رَضِيَ ٱللَّهُ عَنْهُ promised to meet me in the mosque at Fajr Prayer, and I found him there as he promised. So, we headed out and whenever Abu Bakr رَضِيَ ٱللَّهُ عَنْهُ would see a man from a distance, he would greet him with Salam. Then Abu Bakr

رَضِيَ ٱللَّهُ عَنْهُ said, 'Do you not see the good deeds that people are gaining instead of you? Do not let anyone say Salam before you.' So, when we saw a man from afar, we would rush to say Salam to him before he said it to us."

Reported by al-Tabarani in *al-Mu'jam al-Kabir* (880) and al-Albani declared it hasan (*Sahih al-Targhib*, 2702)

Ibn Umar رَضِيَ ٱللَّهُ عَنْهُمَا went out of his way to find people to say *Salam* to.

عن الطُّفَيْلَ بْنَ أُبَيٍّ بْنِ كَعْبٍ أَنَّهُ كَانَ يَأْتِي عَبْدَ اللَّهِ بْنَ عُمَرَ رضي الله عنهما فَيَغْدُو مَعَهُ إِلَى السُّوقِ قَالَ فَإِذَا غَدَوْنَا إِلَى السُّوقِ لَمْ يَمُرَّ عَبْدُ اللَّهِ بْنُ عُمَرَ رضي الله عنهما عَلَى سَقَّاطٍ وَلَا صَاحِبِ بَيْعَةٍ وَلَا مِسْكِينٍ وَلَا أحدٍ إلا يُسَلِّمُ عَلَيْهِ قَالَ الطُّفَيْلُ فَجِئْتُ عَبْدَ اللَّهِ بْنَ عُمَرَ يَوْمًا فَاسْتَتْبَعَنِي إِلَى السُّوقِ فَقُلْتُ مَا تَصْنَعُ بِالسُّوقِ وَأَنْتَ لَا تَقِفُ عَلَى الْبَيْعِ وَلَا تَسْأَلُ عَنِ السِّلَعِ وَلَا تَسُومُ بِهَا وَلَا تَجْلِسُ فِي مَجَالِسِ السُّوقِ فَاجْلِسْ بنا ها هنا نَتَحَدَّثُ فَقَالَ لِي عَبْدُ اللَّهِ يَا أَبَا بَطْنٍ وَكَانَ الطُّفَيْلُ ذَا بَطْنٍ إِنَّمَا نَغْدُو مِنْ أَجْلِ السَّلَامِ نُسَلِّمُ عَلَى مَنْ لَقِينَا.

رواه البخاري في الأدب المفرد (١٠٠٦) وصححه الألباني (صحيح الأدب المفرد ٧٧٤)

Al-Tufayl ibn Ubayy ibn Ka'ab said that he used to visit 'Abdullah ibn 'Umar رَضِيَ ٱللَّهُ عَنْهُمَا and go with him in the morning to the market. And when we went to the market, 'Abdullah ibn 'Umar رَضِيَ ٱللَّهُ عَنْهُمَا did not pass by anyone selling poor or good merchandise or a needy person or anyone but he greeted them with Salam. Al-Tufayl said, "So, I came to 'Abdullah ibn 'Umar رَضِيَ ٱللَّهُ عَنْهُمَا one day and he asked me to follow him to the market. I said to him, 'What will you do in the market when you do not sell or ask about any goods to buy or bargain or sit in the market gatherings? Sit here so we can talk.' He said to me, 'You with the belly [Al-Tufayl had a prominent belly],

> we go out in the morning only for the sake of *Salam*, to greet with *Salam* whomever we meet.'"
>
> Reported by al-Bukhari in *al-Adab al-Mufrad* (1006) and al-Albani declared it sahih (*Sahih al-Adab al-Mufrad*, 774)

Walking the path of love is not always easy. It is sometimes thankless and exhausting. Be ready for it. Like with *Salam*, not everyone will reciprocate. And if you make their reply and approval a condition, your practice of *Salam* will suffer, shrivel, and disappear. It must be done for Allah, for the sake of following this *Hadith*. If people ignore you, you have Allah's reward and the greeting of the angels to satisfy you. Similarly, if you do a loving act to please Allah and bring joy to Muslims and they ignore it or hurt you because of it, do not be discouraged. You did not do it seeking their approval. You did it seeking Allah's approval. Attach yourself to Allah, and you will keep doing good things because His love—unlike that of humanity—never ends or disappoints.

HADITH TWENTY FOUR

الحديث الرابع والعشرون

The sweetness of Iman is in love

قَالَ رَسُولُ اللهِ ﷺ «مَنْ أَحَبَّ أَنْ يَجِدَ طَعْمَ الْإِيمَانِ فَلْيُحِبَّ الْمَرْءَ لَا يُحِبُّهُ إِلَّا لِلّٰهِ عَزَّ وَجَلَّ» وَفِي رواية «مَنْ سَرَّهُ.»

رواه أحمد (٧٩٦٧) وحسنه الألباني (السلسلة الصحيحة ٢٣٠٠) وشعيب الأرناؤوط

The Messenger ﷺ said, «If one would love to find the taste of Iman, let them love someone only for the sake of Allah, Glory be to Him.» In another narration, «If one would be happy to find the taste of Iman.»

Reported by Ahmad (7967). Al-Albani declared it hasan (al-Silsilah al-Sahihah, 2300) and so did Shu'ayb al-Arna'ut

Commentary

Love for Allah's sake guides us to the best love on earth. It rescues us from adverse love and lifts us above our limitations.

The folly of love

We cannot escape love. We are constantly in love with something or other. It literally does not stop. We are constantly in love with ourselves. We also love others based on what brings us benefit and protects us from harm (e.g. we love those who help us but not those who hurt us). We love beauty, but our appreciation of it is idiosyncratic. We love money, but what we do with it varies from one person to another. We plan our days based on love (e.g. what to eat, how to spend our free time, whom to talk to). No matter what we love, we all love for very personal reasons. What and whom we love is an extension of loving ourselves. This is not selfish but the necessity of being dependent humans. Only Allah, the Self-Sufficient, can love without receiving any benefit in return (for more, see *Appendix I*).

If we understand the motivation, we are well poised to examine its consequences. If we love to maximize our benefit, is our love actually accomplishing this? In other words, does what we love help us? And are we expressing our love properly?

It is evident that we sometimes love what harms us and hate what benefits us. Allah explained this when He said:

...وَعَسَىٰٓ أَن تَكۡرَهُواْ شَيۡـٔٗا وَهُوَ خَيۡرٞ لَّكُمۡۖ وَعَسَىٰٓ أَن تُحِبُّواْ شَيۡـٔٗا وَهُوَ شَرّٞ لَّكُمۡۚ وَٱللَّهُ يَعۡلَمُ وَأَنتُمۡ لَا تَعۡلَمُونَ ٢١٦

Perhaps you dislike something good for you and like something bad for you. Allah knows and you do not know.

Al-Baqarah (Q2:216)

He also said:

...فَعَسَىٰٓ أَن تَكۡرَهُواْ شَيۡـٔٗا وَيَجۡعَلَ ٱللَّهُ فِيهِ خَيۡرٗا كَثِيرٗا ١٩

Perhaps you hate something and Allah puts plenty of good in it.

An-Nisa (Q4:19)

These *ayah*s condense one of the most profound realizations, wisdom we would learn after living for many years: we cannot always trust our emotions. Benefit and harm may be hidden from us. We love something to death, thinking that our happiness lies in it, only to discover later that it was the most harmful thing to seek. And the opposite is true: we run away from something as fast and far as we can, and it is the thing that we need the most. Yet, this is not our only handicap. Sometimes, the harms are visible, but we do not want to see them. This is why they say that love is blind. Abu al-Darda' رَضِيَ اللَّهُ عَنْهُ eloquently pointed this out when he said:

قال أبو الدرداء رضي الله عنه: حُبُّكَ الشَّيْءَ يُعْمِي وَيُصِمُّ.

رواه أحمد (٢١٦٩٤) وصحح شعيب الأرناؤوط إسناده

Loving something blinds and deafens.

Reported by Ahmad (21694) and Shu'ayb al-Arna'ut declared its chain sahih

Love can cover up the flaws of what we love. We only see what we like and ignore the warning signs. Our love even blinds us to sincere advice. We are very biased beings when we love and hate.

There is an important lesson for us here. Some of us make love our compass, following it no matter where it leads us, ascribing to it almost magical powers. Love, some believe, guides to the truth, without the need for further evidence: if we love something, then it is good; and if we do not, it must not be. If our hearts point us in a direction, we follow it because love is inherently good. This is romantically attractive, but alas, is mere fantasy. Our hearts are prisoners of our experiences, expectations, weaknesses, knowledge, and surroundings. That is, they are constrained. We are often missing the whole picture. And when we have all the information we need, we often go against it. How many of us are certain that something is wrong and harmful and yet continue to do it? Even continue to love it? We need a nobler love to save us from all of our destructive loves. We need a higher love to save us from selfishness. This is why we need Allah in what we love.

Loving for Allah's sake

Just as loving Allah is unlike any other love, love for Allah's sake is unique. It guards against the folly of love (loving the wrong thing and loving the right thing inappropriately). It does so because Allah inspires this love and guides it. Loving what Allah loves guides us to loving the best of things in ways pleasing to Him. This explains why it is important to follow the Sunnah of

Muhammad ﷺ: it is how we properly express the love of Allah and how we reach it. Allah said:

قُلْ إِن كُنتُمْ تُحِبُّونَ ٱللَّهَ فَٱتَّبِعُونِى يُحْبِبْكُمُ ٱللَّهُ وَيَغْفِرْ لَكُمْ ذُنُوبَكُمْ ۗ
وَٱللَّهُ غَفُورٌ رَّحِيمٌ ﴿٣١﴾

Say, "If you love Allah, then follow me and Allah will love you and forgive your sins. And Allah is All-Forgiving, All-Merciful."

Ali 'Imran (Q3:31)

Some of the People of the Book claimed to love Allah, but they envisioned and practiced this love in ways displeasing to Him. One cannot reach the love of Allah through unsanctioned means. It is a contradiction to do what Allah hates in the name of the love of Allah. It is the same with Bid'ah (innovated and unsanctioned acts of worship). Unless Allah ordained it, it will not bring us closer to Him.

The advantages of love for Allah's sake do not stop there. This love is sublime. It allows us to escape love solely for our own sake. When we love out of self-interest, our love is immature. It is selfish, short-lived, unstable, and may even be destructive. Because of its origin and limitations, such love survives as long as one is receiving personal benefit. Once this stops, love disappears. People will love you as long as they need you, but run away when you need them. Some will forget all the good you have done and hate you because of a single mistake, real or imaginary. Some soon forget you because they are easily bored, some betray your trust for personal gain, and some love and fall out of love for trivial reasons. Some love with such intensity that it turns into intense hatred and venom after a disagreement. Love for Allah's sake is different. It is selfless, just, stable, and uplifting.

When one loves for Allah's sake, they love whom/what pleases Allah regardless of their personal feelings. Their love continues and grows as long as their beloved is pleasing to Allah. And when their beloved displeases Him, they sympathize, conceal their mistakes, and offer advice to rescue them; they do not gloat, feel superior, ignore them when in need, or wish them more harm. They do not cancel one's virtuous past because of a single mistake or a personal quarrel. Their heart moves for Allah, with all the mercy and justice that Allah loves. Such love does not fluctuate with time, is not dependent on worldly favor or benefit, and does not expect anything in return. It is faithful, sincere, and above suspicion and envy. It cannot envy because it does not object to Allah's decisions and gifts. It will not envy because it desires the best for all. How could we love someone and wish them to lose a blessing? Love means wishing the best for your beloved in every way, that they can trust you. The Prophet ﷺ said:

«رؤيا المؤمِنِ جزءٌ مِنْ أربعينَ جُزْءًا مِنَ النبوَةِ وَهِيَ على رِجْلِ طائِرٍ ما لم يُحَدِّثْ بِها فإذا تَحَدَّثَ بِها سقَطَتْ ولا تُحَدِّثْ بها إلّا لبيبًا، أوْ حبيبًا.»

رواه الترمذي (٢٢٧٨) وصححه الألباني (صحيح الجامع ٣٤٥٦)

«A believer's dream is a fortieth portion from prophethood. And it is as if the dream is tied to a bird's leg [i.e. is not fulfilled] as long as he does not share it. But if he shares it, it falls [i.e. happens]. So, do not share it except with one who is wise or beloved.»

Reported by al-Tirmidhi (2278) and al-Albani declared it sahih (*Sahih al-Jami'*, 3456)

You can trust a loved one not to envy you or misinterpret the dream. Love and envy are contradictory. How could we hate something our loved one received? How could we hate something our Beloved gave? Love for Allah's sake rises above our personal feelings, conflicts, and limitations. When love is tied to Him, love is liberated from selfishness and materialism. We love the good in all because Allah loves it, whether this brings us personal gain or not. And we would dislike the evil in all because Allah dislikes it, even if it is in us. When what Allah loves is dearer to the soul than its love, when the source of love is not the self but Allah, we will know how sublime love is.

With this love, we will be better Muslims, better human beings. And we will keep getting better the closer we get to Allah. This love will turn the world into a small heaven. This small heaven is a taste of eternal happiness in Jannah.

Finding the taste of Iman

We saw in *Hadith* One that the sweetness of *Iman* is to be found in love. Love is the culmination of who we are, the best of what we want and would like to be. When we give our love to someone, we are sharing the best and dearest thing that we have. Allah wants us to love Him because it is the greatest human devotion we can give. It is a complete surrender to Allah, where we migrate from ourselves to Him. This is deep and profound. For most of our lives, we live for ourselves. We are the center of our existence. We love and move for our own sake. Loving Allah is the surrender of our ego. We admit that we are not the center, not the most important thing in our lives. We move from a life centered on us to one centered on Allah. This is the profound transition, the great migration. The fruit of this dramatic change is the escape from the trap of personal love to divine love. Instead of surrendering to our self and its dictates (Hawa), we surrender to Allah's love. We move as He wants us, not as we want. We are happiest with His decisions, not ours. We go wherever He wants us to go, and like whatever He wants us to like. This complete surrender is the sweet *Iman* in the *Hadith*. And it is available only through love.

Ibn 'Abbas رَضِيَ اللَّهُ عَنْهُمَا explained how love perches at the highest branch of the tree of *Iman*. It is like the highest fruit on that tree, and you need to climb all the branches to get to it. He said:

قَالَ ابْنِ عَبَّاسٍ رضي الله عنهما: أَحِبَّ فِي اللَّهِ وَأَبْغِضْ فِي اللَّهِ

وَوَالِ فِي اللَّهِ وَعَادِ فِي اللَّهِ فَإِنَّمَا تَنَالُ وِلَايَةَ اللَّهِ بِذَلِكَ وَلَا يَجِدُ عَبْدٌ طَعْمَ الْإِيمَانِ وَإِنْ كَثُرَتْ صَلَاتُهُ وَصِيَامُهُ حَتَّى يَكُونَ كَذَلِكَ.

الإخوان لابن أبي الدنيا (٦٩)

Love for the sake of Allah, hate for the sake of Allah, befriend for the sake of Allah, and befoe for the sake of Allah, for one only becomes a *wali* of Allah by doing this. And one will not find the taste Iman—even with much Salah and fasting—until they behave like this.

Al-Ikhwan by Ibn Abi al-Dunya (69)

Salah and fasting are essential gateways to Allah's love. They are like the trunk of a tree. If they are absent, there is no tree. But as the trunk, they carry the branches and the fruits. And we need to keep climbing to reach them. We need to achieve internal and external surrender to Allah, for the ability to sacrifice for Allah's sake. You become a *wali* of Allah when you put Him before yourself. When you love for His sake, hate for His sake, and move for His sake, you are close to Him. He is dear to you, and you to Him. Love is the consummation of our worship, the consummation of our life. When you give it to Allah, you are His, and He yours.

Love is the best worship

سأل هِشَامُ بْنُ إِسْمَاعِيلَ أُمَّ الدَّرْدَاءِ رضي الله عنها: مَا أَوْثَقُ عَمَلِكِ فِي نَفْسِكِ؟ قَالَت: الْحَبُّ فِي اللَّهِ.

الإخوان لابن أبي الدنيا (٦٤)

Hisham ibn Isma'il asked Umm al-Darda' رَضِيَ اللَّهُ عَنْهَا, "What deed of yours do you trust the most [to be pleasing to Allah]?" She replied, "Love for Allah's sake."

Al-Ikhwan by Ibn Abi al-Dunya (64)

Saturated with love for Allah, one is born anew. They experience the world differently from everyone else. They see everything the way Allah wants them to see it. They do not cease to have personal desires, but their preferences become secondary to Allah. If there is a conflict between the two, they embrace what Allah loves. And it becomes their preference. When Allah's love is strong, it changes the lover, inside out. This is when the love of Allah permeates all aspects of life.

When we love for Allah's sake, we are in fact loving Allah. Makhul said:

قال مَكْحُول: مَنْ أَحَبَّ رَجُلًا صَالِحًا فَإِنَّمَا أَحَبَّ اللهَ.

حلية الأولياء (ج٥ ص١٨٠)

The one who loves a pious man indeed only loves Allah.

Hilyat al-'Awliya' (vol. 5, p. 180)

He is behind our every love, and this is why He is our ultimate love. When we reach this level, the sweetness of *Iman* will reveal itself to us.

HADITH TWENTY FIVE

الحديث الخامس والعشرون

Love others for Allah to love you

قَالَ رَسُولُ اللَّهِ ﷺ «إِنَّ اللَّهَ عَزَّ وَجَلَّ يَقُولُ قَدْ حَقَّتْ مَحَبَّتِي لِلَّذِينَ يَتَحَابُّونَ مِنْ أَجْلِي وَحَقَّتْ مَحَبَّتِي لِلَّذِينَ يَتَصَافَوْنَ مِنْ أَجْلِي وَحَقَّتْ مَحَبَّتِي لِلَّذِينَ يَتَزَاوَرُونَ مِنْ أَجْلِي وَحَقَّتْ مَحَبَّتِي لِلَّذِينَ يَتَبَاذَلُونَ مِنْ أَجْلِي وَحَقَّتْ مَحَبَّتِي لِلَّذِينَ يَتَنَاصَرُونَ مِنْ أَجْلِي.»

رواه أحمد (١٩٤٣٨) وصححه الألباني (صحيح الترغيب ٣٠٢١) وشعيب الأرناؤوط

The Messenger ﷺ said, «Allah, Glory be to Him, says, "My Love is confirmed for those who love each other for My sake, My Love is confirmed for those who purify their love for each other for My sake, My Love is confirmed for those who visit each other for My sake, My Love is confirmed for those who give each other for My sake, and My Love is confirmed for those who champion each other for My sake."»

Reported by Ahmad (19438). Al-Albani declared it sahih (Sahih al-Targhib, 3021) and so did Shu'ayb al-Arna'ut

Commentary

Love for love

As you do and as you are, you shall receive. This is the reciprocal divine law. You see many instances of it spread throughout the Quran and Sunnah. For instance, Allah, the Exalted, said:

...وَلْيَعْفُوا۟ وَلْيَصْفَحُوٓا۟ ۗ أَلَا تُحِبُّونَ أَن يَغْفِرَ ٱللَّهُ لَكُمْ... ﴿٢٢﴾

And let them pardon and overlook. Would you not like Allah to forgive you?

An-Nur (Q24:22)

Reception of Allah's Forgiveness is predicated on our forgiveness. Similarly, the Prophet ﷺ said:

«الرّاحمونَ يرحمُهُمُ الرّحمنُ ارحَموا من في الأرضِ يرحَمْكم من في السَّماءِ.»

رواه الترمذي (١٩٢٤) وصححه الألباني (السلسلة الصحيحة ٩٢٥)

«The merciful receive mercy from the Merciful. Be merciful to those on earth and the One above the sky will be Merciful to you.»

Reported by al-Tirmidhi (1924) and al-Albani declared it sahih (*al-Silsilah al-Sahihah*, 925)

And in the *Hadith*, those who love others for Allah's sake have a promise from Allah to receive His love. This is the highest reward possible: to win the love of Allah is to have everything you ever wanted. Everything else will love you because its Master and Creator is happy with you. All of your worries will disappear, all of your dreams will come true, and your heart will finally receive what will make it forever at peace. Having the love of Allah is having everything.

When Allah looks at those fortunate few who love for His sake, He sees the purest of hearts. They do not love for any worldly return: no praise, no favors, no wealth, and no blood ties. They are moved to love because of Allah. And their love produces the noblest actions. The Prophet ﷺ said:

«زارَ رجلٌ أخًا لَهُ في قريةٍ أخرى فأرصدَ اللَّهُ لَهُ على مَدرجَتِهِ ملَكًا

فلمَّا أتى عليهِ قالَ: أينَ تريدُ؟ قالَ: أريدُ أخًا لي في هذِهِ القريةِ، قالَ: هل لَكَ عليهِ من نعمةٍ تربُّها؟ قالَ: لا غيرَ أنِّي أحببتُهُ في اللَّهِ عزَّ وجلَّ، قالَ: فإنِّي رسولُ اللَّهِ إليكَ بأنَّ اللَّهَ قد أحبَّكَ كما أحببتَهُ فيهِ.»

رواه مسلم (٢٥٦٧)

«A man set out to visit a brother of his in another town, so Allah sent an angel on his way. When the man met the angel, the angel asked him, "Where are you going?" He replied, "I want to visit my brother in this town." The angel asked, "Are you doing it to repay him for a favor [or taking care of a worldly interest by your visit]?" He said, "No, except that I love him for the sake of Allah, the Exalted and Glorious." The angel then said, "I am a messenger of Allah to you [to tell you] that Allah loves you as you love him for His sake."»

Reported by Muslim (2567)

He did not visit because of any worldly reason. He was not returning a favor, visiting out of social obligation, or protecting his interests. These are not necessarily bad motives. But this man was not doing it for any of this. He hoped to receive nothing but the pleasure of Allah. He travelled an unknown distance; and travel then was an ordeal. He faced the hardships of travel for nothing but his love for Allah. And for that he deserved the honor of an angel's visit with the greatest of news that Allah loved him. And the story was immortalized in a *hadith* as an inspiration for millions.

When one loves Allah, their heart beats with Allah's love. They have gentle hearts that love—with utmost delight—everything that Allah loves. This is not something they have to force on themselves: it comes naturally. No one has to remind us to love our favorite food and drink or our favorite smell; we just do. And when the love of Allah penetrates the hearts, it brings in with it everything that Allah loves. Whatever Allah wants becomes what we want. Whatever He decides becomes the best decision. His commands become a joy because they carry us to Him; and His prohibitions become bitterer than death. Physical death is but a transition that leads us back to Him. But sin is alienation from Him, and there is nothing more wretched and lonely than separating from Him. They love Allah so much that they change their plans to fit His, their priorities are His, and the joy of their hearts is hearing His Name and Words (i.e. Quran and *dhikr*). They used to chase after the world to make them happy, but found no real happiness until they came close to Him. He took care of all of their needs, all of their worries, and was their solace and companion when no one else could. They cannot love anyone more than Allah, even their own selves, for they exist only because of Him and for Him. Loving for Allah's sake is as natural to them as loving their own selves.

But love will be tested and will face obstacles. Just like *Iman*, loving Allah and loving for His sake need to be nurtured. The Prophet ﷺ described the lovers in the *Hadith* as purifying their love for each other. They cleanse their hearts from baseless suspicion as soon as it arises. They forgive their beloveds and seek excuses for them, harboring no ill will or hatred in their hearts for them. Abu Qilabah said:

قَالَ أَبو قِلَابَةَ: إِذَا بَلَغَكَ عَنْ أَخِيكَ شَيْءٌ تَكْرَهُهُ فَالْتَمِسْ لَهُ الْعُذْرَ جَهْدَكَ فَإِنْ لَمْ تَجِدْ لَهُ عُذْرًا فَقُلْ فِي نَفْسِكَ لَعَلَّ لِأَخِي عُذْرًا لَا أَعْلَمُهُ.

حلية الأولياء (ج٢ ص٢٨٥)

> When you hear something you hate about your brother, try your best to find an excuse for him. And if you cannot, say to yourself, "Maybe my brother has an excuse that I do not know."
>
> *Hilyat al-Awliya'* (vol. 2, p. 285)

They do not envy the success of their beloveds but wish them all the good they wish for themselves. And when they notice their hearts experiencing negative emotions, they step back to reexamine their *Iman* and strengthen their connection with Allah. If they harm their beloved or deprive them of their rights, they repent to Allah and humbly apologize. They are sincere and honest with those whom they love, doing it to please Allah and gain His love. This is how they keep their love for the pious pure, and because of that, their love for Allah continues to grow.

What love entails

Love is not simply a word we say. It is a state of being, a commitment to what we love. And loving someone for Allah's sake is the greatest of these commitments because it sprouts from the greatest of all loves. The *Hadith* explained that the bond of love manifests itself in moral and physical support to protect the wellbeing of the one that you love. If they see their beloved in financial need, they give immediately without any expectation. They visit them because they miss them and to take care of them. If they are assailed, they console and defend them until they are safe. If they see them committing a mistake, their love moves them to give advice. They cannot sit back and see their beloved drift away from Allah, for this would be too heartbreaking to witness. And they receive no satisfaction from another's affliction. Some, unfortunately, dance with glee when others fail, thinking that their failure somehow translates into their own success. Such a heart suffers from the absence of love, and is distant from Allah's love. We cannot hate the wellbeing of the believers and imagine that Allah loves us. This should be the greatest motivation to combat those destructive feelings and repent from them. If I want Allah's love, I need to love what He loves, and loving the wellbeing of the believers is an essential ingredient.

The aforementioned noble behavior is not limited to the small circle of those whom we know and love. Rather, it is how we are supposed to see the world and react to it.

أَقَامَ طَاوُسٌ عَلَى رَفِيقٍ لَهُ مَرِيضٍ حَتَّى فَاتَهُ الْحَجُّ.

حلية الأولياء (ج٤ ص١٠)

Tawus took care of his sick friend until he missed Hajj.

Hilyat al-Awliya' (vol. 4, p. 10)

Tawus was a Tabi'i (from the second generation) who lived in Makkah, and he put the health of his friend before the performance of (voluntary) Hajj. Hajj is one of the greatest acts of worship. But is it more valuable than the life of a Muslim? When we give (money, aid, time), we should prioritize whom and what Allah loves. Many donate according to their personal preferences, not wondering if this is what Allah loves the most. Many of us champion causes and people based on tribe, color, family ties, citizenship, gender, and the likes. But those with *Iman* champion *Iman*. All other connections disappear: they only see what matters to Allah. Since race, gender, citizenship, color, and tribe are unimportant to Allah, they are unimportant to them. They will stand with a stranger against their dearest relative if the former is more pleasing to Allah. Al-Hasan al-Basri رَحِمَهُ ٱللَّهُ said:

قال الحسن: المؤمن لا يَحيفُ على من يُبغِض ولا يأثَم فيمَن يُحِبّ.

عيون الأخبار (ج٣ ص١٤)

The believer is not unjust with those whom he hates, and he is not driven to sin because of those whom he loves.

'Uyun al-Akhbar (vol. 3, p. 14)

They have emotions like everybody else, but Allah is superior to their emotions. Their devotion to Allah makes them adhere to the truth, no matter where it takes them. They speak the truth and give honest advice because of love and care. We cannot love someone and deprive them of the advice they need. The proverb goes:

أخُوكَ مَنْ صَدَقَكَ النَّصِيحَةَ.

مجمع الأمثال (ج١ ص٢٣)

Your brother is one who is honest in giving you advice.

Majma' al-Amthal (vol. 1, p. 23)

We do not advise each other today as often as we should because we lost the love we have for each other. If we still had it, we would care enough to say the truth even at the risk of angering the advisee. Should I sit back and watch someone spiraling into their own destruction and say nothing because they will get angry? If I love them, I will risk their anger in hope of saving them.

Love for the sake of Allah is challenging and demanding. But the reward is magnificent. This love elevates us to stations that the Prophets of Allah عَلَيْهِمُ السَّلَامُ themselves admire.

قَالَ أَبو مُسْلِمٍ الْخَوْلَانِيِّ لِمُعَاذِ بْنِ جَبَلٍ: وَاللَّهِ إِنِّي لَأُحِبُّكَ لِغَيْرِ دُنْيَا أَرْجُو أَنْ أُصِيبَهَا مِنكَ وَلَا قَرَابَةَ بَيْنِي وَبَيْنَكَ، قَالَ: فَلِأَيِّ شَيْءٍ؟ قُلْتُ: لِلَّهِ، قَالَ: فَجَذَبَ حُبْوَتِي ثُمَّ قَالَ: أَبْشِرْ إِنْ كُنْتَ صَادِقًا فَإِنِّي سَمِعْتُ رَسُولَ اللَّهِ صَلَّى اللَّهُ عَلَيْهِ وَسَلَّمَ يَقُولُ «الْمُتَحَابُّونَ فِي اللَّهِ فِي ظِلِّ الْعَرْشِ يَوْمَ لَا ظِلَّ إِلَّا ظِلُّهُ يَغْبِطُهُمْ بِمَكَانِهِم النَّبِيُّونَ وَالشُّهَدَاءُ» ثُمَّ قَالَ: فَخَرَجْتُ فَأَتَيْتُ عُبَادَةَ بْنَ الصَّامِتِ فَحَدَّثْتُهُ بِحَدِيثِ مُعَاذٍ، فقَالَ عُبَادَةُ بْنُ الصَّامِتِ: سَمِعْتُ رَسُولَ اللَّهِ صَلَّى اللَّهُ عَلَيْهِ وَسَلَّمَ يَقُولُ عَنْ رَبِّهِ تَبَارَكَ وَتَعَالَى «حقَّت مَحَبَّتِي عَلَى الْمُتَحَابِّينَ فِيَّ وحقَّت مَحَبَّتِي عَلَى الْمُتَنَاصِحِينَ فِيَّ وحقَّت مَحَبَّتِي عَلَى الْمُتَزَاوِرِينَ فِيَّ وحقَّت مَحَبَّتِي عَلَى الْمُتَبَاذِلِينَ فِيَّ وَهُمْ عَلَى مَنَابِرَ مِنْ نُورٍ يَغْبِطُهُمُ النَّبِيُّونَ والصديقون بمكانهم.»

رواه أحمد (٢٢٠٦٤) وابن حبان (٢٥١٠) وصححه الألباني (صحيح الترغيب ٣٠١٩)

Abu Muslim al-Khawlani said to Mu'adh ibn Jabal, "By Allah, I love you, not for a worldly favor I will receive from you or kinship between me and you." Mu'adh asked, "Then, for what?" I said, "For Allah." He pulled me by my clothes and said, "Expect the best if you are honest, for I heard the Messenger ﷺ say, 'Those who love each other for the sake of Allah are under the shade of the Throne, where there will be no shade except its shade. The Prophets and the martyrs will admire them and wish for their station.' " Then Abu Muslim al-Khawlani left and met 'Ubadah ibn al-Samit and narrated to him the saying of Mu'adh. He said, "I heard the Messenger ﷺ report that Allah said, 'My love is confirmed for those who love each other for my sake, My love is confirmed for those who advise each other for my sake, My love is confirmed for those who visit each other for my sake, and My love is confirmed for those who give to each other for my sake. They will be on pulpits of light, where the Prophets and the Siddiqs will admire them and wish for their station.' "

Reported by Ahmad (22064) and Ibn Hibban (2510). Al-Albani declared it sahih (*Sahih al-Targhib*, 3019)

They will be under the shade of the Throne and on pulpits of light. The Prophet ﷺ said:

«سَبْعَةٌ يُظِلُّهُمُ اللَّهُ في ظِلِّهِ يَومَ لا ظِلَّ إلَّا ظِلُّهُ» فذكر منهم «ورَجُلانِ تَحابّا في اللَّهِ اجْتَمعا عليه وتَفَرَّقا عليه.»

رواه البخاري (٦٦٠) ومسلم (١٠٣١)

«There are seven that Allah will put under his shade on the Day when there will be no shade except his shade.» He mentioned among them, «...and two who love each other for the sake of Allah; they gathered because of this love and continued to have it until they parted ways.»

Reported by al-Bukhari (660) and Muslim (1031)

Their distinction will be so luminous that it attracts the attention of the best of humanity: the Prophets, Siddiqs, and martyrs. You can only imagine the prestige that even the Prophets would admire and wish for. And their heavenly reward is even greater and more lasting. Those coveted rewards tell us that the path is serious and demanding, but it is also beautiful and gratifying.

Love for the sake of Allah is a badge of honor. It means something. It is not a word we say or a wish we have. Sufyan ibn 'Uyaynah said:

قَالَ سُفْيَانُ بْنُ عُيَيْنَةَ: سَمِعْتُ مُسَاوِرًا الْوَرَّاقَ يَحْلِفُ بِاللَّهِ عَزَّ وَجَلَّ مَا كُنْتُ أَقُولُ لِرَجُلٍ إِنِّي أُحِبُّكَ فِي اللَّهِ عَزَّ وَجَلَّ فَأَمْنَعُهُ شَيْئًا مِنَ الدُّنْيَا.

الإخوان لابن أبي الدنيا (ص ٢٠٢)

I head Musawir al-Warraq swear by Allah and say, "I would not say to a man 'I love you for the sake of Allah, Glory be to Him,' and deny him anything from this world."

Al-Ikhwan by Ibn Abi al-Dunya (p. 202)

When you say it, it means that you love Allah so much that you can now love for His sake. And if you truly love a person because of Allah, you will love them more than the world. So, how can you deny them the world if you love them more than the world? Love is more precious than gold and silver. Abdullah ibn al-Walid said:

قَالَ عَبْدِ اللَّهِ بْنِ الْوَلِيدِ: قَالَ لَنَا أَبُو جَعْفَرٍ مُحَمَّدُ بْنُ عَلِيٍّ: يُدْخِلُ أَحَدُكُمْ يَدَهُ فِي كُمِّ صَاحِبِهِ وَيَأْخُذُ مَا يُرِيدُ؟ قُلْنَا: لَا، قَالَ: فَلَسْتُمْ بِإِخْوَانٍ كَمَا تَزْعُمُونَ.

الإخوان لابن أبي الدنيا (ص ٢٠٣)

Abu Ja'far Muhammad ibn Ali asked us, "Does one of you put his hand in his friend's sleeve [where he keeps his money] and take what he wants?" We said, "No." He said, "Then, you are not brothers as you claim."

Al-Ikhwan by Ibn Abi al-Dunya (p. 203)

This is what loving someone else for the sake of Allah means.

The more you love others, the more Allah loves you

HADITH TWENTY SIX

الحديث السادس والعشرون

قَالَ رَسُولُ اللَّهِ ﷺ «ما تحابّ اثنان في اللهِ إلّا كانَ أفضلَهما أَشدُّهما حبًّا لصاحبِه.»

رواه البخاري في الأدب المفرد (٥٤٤) وابن حبان (٥٦٦) وصححه الألباني (السلسلة الصحيحة ٤٥٠) وفي رواية (إلا كان أحبُّهُما إلى اللهِ أَشدُّهما حبًّا لصاحبِه) (السلسلة الصحيحة ٣٢٧٣)

The Messenger ﷺ said, «No two love each other for Allah's sake except that the best of the two is the one who loves their companion more.»

Reported by al-Bukhari in al-Adab al-Mufrad (544) and Ibn Hibban (566). Al-Albani declared it sahih (Al-Silsilah al-Sahihah, 450). In another narration: (except that the more beloved to Allah of the two is the one who loves their companion more.) (al-Silsilah al-Sahihah, 3273)

Commentary

When the love of Allah is the basis of a relationship, it purifies it and elevates it. It makes kindness and sacrifice the goal, and the love of Allah is the fuel that sustains it.

The more you love Him

Loving Allah has no end. This is not so with anyone else. This is one of the many ways in which the love of Allah is unique. No matter how much we love Allah, we would not have loved Him enough. And no matter how much we worship Allah, we would not have worshipped Him enough. Salman al-Farisi رضي الله عنه said:

قال سلمان الفارسي رضي الله عنه: يُوضَعُ المِيزانُ يومَ القيامةِ فلَوْ وُزِنَ فيهِ السَّمَواتُ والأرضُ لَوَسِعَتْ فتقولُ الملائكةُ: يا رَبِّ لِمَنْ يزِنُ هذا؟ فيقولُ اللهُ تعالى «لِمَنْ شِئْتُ من خَلْقِي.» فتقولُ الملائكةُ: سبحانَكَ ما عَبَدْناكَ حقَّ عِبادَتِكَ، ويُوضَعُ الصِّراطُ مِثْلَ حَدِّ المُوسى، فتقولُ الملائكةُ: مَنْ تُجِيزُ على هذا؟ فيقولُ «مَنْ شِئْتُ من خَلْقِي.» فيقولونَ: سبحانَكَ ما عَبَدْناكَ حقَّ عِبادتك.

رواه الحاكم (٨٧٣٩) وصححه الألباني وقال له حكم الرفع (السلسلة الصحيحة ٩٤١)

The Mizan (Scale) will be set on the Day of Judgment. If the heavens and the earth were to be weighed in it, they would fit in it. The angels will say, "O Rabb, what will this weigh?" Allah, Glory be to Him, will say, «Whomever I wish from My creation.» The angels will say, "Glory be to You, we did not worship you as you deserved to be worshipped." Then the Sirat (Bridge) will be set, thin like a blade. The angels will say, "Whom will you allow to pass on this?" He will say, «Whomever I wish from My creation.» The angels will say, "Glory be to You, we did not worship you as you deserved to be worshipped."

Reported by al-Hakim (8739) and al-Albani declared it sahih and stated that it has the status of a hadith from the Messenger ﷺ (*al-Silsilah al-Sahihah*, 941)

Who is saying this? The angels who worship Allah day and night, without sin and boredom. But when they behold a glimpse of the extent of Allah's Power, they know that their constant worship was not enough to fit the incredible Majesty of the Creator. Whatever we do, we cannot appreciate His Grandeur and Power. Whatever we do, we cannot repay Him for His bounties.

We simply are unaware of all the good that He gifted us and keeps gifting, each second of every day. All our worship cannot adequately thank Him. Yet, He keeps blessing us and forgiving us despite our neglect, shortcomings, and sins. For all that and more, He deserves all of our love. And we can spend our whole life loving Him, and many lives on top of that, and we would not have loved Him enough. (This is, in part, the reason why using Ishq to refer to Allah's love is inadequate. See *Appendix I*.) Ibn Taymiyyah رَحِمَهُ ٱللَّهُ said:

وَاللَّهُ تَعَالَى مَحَبَّتُهُ لَا نِهَايَةَ لَهَا.

مجموع الفتاوى (ج١٠ ص١٣١)

There is no end to the love of Allah.

Majmu' al-Fatawa (vol. 10, p. 131)

The beauty of loving Allah is that once we start our love journey, we will never reach its end. We will continue to discover new depths each day, a new joy at every corner, and with every step. We will know Allah more, love Him more, and strive to be closer to Him. This is the difference between every worldly pleasure and the joy of being close to Allah. Every earthly pleasure is doomed to end, and this saps the joy out of it. We cannot fully enjoy something while knowing that it will end. But the joy of being near Allah will never end. And this makes it the sweetest thing imaginable, and its satisfaction is endless.

Growing our love for Allah requires expanding our love for what pleases Him. It is a loop: as one increases, so does the other. Only when our love for Him falters that we experience emotional distance from what He loves. This happens to be a good and independent test of *Iman*. Check how you feel about what He loves, and it will tell you how you feel about Him. Those who love Allah will have the strongest love for what pleases Him, and they keep themselves close to it. They love spending time in mosques and care for them as they care for their own homes. Their hearts race when they hear the Adhan and the Quran, and cannot imagine spending a day without the blessings of the Quran. They dearly love all those who love Allah and are trying to follow His guidance. They stay close to the scholars and the pious to learn from them and remember Allah. Proximity to what Allah loves enhances the love of Allah, wards off the attacks of Shaytan, and protects from the temptations of the world. When we stay close to what Allah loves, we are close to Him. We need more of what Allah loves around us to keep us on the straight path, to protect us from error.

We can see Allah's Great Mercy in linking love for Him to our love of others. If we desire more of His love, we should strengthen our love for the believers. This is how much Allah loves you and is taking care of you. He made your rights sacred. Every lover of Allah is duty-bound to be the best they can for you. No one can peacefully enter Jannah if they assault you or violate your rights. And kindness to you is one of the keys to Jannah and His love. For that, we should love and thank Him as long as we are alive.

A better you with greater love

The more you love for Allah's sake, the better you are. Why? Because that love comes from loving Allah. As one increases, the other does too. The more one loves their companion, the stronger is their love for Allah. Hence, their *Iman* is greater and their obedience to Allah more complete. And for that, they will take greater care of whom they love. They will even put them before themselves, expecting the reward solely from Allah. Lukewarm responses to their kindness do not change their intention or behavior. Remember, we are doing it for Allah. We are not seeking reward from anyone but Him. You are not waiting for gratitude, praise, reciprocal favors, or money. If we love because of Allah, our acts are because of Him and for Him. The fact that Allah gave us the opportunity to do something good out of love for Him is reward enough. If the door of love opens for you, count yourself among the luckiest on earth, for very few do this today. Many do good today to get something back (money, fame, and to improve their image). But you do it so you would look better before Allah. The difference between the two acts is like the distance between heaven and earth.

Similarly, when there is discord between two lovers, the better of the two is the one who is better to their companion. It is the one who works to restore love to its past vigor. They begin by reviewing their behavior to see if their sin could have been the cause of this rift. The Prophet ﷺ said:

«وَالَّذِي نَفْسُ مُحَمَّدٍ بِيَدِهِ مَا تَوَادَّ اثْنَانِ فَفُرِّقَ بَيْنَهُمَا إِلَّا بِذَنْبٍ يُحْدِثُهُ أَحَدُهُمَا.»

رواه أحمد (٥٣٥٧) وصححه الألباني (صحيح الترغيب ٢٢١٩)

«By the One who has my soul in His Hand, if two who love each other are separated in discord, it is because of a sin that one of the two committed.»

Reported by Ahmad (5357) and al-Albani declared it sahih (*Sahih al-Targhib*, 2219)

Love comes from Allah; sin chases love away. The real reason behind loss of love today—lurking behind other causes of conflict—is sin. Restoring love demands dealing with the main reason for its loss. Repentance and asking Allah for forgiveness are the medicine, followed by apologizing for our mistakes. But if one finds that their beloved is the one who had committed this sin, they rush to give them gentle and loving advice to save them from Allah's anger. They would be happier with their beloved's repentance than if they had discovered gold and silver. They treat their beloved better than they treat themselves. They can do this because Allah's love moves them to do this. As they can put Allah before themselves, they can put others before themselves too. Mus'ab ibn Ahmad ibn Mus'ab said:

قَالَ مصعب بْن أَحْمَد بْن مصعب: قدم أَبُو مُحَمَّد المروزي إلى بغداد يريد مكة فكنت أحب أن أصحبه فأتيته فاستأذنته في الصحبة فلم يأذن لي في تلك السنة ثم قدم سنة ثانية وثالثة فأتيته فسلمت عليه وسألته فَقَالَ: اعزم على شرط يكون أحدنا الأمير لا يخالفه

الآخر، فقلتُ: أنت الأمير، فَقَالَ: يا أبا مُحَمَّد لا بل أنت الأمير، فقلتُ: أنت أسن وأولى، فَقَالَ: نعم، ولا يجب أن تعصيني، فقلت: نعم، فخرجت معه فكان إذا حضر الطعام يؤثرني فإذا عارضته بشيء قَالَ: ألم أشترط عليك أن لا تخالفني؟ فكان هذا دأبنا حتى ندمت على صحبته لما يلحق نفسه من الضرر فأصابنا في بعض الأيام مطر شديد ونحن نسير فَقَالَ لي: يا أبا مُحَمَّد اطلب الميل، فلما رأينا الميل، قَالَ لي: اقعد في أصله فأقعدني في أصله وجعل يديه على الميل وهو قائم قد حنا عَلي وعليه كساء قد تجلل به يظللني به من المطر حتى تمنيت أنى لم أخرج معه لما يلحق نفسه من الضرر فلم يزل هذا دأبه حتى دخلنا مكة.

المنتظم في تاريخ الملوك والأمم (ج١٣ ص١٨-١٩)

Abu Muhammad al-Marwazi passed by Baghdad, intending to travel to Makkah. I loved to accompany him, so I asked his permission to be his companion, but he refused that year. Then he passed by the next year and then the year after that, so I came and made the request [again], and he said, "Do, on the condition that one of us is the Emir and the other does not disobey him." I said, "You are the Emir." He said, "No Abu Muhammad, you are the Emir." I said, "You are older and more worthy." He said, "Yes, and you will not disobey me?" I said, "Yes." So we traveled together. When it was time to eat, he used to favor me with food. And if I objected, he would say, "Did you not promise me that you would not disobey me?" And this was constantly happening until I regretted keeping his company because of the harm he was bringing to himself. One day, heavy rain fell while we were walking, so he said to me, "O Abu Muhammad, head to the milepost." When we saw the milepost, he said to me, "Sit at its bottom." So, he made me sit at its bottom and put his hands on the milepost while standing, leaning over me with a cloak he had over him to protect me

> from the rain until I wished I did not go out with him because of the hardship he was bringing to himself. He continued to behave this way until we arrived at Makkah.
>
> *Al-Muntatham fi Tarikh al-'Umam wa al-Muluk* (vol. 13, pp. 18–19)

This devotion in generosity is devotion in love. It is a race to gain as much of Allah's love while we are still alive. And to that end, one can sacrifice everything on earth to be closer to Allah. This is why and how the people of Allah's love fly higher than everyone else. They are indeed something else. May Allah make us one of them and grace us with their company.

HADITH TWENTY SEVEN

الحديث السابع والعشرون

If you love someone, let them know

قَالَ رَسُولُ اللهِ ﷺ «إِذَا أَحَبَّ الرَّجُلُ أَخَاهُ فَلْيُخْبِرْهُ أَنَّهُ يُحِبُّهُ.»

رواه أبو داود (٥١٢٤) والترمذي (٢٣٩٢) وصححه الألباني (السلسلة الصحيحة ٤١٧)

The Messenger ﷺ said, «If a man loves his brother, he should tell him that he loves him.»

Reported by Abu Dawud (5124) and al-Tirmidhi (2392). Al-Albani declared it sahih (al-Silsilah al-Sahihah, 417)

Commentary

Loving another for Allah's sake is a precious gift. Sharing it is a remarkable blessing. It cements love and rescues us from the loneliness of modern life.

Spreading love

Islam promotes all that spreads love between the believers and eliminates hate. We have seen a demonstration of it in *Hadith Twenty-Three*, and we will see another in *Hadith Twenty-Eight*. In this *Hadith*, the Prophet ﷺ recommended another act that strengthens love: telling others when you love them that you do.

But how do I know when I love someone for Allah's sake?

The telltale sign is that this love stems from loving Allah. When one loves Allah, they view the world with a different lens. What is popular and faddish in the world is not necessarily popular and faddish with them. They love what Allah loves, and they see the way Allah wants them to see (more on that in *Hadith Forty-One*). When they see a person, they do not see ethnicity, citizenship, wealth, education, age, or any other worldly distinction. All people are equal to them in these matters. What they see first and what captures most of their attention later is how close this person is to Allah. If they find them to be close (i.e. their life reflects *Taqwa*), they become dear to them. And the pleasure of Allah remains the scaffold that supports this love. The more this person is pleasing to Allah, the more they love them. And their love for them decreases when they move away from Allah. This is how we know. When we see that our love for another rises and dips because of Allah—and not because of personal reasons or gain—then that is love for Allah's sake.

Now, why should we tell others that we love them? It may be awkward for some of us. Or, it may seem too trivial to mention. But sharing feelings of love serves many benefits. It will delight the recipient when they hear that someone loves them. And what should particularly please them is viewing this announcement as a sign of Allah's love for them (more on that in *Hadith Twenty-Nine*). Hearing, in a single statement, that someone loves you and that Allah may indeed love you will spike the *Iman* of any believer. This blessed testament of love—a few kind words that take seconds to say—brings considerable joy to a Muslim, removes their sadness, and bolsters their *Iman*. Consequently, love between the two will grow. And when this declaration of love becomes common practice, the bonds of brotherhood/sisterhood will be stronger in society as a whole.

Another valuable outcome is that people will be more inclined to accept advice from each other. The reason that many of us are averse to advice is our suspicion that it is an attack disguised as advice. No one likes to be criticized. And we especially hate it from someone who hates you. But advice will be better received when coming from someone who cares for you: we are more likely to heed the advice of those who love us. Additionally, strong love foils the plots of Shaytan. At the onset of an argument or the possibility of discord, lovers know how to preserve their love: they remain humble, they respect each other, forgive each other, and support each other. They know that love for Allah's sake is more significant than any minor disagreement, definitely bigger than their egos. They place this love above their interests because they please Allah before themselves.

Spreading love also has the advantage of combating many of the diseases of the heart. We are often plagued with envy, pride, and greed. At the core of it all, we are selfish; this is why we fight most of the time. But when you know that someone loves you and wants nothing back from you for this love, your heart will change. You will find it harder to envy them, harder to be angry with them. You are more likely to wish them well, to be nicer to them, and to think of them and not only yourself. When we know that someone loves us, and sincerely desires the best for us, we will not be in direct competition with them. This is why the Prophet ﷺ urged that man to let the other know how he felt. It is advice for all of us to let others know, for we will be changing ourselves and society when we do. We would be performing an act of worship that brings us both—I and the one I love—closer to Allah.

Sharing your feelings

It may be hard to share your feelings, but it is important that you do. We are living today in a love-deprived world. When everything got mechanized, automated, and digitized, we lost human interaction and warmth. Moreover, the commercialization of society has reduced our value to what we generate—dollars and profit. We became obsessed with artificial and ephemeral outward glamor. And the globalization of consumerism has turned us into fierce competitors with a winner-take-all attitude. For the sake of this competition—and because of other societal pressures—we separate from our families and loved ones and settle into a lonelier existence. And so, we feel anxious and unloved. And we desperately need to hear that someone loves us. Sincere love, not transactional. Not because they can profit from us, or because they need a favor. It is not about beauty that will fade one day or wealth that I may lose the next day. No. They love us because we deserve this love, because of something in us. When you hear that someone loves for Allah, you will know that they do not want anything back from you. They love you for you. And you will feel closer to them and closer to Allah who made this love possible. This is how we can restore love to a world that has lost it and does not know how to get it back.

Our best example in spreading love is the Prophet ﷺ. He did not hesitate to express his emotions. He announced his love, and by that he made people love Allah.

أَخَذَ رسول الله صلى الله عليه وسلم بِيَدِ مُعَاذٍ فَقَالَ «يَا مُعَاذُ وَاللَّهِ إِنِّي لَأُحِبُّكَ» فَقَالَ مُعَاذٌ: بِأَبِي أَنْتَ وَأُمِّي وَاللَّهِ إِنِّي لَأُحِبُّكَ، فَقَالَ «يَا مُعَاذُ أُوصِيكَ أَنْ لَا تَدَعَنَّ فِي دُبُرِ كُلِّ صَلَاةٍ أَنْ تَقُولَ اللَّهُمَّ أَعِنِّي عَلَى ذِكْرِكَ وَشُكْرِكَ وَحُسْنِ عِبَادَتِكَ.»

رواه أبو داود (١٥٢٢) وابن حبان (٢٠٢٠) واللفظ له وصححه الألباني (التعليقات الحسان ٢٠١٧)

The Prophet ﷺ once held the hand of Mu'adh and said, «O Mu'adh, by Allah I love you.» Mu'adh said, "You are dearer to me than my mother and father, by Allah I love you." So, he said, «O Mu'adh, I am advising you. Do not neglect to say after each Salah, "O Allah, help me to remember you, thank you, and worship you well."»

Reported by Abu Dawud (1522) and Ibn Hibban (2020) and the wording of the hadith is the latter's. Al-Albani declared it sahih (*al-Ta'liqat al-Hisan*, 2017)

Consider the warm introduction that paved the way for this vital teaching. Mu'adh رضي الله عنه probably remembered this advice and practiced it for the rest of his life. Why? Because he heard before it that the Prophet ﷺ loved him, and he taught him this because he loved him. It is one thing to give advice but another to tell people that you care about them. If they know you care, it is easier to receive advice and accept it.

In another *hadith*, the Prophet ﷺ expressed his love to a group from the Ansar.

خرجَ النبيّ صلى الله عليه وسلم يومًا عاصبًا رأسه فتلقاه ذراري الأَنصار وخدمُهم ما هم بوجوه الأَنصار يومئذٍ فقال «والذي نفسي بيده إنّي لأُحبّكم [مرتين أو ثلاثًا].»

رواه ابن حبان (٧٢٦٦) وصححه الألباني (التعليقات الحسان ٧٢٢٢)

The Prophet ﷺ went out one day while he had wrapped his head. He was received by the children and servants of the Ansar—they were not their dignitaries. He said to them, «By the One who has my soul in His Hand, I love you [he said it twice or thrice].»

Reported by Ibn Hibban (7266). Al-Albani declared it sahih (*al-Ta'liqat al-Hisan*, 7222)

Noting that they were not the dignitaries of the Ansar is telling us that it was not done for any worldly consideration. When you say to the least powerful in society that you love them, you are not expecting something back from them. The Prophet ﷺ loved the Ansar, and when he saw their children and servants, he did not hide his affection. It is the weakest and most vulnerable—the ones with broken hearts—who need to hear this the most.

When someone tells you that they love you for Allah's sake, the Sunnah is to make du'a for them to receive Allah's love.

كان رجلٌ عند النبيِّ ﷺ فمر به رجلٌ فقال: يا رسولَ اللهِ إني لأحبّ هذا، فقال له النبيُّ ﷺ «أعلَمْته؟» قال: لا، قال «أعلِمْهُ» قال: فلحقه فقال: إني أحبُّك في اللهِ، فقال: أحبَّك الذي أحببتَني له.

رواه أبو داود (٥١٢٥) وصححه الألباني (صحيح أبي داود ٥١٢٥)

A man was next to the Prophet ﷺ as another man passed them. The first man said, "O Messenger of Allah, I love that man." The Prophet ﷺ asked him, «Did you let him know?» He said, "No." The Prophet ﷺ said, «Let him know.» So, he caught up with him and said, "I love you for Allah's sake." He said back to him, "May the One for whom you loved me love you."

Reported by Abu Dawud (5125) and al-Albani declared it sahih (*Sahih Abi Dawud*, 5125)

This is what we all want. We love what Allah loves so Allah would love us. And when you receive this *du'a*, you know why it was worth it to tell someone that you love them. The warmth of that moment is indescribable, and the shared joy is among the best moments we will experience. This is what the love of Allah does. And we need to have more of these experiences and moments in our lives. If you love someone for Allah's sake, let them know.

HADITH TWENTY EIGHT

الحديث الثامن والعشرون

Give to spread love

قَالَ رَسُولُ اللهِ ﷺ «تَهَادُوا تَحَابُّوا.»

رواه البخاري في الأدب المفرد (٥٩٤) والبيهقي في السنن الكبرى (١١٩٤٦) وحسنه الألباني (صحيح الأدب المفرد ٥٩٤)

The Messenger ﷺ said, «Give presents to each other and you will love each other.»

Reported by al-Bukhari in al-Adab al-Mufrad (594) and al-Bayhaqi in al-Sunan al-Kubra (11946). Al-Albani declared it hasan (Sahih al-Adab al-Mufrad, 594)

Commentary

Giving, in the form of gifts or charity, benefits both the giver and the recipient. One of its most significant consequences is removing hatred and selfishness from the hearts, paving the way for more love and mercy.

The gift of love

A gift may seem like a small gesture, but its impact is great. We have a natural desire for this world. And if it is not excessive and does not distract from Allah, it is blameless. With this in mind, it is natural for us to like gifts and to like those who give them.

We also love kindness and those who show it. Gifts delight us because they express goodwill and reveal someone's care for us. It is also pleasing to receive something new, even a mere trifle.

The benefits of gifting extend to both gifter and giftee. The gift-recipient feels appreciated and loved. The gift may also be something they need, helping to alleviate their hardship and enhance their life. The gift-giver, on their end, is rewarded for the practice of the Sunnah, the worship of spreading love, bringing joy to a fellow Muslim, and helping them in times of need. This worship also combats the stinginess in the self. When we develop gift-giving into a habit, we become used to thinking about others, valuing them more than money, and working for their benefit. As love grows between gifter and giftee, there will be less room for envy, suspicion, backbiting, and enmity. Society as a whole improves from the practice of this seemingly small Sunnah.

Gifts have the incredible effect of changing feelings. Safwan ibn Umayyah رَضِيَ اللَّهُ عَنْهُ accepted Islam after years of opposition to the Prophet ﷺ. As could be expected, years of conflict had left their mark on his heart, and he could not easily move beyond the hatred of the past. The Prophet ﷺ understood this well, and he softened his heart with gifts. This changed him. Safwan said:

قال صفوان ابن أمية: أعطاني رسولُ اللَّهِ ﷺ يومَ حُنينٍ وإنَّهُ لأبغَضُ الخَلقِ إليَّ فما زالَ يعطيني حتّى إنَّهُ لأَحَبُّ الخَلقِ إليَّ.

رواه مسلم (٢٣١٣) والترمذي (٦٦٦) واللفظ له (صحيح الترمذي ٦٦٦)

The Messenger ﷺ gave me on the day of Hunayn while he was the most hated person to me. And he continued to give me until he became the most beloved person to me.

Reported by Muslim (2313) and al-Tirmidhi (666) and the wording is that of al-Tirmidhi (*Sahih al-Tirmidhi*, 666)

This is how much he gave him.

وَأَعْطى رَسولُ اللهِ ﷺ يَومَئذٍ صَفْوانَ بنَ أُمَيَّةَ مِئَةً مِنَ النَّعَمِ ثُمَّ مِئَةً ثُمَّ مِئَةً.

رواه مسلم (٢٣١٣)

The Messenger ﷺ gave Safwan ibn Umayyah one hundred livestock animals, then another hundred, and then another hundred.

Reported by Muslim (2313)

Another narration provides more details of the event and the moment of transformation.

يُقالُ إنَّهُ طافَ مَعَ النَّبيِّ صَلَّى اللَّه عَلَيْهِ وَسَلَّمَ وَالنَّبيِّ صَلَّى اللَّه عَلَيْهِ وَسَلَّمَ يَتَصَفَّحُ الْغَنائِمَ إذْ مَرَّ بِشِعْبٍ مِمّا أَفاءَ اللَّه عَلَيْهِ فِيهِ غَنَمٌ وَإِبِلٌ وَرِعاؤُها مَمْلُوءٌ فَأَعْجَبَ صَفْوانَ وَجَعَلَ يَنْظُرُ إلَيْهِ، فَقالَ رَسُولُ اللَّه صَلَّى اللَّه عَلَيْهِ وَسَلَّمَ «أَعْجَبَك يا أَبا وَهْبٍ هَذا الشِّعْبُ؟» قالَ: نَعَمْ، قالَ: هُوَ لَك وَما فِيهِ، فَقالَ صَفْوانُ: أَشْهَدُ ما طابَتْ بِهَذا نَفْسُ أَحَدٍ قَطّ إلّا نَبيّ وَأَشْهَدُ أَنَّك رَسُولُ اللَّه.

مغازي الواقدي (ج٣ ص٩٤٦)

It was said that Safwan joined the Prophet ﷺ as the latter was inspecting the spoils of war. They passed by a valley that was full of sheep and camels with their shepherds, which was what Allah had given to him from the spoils of war. Safwan admired it and kept staring at it. The Messenger ﷺ asked him, «Abu Wahb, do you admire what is in this valley?» He said, "Yes." He said, «It is all yours.» Safwan said, "I testify that only the soul of a Prophet could be comfortable with such giving. I testify that you are the Messenger of Allah."

Maghazi al-Waqidi (vol. 3, p. 946)

Only a Prophet could give like this! Safwan was still a polytheist, and his heart was attached to this world and its pleasures. What amazed him was that someone like the Prophet ﷺ, who had next to nothing, could give this much. His generous giving convinced Safwan that the Prophet was unlike anyone he had seen or heard about. The Prophet ﷺ was not seeking this world, and his generosity showed how little regard he held for it. This impressed Safwan. Everyone else, kings and powerful men, lived and died for this world except Muhammad ﷺ. Safwan received something he loved with this gift—plenty of livestock—but also received a dose of selflessness, generosity, love, and *Iman*. And this combination changed him. And it changed others too.

سَأَلَ رَجُلٌ النبيَّ ﷺ غَنَمًا بيْنَ جَبَلَيْنِ فأَعْطاهُ إيّاهُ فأتى قَوْمَهُ فَقالَ: أَيْ قَوْمِ أَسْلِمُوا فَواللَّهِ إنَّ مُحَمَّدًا لَيُعْطِي عَطاءً ما يَخافُ الفَقْرَ، فَقالَ أَنَسٌ رضي الله عنه: إنْ كانَ الرَّجُلُ لَيُسْلِمُ ما يُرِيدُ إلّا الدُّنْيا فَما يُسْلِمُ حتّى يَكونَ الإسْلامُ أَحَبَّ إلَيْهِ مِنَ الدُّنْيا وَما عَلَيْها.

رواه مسلم (٢٣١٢)

A man asked the Prophet ﷺ for sheep [that filled the valley] between two mountains, and he gave it to him. So, he returned to his people and said, "My people, embrace Islam. By Allah, Muhammad gives like someone who does not fear poverty." Anas رضي الله عنه said, "One would embrace Islam at first, only desiring this world. But as soon as they became Muslim, Islam would be dearer to them than this world and what it contains."

Reported by Muslim (2312)

Gifts are the gateway to the heart. But they are not the end. When the hearts are clinging to the world, giving them the world removes their need and comforts them. Once they are satisfied, they can see the beauty behind the gift and the beauty of the giver. They move from the material to the spiritual. This is our transformation too. We love gifts because we love this world. But a gift has the power—with the right intention—to transport us into a higher realm.

Righteous giving

As right intentions inspire and bless giving, wrong motives contaminate it. Some give to show off their wealth and broadcast their generosity. Some do it to get something back: return gifts, favors, worldly advancement, and so on. Some reluctantly give out of embarrassment and social obligation. These are not good reasons to give since love is not the motive. Rather than promoting love, these gifts do the opposite: increase resentment and greed.

Gifting as worship—as done by the Prophet ﷺ—is for the material benefit of the recipient, not the giver. Allah said:

وَلَا تَمْنُن تَسْتَكْثِرُ ﴿٦﴾

And do not confer a favor expecting more in return.

Al-Muddaththir (Q74:6)

One of the common practices in Arabia was to gift to receive more favors and gifts. This defeats the purpose of giving. It turns the gift into an exercise in greed, a burden, and a cause for conflict. Thus, Allah forbade it in the Quran.

A gift is supposed to say to others that you value them more than money, that you are thinking about them, and that you love them. It is to assist them, to remove their hardship, to put a smile on their face, and to bring them closer to the love of Allah. It is an act of *Ihsan* that expects nothing in return except from Allah. So when you give, make it for Allah. And do not reduce your reward by demanding human appreciation and reciprocation.

The receiver should also remember that a gift—with the right intention—is an act of love. Someone voluntarily gifted you something: the goodwill in their heart moved them to do so. Appreciate it and do not belittle any gift of love. The Prophet ﷺ said:

«يا نِساءَ المُسْلِماتِ لا تَحْقِرَنَّ جارَةٌ لِجارَتِها ولو فِرْسِنَ شاةٍ.»

رواه البخاري (٢٥٦٦) ومسلم (١٠٣٠)

«O Muslim women, a woman should not look down on a gift she receives from her woman neighbor, even if it were a sheep's hoof.»

Reported by al-Bukhari (2566) and Muslim (1030)

This is a very modest gift, with the least meat, and yet the Prophet ﷺ asked us to appreciate it. It is not what you receive but the sentiment that matters: there is someone out there who loves Allah and loves you. If all we can see is the monetary value of the gift, then we have not yet escaped the material clutches of this world. A gift is a gesture to increase your love for Allah and the believers, not feed your greed and materialism. If you find yourself in the latter category, consistently give more gifts and charity until you find the sweetness of giving. And reward gift-givers with gifts. It is the Sunnah of Prophet ﷺ.

كانَ رَسولُ اللَّهِ ﷺ يَقْبَلُ الهَدِيَّةَ ويُثِيبُ عَلَيْها.

رواه البخاري (٢٥٨٥)

The Messenger ﷺ used to accept gifts and give presents in return.

Reported by al-Bukhari (2585)

When done for Allah, receiving and rewarding a gift become a sweet act that brings about the love of Allah. It links human love to divine love: one leads to the other.

Following the Prophet ﷺ is essentially an act of love: we do it because we love him and we want Allah to love us. Practicing his Sunnah and spreading it should be the same: done with love and so people would love him.

Project

Find someone you love, and give them a gift for the sake of Allah.

HADITH TWENTY NINE

الحديث التاسع والعشرون

The earthly sign of Allah's love

سأل أَبُو ذَرٍّ رَسُولَ اللهِ ﷺ: يَا رَسُولَ اللهِ أَرَأَيْتَ الرَّجُلَ يَعْمَلُ الْعَمَلَ يُحِبُّهُ النَّاسُ عَلَيْهِ قَالَ «تِلْكَ عَاجِلُ بُشْرَى الْمُؤْمِنِ.»

رواه أحمد (٢١٤٠٠) ومسلم (٢٣٩٢) واللفظ لأحمد

Abu Dharr asked the Messenger ﷺ, "What about a man who does something and people love him for it?" He said, «This is hastened good news for the believer.»

Reported by Ahmad (21400) *and Muslim* (2392). *The wording is that of Ahmad*

Commentary

When Allah loves you, He sends you signs of His love. One of these signs is the love people give you. Look beyond their praise to see the pleasure of Allah and His approval.

Divine love and people's love

We have a natural desire to be loved. It is inborn. We need it most when we are young; its absence in those formative years can scar us. Yet we never stop needing it as adults. We always need human connection and intimacy, and it is painful when it is absent. This is the reason we are constantly looking for someone to love who will love us back. This perpetual search is at the core of all our thoughts and efforts.

Human love has its disadvantages. Not everyone we love is ready to receive love or requite it. And if they are, we may not know how to express this love properly. Our love can be excessive or insufficient, misdirected, or tainted with negative emotions and insecurities. Some kill because of love, envy because of love, wreck another's life because of love, or destroy their own lives trying to love another. Love—this powerful and inherent emotion—unleashes the greatest potential for good or evil. Love can be an addiction, more severe than any other addiction. We love something/someone excessively until we believe that we cannot live without it. We seek it to fill the gaps in our life until we become its prisoners: our happiness evaporates without it. We think that we need it because we need love. Yet our love could be misdirected. What we love could be wrong for us, or we could love it with unhealthy intensity and desperation. When we link our love to Allah, we liberate it from earthly constraints, and it can fly free. We are no longer prisoners. And love is no longer a prison.

We have seen in *Hadith Twelve* the connection between loving Allah and loving people. This *Hadith* confirms this connection while adding something important. On the path of love, look for signs of Allah's love. Do not let anything else distract you.

When we are trying to do something good, it seems natural to look for validation, recognition, and even praise. We cannot function without it. Since we are all looking for love, we are looking to receive love with every good thing we do. Our challenge, however, is to decide which love are we seeking. It is easy to slip from seeking Allah's pleasure to hoarding human compliments and praise. If we do, we would be distancing ourselves from real love. Humans—please remember this—are very fickle. They love you and then they hate you for no good reason. You cannot rely on the longevity of human love. If we only invest in their love, we would be wasting our lives and emotions. Rather, love the One who grants all love and controls all hearts. The Prophet ﷺ said:

«من التمس رِضا اللهِ بسخَطِ الناسِ رضِيَ اللهُ عنه وأرْضى عنه الناسَ ومن التَمس رضا الناسِ بسخَطِ اللهِ سخِط اللهُ عليه وأسخط عليه الناسَ.»

رواه ابن حبان (٢٧٦) وصححه الألباني (التعليقات الحسان ٢٧٦)

«The one who seeks Allah's approval though it is upsetting to people, Allah will be pleased with them and will make people pleased with them. And the one who seeks people's approval though it is upsetting to Allah, Allah will be displeased with them and will make people displeased with them.»

Reported by Ibn Hibban (276) and al-Albani declared it sahih (*Al-Ta'liqat al-Hisan*, 276)

You and I do not control our hearts. They can change in an instant. It is such a waste to try to make someone like you but upset Allah in the process. This love will not make you happy, and it will not last. Make Allah happy—religiously and in life—and the right person will love you, and their love will uplift you. Allah will give you all that you need.

Does this mean that we should pay no attention to human praise? The challenge is how to interpret it properly. How do we react when someone heaps praise on us? If we allow it to become our goal and motivation—if we start seeking it and we look forward to it—then we are no longer seeking Allah and no longer sincere in worshipping Him. But we can interpret human approval as a sign descending from the sky that Allah loves us, a reflection of Allah's happiness with what we did. We can see in worldly approval the approval of the Hereafter. In that way, we can value human admiration and praise because it points to something higher and better, not because it is human praise per se. This is what the *Hadith* is teaching us.

But we must distinguish between right and wrong love, and right and wrong people. Not all love is good love, not all love is a sign of divine love, and not everyone who loves you actually loves you. The popularity of celebrities (social media, actors, singers, sports stars, and politicians) is not a sign of divine love. If you want to know why, ask yourself: are they pleasing to Allah? Do people love them for Allah's sake? The fame and admiration many of them receive are superficial and destructive. It is based on loving what Allah hates, and no good comes from that. The challenge is to resist the allure of this artificial love and seek the one that really counts. Suhayl ibn Abi Salih said:

قال سُهَيل بن أبي صالح: كنا بعَرفةَ فمرَّ عمرُ بنُ عبدِ العزيزِ وهو على المَوسمِ فقام الناسُ ينظرون إليه فقلتُ لأبي: يا أبَتِ إني أرى اللهَ يحبُّ عمرَ بنَ عبدِ العزيزِ، قال: وما ذاك؟ قلتُ: لما له من الحُبِّ في قلوبِ الناسِ.

رواه مسلم (٢٦٣٧)

We were in 'Arafah as 'Umar ibn 'Abdul 'Aziz passed by, and he was the Emir of Hajj, and people stood up to catch a glimpse of him. I said to my father, "Father, I think that Allah loves 'Umar ibn 'Abdul 'Aziz." He asked, "Why?" I replied, "Because of the love people have for him in their hearts."

Reported by Muslim (2637)

'Umar ibn 'Abdul 'Aziz رَحِمَهُ ٱللَّهُ received this love because he was pleasing to Allah. And this requires—sometimes—taking unpopular stands, which 'Umar did. If our concern is people's love and popularity, we will seldom do the right thing. But if we intend to please Allah, He will grant us all the love we need. He will bring righteous love closer to us. And it will not be a love that will burden us in this life or the next.

For these reasons, it is crucial not to seek human praise and approval. Al-Nawawi رَحِمَهُ ٱللَّهُ wrote in explanation of the *Hadith*:

هَذَا كُلُّهُ إِذَا حَمِدَهُ النَّاسُ مِنْ غَيْرِ تَعَرُّضٍ مِنْهُ لِحَمْدِهِمْ وَإِلَّا فَالتَّعَرُّضُ مَذْمُومٌ.

شرح النووي على مسلم (ج١٦ ص١٨٩)

This all [i.e. receiving human praise is good] if people praise him without him seeking their praise. Otherwise, seeking it is abhorrent.

Sharh al-Nawawi on Muslim (vol. 16, p. 189)

If praise comes to you without you asking for it or looking forward to it—and your act is pleasing to Allah—then praise Allah. But if you find yourself seeking it and waiting for it, then you are its prisoner. You have polluted your intention.

This is the same attitude we should have with worldly wealth. Hakim ibn Hizam رَضِيَ ٱللَّهُ عَنْهُ said:

قال حَكِيمُ بن حِزام رضي الله عنه: سَأَلْتُ رَسولَ اللَّهِ صَلَّى اللهُ عليه وسلَّمَ فأعْطَانِي ثُمَّ سَأَلْتُهُ فأعْطَانِي ثُمَّ سَأَلْتُهُ فأعْطَانِي ثُمَّ قالَ «يا حَكِيمُ إنَّ هذا المَالَ خَضِرَةٌ حُلْوَةٌ فمَن أَخَذَهُ بسَخَاوَةِ نَفْسٍ بُورِكَ له فِيهِ ومَن أَخَذَهُ بإشْرَافِ نَفْسٍ لَمْ يُبَارَكْ له فِيهِ كَالَّذِي يَأْكُلُ ولَا يَشْبَعُ اليَدُ العُلْيَا خَيْرٌ مِنَ اليَدِ السُّفْلَى.»

رواه البخاري (١٤٧٢)

I asked the Messenger ﷺ and he gave me, then I asked him and he gave me, then I asked him and he gave me and said, "O Hakim, this money is attractive and sweet. Whoever takes it with a generous spirit (i.e. without greed and without looking forward to it), it will be blessed for them. And whoever takes it with greedily craving, it will not be blessed for them but will be like one who eats and does not get full. And the upper (i.e. giving) hand is better than the lower (i.e. receiving) hand."

Reported by al-Bukhari (1472)

In another *hadith*, the Prophet ﷺ said:

«إذا ساقَ اللهُ إليْكَ رِزْقًا من غَيرِ مَسألَةٍ ولا إشْرافِ نَفسٍ فَخُذْهُ فإنَّ اللهَ أعطاكَهُ.»

أخرجه ابن حبان (٣٤٠٣) وصححه الألباني (التعليقات الحسان ٣٣٩٤)

If Allah sends you provision without [you] asking for it and without greedily craving it, then take it because Allah gave it to you.

Reported by Ibn Hibban (3403) and al-Albani declared it sahih (*al-Ta'liqat al-Hisan*, 590)

Similarly, if human praise comes without looking forward to it and without asking for it, then accept it as a sign from Allah. But if it comes because you ran after it or are eagerly waiting for it, there will be no blessing in it.

The greatest motivation

Experiencing the love Allah reveals to us an invaluable truth: the only reward worthy of our life and deeds is the pleasure of Allah. Nothing else comes close, and nothing else satisfies our hearts. Spending our energy and our life attempting to please humans is a tragedy. Our life is the most precious thing we have, while human approval is worth nothing. In comparison to the greatness of Allah, human praise is ephemeral, their promises are a mirage, and they cannot help themselves, let alone help us. Human love ends, eventually. But the love of Allah is inexhaustible. Human love is the shore, whereas Allah's love is deeper than the deepest ocean. The more we love Him, the greater and deeper it gets. Human love does not have the power to save us, but the love of Allah is all the saving we need. If you are going to give your life in exchange for one thing, it must be the love of Allah. Nothing else compares to it, and nothing else is worth it.

When our goal is to reach Allah's love, we will never stop. We will keep going because the source of our inspiration is never-ending. The more we do, the sweeter and more fulfilling it gets. We will not want to stop. On the opposite side, if we are living to collect human praise and approval, we will be frustrated and exhausted. We will discover that we have collected bubbles. And we will regret it, especially when we realize that those who flatter us will abandon us at the first sign of trouble. So, if you want to do something, make it count and let it be for Allah. If you are looking for love, aim for the best and highest, and seek the love of Allah. Love Allah and love *for* Allah. Love people but do not let their love guide you. Allah created you for Him, not for them. Do not wait for people to thank you and appreciate you. Keep your eyes on the Highest. His love is greater than any other. And His pleasure fills the heart more than any other. You will not be truly happy and free until you are close to Him.

HADITH THIRTY

الحديث الثلاثون

Love elevates

قَالَ رَسُولُ اللهِ ﷺ «إنَّ مِن عبادِ اللهِ لَأُناسًا ما هم بأنبياءَ ولا شُهداءَ يغبِطُهم الأنبياءُ والشُّهداءُ يومَ القيامةِ بمكانِهم مِن اللهِ تعالى» قالوا: يا رسولَ اللهِ تُخبِرُنا مَن هم، قال «هم قومٌ تحابُّوا برُوحِ اللهِ على غيرِ أرحامٍ بَيْنَهم ولا أموالٍ يتعاطَوْنَها فواللهِ إنَّ وجوهَهم لَنُورٌ وإنَّهم على نُورٍ لا يخافونَ إذا خاف النّاسُ ولا يحزَنونَ إذا حزِنَ النّاسُ» وقرأ هذه الآيةَ ﴿أَلا إِنَّ أَوْلِياءَ اللهِ لا خَوْفٌ عَلَيْهِمْ وَلا هُمْ يَحْزَنُونَ﴾ [يونس ٦٢]

رواه أبو داود (٣٥٢٧) وصححه الألباني (صحيح أبي داود ٣٥٢٧)

The Messenger ﷺ said, «Among Allah's slaves are people who are not Prophets or martyrs but the Prophets and martyrs will admire them on the Day of Judgment because of their close rank to Allah.» They said, "O Messenger of Allah, would you tell us who they are?" He said, «They are people who love each other for Allah's sake without any kinship between them or wealth they are exchanging. By Allah, their faces are lit and they are upon light. They are not afraid when people are afraid and are not sad when people are sad.» And he read this ayah, ﴾Indeed, the 'Awliya' of Allah will have no fear come upon them and nor will they be sad﴿ [Yunus 62].

Reported by Abu Dawud (3527) and al-Albani declared it sahih (Sahih Abi Dawud, 3527)

Commentary

Loving Allah and for His sake elevates to the highest ranks on the Last Day. The virtue and striving of the lovers will be noted and celebrated, telling all that this is true success.

Love takes you higher

All of us want to be special. We are aware of our talents and abilities, we see the good that we can potentially do, and we hope to do something worthwhile with our life. The recognition we receive for our work validates our worth, and this, in turn, gives meaning to our existence. What we do becomes important because someone else sees it as important and praises us for it. And if they deem what we are doing important and meaningful, then we are important and meaningful. We look for recognition because we are searching for meaning. And the ultimate recognition is love. When someone loves us, we feel valuable and important. Love gives meaning.

Looking for meaning, however, pushes us to sometimes to look for the wrong type of love. If you survey the world today, you will find that value is synonymous with fame and fortune. If you are rich or famous, you are important. You will be admired because you are successful. Why did people conclude that this is success? Because they believe fame and fortune are valuable. So now, anyone who wants to be meaningful and loved must be rich or famous. This is how we define and celebrate success. If we want to redefine success, we must seek recognition from another source. We cannot rely on the world. It does not possess the know-how to tell us how to live nor does it possess the values to tell us our worth.

The need for this redefinition is urgent. In pursuit of worldly success, we are lead to believe that competition—with all the friction and hatred it generates—is how you get ahead in this life. Especially in a globalized capitalist world, this is the only way to succeed. But the *Hadith* offers a counternarrative, one that we need to repeat often so we do not forget it. The truth the *Hadith* reveals is that success comes through love, not hatred. We climb highest in the sight of Allah and reach our greatest worldly and spiritual potential when we allow love to penetrate our hearts, when we purge hatred (envy, greed, and pride) out. Those who love each other for Allah's sake reach a towering position that catches the eyes of the best of humanity: the Prophets and martyrs. Allah elevates them to such heights to showcase their virtue and the excellence of what they did. And the Prophet ﷺ told us about them to inspire us to be among them. That honor is no ordinary honor, and that distinction is unlike any in the world.

That scene in the *Hadith* transports us to a different—and better—reality than the grim one we created here. Those who love each other for Allah's sake may not be famous at all on earth, and they may be struggling financially. By any metric of worldly success, they may be counted as failures. And if the story were to end there, everyone would decide to live selfishly because they see no value in behaving differently. But the *Hadith* comes to offer us a richer understanding of reality. Those who will be celebrated in the next life are the ones who achieve real distinction in this life. They are the real winners, even if most people think otherwise. It is enough that Allah knows who they are and loves them for it. Their sincere love for Allah and each other made even the Prophets of Allah take note of them, and praise them for their excellence. They did not earn distinctions fighting in wars, but they fought their weaknesses and fended off worldly temptations. They did not buy into the dominant narrative of running after this world for meaning and value: they did not believe that they are worth something only if they are rich or famous. They, instead, invested their life trying to please Allah and purifying their hearts. They made the love of Allah their destination, and they tried to reach it in every way possible. They defied what the majority of the world told them about love and meaning. They, instead, took their guidance from Allah and surrendered their hearts to Him. They sought what He loved, and they loved it. They sought whom Allah loved, and they loved them. They did not seek or desire human recognition, for they are waiting for their reward once they meet Allah. And when they do meet Him, He will elevate them because they elevated Him in their lives. He will bring them close to Him because they stayed close to Him in this life. He will proudly display them because He was the greatest love in their hearts. Allah will show humanity what He thought of them, He will show humanity that they are the real winners.

So, if you want distinction and honor, seek it from Allah. If you want value, you will find it with Allah. If you want to feel important, that your life matters, do what Allah loves. If you do love Him, expect the best in this life and the next.

The Iman of the lovers

Why did they deserve such high accolades? The fact that the Prophets will admire their position does not mean that they are higher and better than the Prophets of Allah. The Prophets' station is higher than all. But it does reflect their excellence and high rank. If it catches the attention of the Prophets and they wish for similar honor, you know that their reward is beyond extraordinary. So, why did they deserve it?

We know well the struggles of the Prophets of Allah, and we know their impeccable piety. We also understand the magnitude of the sacrifice of the martyrs: losing wealth, family, and life to please Allah. So, the lovers must have also strived to be so close to Allah. Theirs is not an impossible rank to reach, but it does require sacrifice.

They have to rebel against the world and align themselves with Allah. And this could be lonely at times, and requires much conviction. When everyone else is busy with selfish and material love, they combat their weaknesses and outside pressure to focus on loving Allah. When everyone else is sacrificing for the sake of this world, they look odd as they sacrifice for Allah's sake. When everyone else is trying to elevate themselves (with fame, money, and power), they elevate Allah's Name and Religion. When everyone else builds bonds and friendships based on misguided goals, they do it for Allah and live according to His Will.

They are on a journey to Allah. He is their destination, their Companion, and their Solace. They are not lonely when He is close to them, and they are never weak when He is beside them. They live with Allah, every single day. They move closer to Allah, every single day. That is enough for them, for they find their peace in it, in being close to their Beloved. Distractions away from Him torment them: they feel miserable when they are away from Him. They listen to His comforting Words (the Quran), they pray to Him to keep them strong and faithful, and they immerse themselves in His love each day. This lifelong striving propels them to the highest ranks in Jannah.

The glory of the lovers

They are on pulpits of light, elevated as they elevated themselves above the trivial in this world to reach Allah. The love of Allah binds them together, closer than kinship and friendship. Whereas all other bonds end and break, their love continues to grow. What Allah unites, no human can break. As *Iman* fills their hearts, it illuminates their faces. Internal beauty materializes on their faces and fills their spirits with happiness. What concern could remain once they know that Allah loves them? It is no surprise that they will experience no sadness or fear. The love of Allah eviscerates all pain and insecurity, and all that remains is joy. We do not have to wait till the Hereafter to experience some of the joy. You notice that you are happier and calmer when your *Iman* is strong. When the love of Allah penetrates the heart, it removes other concerns and mollifies our worries. A portion of the joy and peace that awaits the pious in Jannah is available to us right here and now. Walk on this path, and you will see for yourself.

HADITH THIRTY ONE

الحديث الواحد والثلاثون

Marriage and love

قَالَ رَسُولُ اللهِ ﷺ «لَمْ يُرَ لِلْمُتَحَابَّيْنِ مِثْلُ النِّكَاحِ.»

رواه ابن ماجه (١٨٤٧) وصححه الألباني (السلسلة الصحيحة ٦٢٤) وشعيب الأرناؤوط

The Messenger ﷺ said, «There is nothing like marriage for two who are in love with each other.»

Reported by Ibn Majah (1847). Al-Albani declared it sahih (al-Silsilah al-Sahihah, 624), and so did Shu'ayb al-Arna'ut

Commentary

Marriage is the best outlet for expressing and experiencing love for the opposite sex. Whenever it is not possible, one must shun forbidden acts to remain close to Allah. And when other loves clashes with it, the love of Allah should remain the main goal and priority.

Right love, wrong love

Carnal attraction is part of our nature. It is an impulse that Allah created in us. Allah said:

زُيِّنَ لِلنَّاسِ حُبُّ ٱلشَّهَوَٰتِ مِنَ ٱلنِّسَآءِ... ﴿١٤﴾

That which people desire was beautified to them: the love of women.
Ali ʻImran (Q3:14)

Of all the desires that we have—which Allah made appealing—He listed attraction to the opposite sex as the first, indicating its intensity. Something this powerful deserves further attention and understanding.

Allah made the desire for the opposite sex appealing and strong because of the benefits it brings. There is the necessity of human procreation, which this desire ensures. If not for the attraction between the two sexes, there will be little or no procreation. There is also the need for companionship. We need people around us. We cannot live alone. The etymology of the Arabic word "Insan" (human) is derived from Uns (socialization). Humans socialize and need socialization. We need others emotionally and physically. Allah said:

وَمِنْ ءَايَٰتِهِۦٓ أَنْ خَلَقَ لَكُم مِّنْ أَنفُسِكُمْ أَزْوَٰجًا لِّتَسْكُنُوٓا۟ إِلَيْهَا وَجَعَلَ بَيْنَكُم مَّوَدَّةً وَرَحْمَةً... ﴿٢١﴾

And of His signs is that He created mates for you from yourselves so you can find tranquility with them, and He placed affection and mercy between you.
Ar-Rum (Q30:21)

Seeking and finding mates is part of Allah's plan for us. He knows what we need. We have to communicate with others, we need someone to care of us, and we have an emotional need to take care of them. On both the emotional and physical levels, our life feels incomplete without people around us. Sexual attraction brings couples together, and it expands their circle with children and grandchildren. Communities and societies grow because of these unions. Family clusters join each other to form larger unions, and they do together what no individual or smaller groups can. Most of the development in the world—scientific, cultural, agricultural, and industrial—happened because of human aggregation and pooling of resources. The magnet that made all this possible is the sexual and emotional need we have for the opposite sex.

With all the advantages it brings and the needs it fulfills, this intense desire is also a challenge. As it can be used for good, it can be misused and abused, with emotional and physical damages. On the physical side, strong attraction to the opposite sex can lead to illicit relationships and casual sexual encounters, which is disastrous for the individual and society. This is why Allah sternly warned against fornication and adultery and legislated a deterrent punishment for them. Among the harms of this sin is the spread of physical diseases, which could turn into full-blown pandemics. There is also the dissolution of family ties and the ensuing hatred it breeds and spreads. Marital infidelity breaks up families, psychologically damages the betrayer and the betrayed, and scars the children of bitterly divorced parents. The more this spreads, the greater the harm is to the family as the glue that holds society together. And Shaytan knows that the dissolution of the family fulfills his plans. If the family breaks, the doors of *haram* are open again. The Prophet ﷺ said:

«إِنَّ إِبْلِيسَ يَضَعُ عَرْشَهُ عَلَى الْمَاءِ ثُمَّ يَبْعَثُ سَرَايَاهُ فَأَدْنَاهُمْ مِنْهُ مَنْزِلَةً أَعْظَمُهُمْ فِتْنَةً يَجِيءُ أَحَدُهُمْ فَيَقُولُ: فَعَلْتُ كَذَا وَكَذَا، فَيَقُولُ: مَا صَنَعْتَ شَيْئًا قَالَ ثُمَّ يَجِيءُ أَحَدُهُمْ فَيَقُولُ: مَا تَرَكْتُهُ حَتَّى فَرَّقْتُ بَيْنَهُ وَبَيْنَ امْرَأَتِهِ، قَالَ فَيُدْنِيهِ مِنْهُ، وَيَقُولُ: نِعْمَ أَنْتَ فَيَلْتَزِمُهُ.»

رواه مسلم (٢٨١٣)

«Iblis places his throne on water and sends out his units. The closest to him in rank are those who create the greatest dissension. One of them comes and says, "I did so-and-so." And he says, "You have done nothing." Then one of them comes and says, "I did not spare so-and-so until I separated him from his wife." Iblis brings him close to him and says, "You have done well." And he embraces him.»

Reported by Muslim (2813)

There are people who do the same work for Shaytan, and they are the worst. The Prophet ﷺ said:

«ألا أُخْبِرُكُمْ بِخِيارِكُمْ؟» قالوا: بلى، قال: الذينَ إذا رَؤُوا ذكرَ اللهُ أفلا أُخْبِرُكُمْ بِشِرارِكُمْ؟ قالوا: بلى، قال: المشاؤُونَ بِالنَّمِيمَةِ المُفْسِدُونَ بين الأَحِبَّةِ الباغُونَ البُرآءَ العَنَتَ.»

رواه البخاري في الأدب المفرد (٣٢٣) وحسنه الألباني (صحيح الأدب المفرد ٢٤٦)

«Shall I tell you about the best of you?» They said, "Yes." He said, «The ones who remind you of Allah when you see them. Shall I tell you about the worst of you?» They said, "Yes." He said, «The ones who spread secrets to cause enmity, the ones who separate between lovers, the ones who seek to bring difficulty and sin to the innocent.»

Reported by al-Bukhari in *al-Adab al-Mufrad* (323) and al-Albani declared it hasan (*Sahih al-Adab al-Mufrad*, 246)

Shaytan and his human helpers spoil love and separate between lovers, and sin is their sinister tool to destroy love.

There is also the emotional price one pays for pursuing forbidden sexual fulfillment. We are not simply physical beings. We have an essential emotional need that equally seeks fulfillment through an intimate union with another. When this union is flawed (i.e. *haram*), it severely damages us emotionally. When we get physically close to another, we become emotionally invested and attached. Affection sneaks into our hearts, and we begin to see them as long-term companions, adjusting our plans of the present and the future to include them. Our life and theirs intertwine; our hearts come close as our bodies do. A flawed union, however, does not offer stability or peace. It lacks barakah, which is where Shaytan wants to lead us. A flawed union is usually short-term, filled with anxiety, and ends with heartache and resentment. The psychological damage this does is severe. An individual coming out of this ordeal is less trusting, more cynical, less forgiving, and emotionally unavailable.

I heard an excellent parable that perfectly explains this damage. If you take an unused adhesive tape and place it on a surface, it sticks strongly because the glue is new. And it is difficult to remove. If you try to remove it, you will find the separation difficult: residue has stubbornly bonded to the tape. The glue has now been exhausted, and the tape does not adhere to other surfaces or does so poorly. Similarly, every illicit relationship leaves a residue, and every such relationship ends bitterly. One is then left with the pain of the past, carrying it forward to every other relationship they form. Like the tape, they are drained and weak because of the scars of the past (e.g. one who is cheated on cannot trust anymore, and one who is abandoned for another suffers from low self-worth and self-esteem). This is why *haram* can never be an option. It is not medicine for what ails us.

Marriage and love

Men are going to be attracted to women, and women are going to be attracted to men. And we all will fall in love with each other. This love fulfills the physical ends we discussed above, but it also complements us emotionally and psychologically. The *ayah* quoted above in Surah al-Rum signals this complementarity by pointing to the serenity that marriage produces. It is as if, without marriage, one remains in a constant state of restlessness until they find their mate. This restlessness is both physical and emotional. The physical need and agitation are apparent. One with a strong sexual desire cannot rest until they satisfy it. On the emotional side, we need to love and to be loved. We need someone to share our earthly journey with, to talk to when we feel lonely, to help us with our burdens and insecurities, to comfort us when we are anxious, and to support us when we are weak. This companionship produces one of the strongest and most intimate human bonds on earth. And when done right, Allah blesses it with affection and mercy, making it an earthly haven that carries us to Heaven.

When we fall in love, we have the urge to be close to our beloved. And the only appropriate course is what Allah loves. Ibn al-Qayyim رَحِمَهُ ٱللَّهُ wrote:

في أن دواء المحبين في كمال الوصال الذي أباحه رب العالمين. قد جعل الله سبحانه وتعالى لكل داء دواء ويسر الوصال إلى ذلك الدواء شرعا وقدرا فمن أراد التداوي بما شرعه الله له واستعان عليه بالقدر وأتى الأمر من بابه صادف الشفاء ومن طلب الدواء بما منعه منه شرعا وإن امتحنه به قدرا فقد أخطأ طريق المداواة وكان كالمتداوي من داء بداء أعظم منه وقد تقدم حديث طاوس عن ابن عباس رضي الله عنهما عن النبي صلى الله عليه وسلم أنه قال «لم ير للمتحابين مثل النكاح» وقد اتفق رأي العقلاء من الأطباء وغيرهم في مواضع الأدوية أن شفاء هذا الداء في التقاء الروحين والتصاق البدنين وقد روى مسلم في صحيحه من حديث أبي الزبير عن جابر رضي الله عنه أن رسول الله صلى الله عليه وسلم رأى امرأة فأتى زينب فقضى حاجته.

روضة المحبين (ص٢١٢)

The medicine for lovers is in the full physical contact which Allah, the Rabb of all, made permissible. Allah made a cure for each ailment, and He facilitated—religiously and physically—the attainment of that medicine. The one who seeks a cure through what Allah legislated and seek the assistance of the physical means, doing things properly, will attain the cure. But the one who seeks a cure with what Allah prohibited—even if Allah tests them with it physically (i.e. it is available and easy to get)—they will not be cured, and will be like one medicating themselves from a disease with a greater disease. And we have mentioned the hadith of Tawus from Ibn 'Abbas رضي الله عنهما that the Prophet ﷺ said, «There is nothing like marriage for two who are in love with each other.» There is a consensus among wise doctors and among others in discussing medicine that the cure to this ailment is in the meeting of two souls and the intimacy of two bodies. Muslim narrated in his Sahih from the hadith of

Abu al-Zubayr from Jabir رَضِيَ اللَّهُ عَنْهُ that the Messenger ﷺ caught a glimpse of one woman and then went to Zaynab [his wife] to be intimate with her.

Rawdat al-Muhibbin (p. 212)

Satisfying our sexual and emotional needs with *haram* creates greater problems than the ones we are trying to solve. Marriage is what offers the perfect union that meets our physical and emotional needs. In fact, marriage enhances love. The Prophet ﷺ explained in the *Hadith* that there is nothing better for lovers than marriage. This is so because all *haram* routes weaken love and, in time, destroy it and leave regret and hate in its place.

When you are in love, you have the option of nurturing your love and protecting it and yourself, or the option of the ordeal of *haram*. If we seek the forbidden (illicit glance, touch, or encounter), we would be inviting Shaytan into our love. Remember this: *haram* is Shaytan's invitation. When you do it, you are bringing him into your heart, life, and love. And his plot, you have seen, is to destroy love. Shaytan camouflages *haram* as exciting and fulfilling. Unfortunately, many help Shaytan in his scheme by complicating or mocking *halal* while leaving the door of *haram* wide-open. When we follow a forbidden path, the beginning will seem exciting. But the more we pursue it, the more it will torment us. The physical joy of any illicit union will be incomplete, and will diminish in time. It will be followed by feelings of shame, self-hate, fear of disgrace, and fear of damaging this love and losing it. Emotional tranquility, which Allah promised, will never descend. The *ayah* in Surat al-Rum (quoted before) has one more subtle point. Allah places love and mercy among people. Love blossoms because of our obedience to Allah. Allah said:

هُوَ ٱلَّذِيٓ أَيَّدَكَ بِنَصۡرِهِۦ وَبِٱلۡمُؤۡمِنِينَ ﴿٦٢﴾ وَأَلَّفَ بَيۡنَ قُلُوبِهِمۡۚ لَوۡ
أَنفَقۡتَ مَا فِي ٱلۡأَرۡضِ جَمِيعٗا مَّآ أَلَّفۡتَ بَيۡنَ قُلُوبِهِمۡ وَلَٰكِنَّ ٱللَّهَ أَلَّفَ

بَيْنَهُمْ... ﴿٦٣﴾

It is He who supported you with His victory and with the believers. And it is He who brought their hearts together. If you were to spend everything on earth, you would not be able to bring their hearts together, but Allah brought them together.

Al-Anfal (Q8:62-63)

This *ayah* is amazing! No amount of wealth or human effort could have united the Companions as Allah did. Their sacrifice and love for each other were legendary. And their ability to heal the wounds of the past and overcome tribal frictions and isolationism, to become a single and united body, is a testament to the incredible effect of *Iman* when it grows. But what you also notice in this *ayah* is that you and I have no real power to create love. We can behave in ways that enhance love—in fact, we should—but this does not guarantee love. You can do everything in your power for someone to love you yet fail. This is so because love comes from Allah. It is enhanced when we listen to Him. And if we disobey him, we leave our hearts open for Shaytan to steal our love and destroy it. You are not doing your lover a favor when you disobey Allah for their sake; you are killing their love in your heart. As Ibn al-Qayyim رَحِمَهُ ٱللَّهُ explained, when you choose *haram*, you end up with a much bigger problem than the one you started with.

For all this, it is essential to plant the love of Allah firmly in our hearts. If not, carnal and romantic love will overwhelm our hearts and possibly devastate us (more on that when discussing Ishq on page 330). When the Prophet ﷺ directed us to choose a mate, he said:

«تُنْكَحُ المَرْأَةُ لأَرْبَعٍ لِمالِها ولِحَسَبِها وجَمالِها ولِدِينِها فاظْفَرْ بذاتِ الدِّينِ تَرِبَتْ يَداكَ.»

رواه البخاري (٥٠٩٠) ومسلم (١٤٦٦)

«A woman is married for four things: for her wealth, her lineage, her beauty, and her piety. So indeed, do select the pious.»

Reported by al-Bukhari (5090) and Muslim (1466)

These are the reasons why both men and women marry. They look for wealth (which today also includes education and profession), lineage (which includes cultural background), beauty, and piety. Of all of them, the Prophet ﷺ emphasized piety. This does not mean that human love and attraction play no part in choosing a mate. And it does not mean that one should only consider the piety of their potential spouse and nothing else. The fact is there will be greater compatibility, tranquility, and happiness when there is mutual attraction. Al-Tibi, in his commentary on this *hadith*, wrote:

ليس زجرا عن رعاية الجمال بل هو زجر عن النكاح لأجل الجمال المحض مع الفساد في الدين.

شرح المشكاة للطيبي (ج٧ ص٢٢٧١)

It is not a condemnation of seeking beauty but a condemnation of marriage solely based on beauty when [the potential spouse is] impious.

Sharh al Mishkah (vol. 7, p. 2271)

There is further evidence to support this. Al-Mughirah ibn Shu'bah رضي الله عنه said:

قَالَ الْمُغِيرَةِ بْنِ شُعْبَةَ أَتَيْتُ النَّبِيَّ صَلَّى اللهُ عَلَيْهِ وَسَلَّمَ فَذَكَرْتُ لَهُ امْرَأَةً أَخْطُبُهَا فَقَالَ «اذْهَبْ فَانْظُرْ إِلَيْهَا فَإِنَّهُ أَجْدَرُ أَنْ يُؤْدَمَ بَيْنَكُمَا.»

رواه أحمد (١٨٤٢٤) والترمذي (١٠٨٧) وصححه الألباني (صحيح الترمذي ١٠٨٧)

I came to the Prophet ﷺ and told him about a woman I wanted to marry. He said, "Go and look at her, for that is more likely to bring greater agreement between the two of you."

Reported by Ahmad (18424) and al-Tirmidhi (1087) and al-Albani declared it sahih (*Sahih al-Tirmidhi*, 1087)

Marriage exists for emotional and physical fulfillment. If there is no attraction between the couple, their union may not serve its purpose. This is why the Prophet ﷺ asked Al-Mughirah to look at his potential spouse before finalizing his proposal. If he is happy with her piety and appearance—and she with his—then there will be greater harmony in their marriage. But if either of them sees something they dislike, it would be better and easier to terminate their plans at this point rather than after marriage.

The *Hadith* of the chapter has a background story that emphasizes love and attraction as a criterion for marriage.

جاء رجل إلى النبي صلى الله عليه وسلم فقال: يا رسول الله عندنا يتيمة قد خطبها رجلان موسر ومعسر وهي تهوى المعسر ونحن نهوى الموسر.

اللمع في أسباب ورود الحديث (ص٦٠)

A man came to the Prophet ﷺ and said, "O Messenger of Allah, we have an orphan girl and two men proposed marriage to her: one rich and the other poor. She likes the poor one, but we like the rich one."

Al-Luma' fi Asbab Wurud al-Hadith (p. 60)

It is after this inquiry of theirs that the Prophet ﷺ explained that marriage is best for lovers. He was stressing that attraction between the couple—when present—is to be considered in choosing a mate. If a heart is inclined to someone, marrying them gives it the greatest comfort and satisfaction. Conversely, forcing one to marry someone they dislike hurts the couple and leaves them regretful and dissatisfied.

But is attraction the most important criterion? And if not, what is? We see people marrying for different reasons, where what is important to one is not so for another. Not everyone is looking for money, beauty is subjective, and some only want to marry from within their culture while others resent it and marry outsiders. None of these reasons, however, is valid on its own until piety is included. Think about it. If a spouse has everything (beauty and wealth, for instance) but lacks piety, they would ruin the life of their spouse. When piety is absent, manners deteriorate. They will not observe the rights of their spouse as Allah commanded them. Their goals in life would be materialistic and displeasing to Allah. Because of this, they will drag their mate to Hell. But if a spouse has piety and nothing else—a highly unlikely scenario—they would at least guide their mate to Jannah. In addition, their love of Allah would sublimate their character and invite justice and mercy into their behavior. This is why piety is the first and most important condition, and why its absence is disastrous. Once piety is secured, one can seek other qualities that are important to them.

The challenge, however, is how to include what Allah loves in our choices. How do we put piety first? Many of us are primarily seeking physical beauty, and it happens to be the first thing that attracts us to others. Some are attracted to kindness or a sense of humor. This, still, is not piety. Extended interactions (physical and virtual) turn an attraction into feelings of love. When these feelings intensify, they leave no space in the heart for what Allah loves. Hence, we end up marrying whom we are attracted to with no consideration for righteousness. With that choice, our love diverges from Allah's love. And we pay for it later.

We must weld what we love to Allah's love. Even though what we like is important, it is not as essential as the love of Allah. And we have to believe this and practice it every day. We have to grow the love of Allah in our hearts so that it is strong enough to eclipse other loves and desires. When Allah's love is strong, we can subordinate other loves and desires to it. This does not mean, however, that we need to abandon our personal preferences altogether. No! It just means that we will not let our desires and impulses run our lives without giving thought to anything else. It means that if I am attracted to someone beautiful, but they are impious, I will decide right then that they are not the one for me. And if I am not going to marry them, I will put some physical distance between us, avert my gaze, and stop indulging in fantasies about them. With time, this will go away. It means that I know that Allah is dearer to me than anyone and anything else, and I will not lose Him because of anyone else. It means that I know that if I leave something for Allah's sake, that He will grant me something far better than what I left. It means that I know that Allah will give me what will make me truly happy—in this life and the next—when I follow His guidance. If this is firmly planted in the hearts, it will make choosing what is pleasing to Allah easier. Once we set piety as the most important quality in a potential mate, we can also look for beauty, humor, or any other appealing feature. Yes, this, at times, will mean that I will not marry that supermodel or multimillionaire. But we do not need supermodels or multimillionaires to be happy.

Premarital attraction is not the same as postmarital love. Premarital attraction is loving an idea. We imagine them to be one thing, and we fall in love with our construction and imagined reality. But you are not going to know the entire person until you live with them, until you see good and bad times together. Anything before that is pretense. Today, some have premarital relations and live with each other to test their compatibility. This choice, of course, shuns any blessing from Allah, and so is never an option for one who wants Allah's love. A human being is not a car that you test drive to see if you like it. The Islamic etiquettes of engagement provide the proper channels for couples to get to know each other before marriage. But the point here is that you will never know someone until you spend a few years with them. And that relationship is not the same as your premarital attraction and fantasies. Love grows after marriage and evolves into something bigger and more profound. This is why it is crucial not to be trapped by notions of romantic love that we inherit from movies and novels. Love is more complicated than that, and it is much, much deeper than that.

It is also true that love is not the basis of all marriages. 'Umar ibn al-Khattab رَضِيَ ٱللَّهُ عَنْهُ said:

قال عمر بن الخطاب رضي الله عنه: أَقَلُّ الْبُيُوتِ الَّذِي يُبْنَى عَلَى الْحَبِّ وَلَكِنَّ النَّاسَ يَتَعَاشَرُونَ بِالْإِسْلَامِ وَالْإِحْسَانِ.

مساوئ الأخلاق للخرائطي (ص٨٩)

The fewest of all homes are built on love. But people live together with Islam and kindness.

Masawi' al-Akhlaq by al-Khara'itiy (p. 89)

The background of this perceptive comment was a man asking his wife if she loved him. She thought it was best to be honest and let him know that she did not. 'Umar رَضِيَ اللَّهُ عَنْهُ did not like what she did. He wanted her to lie and say that she loved him. It is a harmless lie that the Prophet ﷺ allowed. But what was most important was his assessment of what keeps couples together. Not all homes have love, he said. A couple may marry out of love and then lose it. Or they did not marry for love and were not able to develop it. In either case, should they divorce because they are not in love? 'Umar رَضِيَ اللَّهُ عَنْهُ explained that companionship is greater than that. People stay together to support each other, for religious reasons, and for the good that they see in the other person. We may not call this love, but it is a strong bond that fulfills much of our emotional and physical needs. If every couple needed to be romantically in love like Romeo and Juliet to stay married, many would divorce. Then what happens to them? What happens to the children? What happens if you sacrifice a good spouse for the sake of love that you never find? 'Umar رَضِيَ اللَّهُ عَنْهُ was not asking anyone to stay married if they were sad and miserable. He was pointing out that there are other reasons to remain married besides love. Romantic love is not everything.

Ishq and soulmates

Most of us have watched movies and read novels that valorize romantic love. In fact, it is likely to be the most popular entertainment trope. Whether it is tragic love, unrequited love, or love that conquers all the odds, the idea of finding your ultimate love—your soulmate—is very powerful. And it sells, which is why it is used so often. It is clear that the idea resonates with many of us. And it is not surprising. We are all looking for love. But love in the entertainment industry is a for-profit-product. It is not intended to help us understand or find true love.

The idea of a soulmate—the one person in the world you need to be complete—may have its origins in philosophy. Or maybe philosophers came up with it to explain why some people fall in love. Either way, some philosophers speculated that a soul gets split in half before entry to earth, with each half occupying a different body. For this soul to be complete again, it must unite with its other half or remain forever restless (see *al-Zahrah* by Ibn Dawud al-Dhahiri, p. 53 and *Mukhtasar Tawq al-Hamamah*, by Ibn Hazm pp. 142–143). In Plato's *Symposium* (pp. 22–24), Aristophanes presented a similar view. Humans, he explained, had originally two faces, four hands, and four legs. Zeus, angry with humans, split them in half. Therefore, humans cannot be complete until they once again unite with their other half. It is an entertaining story. But, of course, it is not true. Yet the idea of a soulmate—an all-consuming love that sweeps you off your feet and changes your entire life—is powerful. And with that comes the valorization of sacrificing everything for the sake of your true love, even your life. Dying for love rises to a modern-day martyrdom at par with dying for any noble cause. Movies sell this, we watch it, and we begin to believe it.

This type of excessive love is called Ishq in Arabic. *Appendix I* discusses the aptness of this term when referring to Allah. But it is still problematic when we apply it to humans. Ibn al-Qayyim رَحِمَهُ ٱللَّهُ wrote about Ishq:

هَذَا مَرَضٌ مِنْ أَمْرَاضِ الْقَلْبِ...وَعِشْقُ الصُّوَرِ إِنَّمَا تُبْتَلَى بِهِ الْقُلُوبُ الْفَارِغَةُ مِنْ مَحَبَّةِ اللَّهِ تَعَالَى الْمُعْرِضَةُ عَنْهُ الْمُتَعَوِّضَةُ بِغَيْرِهِ عَنْهُ فَإِذَا امْتَلَأَ الْقَلْبُ مِنْ مَحَبَّةِ اللَّهِ وَالشَّوْقِ إِلَى لِقَائِهِ دَفَعَ ذَلِكَ عَنْهُ مَرَضَ

عِشْقِ الصُّوَرِ وَلِهَذَا قَالَ تَعَالَى فِي حَقِّ يُوسُفَ ﴿كَذَلِكَ لِنَصْرِفَ عَنْهُ السُّوءَ وَالْفَحْشَاءَ إِنَّهُ مِنْ عِبَادِنَا الْمُخْلِصِينَ﴾ [يوسف: ٢٤] فَدَلَّ عَلَى أَنَّ الْإِخْلَاصَ سَبَبٌ لِدَفْعِ الْعِشْقِ وَمَا يَتَرَتَّبُ عَلَيْهِ مِنَ السُّوءِ وَالْفَحْشَاءِ الَّتِي هِيَ ثَمَرَتُهُ وَنَتِيجَتُهُ فَصَرْفُ الْمُسَبَّبِ صَرْفٌ لِسَبَبِهِ وَلِهَذَا قَالَ بَعْضُ السَّلَفِ الْعِشْقُ حَرَكَةُ قَلْبٍ فَارِغٍ يَعْنِي فَارِغًا مِمَّا سِوَى مَعْشُوقِهِ.

زاد المعاد (٢٤٤-٢٤٦)

It is one of the diseases of the heart...Having Ishq of [beautiful] images is only the affliction of hearts that are empty of Allah's love, that have turned away from Him, and that had sought a substitute for Him. If the heart were filled with Allah's love and longing to meet Him, this would push away the disease of Ishq of images. This is why Allah said about Yusuf, ﴿Such We have done to keep away evil and indecency away from him. He is of our sincere servants﴾ [Yusuf: 24]. This is evidence that sincerity protects from Ishq and its consequent evil and indecency, which are its fruits and end results. Protection from the effect is also protection from the cause. And this is why some of the pious predecessors said, "Ishq is the movement of an empty heart," meaning empty of everything else except what they have Ishq for.

Zad al-Ma'ad (pp. 244–246)

Ibn al-Qayyim رَحِمَهُ ٱللَّهُ, among other scholars, considered extreme romantic love a sickness, not a virtue. And it is not difficult to understand why. All hearts are created to love, and we saw before that love is the strongest and most basic human emotion. As such, the heart must love, and it will tirelessly seek love until it finds it. What the heart is looking for, in essence, is the ultimate love, the missing piece that can make it complete. Only Allah can respond to the needs of the heart. No human has the capacity to play that role. A human cannot grant the security the heart needs, answer all its questions, remove all its anxieties, and give it lasting comfort. The heart knows that it is temporal and thus needs the comfort of loving an eternal that does not disappear. When the heart is separated from its love, it dies. And all earthly love is destined to end. So, only the love of the Eternal could cure the heart. Allah is what the heart is seeking, what it needs, and what will give it peace.

Now, when the heart is empty of Allah's love, it will ache for any love to fill its void. When it admires a beautiful human and is sexually attracted to them, the heart will latch onto them and give them all its love. Like someone who is desperately hungry, the heart will voraciously consume this love. But this meal will make it sick. As this love dominates the heart, it will climb to the position reserved for Allah. And so, one will obey the dictates of this love, committing any *haram* for its sake. When love grows big enough, it can literally enslave the heart. Ibn al-Qayyim رَحِمَهُ ٱللَّهُ said:

فَالْإِنْسَانُ عَبْدُ مَحْبُوبِهِ كَائِنًا مَنْ كَانَ.

الجواب الكافي (ص١٨١)

The human is a slave to whom they love, no matter who they are.

Al-Jawab al-Kafi (p. 181)

This takes place when it becomes our ultimate concern and love: we love it more than anything else. Its signs are unmistakable. We live for it, do everything for it, and are constantly thinking about it. It is the thing that makes us happy or sad. This extreme love competes with the love of Allah and prevents it from coming back. This is why that type of love is a disease. It is also agonizing for both body and soul. When one is so attached yet the object of their love—by nature—is unfulfilling, they will be tormented by what they love. When you love someone excessively, but they do not love you back or do not love you as much as you love them; when you love them, but they leave you, willingly or unwillingly; when you love them, and they use the power they have over you to hurt you—this love that is supposed to comfort you brings you pain instead. We cannot ask from a human what they cannot give. No human can love you forever, no human can stay with you forever, and no human can make all your worries go away.

Ishq is a false substitute, a weakness, not an ideal. Ibn al-Qayyim رَحِمَهُ ٱللَّهُ interpreted the "evil" in Surah Yusuf *ayah* 24, quoted above, as *Ishq* and "indecency" as fornication (*al-Fawa'id*, p. 81). Those with *Ikhlas* (sincerity) are saved from it because they surrendered their hearts to Allah, and they seek no greater love than His. Ibn al-Qayyim رَحِمَهُ ٱللَّهُ wrote:

فَلَا يُمْكِنُ أَنْ يَجْتَمِعَ فِي الْقَلْبِ حُبُّ الْمَحْبُوبِ الْأَعْلَى وَعِشْقُ الصُّوَرِ أَبَدًا بَلْ هُمَا ضِدَّانِ لَا يَتَلَاقَيَانِ بَلْ لَا بُدَّ أَنْ يُخْرِجَ أَحَدُهُمَا صَاحِبَهُ فَمَنْ كَانَتْ قُوَّةُ حُبِّهِ كُلُّهَا لِلْمَحْبُوبِ الْأَعْلَى الَّذِي مَحَبَّةُ مَا سِوَاهُ بَاطِلَةٌ وَعَذَابٌ عَلَى صَاحِبِهَا صَرَفَهُ ذَلِكَ عَنْ مَحَبَّةِ مَا سِوَاهُ وَإِنْ أَحَبَّهُ لَمْ يُحِبَّهُ إِلَّا لِأَجْلِهِ أَوْ لِكَوْنِهِ وَسِيلَةً إِلَى مَحَبَّتِهِ أَوْ قَاطِعًا لَهُ عَمَّا يُضَادُّ مَحَبَّتَهُ وَيُنْقِصُهَا وَالْمَحَبَّةُ الصَّادِقَةُ تَقْتَضِي تَوْحِيدَ الْمَحْبُوبِ.

الجواب الكافي (ص١٨١-١٨٢)

> It is impossible for the love of the Highest Beloved and for *Ishq* of [beautiful] images to unite in a heart: they are opposites and they never meet. One of them has to expel the other. If one's love is fully dedicated to the Highest Beloved—whom other than His Love is false and tormenting—that will protect them from loving someone other than Him. And if they love another, they only love them for His sake, or because it is a means to His Love, or because it removes an obstacle to His Love or what decreases it. And true love requires the Tawhid (oneness) of the Beloved.
>
> *Al-Jawab al-Kafi* (pp. 181–182)

The sincere—like everyone else—love their spouses, children, families, friends, and so on. But unlike those afflicted with

Ishq, they do not allow human love to dominate their hearts to the extent that it becomes the love of their life. Allah is the love of their lives. Ibrahim عَلَيْهِ ٱلسَّلَامُ was willing to sacrifice his only son, Isma'il عَلَيْهِ ٱلسَّلَامُ to please Allah. This is a son that he got after years of waiting and praying. Allah did not want Isma'il عَلَيْهِ ٱلسَّلَامُ to die. He wanted Ibrahim عَلَيْهِ ٱلسَّلَامُ to put Allah first, before the dearest human to him. The sincere do not live and die for a human being. No human has the all keys to their happiness. No human can come between them and Allah.

Ishq starts small. It begins with a glance, an admiration, and then a gaze. It grows stronger the longer we stay close to them, especially if alone with them. And it intensifies with conversations, texting, touching, and fantasizing about being intimate with them. The inability to be with the object of one's *Ishq* leads to increased longing, greater obsession, and physical sickness out of sadness and desperation. When one is afflicted with *Ishq*, the only thing they want is to be close to the object of their obsession. If they surrender to their urges and commit *haram*, their problems multiply. And if they do not, they are tormented with desire. *Ishq* is an awful trap. But, fortunately, there is treatment.

Ishq, as we have seen, stems from weakness in loving Allah. The heart is empty of Allah's love, so other loves can easily dominate it. The treatment has to proceed on two fronts: strengthening the love of Allah and weakening the hold of *Ishq*. But we must be ready for a protracted battle, when needed. This disease is an addiction, and it may take a while, and all that we have to escape it. We have to be serious about seeking the cure. If you do not have it, take precautions so that it does not afflict you. This requires taking the following steps to increase our love for Allah and to weaken the likelihood of *Ishq*.

Steps for increasing the love of Allah:

1. Get to know Allah better. The more you know Him, the more that you will love Him.
2. Worship Him more. In extreme cases, devote extended

time for worship. For instance, spend Ramadan (especially the last Ten Nights) in the mosque. Travel for Umrah and spend most of your time in the Haram, praying to Allah to save your heart.

3. Read the Quran and contemplate its meaning
4. Make plenty of du'a for Allah to grant you His love.
5. Remind yourself that only the love of Allah can make you happy.
6. Read the biographies of great Muslims who devoted their lives to Allah and sacrificed so much for His sake.
7. Keep the company of pious Muslims so they would remind you of what is important and help you use your time wisely.

Steps for weakening Ishq:

1. Marry the one you love if they are a good potential spouse. If not, start thinking about marrying someone else.
2. Distance yourself from the object of your *Ishq* if you cannot marry them and do not indulge in fantasies about them.
3. Keep yourself busy with useful work.
4. Lower your gaze and do not look at *haram*.
5. Ask Allah fervently and repeatedly to assist you.
6. Stop listening to music. It only inflames the desire, endlessly talks about love, and sells fantasies that you do not need at this moment.
7. Stop watching movies. They glamorize and exaggerate physical beauty and will weaken your resolve.
8. Ponder the fact that each human is flawed and will decay and die. When you are obsessed with someone, you have an idealized image of them. So, think about their human flaws. Remember also that they will die and leave you. When you start seeing them as the imperfect humans we all are, they will not have such control over you.

The Prophet ﷺ said:

«أتاني جبريلُ فقال: يا مُحمَّدُ عِشْ ما شِئتَ فإنَّك مَيِّتٌ وأحْبِبْ من شِئتَ فإنَّكَ مُفارِقُه واعمَل ما شِئتَ فإنَّك مَجْزِيٌّ بِهِ واعلَم أنَّ شرفَ المؤمنِ قيامُه باللَّيلِ وعِزُّه استِغناؤُه عن النّاسِ.»

رواه الطبراني في المعجم الأوسط (٤٢٧٨) والبيهقي في شعب الإيمان (١٠٥٤١) وحسنه الألباني لغيره (صحيح الترغيب ٧٢٦)

«Jibril came to me and said, "O Muhammad, live as long as you wish, for you will die. Love whomever you wish, for you will leave them. Do whatever you want, for you will be requited for it. And know that the believer's honor is in praying at night, and their strength is in not needing people."»

Reported by al-Tabarani in *al-Mu'jam al-Awsat* (4278) and al-Bayhaqi in *Shu'ab al-Iman* (10541). Al-Albani declared it hasan li-ghayrihi (*Sahih al-Targhib*, 726)

If we heed this hadith, we will know that every love will end except the love of Allah. No love then, except His love, should have power over us. Contemplate the reality of every other love, and it will dawn on you.

9. Consider that *Ishq* is stopping you from reaching the love of Allah, the greatest joy of this life and the next.

As long as you are striving, Allah will assist you. As long as you are trying, Allah will reward you. And you will overcome this addiction and free your heart from it. Start praying to Allah and turning to Him, and you will see the difference insha-Allah.

Forbidden attraction

An attraction could be forbidden because it is excessive, which is the *Ishq* that we discussed. It could also be forbidden because of the one we are attracted to.

We may be attracted to a member of the opposite sex that we cannot marry. The obstacle may be economic, social or cultural. It may be an unrequited attraction, or they may already be married. Whatever the reason, there is no possible way to be with them. Some will fall in love but not have the opportunity to get married, out of either economic pressure or particular circumstances that do not allow it. In both scenarios, there is an attraction but no marriage outlet. Some could be attracted to members of the same sex. We read in classic books in sections on *Ishq* that some men were attracted to younger men and adolescents and fell in love with them. It is possible to be attracted to anyone and even love them. The question is: what do we do with these feelings?

If we accept that love is an absolute good, that we should follow our hearts no matter where they take us, and that everyone deserves to be happy, we will tell everyone to go and be with the one they love. But if we believe that not all love is good and appropriate (e.g. is stalking someone an appropriate form of love?), then love must fulfill certain conditions to be called good. If we believe in Allah and His revelation, there will be no one better than Him to tell us whom to love and how.

What do we do if we find ourselves attracted to someone that we are not supposed to be with? Or there are no *halal* options for us? This attraction, this love, would be our test. And life is full of tests. In this test, Allah forbade something, but we desperately want it. Either we put our earthly love first or put the Greatest Love in existence above it. Sacrificing for Allah is the mark of those who love Him. And we all have to make that choice, sooner or later. All of us face that test. Some of us have greater tests than others; this is true. But the greatest tests are reserved for the best among us.

The only choice is to leave what you love for what Allah loves. If you cannot overcome the feelings you have for them, you can at least stay away from *haram*. I know it is difficult. And I know you can find those who will tell you to do what you feel is right. And I know that this could bring you immediate happiness. But I promise you that this happiness will not last. And I promise you that Allah is better than your friends, your earthly love, and everyone you have ever met. And I promise you that if you stay faithful to Him, He will give you much more than what you give up for His sake. I ask Allah to fill your life with love and *Iman*, and to bless you with loving Him more than anyone else.

HADITH THIRTY TWO

الحديث
الثاني والثلاثون

Sin kills love

قَالَ رَسُولُ اللهِ ﷺ «وَالَّذِي نَفْسُ مُحَمَّدٍ بِيَدِهِ مَا تَوَادَّ اثْنَانِ فَفُرِّقَ بَيْنَهُمَا إِلَّا بِذَنْبٍ يُحْدِثُهُ أَحَدُهُمَا.»

رواه أحمد (٥٣٥٧) وصححه الألباني (صحيح الترغيب ٢٢١٩)

The Messenger ﷺ said, «By the One in whose Hand is my soul, no two love each other and then are separated in discord except that it was because of a sin that one of them committed.»

Reported by Ahmad (5357) and al-Albani declared it sahih (Sahih al-Targhib, 2219)

Commentary

Loving and obeying Allah enhance and secure love. Sin, on the other hand, destroys it. Allah's love is the best way to fix and save our relationships.

Love is connected to Allah

We can think of love as a rope between us and Allah: one end with Allah and the other us. As long as we hold on to that rope, love will flow to us from Allah. If we let go of it, we let go of love itself.

In search for love, humans speculate about its reasons and

obstacles. We want others to love us—which is natural—so we do what we can to please them and win their approval. We also learn from experience what not to do in order to keep their love. But not all that we learn and do for the sake of love is good. We compromise when we should not, and break our moral codes to keep others happy. The pressure of love is strong, and it can make our moral outlook hazy. It is thus important to understand how love develops and dies. If love is so fundamental to our lives, learning how to nurture it is fundamental too.

We have seen before that Allah is the source of all love. He made us conscious beings capable of understanding and experiencing love. And this, by the way, is one of the greatest blessings we have received: to go from nothing to sentient beings, and not any sentient beings but ones with high order thinking and complex emotions. If we experience love, it is because of Allah. And He grants this favor to all humans, enabling us to feel the joy of love. And it is based on their experience of earthly love that humans begin to understand the greater love of Allah and how transcendent and different it is. When Allah reveals who He is to us, we are able to turn our capacity for love towards Him, and with that experience love at an extraterrestrial level. It is with the love of Allah that we reach our fullest potential of love, and it is through loving Allah that we understand what to love and how.

The *Hadith* of the chapter is an essential piece in the jigsaw of love. Sometimes, we are puzzled by the loss of love. Why does it fizzle out? Why does so-and-so dislike me now after we have been so close? Why do I not feel the same for so-and-so as I did before? Or maybe the presence of love is what is puzzling: how come there is love here but not there? There are, of course, social reasons for the flourishing of love and its decline, and these are important to keep in mind. Some of what the previous *hadiths* recommended—like spreading Salam and gift-giving—are examples of these social promoters of love. But there are spiritual—less visible—reasons that are as important, if not more so. And this is where the *Hadith* comes in. It tells us that love is lost because of sin. And since no one will be able to figure this out on their own until Allah tells them, we are very fortunate to learn this *Hadith* from the Prophet ﷺ.

Sin is akin to letting go of the rope that is between us and Allah. This rope is mentioned in the Quran when Allah said:

وَٱعْتَصِمُوا۟ بِحَبْلِ ٱللَّهِ جَمِيعًا وَلَا تَفَرَّقُوا۟ ... ﴿١٠٣﴾

And all of you hold firmly to the rope of Allah and do not divide.

Ali 'Imran (Q3:103)

This rope is Allah's revelation and His obedience. It is what brings you closer to Allah and His love. Now, pause a little and ponder what the *ayah* is asking us to do and its necessary consequences. It is asking us all to come together, to hold on to the purity and edification of Allah's Words, and to do our best not to divide. The necessary outcome of this collective activity is love. And this is why Allah continues the *ayah* by reminding us of this blessing when He said:

...وَٱذْكُرُوا۟ نِعْمَتَ ٱللَّهِ عَلَيْكُمْ إِذْ كُنتُمْ أَعْدَآءً فَأَلَّفَ بَيْنَ قُلُوبِكُمْ فَأَصْبَحْتُم بِنِعْمَتِهِۦٓ إِخْوَٰنًا وَكُنتُمْ عَلَىٰ شَفَا حُفْرَةٍ مِّنَ ٱلنَّارِ فَأَنقَذَكُم مِّنْهَا... ﴿١٠٣﴾

And remember the blessing of Allah upon you when you were enemies, and He brought your hearts together and became—by His grace—brothers, and you were on the edge of the pit of Fire, and He saved you from it.

Ali 'Imran (Q3:103)

Love is the normal corollary of obeying Allah. The enmity between the Companions disappeared when Islam brought them closer together. Those who come closer to Allah, the source of all love, will receive love. Allah said:

إِنَّ ٱلَّذِينَ ءَامَنُوا۟ وَعَمِلُوا۟ ٱلصَّٰلِحَٰتِ سَيَجْعَلُ لَهُمُ ٱلرَّحْمَٰنُ وُدًّا ﴿٩٦﴾

Those who believe and do good deeds, Allah will grant them love.
Maryam (Q19:96)

This is why Islam cannot exist without love. How can it be loveless when the worship of Allah is all based on love? How can it be loveless when those whom Allah loves are spreading love: they love people, and people love them. Love originates with Allah, and the believers transmit it to encompass all. Allah's love reaches everything.

But when we drop our end of the rope, we let go of the source of love. Loss of love is the consequence and the aftermath of sin. We previously discussed that Shaytan aims to divide people and spread hatred among them, the opposite of what Allah intends. As long as people hold firmly to Allah's rope, they will leave no space for Shaytan's plots and interventions. But when they turn away from Allah, they become defenseless. Left exposed, Shaytan manipulates their thoughts and emotions, ignites the worst in them, and sets them against each other to rip each other apart. Hatred is the goal of Shaytan and the weakness of those who listen to him. Hatred is never the outcome of Allah's revelation. In fact, the only way to foil the plan of Shaytan—as the first Islamic generation did—is to embrace Islam in full and allow it to cleanse us of selfishness and greed.

The good news in the *Hadith* is that if two love each other for Allah's sake, Allah will not separate them as long as they obey Him. Their love and friendship will grow more beautiful as they continue to please Allah. They will get to taste in this life a sample of the joy of Heaven, where its people enjoy each other's company with pure love for each other.

Before we move on to the next point, there is a question we need to answer: why do non-Muslims have love? If the *Hadith* is saying that sin separates lovers, why do non-Muslims still enjoy love among themselves? First, Allah did not deny the gift of love to anyone, just like food, drink, and air. Every human, no matter what they believe and how good or bad they are, enjoys Allah's favors, and experiencing love is one of them. Second, not all non-Muslims know Islam sufficiently to be held liable for their choices. Many non-Muslims have not received the true and full message of Islam. Because of this, Allah will be more lenient with their sins compared to people who know Allah well yet stubbornly choose to oppose Him. Third, if non-Muslims commit what Allah hates, their love will also suffer. If they drink and become alcoholics, if they gamble and are addicted to it, if they are unfaithful to their spouses, and if they engage in any criminal activity, they and their families will feel the terrible effects of these sins. In other words, Muslims and non-Muslims alike endanger the love they have when they turn away from Allah. Finally, love has both physical and spiritual foundations. The spiritual foundation is the pleasure of Allah in all of its forms and expressions. The physical foundation includes compatibility between the couple, mutual sympathy, forgiveness, overlooking each other's mistakes, listening to each other, and so on. If a couple manages to secure the physical foundation, they will maintain and nurture their love. But their love will not be as strong as Muslims who have the spiritual foundation as well. But a word of caution is needed here: the spiritual foundation alone is not enough. A man and a woman could be the two most pious in the city and yet remain incompatible. Unless the pious secure and work on the physical side too, their marriage and love will suffer.

How do we solve our problems?

The *Hadith* demystifies the loss of love. There are, of course, physical reasons why love declines and disappears. But the hidden side is elusive and difficult to understand and treat. Why does love go away when it should not, when all of its ingredients are present? And it is harder to understand this loss when it is sudden. But when we realize that sin plays a hidden part in undermining love, we have the medicine we need to protect our love and restore its beauty.

When we start noticing a strain in our relationships, the first thing we should do is take an inventory of our deeds. Have we committed a new sin or neglected a command of Allah? How are we with Allah, in general? Are we close to Him, or have we started to stray away? Is our *Iman* strong, or is it going through a rough patch? If our relationship with Allah is suffering, then this should be our clue that we should rectify our life immediately. The strain in our relationship may be a sign of a bigger underlying problem that we need to fix. If we take care of the more significant issue, the smaller one will rectify itself, insha-Allah. Musa al-Kadhim said:

قال موسى الكاظم: إذا تغير صاحبك عليك فاعلم أن ذلك من ذنب أحدثته فتب إلى الله من كل ذنب يستقم لك وده.

التنوير شرح الجامع الصغير (ج٩ ص٣٧٩)

If your friend['s love] changes, then know that it is because of a sin you committed. So, repent to Allah of all sins, and their love will return.

Al-Tanwir Sharh al-Jami' al-Saghir (vol. 9, p. 379)

Al-Muzani also said:

قال المزني: إذا وجدت من إخوانك جفاء فتب إلى الله فإنك أحدثت ذنبا وإذا وجدت منهم زيادة ود فذلك لطاعة أحدثتها فاشكر الله تعالى.

فيض القدير للمناوي (ج٥ ص٤٣٧)

If you find your friends disliking you, then repent to Allah because you committed a sin. And if you find an increase in love from them, then it is because of a good deed you did, so thank Allah the Highest.

Fayd al-Qadir (vol. 5, p. 437)

What is so beautiful about these sayings is that they help us relate what happens around us to our *Iman* and love of Allah. If something is going wrong in our lives, it prompts us to reexamine and improve our relationship with Allah. Of course, we still need to pursue physical solutions to any problem. But we do not solely focus on the physical side and forget the impact of our spiritual condition on our relationships. This is what distinguishes the believers and grants them greater insights into the universe. Things do not only happen because of physical and observable causes. There is a spiritual realm that is also highly impactful. So, when we receive human love, we do not attribute it all to our excellence and piety, but we realize that Allah was behind it. And we need to thank Him for it. Amazingly, all events in our lives—good or bad—are meant to bring us closer to Allah.

Martial issues

Marital discord is a subset of the loss of love discussed above. And what was said about the solution there applies to solving marital problems as well. I highlight it here, however, because this fact may escape the attention of spouses experiencing trouble in their marriage. The first impulse when there is a problem is to blame the other person and exonerate ourselves of all blame. This is the wrong strategy. The first step, and it should always be the first, is to review our relationship with Allah and improve it. And if you fix what is between you and Allah, He will fix what is between you and people or, at least, make fixing it a lot easier for you. The next step is to inspect how you behaved with your spouse, and rectify any mistakes you made. This will restore love and peace to your marriage insha-Allah. But if you want to wreck your marriage, do nothing but blame your spouse. I am not saying that they are not the one at fault. What I am suggesting is that blaming them takes you nowhere, and they will get defensive and attack you back. Then what? But if you want to save your marriage and your love—and not only save it but enhance it—follow the Prophetic solution. Love is about letting go of our egos and desiring the best for others, especially those closest to us. Love is about surrendering to Allah and loving what He loves. If I love Allah's forgiveness, I should love forgiving others. If I notice that people have flaws, it should not escape me that I am a flawed human and yet I still receive Allah's blessings and love each day. If Allah is generous with me, why I am so stingy with others? Give out some of what Allah gave you. Love for them what you love for yourself. Love as Allah loved you.

HADITH THIRTY THREE

الحديث الثالث والثلاثون

Be moderate in your love

قَالَ رَسُولُ اللهِ ﷺ «أَحْبِبْ حَبِيبَكَ هَوْنًا مَا عَسَى أَنْ يَكُونَ بَغِيضَكَ يَوْمًا مَا وَأَبْغِضْ بَغِيضَكَ هَوْنًا مَا عَسَى أَنْ يَكُونَ حَبِيبَكَ يَوْمًا مَا.»

رواه الترمذي (١٩٩٧) وصححه الألباني (صحيح الجامع ١٧٨)

The Messenger ﷺ said, «Love your beloved moderately, perhaps they will become hated to you someday. And hate whom you hate moderately, perhaps they will become your beloved someday.»

Reported by al-Tirmidhi (1997) *and al-Albani declared it sahih* (*Sahih al-Jami'*, 178)

Commentary

Love and hate tend to run to extremes, and they are destructive when they do. The love of Allah can anchor our emotions and temper our responses, saving us from bringing much harm to ourselves.

Guiding our emotions

Is it true that "all we need is love"? Is it the panacea to our ills? If we could only love each other—the saying goes—all of our problems would go away! Now, we can all agree on how transformative love can be. But is there not a difference between love as raw and untempered emotion and love enlightened by Allah's guidance and revelation?

We run into several problems when we recommend love as a self-sufficient solution. The object of our love, its intensity, duration, and what love entails are all left ambiguous. The fundamental questions of why we love and how we know we are in love remain unanswered. The assumption is that love is good and knows everything: once you fall in love, all of our questions will be answered, and all of our problems will disappear. It is romantically appealing because of the sweeping grand promises it makes and the warmth the promise of love provides. And if you are young or a hopeless romantic, you want to believe this.

But time and experience tell us otherwise, that love is insufficient on its own. We fall in love and then fall out of it. We believe we found our soulmate only to discover later that we were wrong (we discussed the flaws of the soulmate idea previously). Love can make us act foolishly, even destructively. Crimes of passion are committed in the name of love. Unattained love leads to desperation and resentment. Love on its own does not have all the answers.

Love as raw emotion needs guidance. If love is too intense, it could wither away. We could love someone so much that it ends up making us both weary. The way we express our love may also undermine it (e.g. suspicion arising from extreme jealousy). Or we could love the wrong person. Coveting someone's spouse could end a marriage. Love could also be laden with unrealistic expectations. I may fall in love with the idea of this person—what I want them to be—but not with the real person. Love has the potential for beauty, but it is also messy. If it is not supported by wisdom, it will disappoint.

Excessive love and hate

The nature of emotions is that they tend to run to extremes. And they run from one extreme to the other. We can love someone with all our hearts and then hate them with all our hearts. This is the vicissitude that the Prophet ﷺ was cautioning against in the *Hadith*. The instability of love, therefore, requires religious and experiential wisdom to balance it. If emotions run our lives and dictate our reactions without moderation, they can be very destructive. 'Umar ibn al-Khattab رَضِيَ اللَّهُ عَنْهُ said:

قَالَ عُمَرَ بْنَ الْخَطَّابِ رضي الله عنه: لَا يَكُنْ حُبُّكَ كَلَفًا وَلَا بُغْضُكَ تَلَفًا، فقال زيد بن اسلم: كَيْفَ ذَاكَ؟ قَالَ: إِذَا أَحْبَبْتَ كَلِفْتَ كَلَفَ الصبي وإذا أبغضت أحببت لصاحبك التلف.

صحيح الأدب المفرد (١٣٢٢)

"Let not your love be an obsession or your hate a perishment." Zayd ibn Aslam asked, "How is that?" He replied, "When you love, you obsess like a child; and when you hate, you wish for your companion to perish."

Sahih al-Adab al-Mufrad (1322)

The two seemingly opposite reactions are connected. The one who allows their love to grow into an obsession is the same person who allows their dislike to devolve into intense hatred. In both cases, emotions have the upper hand, not any religious concern for piety and justice. It is important for us to love in moderation. When an emotional attachment becomes an obsession, it blinds us and weakens us. We would see then only what we want to see, and we would do everything to get it. When we fail, these intense emotions are channeled as great frustration and anger. This bounce from love and admiration to hatred and the desire to harm is not healthy. This is not true love.

The story of Yusuf عَلَيْهِ السَّلَامُ beautifully encompasses the various types of love and attractions. It deserves a more reflective study and the contemplation of those who are interested in understanding love better. It teaches us, among many things, the harm extreme love leads to. It was the wife of al-'Aziz who fell in such obsessive love with Yusuf عَلَيْهِ السَّلَامُ. Allah said about her love for Yusuf عَلَيْهِ السَّلَامُ:

...قَدْ شَغَفَهَا حُبًّا... ﴿٣٠﴾

His love has filled her heart.
Yusuf (Q12:30)

Though she was married, she allowed her admiration for Yusuf عَلَيْهِ السَّلَامُ to grow beyond the proper bounds until she was willing to risk everything for it. But what did she do when Yusuf عَلَيْهِ السَّلَامُ rebuffed her advances? She threatened him with jail, suggested he be jailed to her husband, and that was where Yusuf عَلَيْهِ السَّلَامُ ended up for several years. Is this love? Or is it an obsession? Scholars suggested that her heart was empty of Allah's love and reverence since she was a disbeliever. Such a heart is open for the development of obsessive attachments and dependence. It also has no qualms about doing all it can to possess what it loves or destroy it when it cannot. The heart of the believer is the opposite of such a heart. In a devout heart, no love can grow bigger than the love of Allah, so no love can become an obsession, a life and death attachment. And since this heart reveres Allah, it will not violate Allah's bounds trying to secure what it loves. Such a heart realizes that if it loses its earthly love, there will always be a compensation for it from Allah, its Greatest Love. Therefore, the religious heart does not obsess in its attachments. Its emotions follow the guidance of Allah.

Extreme love is dangerous in the religious realm too. As we have explained when discussing *Ishq*, our love of Allah is the only love that has no limit to it (see *Appendix I*). Love for everyone else can be dangerously inflated. Exaggerating religious love is more destructive than the obsessive love we just discussed. Take, for instance, what 'Ali ibn Abi Talib رَضِيَ اللَّهُ عَنْهُ said:

قال عليٌّ بن أبي طالب رضي الله عنه: يَهْلَكُ فِيَّ رجلان مُفْرِطٌ في حُبِّي ومُفْرِطٌ في بُغْضِي.

حسنه الألباني في كتاب السنة لابن أبي عاصم (٩٨٤)

Two types of people will perish in relation to me: those who love me excessively and those who hate me excessively.

Al-Albani declared it hasan in *al-Sunnah* by Ibn Abi 'Asim (984)

In another narration, he explained where these extreme reactions would lead the two groups:

قال علي بن أبي طالب رضي الله عنه: لَيُحِبُّنِي قومٌ حتى يَدْخُلوا النارَ فِيَّ ولَيُبْغِضُنِي قومٌ حتى يَدْخُلوا النارَ في بُغْضِي.

صححه الألباني في كتاب السنة لابن أبي عاصم (٩٨٣)

Some people will love me until they enter Hell because of me, and some people will hate me until they enter Hell because of hating me.

Al-Albani declared it sahih in *al-Sunnah* by Ibn Abi 'Asim (983)

Every Muslim should love 'Ali ibn Abi Talib رَضِيَ اللَّهُ عَنْهُ. And this love, like loving the rest of the Companions, is a sign of *Iman*. But some overlove him until they exaggerate his virtues and accept false beliefs about him. Some believed he was God incarnate, and some ascribed infallibility to him and his children. Some only love him and his progeny but hate the remaining Companions. Consequently, they only accept religious guidance attributed to him and his children but reject all other *hadiths* and traditions. This excessive love is a severe deviation from Allah's revealed religion, and it leads to Hell. On the other extreme, the Khawarij hated 'Ali ibn Abi Talib رَضِيَ اللَّهُ عَنْهُ and waged war against him. One of them assassinated him. The Prophet ﷺ denounced in multiple *hadiths* both the killer of 'Ali ibn Abi Talib رَضِيَ اللَّهُ عَنْهُ and the group the killer belonged to.

If these extreme emotions remind us of anything, they should remind us of how people reacted to Jesus عَلَيْهِ السَّلَامُ. Some loved him so much that they considered him to be the son of God, while others loathed him so much that they called him a bastard and a charlatan. Both are serious offenses. But those who love Allah follow His guidance, not their desires and emotions. When they love, they love the way Allah wants them to, without exaggerations or falsifications. And if they hate, they do it in ways that do not upset Allah, without transgressions or falsifications. The hearts and bodies of the believers submit first and foremost to Allah. When they love, their earthly love does not exceed their divine love. They remember that their greatest love and attachment is to Allah.

Love changes

One of the shortsighted assumptions of the soulmate idea is that love and whom you love do not change. Love in that fairytale is imagined as a static and unchangeable reality: once you fall in love, you love forever. But we and whom we love change. Therefore, the relationship itself changes, evolves, and matures. And sometimes, love is not strong enough to survive these changes.

The Prophet ﷺ pointed to the instability of emotions to highlight the need for moderation. If you overlove, you could end up regretting it. And it is so if your hate is extreme. In both cases, you may say and do what you come to regret later. What would you do if you base your worth and happiness on someone's love, and they leave you? Would that not devastate you? How about confiding in someone whom you thought loved you, but they then turn against you and reveal all your secrets? Or suppose when you hated someone, you left no insult in your arsenal unused to let them know how you felt. Later, you found out it was based on a misunderstanding. Or maybe life brings you closer together, and you realize that you now need them. How could you both be friends after what was said and done? If we hate, we must assume that this feeling—and the reasons behind it—may not last. And if we love, we must not let this love be the center of our existence, the be-all and end-all of our happiness.

The following story is illustrative of the unpredictability of love. Ibn 'Abbas رَضِيَ اللَّهُ عَنْهُمَا said:

قال ابن عباس: إنَّ زوجَ بَرِيَرةَ عبدٌ أسودُ يقالُ لهُ مُغيثٌ كأنِّي أنظرُ إليهِ يطوفُ خلفَهَا يبْكي ودُموعُهُ تسيلُ على لحيتِهِ فقال النبيُّ صلَّى اللهُ عليهِ وسلَّمَ لعباسٍ «يا عباسُ ألا تعجَبْ منْ حبِّ مُغيثٍ بَرِيرةَ ومن بُغضِ بريرةَ مغيثًا؟» فقالَ النبيُّ صلَّى اللهُ عليهِ وسلَّمَ «لَو

رَاجَعْتِهِ» قالتْ: يا رسولَ اللهِ تَأْمُرُني؟ قالَ «إِنَّمَا أنَا أَشْفَعُ» قالت لا: حاجةَ لي فِيهِ.

رواه البخاري (٥٢٨٣)

The husband of Barirah was a slave called Mughith. It is as if I can see him now walking behind her crying, with his tears running down his beard. The Prophet ﷺ said to Al-'Abbas, «O 'Abbas, are you not amazed by the love of Mughith for Barirah and the hatred of Barirah for Mughith?» The Prophet of Allah ﷺ said to her, «Why don't you go back to him?» She said, "O Messenger of Allah, are you commanding me to do so?" He said, «I am only interceding.» She said, "I have no need of him."

Reported by al-Bukhari (5283)

She and her husband were slaves. She was freed before he was, and so had the option of staying with him or leaving him. She chose the latter. Notice that the Prophet ﷺ did not compel her to go back to her husband. He ﷺ understood that each human has their own capacity, and he cannot force her to love him or to stay with him. He could only advise. And he did not blame her husband for loving her or crying over her. He understood that this is not something he could control. He ﷺ could only observe and point to the disparity of emotions. If they turn to Allah, He will compensate both of them.

The one whom you love may stop loving you. We have no control over this. But we should not stop loving people because they may abandon us later. Such suspicion is unhealthy and is not the right way to live. What we can do, however, is be balanced in our attachments and detachments. And if we are hurt or confused, we turn to Allah for comfort and support.

This balance—which is based on an intimate relationship with Allah—allows us to love yet remain protected from loss. Ibn 'Umar رَضِيَ اللَّهُ عَنْهُمَا once was asked to divorce his wife. He described the incident:

قال ابنِ عمرَ رضي الله عنهما: كانت تحتي امرأةٌ أحبُّها وكان عمر يكرهُها فقال لي طلِّقْها فأبيتُ فأتى عمرُ رسولَ اللهِ ﷺ فذكر ذلك لهُ فقال لي رسولُ اللهِ ﷺ طلِّقْها.

رواه أبو داود (٥١٣٨) والترمذي (١١٨٩) وصححه الألباني (صحيح أبي داود ٥١٣٨)

I was married to a woman and I loved her, but 'Umar hated her. He asked me to divorce her, but I refused. So, 'Umar went to the Prophet ﷺ and mentioned it to him, and the Prophet ﷺ said to me, «Divorce her.»

Reported by Abu Dawud (5138) and al-Tirmidhi (1189) and al-Albani declared it sahih (*Sahih Abi Dawud*, 5138)

'Umar رضي الله عنه did not ask his son to divorce his wife because of a personal grievance. The Prophet ﷺ interfered and sided with 'Umar رضي الله عنه precisely because the issue was not personal but religious. Had Ibn 'Umar رضي الله عنهما allowed his love for his wife to cloud his judgment and dominate his life, he would not have been able to obey the Messenger ﷺ. This is the balance we need between divine and earthly loves.

Loving someone may not always be under our control. But the growth of this love, its expressions, and where it leads us are. When the Prophet ﷺ advised us against intemperate emotions, he knew the damage they could inflict. For love to be and remain healthy, it always needs Allah.

HADITH THIRTY FOUR

الحديث الرابع الثلاثون

You will be with the ones you love

قَالَ رَجُلٌ: يَا رَسُولَ اللهِ الرَّجُلُ يُحِبُّ الْقَوْمَ وَلَمْ يَبْلُغْ عَمَلَهُمْ؟ فَقَالَ رَسُولُ اللهِ ﷺ «الْمَرْءُ مَعَ مَنْ أَحَبَّ» فَكَانَ أَنَسٌ إِذَا حَدَّثَ بِهَذَا الْحَدِيثِ قَالَ: اللهُمَّ فَإِنَّا نُحِبُّكَ وَنُحِبُّ رَسُولَكَ.

رواه أحمد (١٣٣٨٨) والبخاري (٦١٦٩) ومسلم (٢٦٤٠) وعند البخاري (٣٦٨٨) أن أنسًا قال: فَأَنا أُحِبُّ النَّبِيَّ صَلَّى اللهُ عَلَيْهِ وَسَلَّمَ وَأَبا بَكْرٍ وَعُمَرَ وَأَرْجُو أَنْ أَكُونَ مَعَهُمْ بِحُبِّي إِيَّاهُمْ وَإِنْ لَمْ أَعْمَلْ بِمِثْلِ أَعْمالِهِمْ

A man asked, "O Messenger of Allah, what if a man loves a people but was not able to match their deeds?" The Messenger ﷺ replied, «One will be with those whom they love.» When Anas رضي الله عنه would narrate this hadith, he would say, "O Allah, we love you and love your Messenger."

Reported by Ahmad (13388), al-Bukhari (6169), and Muslim (2640). Al-Bukhari (3688) reported that Anas said, "So, I love the Prophet ﷺ, Abu Bakr, and 'Umar. And I hope to be with them because of my love for them even though I did not do what they did."

Commentary

If we love the righteous, we will be with them in Jannah. If we love what Allah loves and love in ways pleasing to Him, He will not separate us from our beloveds on the Last Day.

With those that you love

When we love someone, we naturally want to be close to them. This takes different forms depending on whom we love. If it is familial love, we want to be around them to enjoy their company and make sure they are happy. When it is romantic love, we additionally desire physical intimacy with our spouses. At times, we can love friends as much family, providing emotional outlets and companionship. Love is the magnet that brings us together.

Emotional and physical proximity lead to spiritual and intellectual proximity. It is the unconscious/conscious adoption of the ideas, character, and behavior of the one we love and spend time with. The more you love someone, the more you like what they say and do. This appreciation, coupled with length of exposure, leaves an imprint on us. We begin to have the same stories, same inside jokes, same experiences, same expressions, and similar ideas. The congruity between lovers, though not always complete, is evident when you scan families and couples to examine their outlook on life, major life plans, and convictions. Love not only brings us physically closer but spiritually and intellectually as well.

The Prophet ﷺ announced in the *Hadith* the cohering effect of love. We are with those we love, he said, and it is so in many ways. When we admire someone, we tend to want to be like them and act like them. We usually copy and imitate those we love and admire. And it works in the other direction too: we tend to develop love and admiration for those that we imitate. Imitation brings the minds and bodies closer, and this, in turn, brings the hearts closer too. So, when the Prophet ﷺ said that we will be with those we love, he was right on many levels. People who love each other tend to get closer in heart, mind, and body. And as they were together on earth, they will be together on the Last Day.

Though the spirit of the *Hadith* is a glad tiding to the believers, it carries in it a warning too. You will be with those you love, the Prophet ﷺ said, no matter who they are. Ibn Hubayrah رَحِمَهُ ٱللَّهُ wrote commenting on this *Hadith*:

فإنه لم يقل المرء مع من أحب من الصالحين خاصة بل أطلقه وهذا عام يتناول الصالحين وغير الصالحين.

الإفصاح (ج٢ ص٧٣)

> He [i.e. the Prophet] did not say that one will only be with the pious whom they love. Instead, he was not specific. Therefore, it is general and includes the pious and the impious.
>
> *Al-'Ifsah* (vol. 2, p. 73)

If loving the pious brings one closer to them and to Jannah, loving the impious brings one closer to them and to Hell. And getting closer to Hell is not where any of us wants to be. And herein lies the warning in the *Hadith*: whom you love matters. The kind of person you want to be in this world is determined largely by the loves of your life. Your inner circle is the people who inspire you and shape your thoughts and plans. They are the same people who will determine where you will be in the next life. If Jannah is your destination, you will love and surround yourself with the pious. But if the impious are our crowd, then our heart will belong to them. And as we choose to be with them here, we will join them on the Day of Judgment. As love makes us one with another on earth, it will do the same in the next life.

One clear inference from the *Hadith* is that we have to be selective in our love, that we have control over our love. This is why we end up in the next life with the ones we love, suggesting responsibility for our choice. We discussed previously that certain aspects of love may be out of our control. I do not control what physical features or personality type I find appealing. But these are not the only determinants of love, and I am not helpless in front of them. Higher loves—mainly the love of Allah—outweigh inferior loves/attractions and guide them. If I find myself attracted to someone who is utterly wrong for me, I do have the means to stem this love at its onset. Distance, contemplating the harms of this love, *du'a*, and seeking better loves are all tools we can use to redirect our hearts. But allowing ourselves a second glance, striking a conversation, seeking them out, and thinking about them only feed our attraction. We have options. We have tools that can channel our emotions towards the pleasure of Allah.

Another inference from the *Hadith* is about acquiring love for the ones Allah loves. When you admire the pious, your heart will be with them. If your heart is not there yet, you can develop your love for them. How? By thinking about the benefits that this love will bring you—including the heavenly reward—and keeping their company. Time, effort, and *du'a* will bring their love to your heart. But when we find our hearts leaping towards the impious, we have to restrain them. Let me be honest. When we admire actors, singers, comedians, sports stars, and social media influencers and celebrities, who are we really admiring? The pious? Are they bringing us closer to Allah? Except for very few of them, what they do is displeasing to Allah. If we take them as our role models and idols, if we imitate them and fashion our lives after theirs, would that not be a sign of love? Would we not have willingly increased the love we have for them? And where is this going to put us on the Day of Judgment? With them, right? So, let us be honest with ourselves: do we want to be resurrected with them? If not, can we nurture love towards what Allah hates and still feel safe?

Loving the pious

The intentions, convictions, and attachments of the heart are its actions. They reflect the state of its *Iman* and wisdom, and are the basis for the actions of the body. Between the two, the actions of the heart are the more foundational and important (for more on this, see *Hearth Therapy* by the author). And none is more fundamental among the many actions of the heart than love. It is the basis for all other actions—internal and external—and it is their natural conclusion. We possess all other emotions because we love, and they all carry us towards what we love. Love is the motivation and destination of all actions.

The Prophet ﷺ distilled the reward of love in the *Hadith*. What do we gain when we love? The questioner in the *Hadith* saw that his actions were not up to the devotion of the righteous, yet he loved them. Will this love help? There may be a hint of concern in the question at the possibility of separation from the beloved. If I love Allah and the Prophet, will I ever be separated from them? Will I be separated from the righteous? From my family? Every lover agonizes over the possibility of separation. Now, if the distress was implicit in the *Hadith* of the chapter, it is not in the following *hadith*.

جَاءَ رَجُلٌ إِلَى النَّبِيِّ صَلَّى اللهُ عَلَيْهِ وَسَلَّمَ فَقَالَ: يَا رَسُولَ اللهِ وَاللهِ إِنَّكَ لَأَحَبُّ إِلَيَّ مِنْ نَفْسِي وَإِنَّكَ لَأَحَبُّ إِلَيَّ مِنْ أَهْلِي وَأَحَبُّ إِلَيَّ مِنْ وَلَدِي وَإِنِّي لَأَكُونُ فِي الْبَيْتِ فَأَذْكُرُكَ فَمَا أَصْبِرُ حَتَّى آتِيَكَ فَأَنْظُرُ إِلَيْكَ وَإِذَا ذَكَرْتُ مَوْتِي وَمَوْتَكَ عَرَفْتُ أَنَّكَ إِذَا دَخَلْتَ الْجَنَّةَ رُفِعْتَ مَعَ النَّبِيِّينَ وَإِنِّي إِذَا دَخَلْتُ الْجَنَّةَ خَشِيتُ أَنْ لَا أَرَاكَ فَلَمْ يَرُدَّ عَلَيْهِ النَّبِيُّ صَلَّى اللهُ عَلَيْهِ وَسَلَّمَ حَتَّى نَزَلَ جِبْرِيلُ بِهَذِهِ الْآيَةِ ﴿وَمَنْ يُطِعِ اللهَ وَالرَّسُولَ فَأُولَئِكَ مَعَ الَّذِينَ أَنْعَمَ اللهُ عَلَيْهِمْ مِنَ النَّبِيِّينَ وَالصِّدِّيقِينَ﴾ [النساء ٦٩]

رواه الطبراني في المعجم الأوسط (٤٧٧) وحسنه الألباني (السلسلة الصحيحة ٢٩٣٣)

A man came to the Prophet ﷺ and said, "O Messenger of Allah, I love you more than myself, I love you more than my family, and I love you more than my children. While I am at home, I remember you, and I cannot wait to come and see you. And when I think about my death and yours, I realize that when you enter Jannah, you will be raised with the Prophets. But if I enter Jannah, I fear that I may not see you." So the Prophet ﷺ did not reply until Jibril came down with this ayah, ﴿And whoever obeys Allah and the Messenger will be with those whom Allah blessed: the Prophets and Siddiqs.﴾ [Al-Nisa' 69]

Reported by al-Tabarani in *al-Awsat* (477) and al-Albani declared it hasan (*al-Silsilah al-Sahihah*, 2933)

First, let us give ourselves time to appreciate the question and the man who asked it. It is humbling to witness such intense love for the Prophet ﷺ. We may think that we love the Prophet and that we are super Muslims, but this *hadith* reminds us how far we have to go before we are at a fraction of the piety of the Companions. May Allah forgive our shortcomings, arrogance, and self-admiration. What comforts the hearts, however, is the answer: the promise of always being with those whom we love. There is no separation and no anxiety if Allah loves you and He immerses you in His mercy. The joy of this *Hadith* must enter every believer's heart. This was what happened with the Companions when they first heard it. Anas رَضِيَ اللهُ عَنْهُ said:

عَنْ أَنَسٍ رضي الله عنه قَالَ: كَانَ يُعْجِبُنَا أَنْ يَجِيءَ الرَّجُلُ مِنْ أَهْلِ الْبَادِيَةِ فَيَسْأَلَ رَسُولَ اللهِ صَلَّى اللهُ عَلَيْهِ وَسَلَّمَ فَجَاءَ أَعْرَابِيٌّ فَقَالَ: يَا رَسُولَ اللهِ مَتَى قِيَامُ السَّاعَةِ؟ وَأُقِيمَتِ الصَّلَاةُ فَصَلَّى رَسُولُ اللهِ فَلَمَّا فَرَغَ مِنْ صَلَاتِهِ قَالَ: «أَيْنَ السَّائِلُ عَنِ السَّاعَةِ؟» قَالَ: أَنَا يَا رَسُولَ اللهِ، قَالَ «وَمَا أَعْدَدْتَ لَهَا؟» قَالَ: مَا أَعْدَدْتُ لَهَا مِنْ كَبِيرِ عَمَلٍ صَلَاةٍ وَلَا صِيَامٍ إِلَّا أَنِّي أُحِبُّ اللهَ وَرَسُولَهُ فَقَالَ رَسُولُ اللهِ صَلَّى اللهُ عَلَيْهِ وَسَلَّمَ «الْمَرْءُ مَعَ مَنْ أَحَبَّ» قَالَ أَنَسٌ: فَمَا رَأَيْتُ الْمُسْلِمِينَ فَرِحُوا بَعْدَ الْإِسْلَامِ بِشَيْءٍ مَا فَرِحُوا بِهِ.

رواه أحمد (١٢٠١٣) والبخاري (٦١٧١)

We used to like it when a Bedouin man would arrive and ask the Messenger ﷺ. So, a nomad came and asked, "O Messenger of Allah, when will the Hour take place?" Then the

> Iqamah for the Salah was called, and the Messenger of Allah prayed. When he finished his Salah, he asked, «Where is the one who asked about the Hour?» The man replied, "It is me, O Messenger of Allah." He asked him, «What did you prepare for it?» He replied, "I did not prepare for it much praying or fasting except that I love Allah and His Messenger." Upon this, the Messenger ﷺ said, «One will be with those whom they love.» Anas said, "I did not witness the Muslims from the time they accepted Islam as happy with anything as they were when they heard this."
>
> Reported by Ahmad (12013) and al-Bukhari (6171)

They have not heard anything more promising since they accepted Islam. Loving Allah and His Prophet is a constant connection that all of us can have no matter how strong or weak our practice is. And we should never let go of this love as long as we are alive.

In essence, loving the Prophet ﷺ and the righteous is loving Allah. Not only is it a good deed, but it is also one of the best deeds that Allah loves. As was discussed, the goal of all of our worship is to inculcate Allah's love in our hearts. When this love inhabits the heart, it transforms it. It fills it with content, generosity, and humility. Having this heart keeps us connected to Allah, even when our physical worship is modest. When the man informed the Prophet ﷺ that he loved people with better deeds than his, he was explaining that he could not rise to the level of their devotion. But his heart was pious, happy with Allah, and close to Him. This internal devotion—love—is like a factory of good deeds that never stops running. And if one keeps producing this love, they will join the righteous whom they love, even if they do not have the same physical deeds. The piety and devotion of the heart is the fastest way to the love of Allah. One with modest worship—performing only the obligations and avoiding the prohibitions—and a devoted heart surpasses by leaps and bounds one with a troubled heart and much more physical worship. The goal is not actions with an empty heart. The goal is a loving heart that produces heartfelt worship.

Will loving the righteous grant us their rank in Jannah? There are two possibilities. The first is that Allah—out of his immense generosity—will unite us in Jannah even if we have fewer good deeds than they do. Love for the pious compensates the shortcomings in physical worship. This helps us appreciate the value of love and how priceless the worship of the heart is. The other possibility is that loving the righteous keeps one close to them, even if we are not at their very rank. So, those who love the Prophet ﷺ will get closer and closer to him in Jannah, but no one will receive his exact rank. In either case, love is a remarkable vehicle to Jannah. It carries people to it, elevates them in it, and keeps them with their beloveds. And the more intense and pure the love is, the higher one would go, getting closer and closer to whom they love.

It is highly recommended to love the righteous. Loving them means loving for Allah's sake, loving because they are pleasing to Him. It means staying close to them to learn from them, emulating their righteousness, and making *du'a* for them. And it must be done in ways pleasing to Allah. If one exaggerates their love (as discussed in *Hadith* Thirty Three), they will depart from Allah's love and be denied the company of the very same people they claim to love. What we love and how we love may not always be pleasing to Allah. We must love what Allah loves, the way Allah loves it. We should seek the path that Allah loves and make it our own. And for that, we must learn what Allah loves.

HADITH THIRTY FIVE

الحديث الخامس الثلاثون

Loving knowledge

عَنْ صَفْوَانَ بْنِ عَسَّالٍ رَضِيَ اللَّهُ عَنْهُ قَالَ: أَتَيْتُ النَّبِيَّ ﷺ وَهُوَ فِي الْمَسْجِدِ مُتَّكِئٌ عَلَى بُرْدٍ لَهُ أَحْمَرَ فَقُلْتُ لَهُ: يَا رَسُولَ اللهِ إِنِّي جِئْتُ أَطْلُبُ الْعِلْمَ، فَقَالَ «مَرْحَبًا بِطَالِبِ الْعِلْمِ إِنَّ طَالِبَ الْعِلْمِ لَتَحُفُّهُ الْمَلَائِكَةُ وَتُظِلُّهُ بِأَجْنِحَتِهَا ثُمَّ يَرْكَبُ بَعْضُهُمْ بَعْضًا حَتَّى يَبْلُغُوا السَّمَاءَ الدُّنْيَا مِنْ حُبِّهِمْ لِمَا يَطْلُبُ.»

رواه الطبراني في المعجم الكبير (٧٣٤٧٧) وابن عبد البر في جامع بيان العلم وفضله (١٦٢) وصححه الألباني (السلسلة الصحيحة ٣٣٩٧)

Safwan ibn 'Assal رَضِيَ اللَّهُ عَنْهُ said, "I came to the Prophet ﷺ while he was reclining in the masjid on his red cloak and said to him, 'O Messenger of Allah, I came to seek knowledge.' He said, «Welcome, O seeker of knowledge! The angels surround the seeker of knowledge and shade him with their wings, and they will pack on top of each other until they reach the lowest sky out of love for what he is seeking.»"

Reported by al-Tabarani in al-Mu'jam al-Kabir (73477) and Ibn 'Abd al-Barr in Jami' Bayan al-'Ilm wa Fadlihi (162). Al-Albani declared it sahih (al-Silsilah al-Sahihah, 3397)

Commentary

Islamic knowledge reveals who Allah is and leads to His love. Its seekers are distinctly close to Allah, the angels revere them, and they receive the prayers of all living creatures.

Spread cheer

Note the enthusiasm in the Prophet's ﷺ welcome. His words were full of joy. He warmly received Safwan and delighted him with the good news of Allah's reward. Pleasant and kind words inject love in the heart of the listener and encourage them to continue doing what Allah loves. When we motivate others to do good, we all come closer to Allah. And we have to do it especially with seeking knowledge. He ﷺ said:

«سَيَأْتِيكُمْ أَقْوَامٌ يَطْلُبُونَ الْعِلْمَ فَإِذَا رَأَيْتُمُوهُمْ فَقُولُوا لَهُمْ: مَرْحَبًا مَرْحَبًا بِوَصِيَّةِ رَسُولِ اللهِ صَلَّى اللهُ عَلَيْهِ وَسَلَّمَ واقْنُوهُم.»

قلت للحكم ما اقنوهم قال علموهم. رواه ابن ماجه (٢٤٧) وحسنه الألباني (صحيح سنن ابن ماجه ٢٤٧)

There will come to you people who will be seeking knowledge. When you see them, say to them, "Welcome, welcome O whom the Prophet ﷺ asked us to take care of," and teach them.

Reported by Ibn Majah (247) and al-Albani declared it hasan (*Sahih Sunan Ibn Majah*, 247)

Why such a heartwarming reception? Well, it speaks to the virtue of seeking knowledge, which we will see shortly. But it also stresses an attitude that we should develop: motivating and nurturing righteousness.

Doing the right thing in life is not easy. It requires sacrifice, and it often makes us unpopular. The truth is heavy. Allah described the Quran and said:

إِنَّا سَنُلْقِي عَلَيْكَ قَوْلًا ثَقِيلًا ﴿٥﴾

We will send down to you heavy words.
Al-Muzzammil (Q73:5)

They are heavy in multiple ways. They are deep, they are rich in meaning, they change anything they come in contact with, and they require sacrifice. Following the Quran is not easy, but it is the best thing for you. Abdullah ibn Mas'ud رضي الله عنه said:

قَالَ عَبْدُ اللَّهِ بن مسعود رضي الله عنه: الحَقُّ ثَقِيلٌ مَرِيءٌ وَالْبَاطِلُ خَفِيفٌ وَبِيءٌ وَرُبَّ شَهْوَةٍ سَاعَةٍ تُورِثُ حُزْنًا طَوِيلًا.

الزهد لهنّاد ابن السَّرِيِّ (ص٢٨٧)

The truth is heavy but healthful, and falsehood is light but diseased. And perhaps an hour's enjoyment leads to long sorrow.

Al-Zuhd by Hannad ibn al-Sarriyy (p. 287)

Everything worthwhile in life requires effort and sacrifice, and it is typically not as enticing as the trivial (think even of wholesome food vs. junk food). But there is a vast difference in the consequences. Humans, unfortunately, are superficial and keen to look for quick gratification. And this makes the truth heavy to adopt, heavy to carry, and heavy to defend. And so the followers of the truth may find themselves burdened and exhausted because of the weight they carry. Knowing this, we should not add to their burden. We must not complicate their lives and sadden them with frowns, harsh words, and mistreatment. We want to unburden them with smiles, encouraging words, and kindness. We should not become the straw that breaks the back of a righteous camel. Assist the righteous to spread righteousness. If you cannot assist them, at least do not harm them.

The *Hadith* has a profound lesson for us if we are trying to follow the truth and feel exhausted. There was no one with greater responsibility and burden than the Prophet ﷺ. Yet, we saw how cheerful he was when he received Safwan رضي الله عنه. This, by the way, was his disposition: he always had a smile on his face. He was cordial all the time. How could one with so much responsibility and worry be so cheerful and kind? The secret is his connection to Allah. Read the sixth *ayah* in Surah al-Muzzammil, the one right after the fifth *ayah* (quoted above). After Allah explained that He will send down heavy words to His Prophet, He spoke about worship, specifically night prayer. Go and read it. It is important. I mean it. Please go and read it. If you do, you will realize that the way to cope with the difficulty of carrying the truth is the worship of Allah. And the heavier the burden, the more worship we need.

I say this because many of us get stuck in the middle phase of carrying the truth. There are three main phases of this journey. The first one is excitement. At this stage, we are eager to spread the truth, teach, call people to Islam, and work on Islamic projects. We have ideas, plans, and are ready to change the world. This phase is beautiful but does not last for long. The second phase begins when we encounter the challenges that accompany what Allah loves, and we lose our enthusiasm, kindness, and patience. The burden makes it harder to smile or find joy in what we are doing. Exhausted, we become harsh, cynical, and disappointed. And it is a dangerous combination to carry the mantle of Islam and yet fail to represent it well. This misrepresentation chases people away and tarnishes the image of Islam itself. So, we have three options if we are at this stage. We can retreat and forget what Allah loves because it is too costly, we can be stuck and miserable, or we can advance to the third phase. In the last stage, we intensify our worship to come closer to Allah. We then uncover the joy of "working for Allah." The difficulties do not disappear, but Allah assists us in overcoming them. And when we feel how close Allah is, it becomes easier to smile and be kind no matter the hardship and worry. So, push until you reach this last stage. And whenever life pushes you back, resist it by marching forward. Fight the burdens of life with heartfelt worship.

Seeking knowledge

Right after obligatory worship, nothing is more beloved to

Allah than seeking knowledge. The famous Tabi'i Mutarrif ibn Abdullah al-Shikhir said:

قال مُطَرِّفِ بْنِ عَبْدِ اللَّهِ بْنِ الشِّخِّيرِ: فَضْلُ الْعِلْمِ خَيْرٌ مِنْ فَضْلِ الْعِبَادَةِ.

المدخل إلى السنن الكبرى للبيهقي (ص٣٠٤)

Extra knowledge is better than Extra worship.

Al-Madhkal ila al-Sunan al-Kubra by al-Bayhaqi (p. 304)

Al-Bayhaqi رَحِمَهُ ٱللَّهُ made this saying the title of one of the chapters in the book above. Under it, he added the saying of Ibn 'Abbas رَضِيَ ٱللَّهُ عَنْهُمَا:

قَالَ ابْنُ عَبَّاسٍ رضي الله عنهما: تَذَاكُرُ الْعِلْمِ بَعْضَ لَيْلَةٍ أَحَبُّ إِلَيَّ مِنْ إِحْيَائِهَا.

المدخل إلى السنن الكبرى للبيهقي (ص٣٠٤)

Discussing matters of knowledge for part of the night is more beloved to me than praying the whole night.

Al-Madhkal ila al-Sunan al-Kubra by al-Bayhaqi (p. 304)

This is so because seeking knowledge is an act of worship. Al-Zuhri رَحِمَهُ ٱللَّهُ made it clear when he said:

قَالَ الزُّهْرِيُّ: مَا عُبِدَ اللَّهُ بِمِثْلِ الْفِقْهِ.

المدخل إلى السنن الكبرى للبيهقي (ص٣٠٨)

Allah is not worshipped with anything like fiqh [i.e. knowledge].

Al-Madhkal ila al-Sunan al-Kubra by al-Bayhaqi (p. 308)

Many may not realize that seeking knowledge is valuable worship of Allah. But studying Islam teaches us what many other acts cannot. The superiority of this worship is what prompted a great scholar like al-Shafi'i رَحِمَهُ ٱللَّهُ to say:

قال الشَّافِعِيّ: طَلَبُ الْعِلْمِ أَفْضَلُ مِنْ صَلَاةِ النَّافِلَةِ.

المدخل إلى السنن الكبرى للبيهقي (ص٣١٠)

Seeking knowledge is better than voluntary Salah.

Al-Madhkal ila al-Sunan al-Kubra by al-Bayhaqi (p. 310)

He even went as far as saying:

قال الشَّافِعِيَّ: لَيْسَ بَعْدَ أَدَاءِ الْفَرَائِضِ شَيْءٌ أَفْضَلُ مِنْ طَلَبِ الْعِلْمِ، قِيلَ لَهُ: وَلَا الْجِهَادُ فِي سَبِيلِ اللَّهِ؟ قَالَ: وَلَا الْجِهَادُ فِي سَبِيلِ اللَّهِ عَزَّ وَجَلَّ.

المدخل إلى السنن الكبرى للبيهقي (ص٣١٠)

"After the performance of the obligations, there is nothing better than seeking knowledge." He was asked, "Not even Jihad for the sake of Allah?" He replied, "Not even Jihad for the sake of Allah."

Al-Madhkal ila al-Sunan al-Kubra by al-Bayhaqi (p. 310)

It is an honor to be connected to Islamic knowledge as a student or a teacher. When you do, you are engaged in one of the most superior acts in life.

قِيلَ لِعَبْدِ اللَّهِ بْنِ الْمُبَارَكِ: لَوْ قِيلَ لَكَ لَمْ يَبْقَ مِنْ عُمُرِكَ إِلَّا يَوْمٌ مَا كُنْتَ صَانِعًا؟ قَالَ: كُنْتُ أُعَلِّمُ النَّاسَ.

المدخل إلى السنن الكبرى للبيهقي (ص٣٠٩)

Abdullah ibn al-Mubarak was asked, "If you were informed that you have only one day to live, what would you do?" He replied, "I would teach people."

Al-Madhkal ila al-Sunan al-Kubra by al-Bayhaqi (p. 309)

Many when asked about their bucket lists—things they want to do before their death—would list travel, adventure, exotic food, and new experiences. Few would say teaching people or learning something new. But our pious predecessors understood the value of knowledge and spreading it. Therefore, they would choose it for their last days on earth.

Why does seeking knowledge have such high distinction? Because it is how we get to love Allah and attain His love. We cannot love what we do not know. We need revealed knowledge to understand who our Creator is. When we know Him in-depth, our love for Him increases. And the more we know Him, the stronger will our love will be. Allah said:

...إِنَّمَا يَخْشَى ٱللَّهَ مِنْ عِبَادِهِ ٱلْعُلَمَـٰٓؤُا۟ۗ... ﴿٢٨﴾

Only the learned are in awe of Allah.

Fatir (Q35:28)

Khashyah in the *ayah* is more than fear (*khawf*). It is fear coupled with veneration, and it is based on knowledge. Allah praised the truly learned who venerate Allah and fear Him, and they do so because they understand His Majesty and Power more than anyone else. This deep knowledge increases their love for Allah. And their love grows as their knowledge does.

Revealed knowledge also details what Allah loves. It tells us how to live the best life on earth, securing all benefits and avoiding all harm. It connects this life to the next, and what we love to what Allah loves. Making these informed choices guides us to Allah's love. And it is not possible to know all this unless Allah teaches us. Allah said:

...وَقَالُوا۟ ٱلْحَمْدُ لِلَّهِ ٱلَّذِى هَدَىٰنَا لِهَـٰذَا وَمَا كُنَّا لِنَهْتَدِىَ لَوْلَآ أَنْ هَدَىٰنَا ٱللَّهُۖ... ﴿٤٣﴾

And they will say, "Alhamdulillah who guided us to this, and we would not have been guided if Allah did not guide us."

Al-A'raf (Q7:43)

Learning is the means to Allah's love. And knowledge coupled with application is true guidance. There is nothing better than this on earth. And if one finds themselves on the path of learning and teaching, they have received the best favor and honor from Allah. The Prophet ﷺ said:

«مَن يُرِدِ اللَّهُ به خَيْرًا يُفَقِّهْهُ في الدِّينِ.»

رواه البخاري (٧١) ومسلم (١٠٣٧)

«When Allah desires good for someone, He gives them fiqh in religion.»

Reported by al-Bukhari (71) and Muslim (1037)

It is a sign of Allah's love and selection when He guides you to what He loves. If you are a seeker of knowledge—you can adopt this intention when reading this book—then appreciate this great gift which Allah chose for you. It is a sign of Allah's love.

On top of all of this, the Prophet ﷺ said:

«مَنْ سَلَكَ طَرِيقًا يَطْلُبُ فِيهِ عِلْمًا سَلَكَ اللهُ بِهِ طَرِيقًا مِنْ طُرُقِ الْجَنَّةِ وَالْمَلَائِكَةُ تَضَعُ أَجْنِحَتَهَا رِضًا لِطَالِبِ الْعِلْمِ وَإِنَّ الْعَالِمَ يَسْتَغْفِرُ لَهُ مَنْ فِي السَّمَاوَاتِ وَمَنْ فِي الْأَرْضِ وَالْحِيتَانُ فِي الْمَاءِ وَفَضْلُ الْعَالِمِ عَلَى الْعَابِدِ كَفَضْلِ الْقَمَرِ لَيْلَةَ الْبَدْرِ عَلَى سَائِرِ الْكَوَاكِبِ إِنَّ الْعُلَمَاءَ وَرَثَةُ الْأَنْبِيَاءِ إِنَّ الْأَنْبِيَاءَ لَمْ يُوَرِّثُوا دِينَارًا وَلَا دِرْهَمًا وَأَوْرَثُوا الْعِلْمَ فَمَنْ أَخَذَهُ أَخَذَ بِحَظٍّ وَافِرٍ.»

رواه أبو داود (٣٦٤١) وصححه الألباني (صحيح أبي داود ٣٦٤١)

«When one pursues a path to seek knowledge, Allah will lead them to a path of the paths of Jannah. The angels lower their wings for the seeker of knowledge out of pleasure for what he is doing. And the inhabitants of the heavens and the earth and the fish in the water ask for forgiveness for the knowledgeable. The superiority of the knowledgeable over the worshipper [without knowledge] is like that of the full moon over the rest of the stars. The learned are the heirs of the Prophets. The Prophets did not bequeath a dinar or dirham but bequeathed knowledge. So, the one who attains it receives plenty of good fortune.»

Reported by Abu Dawud (3641) and al-Albani declared it sahih (*Sahih Abi Dawud*, 3641)

The impact of teaching Islam is so far-reaching that it is almost unimaginable. All creatures sense and receive its blessings. How can one fathom that everyone in the heavens and on earth is making *du'a* for teachers of Islam? Even the animals and the fish at sea? Even ants in their anthills, according to another authentic *hadith*? And the reaction of the angels is something else. They lower their wings for the seeker of knowledge to symbolize respect, love, and admiration.

Royalty is celebrated with salutes and gunfire. But there is nothing more prestigious than receiving the tribute of the angels. In the *Hadith* of the chapter, they throng the seeker of knowledge until they reach the sky. It is important to keep these images in mind. You may be teaching Islam and be completely anonymous. You may do a lot of good work but receive little to zero recognition. Then when you see what the seekers of the world receive, you become sad and deflated. Where is our motivation going to come from? If you see people flocking to a celebrity, remember that the angels of Allah will surround the seeker of knowledge. This is what being a real celebrity is, to have the best of Allah's creation admire you and want to be close to you. When you learn Islam and teach it, you are benefiting everyone on earth, and all living creatures will pray for you. Remembering this blessing is our motivation to keep learning and teaching, even if the world does not reward us for it.

A sign of Allah's love

Some physical signs foretell Allah's love for a person. When one follows Allah's will on earth, it is a sign of Allah's pleasure with Him up above. Ibn Taymiyyah رَحِمَهُ ٱللَّهُ wrote:

قال ابن تيمية: فَمن كَانَ اللهُ يُحِبهُ اسْتَعْملهُ فِيمَا يُحِبهُ.

العبودية (ص١١٣)

When Allah loves someone, He employs them in what He loves.

Al-'Ubudiyyah (p. 113)

Allah reserves His highest honors for the people He loves.

He likes them to be close to Him, so he employs them in doing His work. This is an excellent formula to detect Allah's love. If we want to know if Allah loves us, consider if we are doing what He loves. This is not limited to Islamic knowledge but extends to everything pleasing to Allah. If you are helping others or taking care of your family for Allah's sake, then you are pleasing Allah. If we find, however, that we are not doing what Allah loves, we should change our ways and rush back to Him. We cannot claim Allah's love by doing what He hates.

One of the features of Allah's beloveds is their constant pursuit to come closer to Allah. They seek what Allah loves and do it whenever they can. Their pursuit is endless as Allah's love is endless. And the more of it they have, the more they want. Allah's love is more intense than any other.

HADITH THIRTY SIX

الحديث السادس الثلاثون

Loving whom the Prophet loved

قَالَ عَمْرو بنِ العَاصِ رَضِيَ اللهُ عَنْهُ: يَا رَسُولَ اللهِ مَنْ أَحَبُّ النَّاسِ إِلَيْكَ؟ قَالَ ﷺ «لِمَ؟» قَالَ لِأُحِبَّ مَنْ تُحِبُّ، قَالَ «عَائِشَةُ» قَالَ: مِنَ الرِّجَالِ؟ قَالَ: «أَبُو بَكْرٍ.»

رواه الطبراني في المعجم الكبير (١١٦) وابن حبان (٤٥٤٠) وصححه الألباني (التعليقات الحسان ٤٥٢٣)

'Amr ibn al-'As asked, "O Messenger of Allah, which person do you love the most?" He ﷺ asked, «Why?» He replied, "So I would love whom you love." He answered, «'A'ishah.» He asked, "From among the men?" He replied, «Abu Bakr.»

Reported by al-Tabarani in al-Mu'jam al-Kabir (116) *and Ibn Hibban* (4540). *Al-Albani declared it sahih* (*al-Ta'liqat al-Hisan*, 4523)

Commentary

Loving the Prophet ﷺ naturally means loving whom and what he loved. This love unveils and guides to the best of this life and the next.

Seeking to love

Many of us turn cynical with all the hardship we see. We become convinced that there is little good left in the world and that all people are selfish and hurtful. And though there is indeed plenty of betrayal and ingratitude on earth—and we should protect ourselves from it—painting everyone with the same brush blinds us to the good that is still there. It deprives us of the beneficial company of the righteous. There are people out there who are still worthy of our love and kindness. We just have to find them. Not everyone out there will be worthy of our love. But some are. Do not give up.

When 'Amr ibn al-'As رَضِيَ ٱللَّهُ عَنْهُ asked his question in the *Hadith*, he was seeking the people he should love, the ones most worthy of love. And there are none better than the ones that the Prophet ﷺ loves. They are the best because the best loves them.

Each in this world is attracted to their ilk. Allah said in the Quran:

ٱلْخَبِيثَٰتُ لِلْخَبِيثِينَ وَٱلْخَبِيثُونَ لِلْخَبِيثَٰتِ ۖ وَٱلطَّيِّبَٰتُ لِلطَّيِّبِينَ
وَٱلطَّيِّبُونَ لِلطَّيِّبَٰتِ ۚ... ﴿٢٦﴾

Evil [women, words, or deeds] are for evil men, and evil men are for evil [women, words, or deeds]. And good [women, words, or deeds] are for good men, and good men are for good [women, words, or deeds].

An-Nur (Q24:26)

Virtue seeks virtue, and evil seeks evil. Humans are attracted to what agrees with their nature. Since the Prophet ﷺ is the best of the best, his nature seeks and is comfortable with the best. Discovering his likes—and dislikes—grants us invaluable insight. It is, therefore, of the utmost benefit for us to know this. Whom and what he loved leads us to Jannah. Consider the following *hadith*. Abu Dharr رَضِيَ ٱللَّهُ عَنْهُ said:

قال أبو ذرٍّ رضي الله عنه: أمرني خليلي بسبعٍ أمرني بحُبِّ المساكينِ والدُّنُوِّ منهم وأمرني أن أنظرَ إلى من هو دوني ولا أنظرَ

إلى من هو فوقي وأمرني أن أَصِلَ الرَّحِمَ وإن أَدْبَرَتْ وأمرني أن لا أسألَ أحدًا شيئًا وأمرني أن أقولَ بالحقِّ وإن كان مُرًّا وأمرني أن لا أخافَ في اللهِ لومةَ لائمٍ وأمرني أن أُكْثِرَ من قولِ لا حولَ ولا قوةَ إلا باللهِ فإنهن من كَنْزٍ تحتَ العرشِ.

رواه أحمد (٢١٤١٥) وصححه الألباني (صحيح الترغيب ٢٥٢٥) وشعيب الأرناؤوط

My *khalil* commanded me to do seven things. To love the poor and be close to them. And he commanded me to look at who is below me [in worldly riches] and not to look at who is above me. And he commanded me to be kind to my kin even if they are not closely related [or even if they turn away from me]. And he commanded me not to ask anyone for anything. And he commanded me to speak the truth even if it is bitter. And he commanded me not to fear any criticism in the cause of Allah. And he commanded me to say *La hawla wa quwwata illa bi Allah* often, for it is from a treasure from underneath the Throne.

Reported by Ahmad (21415). Al-Albani declared it sahih (*Sahih al-Targhib*, 2525), and so did Shu'ayb al-Arna'ut

If we love whom he loves, we would be close to the righteous, which helps us emulate them and learn from their wisdom. They would be the best companions, mentors, and friends. And if we love what he loved of food, places, and attire, we would be embracing the most healthful, honorable, and balanced lifestyle. His love unveils and leads to virtue.

Loving what the Prophet ﷺ loved brings us great benefits in this world and the Hereafter. It is also a natural consequence of loving Him. Whenever we love someone, we move closer to what they love. (This is why it is dangerous to love the wrong person.) We are naturally inclined to what brings happiness to our beloveds. What they love also carries their imprint and evokes their memory, becoming an extension of them. It makes us smile whenever we see it. Just think of how much you love the things that make your beloved (parent, spouse, child, or dear friend) happy. Love is a canopy that covers whom we love and what they love. The Companions did not only love the Prophet ﷺ, but they loved what he loved too. Anas ibn Malik رَضِيَ اللَّهُ عَنْهُ said:

قال أنس بن مالك رضي الله عنه: دعا خَيّاطٌ رَسولَ اللَّهِ ﷺ لِطَعامٍ صَنَعَهُ فَذَهَبْتُ مع رَسولِ اللَّهِ ﷺ إلى ذلكَ الطَّعامِ فَقَرَّبَ إلى رَسولِ اللَّهِ ﷺ خُبْزًا مِن شَعِيرٍ ومَرَقًا فيه دُبّاءٌ وقَدِيدٌ فَرَأَيْتُ رَسولَ اللَّهِ ﷺ يَتَتَبَّعُ الدُّبّاءَ مِن حَوْلِ الصَّحْفَةِ فَلَمْ أَزَلْ أُحِبُّ الدُّبّاءَ مِن يَومِئِذٍ فَجَعَلْتُ أجْمَعُ الدُّبّاءَ بيْنَ يَدَيْهِ.

رواه البخاري (٥٤٣٩)

A tailor invited the Messenger ﷺ to a meal he prepared, and I went along with the Messenger ﷺ to that meal. He presented to the Messenger ﷺ barley bread and soup with gourd and cured meat in it. I saw the Messenger ﷺ picking the gourd pieces from around the plate—and I have loved gourd ever since—so I collected the gourd pieces for him.

Reported by al-Bukhari (5439)

Anas رَضِيَ اللَّهُ عَنْهُ loved the Prophet ﷺ so much that he started loving gourd because of the Prophet's love for it. And so would we if our love for the Prophet ﷺ was strong enough: we would love what he loved. It is not really about loving a specific food he liked. But if he asked us to do something or to stay away from another, we would do it because we love him. If he practiced a Sunnah, we would imitate him without hesitation or delay. For instance, 'A'ishah رَضِيَ اللَّهُ عَنْهَا said:

كانَ النبيُّ ﷺ يُعْجِبُهُ التَّيَمُّنُ في تَنَعُّلِهِ وتَرَجُّلِهِ وطُهُورِهِ وفي شَأْنِهِ كُلِّهِ.

رواه البخاري (١٦٨) ومسلم (٢٦٨)

The Prophet ﷺ liked to begin with the right in wearing his shoes, combing his hair, purification, and all of his affairs.

Reported by al-Bukhari (168) and Muslim (268)

Loving the Prophet ﷺ would move us to behave like him, even in the smallest of details. His Sunnah (i.e. way of life) would become our way of life. We would not be asking if an act of worship he maintained is obligatory or voluntary, for love would blur those distinctions and propel us to the joy of companionship. It would not be a burden or a chore to follow him but a delight, for it would emotionally bring us closer to him. And as we get closer to him in this world, we get closer to him in the Hereafter. This is why we should strengthen our love for the Prophet ﷺ. It is easier to follow him when you love him.

Following the Prophet and loving him form a loop. If we want to love him more, we must follow him. And when we do, our love for him will grow. When we practice what he taught, he will be close to us all the time. When we read his *hadith*, he would be talking to us all the time. When we adjust our life-style—in small and big issues—to live more like him, we would be inviting him into our lives and hearts. When we send *Salah* and Salam for him, we become connected to him and he to us. Some understand loving the Prophet ﷺ as the mere repetition of *nasheed* on special occasions. But loving him is much more than what we sing; loving him is living his message and spreading it. We must love him enough for it to change us. If love does not change us at all, is it truly love?

Loving whom they love

Once love starts, it does not stop. It moves you to other loves. This is its nature. The Prophet's love for his late wife Khadijah رضي الله عنها spread to the people she loved.

كان رَسولُ اللَّهِ ﷺ إذا أُتِيَ بِشيءٍ يقولُ «اذْهَبُوا بهِ إلى فُلانةَ فإنَّها كانَتْ صَدِيقَةَ خديجةَ اذهبُوا إلى بيتِ فلانةَ فإنَّها كانَتْ تُحبُّ خديجةَ.»

رواه البخاري في الأدب المفرد (٢٣٢) وحسنه الألباني (١٧٢)

When the Messenger ﷺ was given a gift, he would say, «Take

it to so-and-so for she was a friend of Khadijah, take it to so-and-so for she used to love Khadijah.»

Reported by al-Bukhari in *al-Adab al-Mufrad* (232) and al-Albani declared it hasan (*Sahih al-Adab al-Mufrad*, 172).

This is why 'A'ishah ﵂ became jealous of Khadijah even though she never met her. She said:

ما غِرْتُ على نِساءِ النبيِّ ﷺ إلّا على خَدِيجَةَ وإنِّي لَمْ أُدْرِكْها وَكانَ رَسولُ اللهِ ﷺ إذا ذَبَحَ الشّاةَ فَيَقولُ «أَرْسِلُوا بها إلى أَصْدِقاءِ خَدِيجَةَ» فأغْضَبْتُهُ يَوْمًا فَقُلتُ: خَدِيجَةَ؟ فَقالَ رَسولُ اللهِ ﷺ «إنِّي قدْ رُزِقْتُ حُبَّها.»

رواه مسلم (٢٤٣٥)

I was never jealous of the wives of the Prophet ﷺ as I was jealous of Khadijah, and I never met her. When the Messenger ﷺ would slaughter a sheep, he would say, "Send some of it to the friends of Khadijah." I upset him one day when I said, "Khadijah?" to which he said, «I was gifted her love.»

Reported by Muslim (2435)

Khadijah ﵂ held a special place in the heart of the Prophet ﷺ. His spirit would be lifted when he was reminded of her. When Halah, Khadijah's sister, came to visit the household of the Prophet, her voice and speech reminded him of Khadijah ﵂, and that comforted him (Muslim, 2437). When we love someone, our love extends to what they love. This is proof that our love is strong and true. And this is what makes the question of 'Amr ibn al-'As ﵁ so important. You cannot love the Prophet ﷺ without also loving whom and what he loved.

There is another narration of the *Hadith* in Bukhari and Muslim that explains when this incident took place and adds another name to the list of people that the Prophet ﷺ loved the most.

قال عَمْرُو بْنُ العَاصِ رَضِيَ اللَّهُ عَنْهُ أَنَّ النَّبِيَّ صَلَّى اللهُ عَلَيْهِ وَسَلَّمَ

بَعَثَهُ عَلَى جَيْشِ ذَاتِ السَّلاَسِلِ فَأَتَيْتُهُ فَقُلْتُ: أَيُّ النَّاسِ أَحَبُّ إِلَيْكَ؟ قَالَ «عَائِشَةُ» فَقُلْتُ: مِنَ الرِّجَالِ؟ فَقَالَ «أَبُوهَا» قُلْتُ: ثُمَّ مَنْ؟ قَالَ «ثُمَّ عُمَرُ بْنُ الخَطَّابِ» فَعَدَّ رِجَالًا.

رواه البخاري (٣٦٦٢) ومسلم (٢٣٨٤)

'Amr ibn al-'As ﷺ said that the Prophet ﷺ appointed him to command the army to Dhat al-Salasil. So, when I returned I asked him, "Whom do you love most?" He said, «'A'ishah.» I asked, "From the men?" He replied, «Her father.» I asked, "Then whom?" He replied, «Then 'Umar ibn al-Khattab.» And he enumerated other men.

Reported by al-Bukhari (3662) and Muslim (2384)

The *Hadith* of the chapter adds to this narration the important reason behind asking these questions. 'Amr ibn al-'As ﷺ sought to know whom the Prophet ﷺ loved so he could love them too. This is the natural consequence of *Iman* and the dictate of wisdom. The Prophet ﷺ himself made the link between loving him and loving whom he loved.

كانَ ﷺ يصلِّي فإذا سجدَ وثَبَ الحسنُ والحُسَيْنُ على ظَهْرِهِ فإذا منعوهما أشارَ إليهم أن دَعوهما فلمّا قَضى الصَّلاةَ وضعَهما في حجرِهِ وقالَ «من أحبَّني فليُحبَّ هذينِ.»

حسنه الألباني (السلسلة الصحيحة ٣١٢)

When the Prophet ﷺ prayed, al-Hasan and al-Husayn would jump on his back when he prostrated. When they would attempt to stop them, he would signal to them to let them go. When he concluded his Salah, he put the two in his lap and said, «Whoever loves me, let them love these two.»

Al-Albani declared it hasan (*al-Silsilah al-Sahihah*, 312)

He ﷺ also said about them:

«اللَّهمَّ إنِّي أحبُّهما فأحبَّهما وأحبَّ مَن يحبُّهما.»

رواه الترمذي (٣٧٦٩) وحسنه الألباني (صحيح الترمذي ٣٧٦٩)

«O Allah I love them, so love them and love those who love them.»

Reported by al-Tirmidhi (3769) and al-Albani declared it hasan (*Sahih al-Tirmidhi*, 3769)

He ﷺ said something similar about Usamah ibn Zayd رَضِيَ اللَّهُ عَنْهُ.

«مَن أَحَبَّنِي فَلْيُحِبَّ أُسَامَةَ.»

رواه مسلم (٢٩٤٢)

«If someone loves me, they should love Usamah.»

Reported by Muslim (2942)

Loving the ones the Prophet loved is an extension of our love for him. If we love him, we would surely love the ones he urged us to love. But even if he did not ask, we would willingly love them because they were close to his heart. This is how the Companions were. They put him before themselves, and they put what he loved before what they did. The following story is weak because of its chain. But I wanted to share it with you because the sentiments it conveys are true nonetheless.

فرَضَ عُمَرُ لأسامةَ ثَلاثةَ آلافٍ وخَمسَ مِئةٍ وفرَضَ لابنِه عَبدِ اللهِ ثَلاثةَ آلافٍ فقال لِمَ فَضَّلتَه علَيَّ فواللهِ ما سبَقَني إلى مَشهدٍ قال لأنَّ أباه كان أحَبَّ إلى رسولِ اللهِ مِن أبيكَ وهو أحَبُّ إلى رسولِ الله صلى الله عليه وسلم منك فآثَرتُ حُبَّ رسولِ اللهِ على حُبِّي

رواه الترمذي (٣٨١٣) وضعفه الألباني (ضعيف الترمذي ٣٨١٣)

'Umar assigned three thousand and five hundred [dirhams] as a stipend for Usamah and three thousand as a stipend for his son Abdullah. Abdullah asked, "Why did you give him more? By Allah, he did not get to any battle before me." He replied, "It is because the Messenger of Allah loved his father more than yours, and the Messenger of Allah ﷺ loved him more than you. So, I put the love of the Messenger of Allah before mine."

Reported by al-Tirmidhi (3813) and al-Albani declared it weak (*Da'if al-Tirmidhi*, 3813)

The incident may not have happened exactly as mentioned, and it may be missing some key details. But there is immense beauty in its last sentence, "I put the love of the Messenger of Allah before mine." This is the desire of every Muslim. Loving the Prophet leads to more righteousness and liberates from personal weaknesses. Putting what he loved ahead of ours is how we escape the clutches of our desires and are transformed into servants of Allah. Doing this becomes easier when we are convinced that—because of his piety—what he loved is better than what we love. And if we love as he did, we will be happier and more content.

The virtue of Abu Bakr and his daughter

The Prophet ﷺ is the closest person to Allah, and he loves the closest people to Allah. So, when he revealed that he loved 'A'ishah and her father رَضِيَ اللَّهُ عَنْهُمَا the most, he was announcing and confirming their excellence. Anyone who loves the Prophet ﷺ must also love Abu Bakr and his daughter رَضِيَ اللَّهُ عَنْهُمَا. Those who hate them stand in plain and direct opposition to the Prophet himself, choosing to oppose and hate the people he loved the most. And what does that say about the love they have for the Prophet ﷺ? You cannot claim to love him while hating his wife and his closest Companion.

Our love is the product of our *Iman*. Hating the Companions and those who championed the Prophet ﷺ is a sign of ignorance or weak *Iman*. The Prophet ﷺ said:

«آيَةُ الإيمانِ حُبُّ الأنْصارِ وآيَةُ النِّفاقِ بُغْضُ الأنْصارِ.»

رواه البخاري (١٧) ومسلم (٧٤)

«The sign of Iman is loving the Ansar, and the sign of hypocrisy is hating the Ansar.»

Reported by al-Bukhari (17) and Muslim (74)

One would love the Ansar because they helped the Prophet ﷺ and the Migrants who were in desperate need of shelter and support. Hating them comes only from a heart that hates what they did, and this reveals hypocrisy. If this is the status of loving the Ansar, it is even more so with the Migrants and the Rightly Guided Caliphs. Hating Abu Bakr, 'Umar, and 'A'ishah رَضِيَ اللَّهُ عَنْهُمْ is a clear sign of hypocrisy.

The virtue of Abu Bakr and his daughter رَضِيَ اللَّهُ عَنْهُمَا was well established among early Muslims. Now, between the two, why did the Prophet ﷺ put 'A'ishah before Abu Bakr? Al-Qurtubi رَحِمَهُ اللَّهُ wrote commenting on this:

وإنَّما بدأ النبي صلى الله عليه وسلم بذكر محبة عائشة أولًا لأنَّها محبة جبلية ودينية وغيرها دينية لا جبلية فسبق الأصلي على الطَّارئ.

المفهم لما أشكل من تلخيص كتاب مسلم (ج٦ ص٢٤٤)

The Prophet ﷺ first began with the love of 'A'ishah because her love was [both] natural and religious, while other loves were religious and not natural. So, the natural [or original love] came before the newly acquired.

Al-Mufhim lima 'Ashkal min Talkhis Kitab Muslim (vol. 6, p. 244)

The Prophet ﷺ had multiple reasons to love 'A'ishah رَضِيَ اللَّهُ عَنْهَا. She was his most beloved wife, very close and dear to his heart. She had an amazing personality, and she was outstandingly smart and kind. She was also very devout and exceptionally knowledgeable. He loved her for worldly and religious reasons.

Abu Bakr رَضِيَ اللَّهُ عَنْهُ outranks his daughter religiously. He is the best of this Ummah right after the Prophet ﷺ. Even though the Prophet ﷺ loved him on a personal level, he had greater worldly love for his wife. The combination of the religious and worldly loves brought her closest to the Prophet's heart. But on the religious side, there was no doubt that Abu Bakr رَضِيَ ٱللَّهُ عَنْهُ deserved the greatest religious love and praise. The following *hadith* explains the uniqueness of Abu Bakr رَضِيَ ٱللَّهُ عَنْهُ in Islam.

جَلَسَ رَسولُ اللَّهِ صَلَّى اللهُ عليه وسلَّمَ على المِنبَرِ فقالَ «إنَّ عَبْدًا خَيَّرَهُ اللَّهُ بيْنَ أنْ يُؤْتِيَهُ مِن زَهْرَةِ الدُّنْيا ما شاءَ وبيْنَ ما عِنْدَهُ فاخْتارَ ما عِنْدَهُ» فَبَكَى أبو بَكْرٍ وقالَ: فَدَيْناكَ بآبائِنا وأُمَّهاتِنا، فَعَجِبْنا له وقالَ النَّاسُ: انْظُرُوا إلى هذا الشَّيْخِ يُخْبِرُ رَسولُ اللَّهِ صَلَّى اللهُ عليه وسلَّمَ عن عَبْدٍ خَيَّرَهُ اللَّهُ بيْنَ أنْ يُؤْتِيَهُ مِن زَهْرَةِ الدُّنْيا وبيْنَ ما عِنْدَهُ وهو يقولُ فَدَيْناكَ بآبائِنا وأُمَّهاتِنا، فَكانَ رَسولُ اللَّهِ صَلَّى اللهُ عليه وسلَّمَ هو المُخَيَّرَ وكانَ أبو بَكْرٍ هو أعْلَمَنا به وقالَ رَسولُ اللَّهِ صَلَّى اللهُ عليه وسلَّمَ «إنَّ مِن أمَنِّ النَّاسِ عَلَيَّ في صُحْبَتِهِ ومالِهِ أبا بَكْرٍ ولو كُنْتُ مُتَّخِذًا خَلِيلًا مِن أُمَّتي لاتَّخَذْتُ أبا بَكْرٍ إلَّا خُلَّةَ الإسْلامِ لا يَبْقَيَنَّ في المَسْجِدِ خَوْخَةٌ إلَّا خَوْخَةُ أبِي بَكْرٍ».

رواه البخاري (٣٩٠٤)

The Messenger ﷺ gave a speech from the minbar and said, «Allah gave someone the choice between giving him what he wished from the beauty of this life and what He had [for him], and he chose what He had [for him].» Abu Bakr cried and said, "We would sacrifice our fathers and mothers for you." What he said surprised us, and people said, "Look at this elderly man! The Messenger ﷺ spoke about someone whom Allah gave a choice between the beauty of this life and what He had [for him], and he said we would sacrifice our fathers and mothers for you!" But it was the Messenger ﷺ who was given a choice, and Abu Bakr was the one who knew him best among us. The Messenger ﷺ said, «The most generous one with me in his companionship and wealth is Abu Bakr. If I were to take a *khalil* [i.e. dearest loved one] from my Ummah, I would take Abu Bakr. But he has the love of Islam. There should be no [personal] door leading to the masjid except the door of Abu Bakr رَضِيَ ٱللَّهُ عَنْهُ.»

Reported by al-Bukhari (3904)

A *khalil* is the closest lover to the heart. Love at that stage penetrates the heart to such depths that it fills all of its crevices. It is as if that love soaks the entire heart. The Prophet ﷺ loved Allah to that degree, and Allah adopted him as a *Khalil*, like he did with Ibrahim عَلَيْهِ ٱلسَّلَامُ. The Prophet ﷺ said:

«لَوْ كُنْتُ مُتَّخِذًا خَلِيلًا لاتَّخَذْتُ أَبا بَكْرٍ خَلِيلًا وَلَكِنَّهُ أَخِي وَصاحِبِي وَقَدِ اتَّخَذَ اللَّهُ عَزَّ وَجَلَّ صاحِبَكُمْ خَلِيلًا.»

رواه مسلم (٢٣٨٣)

«If I were to adopt a *khalil*, I would adopt Abu Bakr as a *khalil*. But he is my brother and companion. Allah has adopted your companion [i.e. the Prophet] as a *Khalil*.»

Reported by Muslim (2383)

When the love of Allah fills the heart, it leaves no space for another *khalil*. This is why the Prophet ﷺ could not take any human *khalil*. The Prophet ﷺ could love other humans, and he did. But that comprehensive love, the greatest love of the heart, was reserved only for Allah. But if that space in the Prophet's heart was not occupied, Abu Bakr would be the only one to fill it. This is how outstanding he was: to be the only human candidate who could fill that space and come that close to the heart of the greatest Messenger humanity ever knew.

Worldly love and religious love

We have seen so far how religious love interacts with worldly love. At times, they complement each other, while at other times they clash. And as long as the worldly (or personal) love is not forbidden and does not lead to a forbidden act, such love is permissible and natural. The following story explains this further. 'A'ishah رَضِيَ ٱللَّهُ عَنْهَا said:

عن عائشة رضي الله عَنْها قَالَتْ: قَالَ أَبُو بَكْرٍ رَضِيَ اللَّهُ عَنْهُ يَوْمًا: وَاللَّهِ مَا عَلَى وَجْهِ الْأَرْضِ رَجُلٌ أَحَبَّ إِلَيَّ مِنْ عُمَرَ، فَلَمَّا خَرَجَ رَجَعَ فَقَالَ: كَيْفَ حَلَفْتُ أَيْ بُنَيَّةُ؟ فَقُلْتُ لَهُ فَقَالَ: أَعَزَّ عليَّ والوَلَدُ أَلْوَطُ.

رواه البخاري في الأدب المفرد (٨٤) وحسنه الألباني (صحيح الأدب المفرد ٦١)

Abu Bakr رَضِيَ ٱللَّهُ عَنْهُ once said, "By Allah, there is no one on this earth that I love more than Umar." When he left and came back, he asked, "What did I swear to, my daughter?" I told him what he said. He then said, "No, dearer to me. One's child is closer to the heart."

Reported by al-Bukhari in *al-Adab al-Mufrad* (84) and al-Albani declared it hasan (*Sahih al-Adab al-Mufrad*, 61)

'Umar was the best person right after Abu Bakr رَضِيَ ٱللَّهُ عَنْهُمَا. Abu Bakr's *Iman* and piety created this intense love for 'Umar. But no matter how strong our religious love for someone may grow, the worldly love we have for our spouses and children keeps them closest to our hearts. And there is no contradiction between the two loves. Each has different causes, and each can exist and grow independently of the other (i.e. we can love another personally but not religiously or religiously but not personally). Love is strongest, however, when both types of loves combine, such as when we love our pious family members or personally like righteous friends. But as these loves can combine, they can also clash and diverge. When our instinctual love—meaning what is embedded in our nature—pulls us away from Allah, our religious (acquired) love must be strong enough to favor Allah. This is what the following *ayah* is referring to. Allah said:

قُلْ إِن كَانَ ءَابَآؤُكُمْ وَأَبْنَآؤُكُمْ وَإِخْوَٰنُكُمْ وَأَزْوَٰجُكُمْ وَعَشِيرَتُكُمْ وَأَمْوَٰلٌ ٱقْتَرَفْتُمُوهَا وَتِجَٰرَةٌ تَخْشَوْنَ كَسَادَهَا وَمَسَٰكِنُ تَرْضَوْنَهَآ أَحَبَّ إِلَيْكُم مِّنَ ٱللَّهِ وَرَسُولِهِۦ وَجِهَادٍ فِى سَبِيلِهِۦ فَتَرَبَّصُوا۟ حَتَّىٰ يَأْتِىَ ٱللَّهُ بِأَمْرِهِۦ... ﴿٢٤﴾

> Say, "If your parents, children, siblings, spouses, your family, the wealth you collected, the business you fear its decline, and homes you cherish are more beloved to you than Allah, His Messenger, and Jihad in His sake, then wait until Allah brings His punishment.
>
> At-Tawbah (Q9:24)

This is why we must strive to love Allah. If we do not, we will not have the strength to choose Him. The good news is that if we strive, we can reach the point where our love for Him can surpass loving our children and wealth, even loving ourselves. Our religious love has this power and this great potential. It just needs nurturing. And if we do, what happens next will amaze us.

HADITH THIRTY SEVEN

الحديث السابع الثلاثون

Loving to hear about Allah

كَانَ رَجُلٌ مِنَ الأَنْصَارِ يَؤُمُّهُمْ فِي مَسْجِدِ قُبَاءَ فَكَانَ كُلَّمَا افْتَتَحَ سُورَةً يَقْرَأُ لَهُمْ فِي الصَّلَاةِ يَقْرَأُ بِهَا افْتَتَحَ بِـ﴿قُلْ هُوَ اللَّهُ أَحَدٌ﴾ حَتَّى يَفْرُغَ مِنْهَا ثُمَّ يَقْرَأُ بِسُورَةٍ أُخْرَى مَعَهَا وَكَانَ يَصْنَعُ ذَلِكَ فِي كُلِّ رَكْعَةٍ فَكَلَّمَهُ أَصْحَابُهُ فَقَالُوا: إِنَّكَ تَقْرَأُ بِهَذِهِ السُّورَةِ ثُمَّ لَا تَرَى أَنَّهَا تُجْزِيكَ حَتَّى تَقْرَأَ بِسُورَةٍ أُخْرَى فَإِمَّا أَنْ تَقْرَأَ بِهَا وَإِمَّا أَنْ تَدَعَهَا وَتَقْرَأَ بِسُورَةٍ أُخْرَى، قَالَ: مَا أَنَا بِتَارِكِهَا إِنْ أَحْبَبْتُمْ أَنْ أَؤُمَّكُمْ بِهَا فَعَلْتُ وَإِنْ كَرِهْتُمْ تَرَكْتُكُمْ، وَكَانُوا يَرَوْنَهُ أَفْضَلَهُمْ وَكَرِهُوا أَنْ يَؤُمَّهُمْ غَيْرُهُ فَلَمَّا أَتَاهُمُ النَّبِيُّ ﷺ أَخْبَرُوهُ الخَبَرَ فَقَالَ «يَا فُلَانُ مَا يَمْنَعُكَ مِمَّا يَأْمُرُ بِهِ أَصْحَابُكَ وَمَا يَحْمِلُكَ أَنْ تَقْرَأَ هَذِهِ السُّورَةَ فِي كُلِّ رَكْعَةٍ» فَقَالَ: يَا رَسُولَ اللهِ إِنِّي أُحِبُّهَا، فَقَالَ رَسُولُ اللهِ ﷺ «إِنَّ حُبَّهَا أَدْخَلَكَ الجَنَّةَ.»

رواه الترمذي (٢٩٠١) وصححه الألباني (صحيح الترمذي ٢٩٠١)

There was a man from the Ansar who led them in Salah at Masjid Quba'. And every time he recited a Surah for them during Salah, he would begin by reciting *Qul Huwa Allahu Ahad* until he finished it, then he would recite another Surah with it. He used to do this in each Rak'ah. His companions talked to him and said, "You recite this Surah but see it is not enough unless you read another. You should either recite it [by itself] or leave it and recite another Surah." He said, "I will not leave it. If you would like me to lead you with it, then I will do so. But if you do not like it, then I will leave you." They considered him to be the best among them, and they disliked the idea of someone else leading them. So when the Prophet ﷺ came to them, they informed him of what had happened and he said, «O so-and-so, what prevents you from doing what your companions told you to do? And why do you recite this Surah in every Rak'ah?» He said, "O Messenger of Allah, I love it." So the Messenger of Allah ﷺ said, «Its love has admitted you to Jannah.»

Reported by al-Tirmidhi (2901) and al-Albani declared it sahih (Sahih al-Tirmidhi, 2901)

Commentary

When you love someone, you frequently talk about them, love to hear from them, and about them. When we love Allah, there would be nothing sweeter and more comforting than Him talking about Himself.

Loving the Quran

Romantic love is a staple in classical literature, poetry, and art. Even today, novels, movies, series, and songs center on the ups and downs of love: the excitement of loving someone and the agony of losing them. We hear there how a lover impatiently waits to hear from their beloved, to see them, and to be near them. And we see how their union brings immense joy to them. Their love transforms anything they receive from their lover into a priceless possession, a source of bliss that reminds them of their beloved and the love they share. Now, imagine with me, lovers separated by long-distance for a protracted time. Imagine them eagerly awaiting a letter—or a text—from their beloved, and the happiness they feel when they hear from them. Now, I want you to imagine with me the joy those who love Allah will feel when they read and hear the Quran.

Allah is greater than anyone else. He is Perfect in His qualities, Perfect in His gifts, and Perfect in His promises. And His love is greater than any other love. And so, the bliss and comfort His beloveds receive from His Words and the longing they have for them are greater than what other lovers experience. They hear in His Words the eternal wisdom that answers all of their questions. They discover in them the final truth that gives them peace. They receive in them the assurance they constantly need to feel safe and fortunate. There is no other book like it, and no one can speak to their hearts like the One who created them. The Quran, to them, is more important than food and drink. Their bodies can survive without them for days, but their souls cannot withstand to be separated from their Creator. The Quran is their comforter, their solace, their answer, their companion, their hope, their advisor, and their treasure. When they stay away from it, their souls shrivel. And when they come back to it, life itself returns to their soul. It is their daily fuel that fights all the demons of this world. Without it, they stand defenseless. With it, they can take the entire world. Every time they read it, they discover something new. Every time they come to it with a problem, they discover in it the light that guides them to safety. How can you stay away from a book like this? They long for it because it is the Words of the One they love. Whenever they miss Allah and long to see Him, they rush to the Quran. These are the actual words of the One they love and Who loves them. How much joy do the Words of the Beloved bring to these parched hearts? Like a child who is only comforted by the sound of his loving mother, only the Words of their Greatest Love can make them this happy.

The Quran is Allah's revelation to humanity. It tells them who He is, and invites them to His Forgiveness and Mercy. It invites them to His love: to love Him and be loved by Him. The Quran is intimately linked to attaining the love of Allah (see also *Hadith Sixteen*). Ibn Rajab رَحِمَهُ ٱللَّهُ said:

قال ابن رجب: ومن أعظم ما تحصل به محبة الله تعالى من النوافل تلاوة القرآن وخصوصاً مع التدبر قال ابن مسعود: لا يسأل أحدكم عن نفسه إلا القرآن فمن أحب القرآن فهو يحب الله ورسوله.

إختيار الأولى في شرح حديث اختصام الملأ الأعلى (ص١٣٠)

And of the greatest voluntary deeds that bring the love of Allah is the recitation of the Quran, especially with reflection. Ibn Mas'ud رَضِيَ اللَّهُ عَنْهُ said, "Do not ask yourself about anything except the Quran. The one who loves the Quran loves Allah and His Messenger."

Ikhtiyar al-Awla (p. 130)

If you read the Quran regularly and you understand it, you will love Allah. And according to the great Companion and teacher of the Quran, Ibn Mas'ud رَضِيَ اللَّهُ عَنْهُ, if you love Allah, you would not be able to stay away from the Quran. How can one love Allah and bear to stay away from His Words? Ibn Mas'ud رَضِيَ اللَّهُ عَنْهُ gave us invaluable advice: if you want to love Allah, start with the Quran. It is one of the easiest and most fulfilling paths towards the love of Allah.

Another cherished gem that can be gleaned from what Ibn Mas'ud said is to interrogate our loves and behaviors. Do we truly love Allah? What evidence do we have of this? What is it that I love in this life? If you want a hint, look at what you love to talk about and listen to. Look at how you spend your time. What do you enjoy doing? Now, is Allah part of any of this? The answer to these questions will raise our awareness of the direction of our life, the good and the bad in it. Once we can clearly see it, we can try to change it.

The virtue of Surat al-Ikhlas

The Companions were especially close to the Quran. The love the Companion had in the *Hadith* for Surah al-Ikhlas was not unique. Another Companion did something similar.

بَعَثَ النبيُّ ﷺ رَجُلًا على سَرِيَّةٍ وكانَ يَقْرَأُ لأصْحابِهِ في صَلاتِهِمْ فَيَخْتِمُ بـ﴿قُلْ هو اللَّهُ أحَدٌ﴾ فَلَمّا رَجَعُوا ذَكَرُوا ذلكَ للنبيِّ ﷺ فَقالَ «سَلُوهُ لأيِّ شيءٍ يَصْنَعُ ذلكَ» فَسَأَلُوهُ فَقالَ: لأنَّها صِفَةُ الرَّحْمَنِ وأنا أُحِبُّ أنْ أقْرَأَ بها، فَقالَ النبيُّ ﷺ «أخْبِرُوهُ أنَّ اللَّهَ يُحِبُّهُ.»

رواه البخاري (٧٣٧٥) ومسلم (٨١٣)

The Prophet ﷺ sent a man as head of an army expedition, and he used to lead them in Salah and conclude his reading with *Qul Huwa Allahu Ahad*. When they returned, they mentioned this to the Prophet ﷺ, and he said, «Ask him why he did it?» They asked him and he replied, "Because it has the attributes of the Most Merciful and I love to read it." The Prophet ﷺ said, «Let him know that Allah loves Him.»

Reported by al-Bukhari (7375) and Muslim (813)

There is a third narration that may point to yet another man.

كان رَجُلٌ مِنْ أَصْحَابِ النَّبِيِّ صَلَّى اللهُ عَلَيْهِ وَسَلَّمَ لَا يَقْرَأُ سُورَةً فِي مَكْتُوبَةٍ وَلَا نَافِلَةٍ إِلَّا قَرَأَ بَعْدَهَا ﴿قُلْ هُوَ اللَّهُ أَحَدٌ﴾ فَذَكَرَ ذَلِكَ لِلنَّبِيِّ صَلَّى اللهُ عَلَيْهِ وَسَلَّمَ فَقَالَ «لِمَ تَفْعَلُ ذَلِكَ» فَقَالَ: إِنِّي أُحِبُّهَا، فَقَالَ «إِنَّ اللَّهَ قَدْ أَحَبَّكَ بِحُبِّكَ إِيَّاهَا.»

الآثار لأبي يوسف (١٣٢)

A Companion of the Prophet ﷺ would not recite a Surah in an obligatory or voluntary prayer but he would read *Qul Huwa Allahu Ahad* after it. This was brought to the attention of the Prophet ﷺ and so he asked him, «Why do you do this?» He replied, "I love it." He said to him, «Indeed, Allah loves you because of your love for it.»

Al-'Athar by Abu Yusuf

This Surah is about Allah and His Perfect Attributes, and there is no other Surah like it. It packs—in short and clear sentences—significant truths about the Creator: His Oneness,

Uniqueness, Greatness, and our need for Him. Those who love Allah find immense peace and comfort in it. It reminds them that Allah is sufficient for them and can take care of all of their needs (al-Samad). Since no one is like Him or is equal to Him, they remain faithful to Him despite what others say and do. His supremacy in existence translates into His supremacy in their hearts. Whenever they miss Him and long for Him, they read this Surah and they hear about their Beloved. As they keep reading it, their love and longing for Him grows. Nothing will truly satisfy them except gazing upon His Honorable Face in Jannah. But until then, they stay close to His Words, and they repeat the *ayahs* that describe Him, impatiently waiting for the day when they will hear His words with their own ears and see Him with their own eyes. This is the greatest bounty in Jannah.

The Companion loved this Surah—as he stated in the *hadith*—because it described the Most Merciful. When our love for the Most Merciful grows, so will our love for the Quran and the *ayahs* that describe Allah, especially al-Ikhlas.

This short Surah is equal to one third of the Quran. The Prophet ﷺ said:

«احْشُدُوا فَإِنِّي سَأَقْرَأُ عَلَيْكُمْ ثُلُثَ الْقُرْآنِ» فَحَشَدَ مَنْ حَشَدَ ثُمَّ خَرَجَ نَبِيُّ اللهِ صَلَّى اللهُ عَلَيْهِ وَسَلَّمَ فَقَرَأَ ﴿قُلْ هُوَ اللهُ أَحَدٌ﴾ ثُمَّ دَخَلَ فَقَالَ بَعْضُنَا لِبَعْضٍ: إِنِّي أُرَى هَذَا خَبَرٌ جَاءَهُ مِنَ السَّمَاءِ فَذَاكَ الَّذِي أَدْخَلَهُ ثُمَّ خَرَجَ نَبِيُّ اللهِ صَلَّى اللهُ عَلَيْهِ وَسَلَّمَ فَقَالَ «إِنِّي قُلْتُ لَكُمْ سَأَقْرَأُ عَلَيْكُمْ ثُلُثَ الْقُرْآنِ أَلَا إِنَّهَا تَعْدِلُ ثُلُثَ الْقُرْآنِ.»

رواه مسلم (٨١٢)

«Gather, for I will recite one-third of the Quran for you.» So, people gathered. Then the Prophet of Allah ﷺ came out and recited *Qul Huwa Allahu Ahad*, and then he entered his house. We said to each other, "He must have gone inside because of some news he received from above." The Prophet of Allah ﷺ then came out and said, «I told you that I will recite for you one-third of the Quran. Indeed, it is equivalent to one-third of the Quran.»

Reported by Muslim (812)

It encapsulates one-third of the Quran: Tawhid. And if we know that the highest goal of the Quran is to teach us who Allah is, we would understand why this Surah is so significant. The Prophet ﷺ also said about it:

«مَن قرأَ ﴿قُل هوَ اللهُ أحدٌ...﴾ حَتَّى يَخْتِمَها عَشر مَرَّاتٍ بَنى اللهُ لَهُ قَصْرًا في الجَنَّة.»

رواه أحمد (١٥٦١٠) وحسنه الألباني (السلسلة الصحيحة ٥٨٩)

«Allah will build a palace in Jannah for the one who reads *Qul Huwa Allahu Ahad* till the end ten times.»

Reported by Ahmad (15610) and al-Albani declared it hasan (*al-Silsilah al-Sahihah*, 589)

This Surah is part of the morning and evening *dhikr* of Allah, part of the pre-sleep *dhikr*, and one of the protective and healing trio of Surahs (with al-Falaq and al-Nas). This Surah is the companion of those who remember Allah often. It nurtures the love of Allah in their hearts every single day. The more they read it—and the rest of the Quran—the more they can stay devoted to Allah, and the safer they are from the temptations of the world. It keeps them close to Allah, and Allah close to them.

HADITH THIRTY EIGHT

الحديث الثامن الثلاثون

Spend from what you love to attain love

لَمَّا نَزَلَتْ ﴿لَنْ تَنَالُوا الْبِرَّ حَتَّى تُنْفِقُوا مِمَّا تُحِبُّونَ﴾ [آل عمران ٩٢] جاءَ أَبُو طَلْحَةَ إِلَى رَسُولِ اللهِ ﷺ فَقَالَ: يَا رَسُولَ اللهِ يَقُولُ اللهُ تَبَارَكَ وَتَعَالَى فِي كِتَابِهِ ﴿لَنْ تَنَالُوا الْبِرَّ حَتَّى تُنْفِقُوا مِمَّا تُحِبُّونَ﴾ وَإِنَّ أَحَبَّ أَمْوَالِي إِلَيَّ بَيْرُحَاءَ - وَكَانَتْ حَدِيقَةً كَانَ رَسُولُ اللهِ ﷺ يَدْخُلُهَا وَيَسْتَظِلُّ بِهَا وَيَشْرَبُ مِنْ مَائِهَا - فَهِيَ إِلَى اللهِ عَزَّ وَجَلَّ وَإِلَى رَسُولِهِ صَلَّى اللهُ عَلَيْهِ وَسَلَّمَ أَرْجُو بِرَّهُ وَذُخْرَهُ فَضَعْهَا أَيْ رَسُولَ اللهِ حَيْثُ أَرَاكَ اللهُ، فَقَالَ رَسُولُ اللهِ ﷺ «بَخٍ يَا أَبَا طَلْحَةَ ذَلِكَ مَالٌ رَابِحٌ قَبِلْنَاهُ مِنْكَ وَرَدَدْنَاهُ عَلَيْكَ فَاجْعَلْهُ فِي الْأَقْرَبِينَ» فَتَصَدَّقَ بِهِ أَبُو طَلْحَةَ عَلَى ذَوِي رَحِمِهِ.

رواه البخاري (١٤٦١) ومسلم (٩٩٨)

When the ayah ﴾You will not attain righteousness until you spend from what you love﴿ [Ali Imran 92] was revealed, Abu Talhah came to the Messenger ﷺ and said, "O Messenger of Allah, Allah the Most Blessed and High said in His Book, ﴾You will not attain righteousness until you spend from what you love﴿, and my most beloved wealth to me is Bayruha'—a garden that the Messenger ﷺ used to frequent, seek shade in it, and drink from its water—and I give it to Allah, Glory be to him, and to His Messenger ﷺ seeking its reward and investment [with Allah]. So, put it, O Messenger of Allah, wherever Allah directs you." The

Messenger ﷺ said, «Amazing, O Abu Talhah! That is profitable wealth. We accept it from you and return it to you, so give it to relatives.» So, Abu Talhah donated it to his relatives.

Reported by al-Bukhari (1461) *and Muslims* (998)

Commentary

The love of Allah and the love of the world are polar opposites. In order to love Allah, we have to be willing to sacrifice the world for His sake. Only then would we be liberated from the shackles of greed and selfishness, and we would taste the sweetness of nearness to Allah.

Giving from what we love

Abu Talhah رَضِيَ اللَّهُ عَنْهُ was of the wealthiest in Madinah, and his wealth was made up of palm-trees in the lands he owned. The best of his gardens was Bayruha'. It was close to the Madinah Mosque, and had a freshwater well in it that the Prophet ﷺ loved to drink from. That made it even more precious in Abu Talhah's eyes. When Allah revealed the *ayah* urging charity from what we love, it moved Abu Talhah. He gave away the thing he loved the most for the sake of Allah. He did not have to give anything, and he did not have to give the thing he loved the most. But he chose the dearest of his possessions. He wanted to attain righteousness, and that beautiful garden was a small price to pay in his eyes. When something matters to us, it is easy to sacrifice for its sake. And Allah mattered to him.

Why did Allah state that spending from what we love is a condition for righteousness? It has to do with our nature and what we love. We have an intense love for wealth and this world. Allah said:

وَتُحِبُّونَ ٱلْمَالَ حُبًّا جَمًّا ﴿٢٠﴾

And you love wealth an immense love.
Al-Fajr (Q89:20)

Humans love wealth in all of its forms: gold and silver, mansions and estates, cars and clothes, and all the luxury money can buy. And this is not something that easily goes away as we age. The Prophet ﷺ said:

«قَلبُ الشَّيخِ شابٌّ على حبِّ اثنتيْنِ طولُ الحياةِ وحُبُّ المالِ.»

رواه البخاري (٦٤٢٠) ومسلم (١٠٤٦)

«The heart of an elder is still young in loving two things: long life and love of money.»

Reported by al-Bukhari (6420) and Muslim (1046)

This love—when immoderate and unchecked—has dire consequences. The Prophet ﷺ said:

«ما ذِئبانِ جائعانِ أُرْسِلا في غنَمٍ بأفسدَ لَها من حِرصِ المَرءِ على المالِ والشَّرَفِ لدينِهِ.»

رواه الترمذي (٢٣٧٦) وصححه الألباني (صحيح الترمذي ٢٣٧٦)

«Two hungry wolves let loose among sheep will not do more harm to it than the harm one's desire for wealth and recognition does to their religion.»

Reported by al-Tirmidhi (2376) and al-Albani declared it sahih (*Sahih al-Tirmidhi*, 2376)

Can we picture the carnage? The two hungry wolves will devastate the flock, soaking the ground with their blood. Nothing will be left alive. If one allows their craving for money and fame to grow rampant, they will destroy their religion. One will commit every sin to get richer. Their heart will be so saturated with the love of this world that it will leave no space for Allah. The test of wealth is serious and severe. The Prophet ﷺ said:

«إنَّ لكلِّ أمَّةٍ فتنةً وفتنَةُ أمَّتي المالُ.»

رواه الترمذي (٢٣٣٦) وصححه الألباني (صحيح الترمذي ٢٣٣٦)

«Each Ummah has a fitnah [test or a source of temptation], and the fitnah of my Ummah is wealth.»

Reported by al-Tirmidhi (2336) and al-Albani declared it sahih (*Sahih al-Tirmidhi*, 2336)

It is this Ummah's greatest temptation. And you can see what it did to other nations before us. They kept running after this world until it blinded their eyes and put a seal on their hearts. They ran away from Allah to amass the money they so desired, no matter the consequences. What they could not see, however, was how what they loved was destroying them. The love of Allah opens our eyes, but the love of the world blinds us. The Prophet ﷺ said:

«إذا رأيْتَ اللهَ يُعْطي العبدَ مِنَ الدُّنيا على مَعاصيه ما يُحِبُّ فإنَّما هو استِدراجٌ ثمَّ تلا رسولُ اللهِ ﴿فَلَمّا نَسُوا ما ذُكِّرُوا بِهِ فَتَحْنا عَلَيْهِمْ أَبْوابَ كُلِّ شَيْءٍ حَتّى إِذا فَرِحُوا بِما أُوتُوا أَخَذْناهُمْ بَغْتَةً فَإِذا هُمْ مُبْلِسُونَ﴾ [الأنعام ٤٤]»

رواه أحمد (١٧٣١١) وقال الألباني أن إسناده قوي (السلسلة الصحيحة ٤١٣)

«When you see Allah giving one what they love from this world despite their sins, they are being led on. Then the Messenger ﷺ recited, ﴾When they forgot what they were reminded of, we opened for them the doors of everything. Then when they were happy with what they were given, we destroyed them suddenly, and they became hopeless﴿ [Al-An'am 44]»

Reported by Ahmad (17311) and al-Albani declared its chain strong (*al-Silsilah al-Sahihah*, 413)

Imagine one running after the world and winning so much of it, thinking all along that they are lucky. Their material fixation blinds them to the irony of receiving more wealth while sinning. This alone should wake them up. But the world is intoxicating.

The stark danger of wealth explains the warning in the Quran against its temptations, the cautionary tales of past nations who did not heed this advice, and the command to spend for

Allah's sake. This spending is not because Allah needs it, but because we do. Allah said:

خُذْ مِنْ أَمْوَٰلِهِمْ صَدَقَةً تُطَهِّرُهُمْ وَتُزَكِّيهِم بِهَا... ﴿١٠٣﴾

Take from their wealth a charity that purifies them and blesses them.

At-Tawbah (Q9:103)

The intent of charity is the cleansing of the soul from stinginess and greed, from the worldly obsession that comes from running after money. Allah knows very well the hold that money has on us, how much we love it and are willing to sacrifice for it. And Allah wants us to change, to adopt a higher and nobler love. This is why He asks us to spend from the wealth that we love. When we do, another love takes its place. Ibn Mas'ud رَضِيَ ٱللَّهُ عَنْهُ said commenting on *ayah* 177 from Surah al-Baqarah:

قولُه تعالَى ﴿وَآتَى الْمَالَ عَلَى حُبِّهِ﴾ [البقرة ١٧٧] قال ابنُ مسعودٍ رضي الله عنه: أن تؤتِيَه وأنت صحيحٌ شحيحٌ تأملُ العيشَ وتخشَى الفقرَ.

تفسير ابن أبي حاتم (١٥٤٦)

Allah's saying, ﴾And he gave wealth despite loving it﴿ [al-Baqarah 177]. Ibn Mas'ud رَضِيَ ٱللَّهُ عَنْهُ said, "You give it while you are healthy and stingy, hopeful of living and afraid of poverty."

Tafsir Ibn Abi Hatim (1546)

This is taken from the following *hadith*.

جاءَ رَجُلٌ إلى النبيِّ ﷺ فقالَ: يا رَسولَ اللَّهِ أيُّ الصَّدَقَةِ أَعْظَمُ أَجْرًا؟ قالَ «أَنْ تَصَدَّقَ وأَنْتَ صَحِيحٌ شَحِيحٌ تَخْشى الفَقْرَ وتَأْمُلُ الغِنى ولا تُمْهِلُ حتّى إذا بَلَغَتِ الحُلْقُومَ قُلْتَ لِفُلانٍ كَذا ولِفُلانٍ كَذا وقدْ كانَ لِفُلانٍ.»

رواه البخاري (١٤١٩) ومسلم (١٠٣٢)

A man came to the Prophet ﷺ and asked, "O Messenger of Allah, which charity has the greatest reward?" He replied, «When you give while you are healthy and stingy, afraid of poverty and hoping to be rich. And you do not wait until the soul reaches the throat and then say, "So-and-so gets this, and so-and-so gets that," and it is already for so-and-so.»

Reported by al-Bukhari (1419) and Muslim (1032)

We love wealth, and we love it especially when we are hopeful of a long and healthy life. If we manage to sacrifice some of it despite our natural selfishness, we will free ourselves from the hold of wealth, purify our souls from the impurities of greed, and increase our love for Allah and the Hereafter. You are not going to give up something dear to you except for something dearer. The act of giving itself develops this new love.

This is the purpose of spending. We are giving to Allah to treat our souls. We are not giving to unload our junk. Allah gave us a valuable reminder about the quality of what we spend when He said:

يَـٰٓأَيُّهَا ٱلَّذِينَ ءَامَنُوٓا۟ أَنفِقُوا۟ مِن طَيِّبَـٰتِ مَا كَسَبْتُمْ وَمِمَّآ أَخْرَجْنَا لَكُم
مِّنَ ٱلْأَرْضِ ۖ وَلَا تَيَمَّمُوا۟ ٱلْخَبِيثَ مِنْهُ تُنفِقُونَ وَلَسْتُم بِـَٔاخِذِيهِ إِلَّآ أَن
تُغْمِضُوا۟ فِيهِ ۚ وَٱعْلَمُوٓا۟ أَنَّ ٱللَّهَ غَنِىٌّ حَمِيدٌ ﴿٢٦٧﴾

O you who have Iman, spend from the good that you earned and from what We produced for you from the ground. And do not seek what is lowly among it to spend, while you would not take it unless your eyes were closed. And know that Allah is Self-Sufficient and Praiseworthy.

Al-Baqarah (Q2:267)

It is better to donate our old belongings than throw them away. But the giving we aspire to, the one that will uplift us, comes from what we love. We give from what we love to Whom we love to gain what we love.

Kindness to those closest to us

When we speak of love and good manners, many imagine it as an attitude we show to strangers. We fail to realize that our families deserve our greatest kindness. It may be that our proximity to them blinds us to their needs, or maybe our interactions create friction and tension that harden our hearts towards them. But this is all the more reason that we show greater love to our families, close and extended. It is truly lopsided piety when one is cordial with nonrelatives but denies their family the love and compassion they need. It is, of course, important to treat strangers kindly, especially when they are vulnerable and in need. But our kin have greater rights over us, and we cannot be right with Allah unless we do right by them. Sometimes this is more challenging than kindness towards nonrelatives. But remember that there is a lot more reward when things are difficult. When doing the right thing is challenging, it removes more of our sins and carries us closer to Allah. So, do not let the difficulty deter you. Let it motivate you.

Kindness to our relatives is doubly rewarded: it is both charity and kindness to our kin (*Silat al-Rahim*). Thus, the Prophet ﷺ directed Abu Talhah to give his charity to his needy relatives. Its purpose is to please Allah. It does not matter who will appreciate the gift or how people treated us in the past. What matters is that Allah will reward you. Humans are incapable of compensating you adequately and fully for your kindness. So, do not seek your reward from them. Only Allah has the reward you want and need.

Loving the Hereafter

Loving this world competes with love for Allah and the Hereafter. The Prophet ﷺ said:

«مَنْ أحبَّ دُنْياهُ أَضَرَّ بِآخِرَتِه ومَنْ أحبَّ آخِرَتَهُ أَضَرَّ بِدُنْياهُ فآثِرُوا ما يَبْقى على ما يَفْنى.»

رواه أحمد (١٩٦٩٧) وابن حبان (٧٠٩) وصححه الألباني (صحيح الموارد ٢٠٩٣)

«The one who loves their world will harm their hereafter, and the one who loves their hereafter will harm their world. So, give preference to what lasts over what perishes.»

Reported by Ahmad (19697) and Ibn Hibban (709) and al-Albani declared it sahih (*Sahih al-Mawarid*, 2093)

Each love leads to different ends and paths in life. Each creates different concerns and actions. Loving the Hereafter elevates us as Muslims and human beings: it lets us focus on the meaningful and disregard the trivial. The best among us are those who devote their lives to reaching the happiness of the Hereafter.

قِيلِ لرسولِ اللهِ ﷺ: أَيُّ النَّاسِ أفضلُ؟ قال «كُلُّ مَخْمومِ القَلْبِ صَدوقِ اللِّسانِ» قالوا: صدوقُ اللسانِ نَعرِفُه فما مخمومُ القلبِ؟ قالَ «هُوَ التَّقِيُّ النَّقِيُّ لا إِثْمَ فِيهِ ولا بَغْيَ ولا غِلَّ ولا حَسَدَ» قلنا: يا رسولَ اللهِ فمَن على أَثَرِهِ؟ قال «الذي يَشْنَأُ الدُّنيا ويُحِبُّ الآخِرَةَ.»

رواه البيهقي في شعب الإيمان (٤٤٦) وصححه الألباني (صحيح الترغيب ٢٩٣١)

The Messenger ﷺ was asked, "Who is the best of people?" He said, «Everyone with a *makhmum* [clean] heart and truthful tongue.» They asked, "We know the truthful tongue, but what is a *makhmum* heart?" He answered, «It is the pious and pure one, with no sin, aggression, hatred, and envy in it.» We said, "O Messenger of Allah, then who?" He said, «The one who hates this world and loves the Hereafter.»

Reported by al-Bayhaqi in *Shu'ab al-Iman* (446) and al-Albani declared it sahih by (*Sahih al-Targhib*, 2931)

What does it mean to hate this world? The Prophet ﷺ did not hate everything on earth. In fact, he said:

«حُبِّبَ إلي منَ الدُّنيا النساءُ والطِّيبُ وجُعِلَ قرةُ عيني في الصلاةِ.»

رواه النسائي (٣٩٤٩) وصححه الألباني (صحيح النسائي ٣٩٤٩)

«Women and perfume were made beloved to me from this world. And my greatest joy is in Salah.»

Reported by al-Nasa'i (3949) and al-Albani declared it sahih (*Sahih al-Nasa'i*, 3949)

It is natural to love and be attracted to the beauty of this world. Allah put it there as a blessing and a favor. Allah also did not ask us to stay away from *halal* or hate it. And if we realize that *halal* is the means of avoiding *haram*, which Allah hates, we will know that *halal* is actually praiseworthy and desirable. What brings us closer to Allah deserves our love. Hating the world means hating the unlawful and what is distracting in it. The problem is obsessively running after it, favoring it over the Hereafter. This is why the Prophet ﷺ repeatedly reminded us of the true value of this world. The Prophet ﷺ said:

مرَّ رسولُ اللهِ صلَّى اللهُ عليه وسلَّمَ بالسوقِ داخلًا من بعضِ العاليةِ فمرَّ بجَدي أَسَكَّ ميتٍ فتناوله فأخذ بأُذُنِه ثم قال «أيكم يحبُّ هذا له بدرهمٍ؟» فقالوا: ما نحبُّ أنه لنا بشيءٍ وما نصنعُ به، قال «أتحبّون أنه لكم؟» قالوا: لا، قال «ذلك لهم» ثلاثًا، فقالوا: لا واللهِ لو كان حيًّا لكان عيبًا فيه أنه أَسَكٌّ فكيف وهو ميتٌ؟ قال «فواللهِ لَلدُّنيا أهونُ على اللهِ من هذا عليكم.»

رواه مسلم (٢٩٥٧)

The Prophet ﷺ was coming from al-'Aliyah. He passed by the market and saw in it a dead short-eared young goat. He grabbed it by the ear and asked, «Who among you would love that this be his in return for a dirham [coin]?» They replied, "We would not love that it be ours even if it were free. What would we do with it?" He asked again, «Do you love that it be yours?» They replied, "No." He said that to them three times. They replied, "No, by Allah! If it were alive, it would be defective because it is earless, so how about when it is dead!" He said, «By Allah, this world is paltrier to Allah than this [dead animal] to you.»

Reported by Muslim (2957)

We are encouraged to work to earn a living and support our family and children. With the right intention, work becomes an act of worship. But most do not stop there. They collect much more than they need—often from *haram* sources—and they allow the pursuit of wealth to distract them from the Hereafter. The following *hadith* puts it all in perspective. The Prophet ﷺ said:

«أيُّكم يُحبُّ أن يغدوَ كلَّ يومٍ إلى بُطْحانَ أو إلى العقيقِ فيأتيَ منهُ بناقتَينِ كَوْماوَيْنِ بغيرِ إثمٍ ولا قطعِ رحمٍ؟» قالوا: كلُّنا يا رسولَ اللهِ، قال «فلأن يغدُوَ أحدُكُم كلَّ يومٍ إلى المسجدِ فيعلمُ او يقرأُ آيتَينِ مِن كتابِ اللهِ خيرٌ لهُ مِن ناقتَينِ وإنْ ثلاثٌ فثلاثٌ مثلُ أعدادِهنَّ.»

رواه مسلم (٨٠٣)

«Who among you would like to head each morning to Buthan or al-'Aqiq and come back with two big-humped she-camels without being guilty of sin or severing ties of kinship?» They replied, "All of us, O Messenger of Allah." He said, «If any of you heads each morning to the masjid and learns or reads two ayahs from the Book of Allah, it would be better for them than two she-camels. And if three, then three like their numbers.»

Reported by Muslim (803)

Yes, it is permissible to acquire those camels (or cars for us today). But few of us are as excited about learning an *ayah* as we would be when we buy a new car. The Prophet ﷺ wanted to change these preferences in our hearts and cleanse them from worldly obsession. Otherwise, this obsession becomes a disease that dooms us in this life and the next. The Prophet ﷺ said:

«يُوشِكُ الأممُ أن تَداعَى عليكم كما تَداعَى الأَكَلةُ إلى قَصْعتِها» فقال قائلٌ: ومن قِلَّةٍ نحن يومئذٍ؟ قال «بل أنتم يومئذٍ كثيرٌ ولكنَّكم

غُثاءٌ كغُثاءِ السَّيلِ ولينزِعَنَّ اللهُ من صدورِ عدوِّكم المهابةَ منكم وليقذِفَنَّ اللهُ في قلوبِكم الوهْنَ» فقال قائلٌ: يا رسولَ اللهِ وما الوهْنُ؟ قال «حبُّ الدُّنيا وكراهيةُ الموتِ.»

رواه أبو داود (٤٢٩٧) وصححه الألباني (السلسلة الصحيحة ٩٥٨)

«People are about to invite each other [to attack you] like people invite each other to a meal.» So someone said, "Will we be few at time?" He replied, «No, you will be plenty then, but you will be like the dregs of a stream. And Allah will remove from the chest of your enemies any fear they have for you and will place weakness in your hearts.» Someone asked, "What is this weakness [meaning where does it come from] O Prophet of Allah?" He replied, «Love of the world and hatred of death.»

Reported by Abu Dawud (4297) and al-Albani declared it sahih (*al-Silsilah al-Sahihah*, 958)

Love of the world here is condemnable. It produces weakness in faith and hatred of meeting Allah. Loving the world in moderation, with our eyesight on the life to come, does not do that. There lies the difference between obsessive love and healthy love. In the first, we sacrifice Allah for the sake of the world. In the second, we give up the world to please Allah. What we love most wins.

What will help us make the emotional transition to the Hereafter is to know what happens after death. Those devoted to Allah never want to return to this world. They realize that what Allah has is incomparable to this meager world. The Prophet ﷺ said:

«ما علَى الأرضِ من نفسٍ تموتُ ولَها عندَ اللَّهِ خيرٌ تُحبُّ أن ترجِعَ إليكم ولَها الدُّنيا إلَّا القَتيلُ فإنَّهُ يُحبُّ أن يرجِعَ فيُقتلَ مرَّةً أخرَى.»

رواه البخاري (٢٧٩٥) ومسلم (١٨٧٧) والنسائي (٣١٥٩) واللفظ له

«If a soul dies on earth and it has something good waiting for it with Allah, it would not love to come back to you, even if it had the world in return. Except for the martyr. They would love to come back and be killed another time.»

Reported by al-Bukhari (2795), Muslim (1877), and al-Nasa'i (3159), and the wording is his

Gaining the favors of the Hereafter requires devotion to Allah, and this takes one away from excessive worldly pursuits. Conversely, winning more of this world requires devotion to it, and this takes one away from Allah. The two are opposite projects in life. And they lead to very different results. Thu al-Nun عَلَيْهِ السَّلَامُ said:

قال ذو النُّونِ عليه السلام: اعْلَمُوا أَنَّ الْمُحِبَّ لِلَّهِ عَزَّ وَجَلَّ لَا يَعْظُمُ عِنْدَهُ الْإِيثَارُ لِلَّهِ لِأَنَّهُ لَيْسَ شَيْءٌ عِنْدَهُ أَعْظَمَ مِنَ اللَّهِ فَيَنْبَغِي لِلْمُحِبِّ لِلَّهِ أَنْ يُرَى عَلَيْهِ أَثَرُ ذَلِكَ مِنْ رَفْضِ الدُّنْيَا لِأَنَّهُ مِنَ الْمُحَالِ أَنْ يَجْتَمِعَ فِي الْقَلْبِ حُبُّ اللَّهِ مَعَ حُبِّ الدُّنْيَا فَمَنْ أَحَبَّ اللَّهَ لَمْ يَنْظُرْ إِلَى مَا يَنَالُهُ مِنَ الدُّنْيَا وَلَا تَكُونُ لَهُ حَاجَةٌ إِلَى غَيْرِ مَنْ أَحَبَّ.

الزهد الكبير للبيهقي (ص٧٧)

Know that Allah's beloved does not consider any sacrifice for Allah's sake to be too big because, for them, there is nothing greater than Allah. Allah's beloved must exhibit this by turning away from the world, for it is impossible for the heart to combine the love of Allah and the love of the world. The one who loves Allah does not pay attention to what they get from this world, and they do not have a need for anyone except the One they love.

Al-Zuhd al-Kabir by al-Bayhaqi (p. 312)

Loving Allah makes sacrificing this world possible. And it is a worthwhile trade. But when the love of this world dominates the heart, it will abandon Allah for this world. And it would be its greatest loss.

If we want to conquer this world and surrender to Allah, we

must spend from what we love. In fact, the entire Shari'ah leads to that end. Ibrahim ibn Adham said:

قَالَ إِبْرَاهِيمُ بْنُ أَدْهَمَ: الْوَرَعُ يَبْلُغُ بِالْعَبْدِ إِلَى الزُّهْدِ فِي الدُّنْيَا وَالزُّهْدُ يَبْلُغُ بِهِ إِلَى حُبِّ اللَّهِ عَزَّ وَجَلَّ.

الزهد الكبير للبيهقي (ص٣١٢)

> *Wara'* [i.e. leaving haram and doubtful matters] leads one to *Zuhd* [i.e. turning away from the world]. And turning away from the world leads one to love Allah, Glory be to Him.
>
> *Al-Zuhd al-Kabir* by al-Bayhaqi (p. 312)

The first step is abandoning *haram* and performing the obligations. This blocks the greatest worldly harm. Declining the impermissible creates the first distance between us and the world. This distance grows further when we avoid doubtful matters. As we keep moving away from the world, our worship moves us closer to Allah. And as our love for this world decreases, our love for Allah grows. The last stage is leaving unnecessary *halal* that distracts from Allah. Eventually, and if we are consistent, we will love Allah and desire His rewards more than we want anything in this life. This is when the love of Allah becomes our greatest possession and joy. But to get it, we have to start giving from what we love.

HADITH THIRTY NINE

الحديث التاسع الثلاثون

Loving our hometowns

كَانَ النَّبِيُّ ﷺ إِذَا قَدِمَ مِنْ سَفَرٍ فَنَظَرَ إِلَى جُدُرَاتِ المَدِينَةِ أَوْضَعَ رَاحِلَتَهُ وَإِنْ كَانَ عَلَى دَابَّةٍ حَرَّكَهَا مِنْ حُبِّهَا.

رواه البخاري (١٨٠٢)

When the Prophet ﷺ would return from a trip and see the walls of Madinah, he would speed up his camel, and if he were on another animal, he would prompt it to speed up, out of his love for Madinah.

Reported by al-Bukhari (1802)

Commentary

We can love a city for religious or worldly reasons, or both. The best cities on earth are Makkah and Madinah. Allah loves them, blessed them, and they deserve the love of every Muslim.

Loving Makkah and Madinah

Makkah and Madinah conjure up the memory of Islam itself. And for that, their love is in the blood of every Muslim. Makkah houses the first and best Masjid on earth, and Madinah is the beacon of Islam. The revelation commenced in Makkah and blossomed in Madinah. And from Madinah, it radiated to the rest of the world. No matter where we come from, our spiritual roots are in Makkah and Madinah. They are our home, our destination, and our dream.

Makkah was the birthplace of the Prophet ﷺ, so he naturally loved it. But it was much more than that. Makkah is the best city on earth. The following *hadith* sums it well. The Prophet ﷺ said:

«واللَّهِ إنَّكِ لخيرُ أرضِ اللَّهِ وأحبُّ أرضِ اللَّهِ إلى اللَّهِ ولولا أنِّي أُخرِجتُ منكِ ما خرجتُ.»

رواه الترمذي (٣٩٢٥) وصححه الألباني (صحيح الترمذي ٣٩٢٥)

«By Allah, you are the best of Allah's lands and the most beloved of Allah's lands to Him. And were it not that I was forced to leave you, I would not have left.»

Reported by al-Tirmidhi (3925) and al-Albani declared it sahih (*Sahih al-Tirmidhi*, 3925)

You can feel the longing in this farewell. Just before his exit from his hometown, the Prophet ﷺ paused to take what he thought was his last look and told of his love for the Mother of all Cities. It was not just that he grew up there and spent all of his life. It was more than that. It is the land that Allah loves the most, and leaving what Allah loves is difficult. But the Prophet ﷺ sacrificed the beauty and comfort of Makkah for the sake of a greater love: the spread of Islam. Allah commanded him to migrate because what Allah loved was elsewhere. And he pursued what Allah loved no matter where it took him.

We all have hometowns that we love. Leaving such a place feels like uprooting a plant: a severance of connections and memories that leaves us empty for a long time. Some of us leave our hometowns willingly, while others are forced out. If the former is difficult, the latter is traumatizing. But we have solace in the life of the Prophet ﷺ who was chased out and they even tried to kill. There are people today who are expelled from their homes and flee for their lives. In those unbearable times, remember your Prophet. Allah protected him and gave him refuge in another blessed land. It was not easy. But it bore the most excellent fruit later. And so, if you ever find yourself in a situation like that, remember that Allah can give you more than what the transgressors are trying to take away from you.

The second best place on earth is Madinah, the city of the Prophet ﷺ. He built his Masjid there, and Islam spread from it to the rest of the Peninsula and beyond. But it was challenging. Not only was it a new city that needed adjustment, but it was not as well to do as Makkah. And it was not healthful because of its infamous plagues. Therefore, the Prophet ﷺ made the following *du'a*:

«اللهم إنَّ إبراهيمَ خليلَك وعبدَك ونبيَّك دعاك لأهلِ مكةَ وأنا محمدٌ عبدُك ورسولُك أدعوك لأهلِ المدينةِ مثلَ ما دعاك إبراهيمُ لمكةَ ندعوك أن تبارِكَ لهم في صاعِهم ومُدِّهم وثمارِهم اللهم حَبِّبْ إلينا المدينةَ كما حَبَّبتْ إلينا مكةَ واجعلْ ما بها من وباءٍ بخُمَّ اللهم إني حرَّمتُ ما بين لابتَيها كما حرَّمتَ على لسانِ إبراهيمَ الحرَمَ.»

رواه أحمد (٢٢٦٣٠) وصححه الألباني (صحيح الترغيب ١١٩٨)

«O Allah, Ibrahim—Your Khalil, Your servant, and Your Prophet—prayed to You for the sake of the people of Makkah. And I am Muhammad—Your servant and Your Messenger—and I am praying to You for the sake of the people of Madinah as Ibrahim prayed to You for Makkah. We pray to You that You bless their sa' and mudd [i.e. the food they measure] and their harvest. O Allah, make us love Madinah as You made us love Makkah, and transfer its plague to Khumm [i.e. outside Madinah]. O Allah, I forbid [i.e. declare sacred] what is between its mountains as You forbade on the tongue of Ibrahim the Haram [of Makkah].»

Reported by Ahmad (22630) and al-Albani declared it sahih (*Sahih al-Targhib*, 1198)

The Prophet ﷺ declared Madinah a *haram* like Makkah. And He asked Allah to put barakah in it, remove its plagues, and make it close to the hearts of the believers. This is your city, O believers! The city that your Prophet loved. How much did he love it? When he would come back from his travels and catch a glimpse of Madinah, he would rush back to it because he could not stay away anymore. How could the hearts of the believers not long for Madinah after hearing this? How could anyone stay away from it? Can anyone stay away from their heart? The Prophet's ﷺ longing would show itself repeatedly when he came back to it.

أَقْبَلْنَا مَعَ النَّبِيِّ صَلَّى اللهُ عَلَيْهِ وَسَلَّمَ مِنْ غَزْوَةِ تَبُوكَ حَتَّى إذا أَشْرَفْنَا على الْمَدِينَةِ قالَ «هَذِهِ طَابَةُ وَهَذَا أُحُدٌ جَبَلٌ يُحِبُّنَا وَنُحِبُّهُ.»

رواه البخاري (٤٤٢٢)

We were heading back with the Prophet ﷺ from the battle of Tabuk. When we reached the outskirts of Madinah, he said, «This is Tabah. And this is Uhud, a mountain that loves us and we love it.»

Reported by al-Bukhari (4422)

Tabah is another name for Madinah, which means the Fragrant or the Pure. And it is both fragrant and pure. And what about the Mountain of Uhud? You gaze at this majestic mountain, and you remember it shaking beneath the feet of the Prophet ﷺ. It loved him, and he loved it. It is not a figure of speech: Uhud feels. Everything around us has consciousness and glorifies Allah, even if we do not sense it. Allah said:

...وَإِن مِّن شَيْءٍ إِلَّا يُسَبِّحُ بِحَمْدِهِۦ وَلَٰكِن لَّا تَفْقَهُونَ تَسْبِيحَهُمْ... ﴿٤٤﴾

And there is not a thing except that it glorifies and praises Allah, but you do not comprehend their glorifications.

Al-Isra (Q17:44)

Things around you have emotions and can love. And they

love the believers. Allah said after the demise of Pharoah and his soldiers:

فَمَا بَكَتْ عَلَيْهِمُ ٱلسَّمَآءُ وَٱلْأَرْضُ... ﴿٢٩﴾

The heavens and the earth did not cry over them.

Ad-Dukhan (Q44:29)

This tells you that they cry over the believers. So, if you want everything to love you—literally everything—then love Allah, and even the walls of your house will love you.

Praying in Makkah and Madinah is unlike praying anywhere else. The Prophet ﷺ said:

«صلاةٌ في مَسْجِدِي أفضلُ من ألفِ صلاةٍ فِيما سِواهُ إلا المسجِدَ الحرامَ وصلاةٌ في المسْجِدِ الحرامِ أفضلُ من مِائةِ ألفِ صلاةٍ فِيما سِواهُ.»

رواه أحمد (١٤٦٩٤) وصححه الألباني (صحيح الجامع ٣٨٣٨)

«A single Salah in my Masjid is better than a thousand elsewhere, except al-Masjid al-Haram [in Makkah]. And a single Salah in al-Masjid al-Haram is better than a hundred thousand elsewhere.»

Reported by Ahmad (14694) and al-Albani declared it sahih (*Sahih al-Jami'*, 3838)

The extraordinary reward for praying in these two masjids is a reflection of Allah's love for them and the virtue of the two blessed cities. These two Masjids—in addition to al-Aqsa in Jerusalem—are the only three masjids of extraordinary virtue. Abu Dharr رضي الله عنه once asked the Messenger ﷺ:

عن أبي ذر رضي الله عنه قال: قُلْتُ: يا رَسُولَ اللَّهِ أَيُّ مَسْجِدٍ وُضِعَ فِي الأَرْضِ أَوَّلَ؟ قالَ «الْمَسْجِدُ الْحَرامُ» قالَ: قُلْتُ: ثُمَّ أَيٌّ؟

قالَ «الْمَسْجِدُ الأَقْصَى» قُلْتُ: كَمْ كانَ بَيْنَهُما؟ قالَ «أَرْبَعُونَ سَنَةً ثُمَّ أَيْنَما أَدْرَكَتْكَ الصَّلاةُ بَعْدُ فَصَلِّهْ فَإِنَّ الْفَضْلَ فِيهِ.»

رواه البخاري (٣٣٦٦)

"O Messenger of Allah, what masjid was built first on earth?" He answered, «Al-Masjid al-Haram.» I asked, "Then?" He answered, «Al-Masjid al-Aqsa.» I asked, "How many years were there between the two?" He answered, «Forty years. If you are elsewhere, whenever it is time to pray, then pray, for the virtue is in doing that.»

Reported by al-Bukhari (3366)

The Messenger ﷺ was telling Abu Dharr that these two masjids—in addition to his masjid—are the only ones of distinction. Besides them, all others are equal in virtue: when it is time to pray, pray in anyone of them.

The three also share the distinction of being the only masjids worthy of traveling to. The Prophet ﷺ said:

«لا تُشَدُّ الرِّحالُ إِلَّا إِلى ثَلاثَةِ مَساجِدَ الْمَسْجِدِ الحَرامِ وَمَسْجِدِ الرَّسُولِ صَلَّى اللهُ عَلَيْهِ وَسَلَّمَ وَمَسْجِدِ الأَقْصَى.»

رواه البخاري (١١٨٩)

«Travel should not be initiated except to three masjids: al-Masjid al-Haram, the Masjid of the Messenger ﷺ, and Masjid al-Aqsa.»

Reported by al-Bukhari (1189)

These are the best three masjids on earth. And for that, they deserve the love of every Muslim.

For al-Aqsa, according to one *hadith*, a single *Salah* in it is worth two hundred and fifty (*Sahih al-Targhib*, 1179). In another *hadith*, Prophet Sulayman عَلَيْهِ السَّلَام prayed to Allah to forgive all the sins of one who visits al-Aqsa solely for the sake of Allah (*Sahih al-Targhib*, 1178). In these difficult times, we need to revive the love of al-Aqsa in our hearts and the hearts of our children and renew our attachment to it.

Loving our hometowns

We have personal and religious reasons for loving any place on earth. We love our hometowns, scenic areas, vacation destinations, and anywhere we can shop. Religiously, we love masjids and institutions of religious learning. The religious and personal can sometimes coincide as well as clash. We can love our Umrah or Hajj trip because it brings us closer to Allah and because it is a vacation or an opportunity to shop. And as long as the main motivation for this trip is religious, we can love Makkah and Madinah for both reasons. We love going to masjids because they are the houses of Allah, and they are where we meet friends and socialize. Similarly, as long as the religious reason is the dominant one, the two loves can coexist without contradiction. We can love scenic routes because they are naturally appealing and because they remind us of Allah's Beauty. Our hometowns may be places of impiety, pitting religious and natural loves against each other. If continued residence in any place, no matter our personal feelings, is religiously harmful, migration to a more pious area is mandated. Religious love, in this case, must take precedence. This is why many of the Prophets of Allah عَلَيْهِمُ السَّلَامُ migrated and left everything behind for the sake of Allah.

This leads us to comment briefly on nationalism. The nationalism I am referring to is not the natural love we have for our birthplace. What I mean by it is the modern political construct that unites people as citizens in a specific geographic area, binding them to the land and its political system, and distinguishing them from different citizens in different regions. Islamic love and belonging are much broader and more merciful than the nationalist one. We love any pious land even if we were never to set foot in it, and we migrate from a sinful land even if we were born there. We are not servants of lands but servants of Allah. And as servants of Allah, we move wherever we may be more pleasing to Him. We cannot love a sinful co-citizen more than we love a pious non-citizen. I may personally love my co-citizen because we share the same language, culture, and cuisine. But if they are displeasing to Allah, I cannot put them ahead of the pious just because the latter was born in a different country. We can love our homeland as much as we want. But we cannot love it more than we love Allah and what Allah loves.

HADITH FORTY

الحديث الأربعون

Loving Iman and righteousness

لَمَّا كَانَ يَوْمُ أُحُدٍ وَانْكَفَأَ الْمُشْرِكُونَ قَالَ رَسُولُ اللَّهِ ﷺ «اسْتَوُوا حَتَّى أُثْنِيَ عَلَى رَبِّي» فَصَارُوا خَلْفَهُ صُفُوفًا فَقَالَ «اللَّهُمَّ لَكَ الْحَمْدُ كُلُّهُ اللَّهُمَّ لَا قَابِضَ لِمَا بَسَطْتَ وَلَا بَاسِطَ لِمَا قَبَضْتَ وَلَا هَادِيَ لِمَا أَضْلَلْتَ وَلَا مُضِلَّ لِمَنْ هَدَيْتَ وَلَا مُعْطِيَ لِمَا مَنَعْتَ وَلَا مَانِعَ لِمَا أَعْطَيْتَ وَلَا مُقَرِّبَ لِمَا بَاعَدْتَ وَلَا مُبَاعِدَ لِمَا قَرَّبْتَ اللَّهُمَّ ابْسُطْ عَلَيْنَا مِنْ بَرَكَاتِكَ وَرَحْمَتِكَ وَفَضْلِكَ وَرِزْقِكَ اللَّهُمَّ إِنِّي أَسْأَلُكَ النَّعِيمَ الْمُقِيمَ الَّذِي لَا يَحُولُ وَلَا يَزُولُ اللَّهُمَّ إِنِّي أَسْأَلُكَ النَّعِيمَ يَوْمَ الْعَيْلَةِ وَالْأَمْنَ يَوْمَ الْخَوْفِ اللَّهُمَّ إِنِّي عَائِذٌ بِكَ مِنْ شَرِّ مَا أَعْطَيْتَنَا وَشَرِّ مَا مَنَعْتَ اللَّهُمَّ حَبِّبْ إِلَيْنَا الْإِيمَانَ وَزَيِّنْهُ فِي قُلُوبِنَا وَكَرِّهْ إِلَيْنَا الْكُفْرَ وَالْفُسُوقَ وَالْعِصْيَانَ وَاجْعَلْنَا مِنَ الرَّاشِدِينَ اللَّهُمَّ تَوَفَّنَا مُسْلِمِينَ وَأَحْيِنَا مُسْلِمِينَ وَأَلْحِقْنَا بِالصَّالِحِينَ غَيْرَ خَزَايَا وَلَا مَفْتُونِينَ اللَّهُمَّ قَاتِلِ الْكَفَرَةَ الَّذِينَ يُكَذِّبُونَ رُسُلَكَ وَيَصُدُّونَ عَنْ سَبِيلِكَ وَاجْعَلْ عَلَيْهِمْ رِجْزَكَ وَعَذَابَكَ اللَّهُمَّ قَاتِلِ الْكَفَرَةَ الَّذِينَ أُوتُوا الْكِتَابَ إِلَهَ الْحَقِّ.»

رواه أحمد (١٥٤٩٢) والحاكم (١٨٦٨) وصححه الألباني (صحيح الأدب المفرد ٥٤١)

When the polytheists left on the Day of Uhud, the Messenger of Allah ﷺ said, «Form straight rows so that I can praise my Rabb.» They lined up behind him and he said, «O Allah, all praise belongs to You. O Allah, none can contract what You expand nor expand what You contract. None can guide whom You misguide nor misguide whom You guide. None can give what You withhold nor withhold what You give. None can bring near what You put far nor put far what You bring near. O Allah, grant us abundance from Your blessings, mercy, favor, and provision. O Allah, I ask You for the lasting blessing that does not change or depart. O Allah, I ask You for blessing on the Day of Poverty and security on the Day of Fear. O Allah, I seek refuge with You from the evil of what You gave us and what you withheld. O Allah, make us love Iman and beautify it in our hearts; make us hate disbelief, rebellion, and disobedience; and make us of the guided. O Allah, make us die as Muslims, live as Muslims, and join us with the righteous, neither disgraced nor tempted. O Allah, fight the disbelievers who deny Your Messengers and deter people from Your path and send Your severe punishment over them. O Allah, fight the disbelievers who were given the Book, O the True Ilah.»

Reported by Ahmad (15492) and al-Hakim (1868). Al-Albani declared it sahih (Sahih al-Adab al-Mufrad, 541)

Commentary

What we love and hate determines the paths we take. Loving *Iman* and piety is essential to following the truth and resisting temptations. Asking for this love should be one of our frequent prayers.

Praising Allah at all times

This *du'a* is remarkable! What makes it even more impressive is the circumstances surrounding it. The Prophet ﷺ prayed it right after burying the dead of Uhud. He said it while the battle wounds were still fresh and the emotional pains even deeper. It is precisely because of all of this that this *du'a* was needed.

The Prophet ﷺ began the *du'a* with praising and thanking Allah. It was the common practice of the Prophet ﷺ to praise and thank Allah all the time, no matter what.

كانَ رسولُ اللَّهِ صلَّى اللَّهُ عليهِ وسلَّمَ إذا رأى ما يُحبُّ قالَ «الحمدُ للَّهِ الَّذي بنِعمتِهِ تتمُّ الصَّالحاتُ» وإذا رأى ما يكرَهُ قالَ «الحمدُ للَّهِ علَى كلِّ حالٍ.»

رواه ابن ماجه (٣٨٠٣) وحسنه الألباني (صحيح ابن ماجه ٣٨٠٣)

When the Messenger of Allah ﷺ would see [or encounter] what he loved, he would say, «*Alhamdulillah* by whose bounty good things are done.» And if he would see [or encounter] what he hated, he would say, «*Alhamdulillah* in every situation.»

Reported by Ibn Majah (3803) and al-Albani declared it hasan (*Sahih Ibn Majah*, 3803)

It is easy to see why we are thanking Allah during good times. But for the bad ones too? Yes, even the bad times. Allah deserves our gratitude no matter what is happening at any moment. What seems like hardship and misfortune is, in fact, a blessing. It is just that the blessing is hiding beneath the veneer of the test. Does Allah send anything bad, or could anything bad come from Him? Are our sins not forgiven through hardship? Do they not teach us patience and humility? Do they not open our eyes and send us back to Allah? Hardship transforms us into better Muslims and humans. It is just difficult sometimes to see this and appreciate it while in the midst of it. Praising and thanking Allah reminds us to look for the hidden blessing, to extract it, and turn every misfortune into a gift.

Consider the Prophet's ﷺ praise of Allah right after the pain of Uhud. Were not so many Muslims just killed? Was this not a defeat? It is a defeat only if it defeats you and steals you away from Allah. Were those killed not martyrs, blessed with such death? Were they not happier with Allah than they ever were on earth? Their departure was sad, but their destination is beautiful. When you thank Allah despite your pain, He allows you to see the other side of the story. Uhud taught Muslims a valuable lesson. It taught them the necessity of listening to the commands of the Prophet ﷺ. If you disobey him, you would be leaving Allah's care. It taught them to put the Hereafter before worldly gains and the Will of Allah before their desires. It prepared them for the death of the Prophet ﷺ so they could carry the message after his painful departure. These are lessons for us too. This is why he stood up and thanked Allah, dedicating all praise to Him. Even if you cannot see the benefits of a test, they are there. Thanking Allah opens our hearts and minds so we can see them.

Surrendering before Allah

It is such a beautiful *du'a*! The Prophet continued his praise of Allah by enumerating His Perfect Qualities, contrasting them with our weakness. He is the only One who gives and the only One who guides. If He holds something back, no one else can grant it. If you want something that is far, He can bring it near. And if you want something near to be gone, Allah can take it away. So, ask Him alone for what you want. And accept and submit to Him when He decides.

Surrendering to Allah is the best way to deal with a setback. It allows you to accept that what happened was destined and inevitable, so nothing could have been done to stop it. Regret and self-blame are meaningless when something cannot be avoided. The second thing it does is that it supplies you with hope and energy, coming from your faith in Allah and reliance on Him. Whenever you fall, you can get back up because Allah is always there, willing to help, and promising the best. Allah is bigger than any setback.

The Prophet ﷺ would rush to Allah whenever something distressed him.

كان النَّبيُّ ﷺ إذا حَزَبَه أمْرٌ صَلّى.

رواه أبو داود (١٣١٩) وحسنه الألباني (صحيح أبي داود ١٣١٩)

When something would distress the Prophet ﷺ, he would pray.

Reported by Abu Dawud (1319) and al-Albani declared it hasan (*Sahih Abi Dawud*, 1319)

Praying unburdens us from worry and sadness. And it injects us with energy and the hope that it all will be better with Allah's help. *Salah* redirects our attention to the Hereafter. When one's gaze is focused solely on this world, their problem gets amplified, especially when no solution and compensation seem possible. But the Hereafter opens the door wide open for a resolution to our problems. First, all worldly problems have expiration dates, so a day will come when your problem and the hurt you feel will end. Second, whatever we lose or lack here will be available there. You see this refocus on the Hereafter in the *Hadith*. The Prophet ﷺ asked Allah for the eternal blessing, highlighting the shifting fortunes of this world. If we lose some of Allahs' blessings here—as they did in Uhud—remember that this is the nature of life on earth. So, set our eyes on the Hereafter, where Allah will compensate you for your losses, and you will never experience another loss. Suppose you experience fear and lack of security—like what happened in Uhud. Remember then that the Day of Judgment is far more terrifying. If Allah saves you from it, you will never be afraid again. Worldly problems pale in comparison to the rewards and trials of the Hereafter. This is another benefit of hardships: they expose the sour reality of our worldly life and ask us to set our sights on the Hereafter. The *du'a* of the Prophet ﷺ alerted the Companions to the Hereafter as their pursuit and destination. As long as they lived seeking Allah, all the hardship they encountered on the road to Allah was minuscule. Remembering Allah makes everything easier. Remembering Allah takes your problems away.

Praying for love

I will not be telling you anything new when I say that life is challenging. As long as you are alive, you are going to keep facing things that you like and things that you hate. You will be tempted in so many ways to stray away from Allah's path and pursue something else out of greed, lust, frustration, doubt, and anger. And unless Allah saves us, we will be lost. Unless we love *Iman*, we will not pursue it. If we do not distaste disbelief and disobedience, they will drag us to Hell. Thus, the prayer of the Prophet ﷺ to make *Iman* beloved to us and disbelief and sin hateful.

Loving righteousness is one of Allah's greatest favors. Allah said:

...وَلَٰكِنَّ ٱللَّهَ حَبَّبَ إِلَيْكُمُ ٱلْإِيمَٰنَ وَزَيَّنَهُۥ فِى قُلُوبِكُمْ وَكَرَّهَ إِلَيْكُمُ ٱلْكُفْرَ وَٱلْفُسُوقَ وَٱلْعِصْيَانَ ۚ أُو۟لَٰٓئِكَ هُمُ ٱلرَّٰشِدُونَ ۝٧

But Allah made Iman beloved to you and beautified it in your hearts, and He made disbelief, major sins, and small sins hateful to you. Those are the guided ones.

Al-Hujurat (Q49:7)

This is what makes following Allah and His Prophets easier. This is what makes turning away from temptations possible. It is in our nature to love righteousness, a divine gift of recognizing the truth and desiring it. When we pursue the truth, our love for it grows. But there are obstacles on our path. And our hawa (desire) stands in the way. So do the whispers of Shaytan and the pressure from our environment and friends. If our love for the truth is not greater and stronger, we will surrender to other influences and become another victim of Shaytan.

The problem with sin is not only the act but also how it changes us. It transforms what was abhorrent and unthinkable before to something likeable and desirable. One of the evil consequences of sin is the inability to see it as sin anymore, the collapse of the moral and ethical fences that kept it safe from Allah's anger. When sin becomes a practice—a new normal—its love settles in the heart. If that happens, we will hate the *Iman* that forbids it. Loving sin is the greatest misfortune. Allah said:

سَأَصْرِفُ عَنْ ءَايَٰتِيَ ٱلَّذِينَ يَتَكَبَّرُونَ فِي ٱلْأَرْضِ بِغَيْرِ ٱلْحَقِّ وَإِن يَرَوْا۟ كُلَّ ءَايَةٍ لَّا يُؤْمِنُوا۟ بِهَا وَإِن يَرَوْا۟ سَبِيلَ ٱلرُّشْدِ لَا يَتَّخِذُوهُ سَبِيلًا وَإِن يَرَوْا۟ سَبِيلَ ٱلْغَيِّ يَتَّخِذُوهُ سَبِيلًا ۚ ذَٰلِكَ بِأَنَّهُمْ كَذَّبُوا۟ بِـَٔايَٰتِنَا وَكَانُوا۟ عَنْهَا غَٰفِلِينَ ﴿١٤٦﴾

I will turn away from My signs those who are arrogant without right on earth. And if they were to see every sign, they will not believe in it. And if they were to see the path of guidance, they will not follow it. And if they were to see the path of misguidance, they will follow it. This is because they disbelieved in Our signs and were heedless of them.

Al-A'raf (Q7:146)

Those people earned their blindness; they willingly chose it! When one walks away from the straight path, they start liking corruption and hating piety. This is the calamity when the heart turns towards sin and away from Allah. The prayer to make *Iman* beloved to us is a plea to Allah to save us from the temptations that lie ahead and keep our hearts close to Him. He is the only One who can save us.

As we go through life and face its tests, we will have to keep making the right choices. We will make these choices based on what we love. If Allah grants us the right love, we will make the right choices. And every time we do, we will discover more of Allah's love. Worship becomes an opportunity to get closer to Him, another act of love that fills our life with meaning. And we would see sin as it truly is: a deprivation of love that destroys everything around it.

Love vs. morality

The last part of the *du'a* was reserved for those who oppose Allah. At the time, Muslims had just finished fighting the disbelievers. They stood up to their corruption and injustice, trying to please Allah, and it cost them. They saw firsthand the danger of the enemies of Allah when they attempted to extinguish the light of faith. If they had their way, they would have obliterated Islam and Muslims, up to the last person. Stopping their evil was a necessity; in fact, a great benefit to all. It is to the advantage of the disbelievers when their aggression stops: they cease accumulating sin. And it saves everyone else from their misguidance and torment. Not only do they reject the truth, but they deter people from it and punish them when they follow it. The *du'a* of the Prophet ﷺ against them is a request for their evil to cease in a way that teaches them and everyone else the folly of opposing Allah. When they see the disastrous outcome of their evil pursuits, they will rethink the choices they make.

Does asking for punishment contradict love? This question is a subset of the greater discussion of the relationship between love and hate (see *Hadith One* and *Appendix II*). Consider the following question: does the fact that Allah punishes contradict the fact that He loves? If we see a contradiction, it stems from our definitions and assumptions.

There is a divine definition of love, and there is the human attempt to define it and understand it. And the two do not always agree. What we think and conclude is love is not always the love that Allah desires for us. Love, for some, is a permissive state that allows everything. They claim that as long as love is making people happy and is not hurting anyone, it should be celebrated. The question is, however, how do we know that it is not harming anyone? Righteous love is loving the truth, and it is Allah who teaches us what the truth is. And Allah truly knows what is harmful. Loving falsehood and oppression—though technically love—is hardly a thing that any decent person would praise. Not every choice based on love can be celebrated. Love cannot decide its own parameters of morality. If love is letting everyone construct their morality, if love justifies everything and is the embrace of everything, then this would lead to the dissolution of love itself. Love must have boundaries. If you love something, you must hate its opposite. If you claim to love something and its complete opposite, then you love nothing at all.

Love operates within the natural boundaries Allah made, and cannot transcend them. Love is connected to an array of other emotions and operates in tandem with them. We love something and fear losing it, and we become angry when someone attempts to take it from us. We cannot extract love from this web of emotions, which includes hate. In addition to natural boundaries, there are divine boundaries. If we argue against divine moral boundaries, we lose the ability to set any permanent moral codes in life. Everything then would be up for grabs: what is wrong today is right tomorrow and vice versa. If we accept divine boundaries, we must oppose transgressions against them. Love would require it. If I love the best for others, I would wish that they follow Allah. But would they be able to follow Allah without a deterrence that anticipates and stops transgressions? Without us seeing the dire consequence of going against Allah? The *du'a* of the Prophet ﷺ for punishment is a protection and preservation of the truth. He made that *du'a* because he loved Allah and loved the best for people. And if the only way to stop some falsehood is through punishing those who champion it, then such punishment is a consequence of love and not its opposite.

When Allah created this earth, He placed on it things He loved and things He did not. Its purpose was for Allah's beloveds to change what He hates with what He loves. Striving elevates us, allows us to reach heights in Allah's love that would not be possible without struggle and sacrifice. Those who sacrifice attain the love of Allah. And when they receive Allah's love, there will be no limit to the favors they will see.

HADITH FORTY ONE

الحديث الواحد والأربعون

The way to His love

قَالَ رَسُولُ اللهِ ﷺ «إنَّ اللَّهَ قالَ: مَن عادى لي ولِيًّا فقَدْ آذَنْتُهُ بالحَرْبِ وما تَقَرَّبَ إلَيَّ عَبْدِي بشيءٍ أحَبَّ إلَيَّ ممّا افْتَرَضْتُ عليه وما يَزالُ عَبْدِي يَتَقَرَّبُ إلَيَّ بالنَّوافِلِ حتّى أُحِبَّهُ فإذا أحْبَبْتُهُ كُنْتُ سَمْعَهُ الذي يَسْمَعُ به وبَصَرَهُ الذي يُبْصِرُ به ويَدَهُ الَّتي يَبْطِشُ بها ورِجْلَهُ الَّتي يَمْشِي بها وإنْ سَأَلَنِي لَأُعْطِيَنَّهُ ولَئِنِ اسْتَعاذَنِي لَأُعِيذَنَّهُ وما تَرَدَّدْتُ عن شيءٍ أنا فاعِلُهُ تَرَدُّدِي عن نَفْسِ المُؤْمِنِ يَكْرَهُ المَوْتَ وأنا أكْرَهُ مَساءَتَهُ.»

رواه البخاري (٦٥٠٢)

The Messenger of Allah ﷺ said, «Allah said, "I have declared war on the one who hurts my *Wali*. My servant will not come closer to me with something I love more than what I obligated on them. And My servant will continue to come closer to me with voluntary worship until I love them. And when I love them, I will be their hearing by which they hear, their sight by which they see, their hands by which they take, and their legs by which they walk. If they ask Me, I will give them. And if they seek My protection, I will protect them. And I do not hesitate in something I am doing as much as I hesitate with the soul of the believer: they hate death and I hate to upset them."»

Reported by al-Bukhari (6502)

Commentary

Allah's obedience is the path that leads to His love. Once Allah loves you, you will see wonders.

The Wali of Allah

What does it mean to be a *wali* of Allah? And how does one become one? Many are confused over the credentials of a *wali*. It is all wrapped in mystery. They attribute it to eccentric personalities, outliers who speak in riddles and exist on the edge of Shari'ah. But this is not at all what a *wali* is.

Linguistically, *wali* carries the meaning of proximity (see *Appendix III*). When someone or something is a *wali* of another, they follow each other or are next to each other without separation (see, for example, *Mufradat al-Fadh al-Quran* by al-Raghib al-Asfahani). Ibn Rajab رَحِمَهُ ٱللَّهُ wrote:

وَأَصْلُ الْوِلَايَةِ الْقُرْبُ وَأَصْلُ الْعَدَاوَةِ الْبُعْدُ.

جامع العلوم والحكم (ج٢ ص٣٣٥)

> The basis of *wilayah* (being a *wali*) is proximity, and the basis of enmity is remoteness.
>
> *Jami' al-'Ulum wa al-Hikam* (vol. 2, p. 335)

Since proximity leads to love, support, and caretaking, *wali* carries these meanings too: lover, supporter, and caretaker. A *wali* of Allah is one who is close to Allah, a proximity founded on love (as the *Hadith* affirms). They love Allah dearly, champion His religion, and sacrifice what they love for His sake. Allah loves them back, protects them, and takes care of them. It is a connection based on love.

Every Muslim—in correspondence to the strength of their

Iman—has their portion of being a *wali* of Allah. The portions vary significantly, however, as *Iman* varies. When *Iman* is strong, so is the love of Allah and the observance of what He loves. The *wali* then receives the full blessings of Allah's love. Weakness of *Iman*, however, produces weak love that receives few of these blessings.

One of the prominent signs of Allah's love for His *wali* is how strongly He defends them. Allah declared war in the *Hadith* against those who oppose and hurt His *wali*. Allah's care for the believers is abundant in the Quran. Allah said:

إِنَّ ٱللَّهَ يُدَٰفِعُ عَنِ ٱلَّذِينَ ءَامَنُوٓاْۗ... ﴿٣٨﴾

Indeed, Allah defends the believers.

Al-Hajj (Q22:38)

He defends them because of their devotion and faith. They let go of everything else to be with Him, and He defends them from all that seeks them harm. The believers receive an ever-increasing portion of Allah's assistance as their *Iman* grows. Allah said:

يَٰٓأَيُّهَا ٱلَّذِينَ ءَامَنُوٓاْ إِن تَنصُرُواْ ٱللَّهَ يَنصُرۡكُمۡ وَيُثَبِّتۡ أَقۡدَامَكُمۡ ﴿٧﴾

O you who believe, if you champion Allah, He will champion you and make you steadfast.

Muhammad (Q47:7)

And He also said:

...وَلَيَنصُرَنَّ ٱللَّهُ مَن يَنصُرُهُۥٓۚ... ﴿٤٠﴾

And Allah surely will champion the one who champions Him.

Al-Hajj (Q22:40)

The more we rely on Allah and seek His help, the more that He helps us. But if we turn away from Him in disobedience, we leave ourselves vulnerable without Allah's support.

How does Allah defend the believers? In every way and whenever they need Him. He defends their honor and reputation, their physical and emotional wellbeing, their family and wealth, and their *Iman*. He defends them with His proofs and signs, with His angels and miracles (i.e. *karamah* for the *wali*), with circumstances that favor them, and with natural causes. He defends them in perceptive and imperceptive manners, in ways they know and in ways they cannot imagine. They are Allah's beloveds, and Allah takes care of the ones He loves.

Imagine the warmth and comfort of knowing that Allah is taking care of you. Not only that, but He is threatening your enemy with war if they hurt you. Is there something more threatening than Allah waging war against someone? Allah's firm stance is a reflection of how much He loves His *wali* and how much He hates it when they are hurt. Why do they deserve such special treatment? They strive until they love Allah more than anyone else, and sacrifice more than anyone else. Allah's wali withdraws from other loves to the love of Allah. They cleanse their hearts and bodies from sin and adorn themselves with the best of manners. They remind you of Jannah when you see them. They remind you of Allah. The Prophet ﷺ said:

«أولياءُ اللهِ تعالى الذينَ إذا رُؤُوا ذُكِرَ اللهُ تعالى.»

حسنه الألباني (صحيح الجامع ٢٥٥٧)

«The *walis* of Allah are those whom when seen, Allah is remembered.»

Al-Albani declared it hasan (*Sahih al-Jami'*, 2557)

Their humility, their worship, their manners, and their appearance remind people of Allah whenever they see them. The love of Allah has so saturated their hearts and bodies that they exude *Iman* wherever they go.

Hurting a *wali* of Allah is a serious offence. In fact, hurting any Muslim is a serious offence, but it is more so for a *wali*. They spend greater time in devotion and obedience to Allah. How can you hate such a person or wish them harm? Opposition to Allah Himself likely motivates opposition to them. You cannot hate a *wali* except if religious hatred is behind it. Personal grievances are something else. If one quarrels with a *wali* over worldly matters, they are not opposing Allah. A *wali* is a fallible human who can commit injustice. Some of the Companions—the best of the *walis* of Allah—would sometimes disagree and become upset with each other. Similarly, a *wali* of Allah can make mistakes, and one can rightfully be angry with them. If, however, a *wali* is innocent and blameless and yet they are hurt, one does risk the anger of Allah. The following story explains this.

أَتى أَبو سُفْيان على سَلْمانَ وَصُهَيْبٍ وَبِلالٍ في نَفَرٍ، فَقالوا: واللَّهِ ما أَخَذَتْ سُيُوفُ اللهِ مِن عُنُقِ عَدُوِّ اللهِ مَأْخَذَها، قالَ: فَقالَ أَبُو بَكْرٍ: أَتَقُولونَ هذا لِشيخِ قُرَيْشٍ وَسَيِّدِهِمْ؟ فأتى النبيَّ ﷺ فأَخْبَرَهُ فَقالَ «يا أَبا بَكْرٍ لَعَلَّكَ أَغْضَبْتَهُمْ لَئِنْ كُنْتَ أَغْضَبْتَهُمْ لقَدْ أَغْضَبْتَ رَبَّكَ» فَأَتاهُمْ أَبُو بَكْرٍ فَقالَ: يا إِخْوَتاهْ أَغْضَبْتُكُمْ، قالوا: لا يَغْفِرُ اللَّهُ لكَ يا أَخِي.

رواه مسلم (٢٥٠٤)

Abu Sufyan passed by Salman, Suhayb, and Bilal while they were in a gathering, and they said, "By Allah, the swords of Allah did not strike the neck of the enemy of Allah as they should have." Abu Bakr said to them, "Do you say this to the head of Quraysh and its master?" Then he went to the Prophet ﷺ and told him what happened. The Prophet said to him, «O Abu Bakr, perhaps you made them angry. If you made them angry, then you made your Rabb angry.» Abu Bakr went to them and said, "My brothers, did I make you angry?" They replied, "No, may Allah forgive you our brother."

Reported by Muslim (2504)

Abu Bakr رَضِيَ اللَّهُ عَنْهُ is the best *wali* in this Ummah. Yet, the Prophet ﷺ feared that he may have made Allah angry by upsetting the other Companions. And you see the sublime manners of the Companions: Abu Bakr رَضِيَ اللَّهُ عَنْهُ rushing to restore the love, and the three responding with a gracious *du'a* and comforting words.

It is so beautiful to have Allah be so close to you that He is the One who is taking care of you. This is available to us all. If we want Allah to take care of us, we have to come closer to Him. If we run away from Him, we will be running into the troubles of the world. Allah said:

إِن يَنصُرۡكُمُ ٱللَّهُ فَلَا غَالِبَ لَكُمۡۖ وَإِن يَخۡذُلۡكُمۡ فَمَن ذَا ٱلَّذِي يَنصُرُكُم مِّنۢ بَعۡدِهِۦۗ وَعَلَى ٱللَّهِ فَلۡيَتَوَكَّلِ ٱلۡمُؤۡمِنُونَ ١٦٠

If Allah champions you, no one can defeat you. And if He forsakes you, who can champion you besides Him? So, let the believers rely on Allah alone.

Ali ʿImran (Q3:160)

Allah is waiting for us. We just have to take the first step.

The path to Allah's love

Every destination has a path. And the path to Allah's love is in His revelation. The whole Shariʿah was sent down to guide us to the love of Allah. Allah said about the *walis* of Allah:

أَلَآ إِنَّ أَوۡلِيَآءَ ٱللَّهِ لَا خَوۡفٌ عَلَيۡهِمۡ وَلَا هُمۡ يَحۡزَنُونَ ٦٢ ٱلَّذِينَ ءَامَنُواْ وَكَانُواْ يَتَّقُونَ ٦٣

Indeed, there is no fear or sadness for the *walis* of Allah. They are the ones who have Iman and Taqwa.

Yunus (Q10:62–63)

This is Allah's definition—Glory be to Him—of who is a *wali* and how to become one. The *Hadith* complements the *ayah* by explaining the progressive ascension towards Allah's love.

The first step in the path is adherence to the obligations, the top priority of Taqwa. Included in that is avoiding the prohibitions, since avoiding them is also an obligation. Allah loves obligatory acts the most, and this is why He made them a must for everyone. We need them. The five daily prayers are indispensable. They nurture *Iman* and keep our connection to Allah vibrant. They teach us patience and help us overcome life's problems. If our *Iman* is suffering, if our love of Allah is weak, we should focus on improving our *Salah*. Similarly, the rest of the obligations—especially the pillars—are the keys of love. They are the foundations. When these foundations falter, the entire structure is weak. Adhering to the obligations—and avoiding *haram*—is the first step towards solving any spiritual, emotional, and mental problems and anguish.

The *Hadith* provides us with an essential master plan. If you want Allah, here is the way and the steps. And it sets our priorities. If there is ever a clash between obligatory and voluntary acts, the obligations come first because Allah's love for them is greater. If we want to progress into the recommended acts, make sure they are resting on the secure foundation of obligatory ones. It is unproductive to engage in the voluntary—especially when it consumes our time—while the obligations are missing. How could a building have a tenth floor without a first? At times, we may prefer some recommended acts to obligatory ones. Yet, the *Hadith* teaches us to place what Allah loves before what we do. It is important when worshipping Allah to prioritize Allah's loves, not ours. If we get our priorities straight, we would proceed with sure and guided steps towards Allah.

The second step towards Allah is the recommended acts. When the obligations are performed well, they plant in us the desire to do more. And since they made worship a habit, it is easier to do more of it. We are more likely to pray voluntary *Salah* when the obligatory *Salah* has become a fixture, an anchor to which voluntary *Salah* can attach. The obligations introduce the love of Allah, and voluntary worship develops it. Unlike the obligations, voluntary worship is based on choice, the desire to do them. This signals a higher commitment to Allah. The *Hadith* describes a persistent and continued performance of voluntary worship until Allah loves this person. With consistency and striving comes the gradual buildup of practice, certainty, and love. With every good deed, we draw near to Allah. Every day, we conquer our desire and Shaytan. Every day, we love Allah more.

Ibn Rajab رَحِمَهُ ٱللَّهُ remarked that the greatest voluntary acts that bring the love of Allah are (1) the frequent reading and listening to the Quran with understanding and reflection, (2) the *dhikr* of Allah with the tongue and heart, and (3) loving whom Allah loves and hating whom Allah hates (*Jami' al-'Ulum wa al-Hikam*, vol. 2, pp. 342–343). We can confidently add night prayer to his list. Also, charity and helping others. These acts grant us the opportunity to be in solitude with Allah, to enjoy listening to His Words and talking to Him. They teach us to rely on Him alone and ask Him for what we want. They are our daily nourishment that connects us emotionally to Allah. With time, they become indispensable. They cleanse us from material obsession and open our hearts for Allah.

The path of love is not a mystery. We do not need to travel to meet a recluse guru at the top of a mountain to learn it. And we do not need to learn special *dhikr* or act that only a select and lucky few have had the privilege to learn. No. It is available to everyone. Allah revealed it, in plain words, to all. Ibn Rajab رَحِمَهُ ٱللَّهُ said:

لَا طَرِيقَ يُوصِّلُ إِلَى التَّقَرُّبِ إِلَى اللَّهِ تَعَالَى وَوِلَايَتِهِ وَمَحَبَّتِهِ سِوَى طَاعَتِهِ الَّتِي شَرَعَهَا عَلَى لِسَانِ رَسُولِهِ فَمَنِ ادَّعَى وِلَايَةَ اللَّهِ وَمَحَبَّتَهُ بِغَيْرِ هَذَا الطَّرِيقِ تَبَيَّنَ أَنَّهُ كَاذِبٌ فِي دَعْوَاهُ.

جامع العلوم والحكم (ج٢ ح٣٣٦)

There is no way that leads closer to Allah, to becoming His *wali*, and to His love except through His obedience that He legislated on the tongue of His Messenger. So, if one claims to be a *wali* of Allah and to love Him through a path other than this, it would be clear that they are lying in their claim.

Jami' al-'Ulum wa al-Hikam (vol. 2, p. 336)

If you want Allah to love you, follow the guidance that He revealed to Muhammad ﷺ. Stay close to the obligations and recommendations, and your love for Allah will blossom. Some get excited only when they think that the path is mysterious, with guarded knowledge that needs initiation and pledges. But Allah's love is there for all, taught to all, and available to all in the clearest language. His love is the nourishment of the soul. It is an essential need, and it must be available to all, just as food and drink are. It is even more important than that.

Loving Allah until He is everything

One can continue to worship Allah—with heart and body—until Allah's love fills their heart. When that happens, Allah becomes their greatest joy, their greatest concern, and their greatest companion. He is with them all the time. When they are sad, they turn to Him for comfort, to heal their hearts. When they are happy, they praise Him for His never-ending blessings. When they are overwhelmed and overpowered, they seek Him for help and support. They believe He alone can fulfill all their needs, so they ask Him first and place all their hope and trust in Him. Their hearts are liberated from human dependence, and see only Allah as their Master. They see the weakness and helplessness of all humans, and realize that Allah has all the power, wisdom, and knowledge. They rely on Him and need no one else. They worship Him as if they can see the Day of Judgment, where people are separating into the party of Heaven and the party of Hell. They know they can never do enough to worship and thank Him. His Mercy alone will rescue them. They love Him for His favors, they love Him for His unmatched qualities, and they love Him because their life means nothing without Him. They worship Him as if they can see Him, and they cannot wait to see Him in Jannah. To them, He is everything. And to Him, they are the best of His creation.

When the love of Allah saturates their hearts, it flows to their senses. They are embarrassed to use their senses in what upsets Allah. They preserve them for what pleases the One who made them. When they move, they move for Allah; and when they take and give, they do so for Allah. They also "see Allah" in everything. They see His signs wherever they look. They see His Power, Wisdom, Mercy, and Design. They see His Will in whatever happens. He is extremely close to them. He is above His Throne—glory be to Him—but everything they see, hear, and encounter reminds them of Him.

Allah loves them so much that He guards their hearts and their love by protecting their senses. He guides their eyes, ears, limbs, hearts, and thoughts towards what He loves and away from what He hates. And He assists them so they see, hear, and can do what others typically cannot.

Their station with Allah is so high that if they ask Him, He will give them what they desire. He does not say no to them because they do not say no to Him. He protects them because they protect their hearts and bodies from what Allah hates, and they protect and defend His religion. Imagine if Allah Himself is ready to give you what you want! What honor is this! What happiness is this! If we can get all this from Allah, do we need anyone else? So, why would we listen to anyone but Him, worship anyone but Him, or ask anyone but Him? When you love Allah, He will show you that He is the only One you need.

This is how much Allah cares

We all will die; this is how we pass on to the next life. Though it is inevitable, it is still hard to accept and harder to experience (see *Hadith* Fourteen). The believer may have mixed feelings about death. On the one hand, death brings relief from the trials, temptations, and hardships of this life. It is the passageway to the Hereafter, Jannah, and meeting Allah. All this makes death very desirable. On the other hand, we have a natural aversion to death. It is the ultimate separation. We leave our loved ones and everything we know. And the soul separates from the body to enter a new realm which has never experienced and is not sure about its fate in it.

Allah told us in the *Hadith* that He does not hesitate in doing something as much as He does when taking the soul of the believer. Allah's hesitation—and all of His attributes—do not resemble human hesitation. Humans hesitate because they are not sure of the outcome of their decisions, do not have all the facts they need to make the right choice, and lack the resolve and patience to make the right but difficult choices. Allah is free from all of these imperfections. Allah's knowledge is complete and encompasses past, present, and future. And Allah is All-Powerful, so He does what He does unopposed. Allah's hesitation is different. It comes from His Care and Mercy. Allah loves two things but only one can happen.

Allah decreed death to move us from this world to the next. In that sense, Allah loves it since it is part of His plan for us. Yet, Allah hates what His devout believers hate, and He does not wish to upset them. So, death is beloved and unbeloved to Allah. His hesitation is in disliking the discomfort of the believers while knowing that death is necessary and best.

What all this tells us is how deeply Allah cares about the believers and their feelings. And this is out of love for them. Why would the All-Mighty, the First and the Last, care so much about such a weak and insignificant being? What are we compared to Allah? Imagine if our greatest hesitation was about removing an ant from its house! We to Allah are lesser than ants to humans. This is why Allah is so great. He does not need us, yet He cares so deeply about us and desires our happiness. If we develop this intimate relationship with Allah, we will receive the highest honor and care in existence. Allah would love us so much that He would not want to upset us. When Allah is your *wali* and you are His, you will live in bliss, die in bliss, and be resurrected in bliss. To that we say, as Allah said:

لِمِثْلِ هَـٰذَا فَلْيَعْمَلِ ٱلْعَـٰمِلُونَ ﴿٦١﴾

For the like of this let the strivers strive.

As-Saffat (Q37:61)

HADITH FORTY TWO

الحديث الثاني والأربعون

Never-ending love

قَالَ رَسُولُ اللهِ ﷺ «أتاني جبريلُ فقال يا مُحَمَّدُ عِشْ ما شِئتَ فإنَّك مَيِّتٌ وأَحْبِبْ من شِئتَ فإنَّكَ مُفارِقُه واعمَل ما شِئتَ فإنَّك مَجْزِيٌّ بهِ واعلَم أنَّ شرفَ المؤمنِ قيامُه باللَّيلِ وعِزُّه استِغناؤُه عن النّاسِ.»

رواه الطبراني في المعجم الأوسط (٤٢٧٨) والبيهقي في شعب الإيمان (١٠٥٤١) وحسنه الألباني لغيره (صحيح الترغيب ٧٢٦)

The Messenger of Allah ﷺ said, «Jibril came to me and said, "O Muhammad, live as long as you wish, for you will die. Love whomever you wish, for you will leave them. Do whatever you want, for you will be requited for it. And know that the believer's honor is in praying at night, and their strength is in not needing people."»

Reported by al-Tabarani in al-Mu'jam al-Awsat (4278) and al-Bayhaqi in Shu'ab al-Iman (10541). Al-Albani declared it hasan li-ghayrihi (Sahih al-Targhib, 726)

Commentary

All are destined to end, except for Allah. His love is unique, and it gives meaning to everything else.

Live whatever way you want

The choice is ours. How do you want to live and what you want to do with your life? Who do you love and would like to love you back? We have the choice, and each choice has very different consequences.

Living the way we want is a modern rallying cry. It is the ultimate freedom. No one can tell us how to live: neither parents, culture, nor society. It is imagined as a discovery of your true self, living authentically in pursuit of what you love, not what others force on you. For some, it is a rebellion against injustice and antiquated rules. It is exhilarating because it is liberating, because you can build your life anew. You can imagine a better world and construct it on the ruins of the old. It is especially appealing to anyone who feels they are living under oppressive conditions. Living as you like is to be able to breathe...finally.

As appealing as this may sound, it is not without its problems. The liberation in this idea is individualistic and western in flavor. It pits the individual against society, the modern against tradition, and the secular against religion. This is its general bent, even though not all who are swept by it are secular or anti-tradition. But it is unmistakably clear that the authority is with the individual. Each person decides for themselves, on their own. Power is wrested from the divine and assigned to humans, to their reasoning or emotions. Doing whatever we like has deep philosophical and religious roots and implications. It is not just about what career to pick, whom to marry, or where to live. It is about who decides right and wrong. And here, humans do, not Allah.

In reality and beyond idealism, there are always pressures that force to conform, to act in specific ways but not others. We just have learned to live with them and not to notice them. You cannot dress whatever way you want, I mean whatever wild way you want. There are always limits, and if we ignore the limits, we pay the price: economically, socially, and legally. You have to dress a certain way to get a job, to fit in society, and not be arrested. There are always limits. We do not get to do whatever we want. They tell us that so we would believe it, but there are still limits set for us, and we tacitly accept them. Do you know who the real maverick is? The one who truly does whatever they want? The homeless who lives outside of society, or the off-the-grid recluse who withdraws to the woods. Everyone else has to follow the rules of the game.

The real revolutionary today is the follower of Allah. I do not mean the follower of a culture that they believe is religion, or traditions that masquerade as the true religion. I mean the follower of Allah the way He wants to be worshiped, which is revealed in the Quran and Sunnah. This person is going against a global thrust of materialism, hedonism, self-obsessiveness, and fatal cynicism. They embrace meaning in a world that is moving towards nihilism. They embrace Allah in a world that is running away from Him and paying the price for it. Today, you are penalized for following and speaking the truth and celebrated if you are false and for falsehood. Real liberation today is not from religion, but from the system that oppresses people. If we do not choose Allah as our Master, another will take His place. And they will not be forgiving, merciful, or wise.

Whatever we choose has consequences. And we will see them in this life and the next. Eat whatever you want, and drink whatever you want. There will be consequences: physical, social, familial, and financial. Abstaining from alcohol is not like drinking it, and sobriety is not the same as alcoholism. Eating healthy and exercising is not like bad diet and a sedentary lifestyle. Each choice leads to a different path. And our life will be different because of it. Sin is the same.

Surrender to Allah and obey Him, and it will lead you to the best this life has to offer. You will understand the meaning of this life and be liberated from false gods and prophets. You will be liberated from Shaytan and see through his plots: you will see the puppeteer behind the puppets. You will learn how to rise above your desires and weaknesses. And Allah will be beside you. And in the Hereafter, you will live close to Him forever.

But if we rebel against Allah, we will pay for it here first. We will make the worst choices, follow the worst paths, and suffer with each choice. Everything else will enslave us, and Shaytan will dominate us. We will be miserable, and will grow more miserable with each sin. And in the Hereafter, it will be even worse. So yes, we can do whatever we want. But we will see the consequences. We will meet our choices.

Anticipating death may be one of the few things to convince us to make the right choices. The finality of life shows its triviality. You will see everything in a new light when you know it is going to end. When you remember death, life will have a new meaning. What seemed important will stop being important. What you thought you could delay will become urgent. Our goals will mature. There is great wisdom in remembering death. Many run away from it. But it can teach us so much. And its lessons lead back to Allah. If everything is going to end, we desperately need the Only One who will not. He is the Only One who can give our life meaning.

All love will end

Separation from our loved ones is probably one of the hardest things in life. But we must separate from them. This fact will force us to reevaluate our love.

The first lesson is that if we must separate, then we must learn to be less attached. We cannot be so dependent on something that will not last. This prevents every earthly love from ballooning to dominate our life. We will love, but we will do it with moderation and anticipation of its impermanence. This allows us to deal with loss, too. If you know you have to lose something, you will be more prepared for it. Loss is like the day and the night, summer and winter. It must happen. But is this enough? Is this knowledge sufficient to curb pain and bring happiness? How can we accept the loss of all that we love?

We live for love. If you read the rest of the book, you know how much we need it. The possibility of all love ending is the death of all hope and joy. Fortunately, one love defies this rule.

The love of Allah. It cannot end. And because of this love, all other loves survive.

What is exceptional about Allah's love is that it is inexhaustible. It covers all creation and is there as long as we need it. There is more of it the more we take. It is always with us. It is our solace when we lose other earthly loves. When we feel alone, Allah is there to carry our burden and comfort our hearts. We can make it through anything if He is with us. He is beside us in every difficulty, and with us when we pass from this life to the next. We leave all of our loved ones behind when we die except Him. He is with us in our graves. And He is with us when we come back to life. On the day when loved ones will run away from each other, He brings you closer to Him. Allah said:

يَوْمَ يَفِرُّ ٱلْمَرْءُ مِنْ أَخِيهِ ﴿٣٤﴾ وَأُمِّهِۦ وَأَبِيهِ ﴿٣٥﴾ وَصَٰحِبَتِهِۦ وَبَنِيهِ ﴿٣٦﴾
لِكُلِّ ٱمْرِيٍٕ مِّنْهُمْ يَوْمَئِذٍ شَأْنٌ يُغْنِيهِ ﴿٣٧﴾

On the Day when a man will run away from his brother, and his mother and father, and his wife and children. Each will have their own worry to consume them.

'Abasa (Q80:34–37)

When we know that Allah's love is greater than any other love, we will not put anyone before Him in our hearts. We will not choose anyone else over Him.

His love saves every other love. Allah said:

ٱلْأَخِلَّآءُ يَوْمَئِذٍۭ بَعْضُهُمْ لِبَعْضٍ عَدُوٌّ إِلَّا ٱلْمُتَّقِينَ ﴿٦٧﴾

Loved ones will be enemies of each other on that Day, except for the pious.

Az-Zukhruf (Q43:67)

His love unites and connects. All other loves, when not based on His, evaporate. If we are righteous, Allah joins us with our loved ones in Jannah. He said:

وَٱلَّذِينَ ءَامَنُوا۟ وَٱتَّبَعَتْهُمْ ذُرِّيَّتُهُم بِإِيمَٰنٍ أَلْحَقْنَا بِهِمْ ذُرِّيَّتَهُمْ... ﴿٢١﴾

For those who believe and whose offspring follow them in faith, we will unite them with their offspring.

At-Tur (Q52:21)

We will see them again, and this eliminates the finality of death. When we die, we transition, we travel, but we do not lose each other. Allah's love keeps us connected forever. If we know this, we can overcome every loss in this world. Every loss is a temporary separation that will end one day. The real tragedy is losing His love. If we do not have it, we will lose every other love we have. If we sacrifice His love for someone else, we will lose it all. He is the source of all love, and all love returns to Him.

Dignity and strength

All of us search for honor and dignity. Some find it in wealth, some in education, and others in lineage. But real honor resides with Allah. He said:

مَن كَانَ يُرِيدُ ٱلْعِزَّةَ فَلِلَّهِ ٱلْعِزَّةُ جَمِيعًا... ﴿١٠﴾

Whoever desires honor, then all honor belongs to Allah.

Fatir (Q35:10)

And those who believe in Allah receive honor from Him. Allah said:

وَلِلَّهِ ٱلْعِزَّةُ وَلِرَسُولِهِۦ وَلِلْمُؤْمِنِينَ وَلَٰكِنَّ ٱلْمُنَٰفِقِينَ لَا يَعْلَمُونَ ﴿٨﴾

And to Allah belongs honor, and to His Messenger and the believers. But the hypocrites do not know.

Al-Munafiqun (Q63:8)

The honor of the believer, as the *Hadith* states, is in night prayer. This *Salah* teaches us how to be alone with Allah. It lifts us above worldly plains and connects us to the heavens. In it, we are conversing with Allah, the Highest, and surrounded by angels. We learn in this heavenly encounter to give all our problems and concerns to Him. We learn that if we ask Him, He listens. If we rely on Him, He helps. If we need Him, He is always there. And this is real dignity. We are close to the Greatest, and He is listening to us. We take every problem to Him, and He makes it small. We take every worry, and He makes it better. We are not weak next to Him, and are not lost as long as He guides us. We do not need anyone else but Him. This is the dignity of the believer. And night prayer is the path to it. When you are alone with Allah, you learn who He is and who you are.

As we acquire our honor from Allah, we derive our strength from Him. We are, by nature, weak. We need others. When we rely on other humans, our heart partially submits to them. We feel indebted, and we can compromise our beliefs to fulfill our needs. This is clear weakness. When we trust another human to help us, we are trusting someone as weak as us. When we rely on creation, we forget the Creator. And this is weakness in *Iman*. Strength is in depending on Allah alone. When you have Him, you do not need anyone else. He will bring everyone else to you. When you trust Allah, you are trusting the greatest power. And this is the strength that every believer can have. The more you rely on Allah, the stronger you will be on earth. And the more you rely on people, the weaker.

The end is a beginning

I conclude this book with a *hadith* on the end of everything. But embedded in it, as we have seen, is the realization that nothing ends with Allah. And so, the end of this book is not an end but a beginning. It is the start of another journey. It is when you take what you read here and move closer to Allah. You will find Allah's love when you read the Quran and *hadith*. You will feel it when you make *du'a*. You will see it when you look at the world around you. Let it be your path and destination. Let your love of Allah grow and inspire you to meet Him. Spread love all around you. Feel His love when you worship, and let others feel His love by how you treat them. Ask Him for His love, and ask Him to spread love through you. May you love Allah, and may Allah love you back.

APPENDIX I
What is love?

Definition

If you are reading this after finishing the entire book, you must wonder how—in a book about love—we are coming to its definition at its end. Well, my answer is: do we need a definition for love? So far, in life and this book, you have been operating without a definition. Yet, you understand what it means. All of us have a sense of what love is. Ibn al-Qayyim is of the opinion that there are things—such as love—that do not need to be defined (*Madarij al-Salikin* vol. 3, p. 11). We all know what it is; we have experienced it. Attempting to define it only obscures it. After he goes through many of its definitions, he explains that they all fall short. Each, when attempting to define love, captured one thing but missed another. Definitions are there to provide clarity. But when something is already clear, there is no need for a definition (*Tariq al-Hijratayn*, p. 674). Ibn Hajar رَحِمَهُ ٱللَّهُ agreed that a definition is elusive and that it is something felt and not fully articulated (*Fath al-Bari*, vol. 10, p. 462). This opinion can be traced all the way back to al-Qushayri رَحِمَهُ ٱللَّهُ in his *Risalah*, where he declared that love, as a self-evident truth—is in no need of a definition. Its best definition is itself: love is love. Anything else is incomplete and obscuring. This is a valuable point about self-evident truths. Allah spoke about love in the Quran without defining it because we understand what love is. The Prophet ﷺ did the same. We all know what love is because we all experience it. When something is so plain and universal, it does not need clarification.

The Arabic language has sixty different words for love, according to Ibn al-Qayyim رَحِمَهُ ٱللَّهُ in his book on love (*Rawdat al-Muhibbin*, pp. 25–26). Not all of them, however, are names for love. They describe the development of love, its conditions, consequences, and the different stages of love. The main word for love is *Hubb*. Ibn al-Qayyim رَحِمَهُ ٱللَّهُ, and al-Qushayri رَحِمَهُ ٱللَّهُ before him, connected the etymology of "Hubb" to the experience of love. "Hubb" comes from:

1. Purity and clarity. The devotion of the lover to their beloved is compared to the purity of color;
2. Agitation. This is so because love causes the agitation or movement of the heart;
3. Firmness in place. Love, when true, settles in the heart and does not leave;
4. The kernel of fruit, the innermost. Love reaches the deepest parts of the heart, and the lover gives their innermost to their beloved;
5. A big vessel that gets completely filled with no space left. When love enters the heart, it fills it all and leaves no space for anything else;
6. A stand made up of four legs that carries and supports a jar. The lover carries the weight of love like four legs carrying heavy objects.

Ibn al-Qayyim رَحِمَهُ ٱللَّهُ added that *Hubb* is made up of two letters: Ha and Ba. Ha is pronounced from the lowest part of the throat while Ba comes from the lips, moving as you pronounce the word from one end to the other. And so is love the beginning and the end: it begins with an admiration and an inclination until the entire being is consumed by it (*Madarij al-Salikin*, vol. 3, p. 12).

Why people love?

Al-Qadi 'Iyad رَحِمَهُ ٱللَّهُ boiled down the reasons of love to three:

1. Physical (outer) beauty that people behold with their eyes (beautiful vista), ears (beautiful sound), and tongues (delicious food and drink);
2. Nonphysical (internal) beauty that people behold with their minds (good manners, morality, uprightness);
3. The benefactor and the benefit they bring, for a soul is

naturally attracted to anyone who helps it. (*Al-Shifa*, vol. 2, p. 66)

Al-Ghazali رَحِمَهُ ٱللَّهُ added two more reasons:

1. We love ourselves and our continued existence. Anything that supports this existence is loved as well;
2. Compatibility between lovers. This, sometimes, is hidden and cannot be explained. Two could love each other, not out of beauty or particular gains, but simply because their souls are connected and compatible (*Ihya' 'Ulum al-Din*, vol. 6, pp. 11–18).

He went on to affirm that Allah deserves our greatest love based on these five reasons. He has the greatest Outer and Inner Beauty, He is the only true Benefactor, He is the sole cause of our existence, and He is the closest to us.

Ibn al-Qayyim رَحِمَهُ ٱللَّهُ listed ten reasons that bring about the love of Allah (*Madarij al-Salikin*, vol. 3, pp. 381–383). They are:

1. Reading the Quran with comprehension and contemplation. It is the kind of reading that seeks to understand the intent of the Quran (i.e. what Allah wants you to do). It is exactly like memorizing and studying a book to understand its author's intent.
2. Drawing closer to Allah with voluntary acts after performing the obligatory ones.
3. Continued remembrance of Allah with tongue, heart, deeds, and in all conditions and states. One will receive Allah's love in proportion to how much they remember Allah.
4. Favoring what He loves over what you love, and ignoring your desire to please Him. In addition, ascending to do what He loves even if the climb is difficult.
5. Contemplating His Names and Attributes. The heart that understands them, connects with Allah through them. Witnessing their effects in creation necessarily leads to

the love of Allah.

6. Witnessing His favors, gifts, and internal and external bounties.
7. The complete humility of the heart before Allah. This is one of the most wondrous of all the reasons.
8. To be alone with Him when He comes down at the last third of the night: speaking to Him, reading His Words, being attentive and humble with heart and body, and concluding it all with repentance and asking for His forgiveness.
9. Keeping the company of those who love Allah and learning from them. And not speaking unless you know there is benefit in what you will say.
10. Avoiding anything that stands between the heart and Allah.

Love at first sight

When considering the multiple causes of love and how profound it is, love at first sight seems like a tiny fraction of the reality of love. Not every claim to love at first glance is genuine. But if the claimant is honest, their love is for external beauty, and there are layers of love that have not been experienced. Physical beauty could be the antecedent to greater love when it is reinforced with inner beauty, or it could be the only cause of attraction. If it is the latter, it will prove to be flimsy. The marketing of "love at first sight" as true love is a disservice to how deep love is.

Types of love

The first and the most significant is the love of Allah. This is the greatest and the most fulfilling love. As Allah is the First and the Last, this love is the first and the last, the beginning and the end. It is why we were created and our goal. It drives the righteous to Jannah and unlocks its gates. Allah made the universe for this love, and Allah's beloveds are the best and noblest of Allah's creation.

Loving Allah is more than a claim or a fuzzy feeling. Loving Allah is incomplete and insufficient until one loves what Allah loves. Ibn al-Qayyim رَحِمَهُ ٱللَّهُ wrote:

وَهَاهُنَا أَرْبَعَةُ أَنْوَاعٍ مِنَ الْمَحَبَّةِ يَجِبُ التَّفْرِيقُ بَيْنَهَا وَإِنَّمَا ضَلَّ مَنْ ضَلَّ بِعَدَمِ التَّمْيِيزِ بَيْنَهَا أَحَدُهَا مَحَبَّةُ اللَّهِ وَلَا تَكْفِي وَحْدَهَا فِي النَّجَاةِ مِنْ عَذَابِ اللَّهِ وَالْفَوْزِ بِثَوَابِهِ فَإِنَّ الْمُشْرِكِينَ وَعُبَّادَ الصَّلِيبِ وَالْيَهُودَ وَغَيْرَهُمْ يُحِبُّونَ اللَّهَ الثَّانِي مَحَبَّةُ مَا يُحِبُّ اللَّهُ وَهَذِهِ هِيَ الَّتِي تُدْخِلُهُ فِي الْإِسْلَامِ وَتُخْرِجُهُ مِنَ الْكُفْرِ وَأَحَبُّ النَّاسِ إِلَى اللَّهِ أَقْوَمُهُمْ بِهَذِهِ الْمَحَبَّةِ وَأَشَدُّهُمْ فِيهَا الثَّالِثُ الْحُبُّ لِلَّهِ وَفِيهِ وَهِيَ مِنْ لَوَازِمِ مَحَبَّةِ مَا يُحِبُّ وَلَا تَسْتَقِيمُ مَحَبَّةُ مَا يُحِبُّ إِلَّا فِيهِ وَلَهُ الرَّابِعُ الْمَحَبَّةُ مَعَ اللَّهِ وَهِيَ الْمَحَبَّةُ الشِّرْكِيَّةُ وَكُلُّ مَنْ أَحَبَّ شَيْئًا مَعَ اللَّهِ لَا لِلَّهِ وَلَا مِنْ أَجْلِهِ وَلَا فِيهِ فَقَدِ اتَّخَذَهُ نِدًّا مِنْ دُونِ اللَّهِ وَهَذِهِ مَحَبَّةُ الْمُشْرِكِينَ وَبَقِيَ قِسْمٌ خَامِسٌ لَيْسَ مِمَّا نَحْنُ فِيهِ وَهِيَ الْمَحَبَّةُ الطَّبِيعِيَّةُ وَهِيَ مَيْلُ الْإِنْسَانِ إِلَى مَا يُلَائِمُ طَبْعَهُ كَمَحَبَّةِ الْعَطْشَانِ لِلْمَاءِ وَالْجَائِعِ لِلطَّعَامِ وَمَحَبَّةِ النَّوْمِ وَالزَّوْجَةِ وَالْوَلَدِ فَتِلْكَ لَا تُذَمُّ إِلَّا إِذَا أَلْهَتْ عَنْ ذِكْرِ اللَّهِ وَشَغَلَتْ عَنْ مَحَبَّتِهِ كَمَا قَالَ تَعَالَى {يَاأَيُّهَا الَّذِينَ آمَنُوا لَا تُلْهِكُمْ أَمْوَالُكُمْ وَلَا أَوْلَادُكُمْ عَنْ ذِكْرِ اللَّهِ} [سُورَةُ الْمُنَافِقُونَ: ٩] وَقَالَ تَعَالَى {رِجَالٌ لَا تُلْهِيهِمْ تِجَارَةٌ وَلَا بَيْعٌ عَنْ ذِكْرِ اللَّهِ} [سُورَةُ النُّورِ: ٣٧].

الجواب الكافي (ص١٨٩-١٩٠)

It is necessary to distinguish between four types of love. Those who got misguided were misguided because they did not distinguish between them. The first is loving Allah. This is insufficient on its own to save from the punishment of Allah and to win His reward since the polytheists, the Worshippers of the Cross, the Jews, and others love Allah. The second is loving what Allah loves. This is the love that makes one a Muslim and extracts them from disbelief. The most beloved to Allah are the ones who are best in this love and strongest in it. The third is loving people and things for Allah's sake, which is one of the necessary consequences of loving what He loves. Loving what Allah loves would not be complete until [one loves] people and things for His sake. The fourth is loving [others] alongside Allah. This is the polytheistic love. Anyone who loves something alongside Allah, not for Allah or His sake, then they have adopted that thing as a rival besides Allah. This is the love of the polytheists. There remains a fifth type that is not related to this [discussion] and that is natural love, which is one's inclination to what agrees with their nature, like the thirsty loving water, the hungry food, loving sleeping, a wife, and a child. These are not condemned unless they distract from the remembrance of Allah and distance from His love as Allah said, ﴾O you who have Iman, let not your wealth and children distract you from the remembrance of Allah﴿ [Al-Munafiqun 9] and He said, ﴾Men who do not let commerce and selling distract them from remembering Allah﴿ [Al-Nur 37].

Al-Jawab al-Kafi (pp. 189–190)

The definition of loving Allah includes loving what He loves and loving for His sake. When one of the two or both are missing, the love of Allah itself is weak and compromised. Ibn al-Qayyim رَحِمَهُ ٱللَّهُ explained the other two loves—the natural and the polytheistic—when he wrote:

المحبة المشتركة ثلاثة أنواع أحدها محبة طبيعية مشتركة كمحبة الجائع للطعام والظمآن للماء وغير ذلك وهذه لا تستلزم التعظيم والنوع الثاني محبة رحمة وإشفاق كمحبة الوالد لولده الطفل ونحوها وهذه أيضاً لا تستلزم التعظيم والنوع الثالث محبة أُنس وإلف وهى محبة المشتركين في صناعة أو علم أو مرافقة أو تجارة أو سفر بعضهم بعضاً وكمحبة الإخوة بعضهم بعضاً فهذه الأنواع الثلاثة هي المحبة التي تصلح لخلق بعضهم من بعض ووجودها

فيهم لا يكون شركاً في محبة الله سبحانه ولهذا كان رسول الله صلى الله عليه وسلم يحب الحلواءَ والعسل وكان أحب الشراب إليه الحلو البارد وكان أحب اللحم إليه الذراع وكان يحب نساءه وكانت عائشة رضي الله عنها أحبهن إليه وكان يحب أصحابه وأحبهم إليه الصديق رضي الله عنه وأما المحبة الخاصة التي لا تصلح إلا لله وحده ومتى أحب العبد بها غيره كان شركاً لا يغفره الله فهي محبة العبودية المستلزمة للذل والخضوع والتعظيم وكمال الطاعة وإيثاره على غيره فهذه المحبة لا يجوز تعلقها بغير الله أصلاً وهي التي سوَّى المشركون بين آلهتهم وبين الله فيها.

طريق الهجرتين (ص٢٩٥-٢٩٦)

Common love is of three kinds. The first is natural and common love, like the hungry loving food, the thirsty water, and so on. This love does not require exaltation. The second is a love of mercy and kindness, like a parent loving their young child and so on. This too does not require exaltation. The third is a love of affability and sociability. This is the love between companions in an industry, discipline of knowledge, company, business, travel, and love between brothers. These three types of love are suitable for creation, between each other, and its presence among them is not Shirk in loving Allah. This is why the Messenger ﷺ used to love sweets and honey, the most beloved drink to him was the sweet and cold one, the most beloved meat to him was the shoulder, he loved his wives and 'A'ishah رَضِيَ اللَّهُ عَنْهَا was the most beloved among them to him, and he loved his Companions and the most beloved among them to him was al-Siddiq رَضِيَ اللَّهُ عَنْهُ. As for the special love that is only suitable for Allah alone and once one loves another with it, it would be Shirk that Allah does not forgive, it is love that is worship and which requires humility, submission, exaltation, complete obedience, and favoring Him over others. This love

> cannot be given to other than Allah, and this is the love that the polytheists equated their idols with Allah in it.
>
> *Tariq al-Hijratayn* (pp. 295–296)

Natural love is permissible by default because it is not religious in nature and does not have the components of worship. It is disallowed only when it distracts away from Allah. Love that is worship—the one only Allah deserves and which becomes Shirk when given to another—is love that leads to exaltation of the object of love and submission to it. This submission includes its worship (e.g. prostration, *du'a*, and full obedience), internal and external veneration, and putting it ahead of others. The polytheists devote some of their worship to their idols, grant them veneration that is fitting only for a deity, and they hold them very close to their hearts. Righteous love is the basis of Tawhid, as is corrupt love the basis of Shirk.

The second major love is love among creation. We encountered above the causes of this love and examples of it. This love divides into natural (worldly) love and religious (spiritual) love. It is dubbed natural when it is based on mundane reasons (e.g. blood relations, favors, and sexual attraction), and it is religious when motivated by religion (love for the sake of Allah, as discussed previously). These two types of love—the natural and religious—can diverge or intersect in different proportions. For example, we love a relative naturally. If the relative is pious, we love them religiously too. If the relative is impious, they will receive only natural love but not the religious one. We love a religious scholar that we have never met religiously but not naturally. If a Muslim wrongs us in some manner, we will develop natural dislike (or hate) for them but remain religiously connected to them (i.e. still have basic love for them despite their offence because they are still Muslims and Allah loves this about them). In other words, even if we happen to hate them for one reason, we love them for another. If a non-Muslim shows us kindness, we will develop natural love for them but not religious love (see *Appendix III*). Overall, we can love for religious and natural reasons or only for one of the two.

Allah's love is unique

Allah is the only one who deserves to be loved for Himself. Everything else is loved because of something else. This is a significant distinction in love between Allah and His creation. When we love a created being, our love for it is not complete, whole, or final. It is incomplete because we cannot love everything about it since it is not perfect. It is not whole because we can love something else, or many, as we love it: they have similar features that would cause you to have a similar love for them. And it is not final because each love for a created being is because of something else, linked in a chain that leads somewhere else. The final destination of love, where there is no longer someone or something else, is Allah. Let us explore this further.

Whatever we love religiously, we love it because of Allah. We love the Prophets, the Angels, and pious humans because Allah loves them. This is clear and easy to understand. So religiously, what we love leads back to Him.

Worldly love follows a similar chain. All human love is connected to a cause and leads to another. Let us take food as an example. We love food because it keeps us alive. We also love food because it pleases us. Why do we love pleasure? Because it enhances our life. Food both preserves and improves our existence. So does marriage. We love our spouses and children because they provide us with companionship, enhance our lives, and we rely on them. We need them to continue to exist. Our children are an extension of our lives and dreams, and family helps us overcome the hardships of life. Like food, marriage is about preserving and enhancing our existence. Everything we love in this world is loved for the same reason.

Why do we want to preserve our existence? What meaning does it have? If we exist simply for the sake of survival, then our life has no meaning. Our existence is meaningless on its own and cannot give meaning to itself. This is why we continuously look for the purpose of life. And if our only concern is to ensure our existence, we would not hesitate to erase the presence of others to survive (e.g. kill the competition). Thus, our life cannot impart morality. We need something else to give us meaning and direction. And it can only be the Creator. He granted us life, and why He did so is what gives it meaning. Once we reach the Creator, the chain stops.

If we love our existence and everything that protects and enhances it, then our love for Allah must be the greatest. This was al-Ghazali's argument (*Ihya' 'Ulum al-Din*, vol. 6, pp. 11–18). Allah is the One who gave us life. Without Him, we would cease to be. And He is the One who preserves it and sustains it. Everything that we do and collect to stay alive is His and by His Will. If we love those who save our lives and feel indebted to them, would we not love the One who created life itself and continues to support it?

If we look at the five reasons for love discussed previously, we find that Allah deserves ultimate love in each. We love our life, and it was Allah who created it and gave us everything we enjoy in it. We love outer beauty, but is not Allah the Most Beautiful? When the believers behold His Splendor with their eyes in Jannah, they forget all the beauty of Jannah compared to His. All the beauty we see in this life is His work, and it reminds us every time we see it of the beauty of its Maker. Just imagine the Beauty of the One who made it all. Inner beauty, similarly, belongs all to Allah. Allah has the best qualities. If we love honesty, mercy, kindness, and forgiveness, then Allah has the ultimate of each. And He is the One who created in us and taught us the beauty of character. If you ever loved someone because of their lofty manners, you must love Allah more because He gave it to them. And it is so with any human help and benefit: the true Helper and Benefactor is Allah. Who put the desire to help in their hearts? Who enabled them to help you? Any gift comes truly from Allah; humans are channels through which the bounties of Allah flow. And if we are talking about compatibility, who is closer to us than the One who made us, who is with us all the time? No one knows you better than Allah. He remembers about you what you forgot. If we ponder this, we will find that any worldly love is a call back to the love of Allah. It is He who gave all. He started it all, and to Him all of us return.

Stating that Allah is the only One who deserves to be loved for Himself is like saying that He is the only Provider, only He is Perfect, He alone should be worshipped, and He alone should be obeyed entirely. Humans, out of ignorance and selfishness, will ask you to do what harms you. Humans seek you to benefit from you, but Allah seeks you to benefit you; you do not benefit Him. For that, He alone deserves complete, unqualified, and maximum love. This love naturally leads to complete obedience: following what your Ultimate Beloved loves. No one should receive this level of love and authority except Allah. This is why Ibn Taymiyyah رَحِمَهُ ٱللَّهُ stated that loving other than Allah for Himself, giving them that type of complete love, is shirk.

فَإِنَّ مَحَبَّةَ الشَّيْءِ لِذَاتِهِ شِرْكٌ فَلَا يُحَبُّ لِذَاتِهِ إِلَّا اللَّهُ.

مجموع الفتاوى (ج١٠ ص٦٠٧)

> Loving something for itself is shirk. Only Allah can be loved for Himself.
>
> *Majmu' al-Fatawa* (vol. 10, p. 607)

Humans can only be loved partially and obeyed partially. They are loved because they lead to something else. And Allah is the end of all roads, the end of all loves, and the end of all pursuits. He is our destination. We just do not realize it. If you have Him, you will have everything. If you lose Him, you remain without a destination, with incomplete love. Only the love of Allah makes us whole.

Ishq

In the pursuit of the love of Allah, some refer to their affection for Allah as *Ishq*. They intend to express with it the intensity of an all-consuming passion. It is quite common in some circles and some literature on soul purification. This term, however, is not without its problems, raising concerns about its appropriateness. Al-Qushayri رَحِمَهُ ٱللَّهُ in his *Risalah* recorded what he heard al-Daqqaq, his teacher and father-in-law, say about *Ishq*:

سمعت الأستاذ أبا عَلِي الدقاق رَحِمَهُ اللَّهُ تَعَالَى يَقُول: العشق مجاوزة الحد فِي المحبة والحق سبحانه لا يوصف بأنه يجاوز الحد فلا يوصف بالعشق ولو جمع محاب الخلق كلهم لشخص واحد لَمْ يبلغ ذَلِكَ استحقاق قدر الحق سبحانه فلا يقال إِن عبدا جاوز الحد فِي محبة اللَّه تَعَالَى فلا يوصف الحق سبحانه بأنه يعشق ولا العبد فِي صفته سبحانه بأنه يعشق فنفى العشق ولا سبيل لَهُ إِلَى وصف الحق سبحانه لا من الحق للعبد ولا من العبد للحق سبحانه.

الرسالة للقشيري (ج٢ ص٤٨٨)

Ishq is exceeding the limits in love [i.e. excessive]. And al-Haqq, Glory be to Him, cannot be described as exceeding limits, so He is not to be described with *Ishq*. And if all the love that belongs to all creation were to be gathered in one person, it would not be what al-Haqq deserves, Glory be to Him. So, it cannot be stated that someone has exceeded the limits of loving Allah. Thus, Allah is not to be described as having *Ishq* for someone nor the slave [of Allah] that they have *Ishq* for Allah. So, *Ishq* is negated. There is no way for it to describe al-Haqq, Glory be to Him: neither from the al-Haqq to the slave nor from the slave to al-Haqq.

Al-Risalah (vol. 2, p. 488)

This may be one of the earliest critiques of the term: al-Daqqaq died in the year 405 Hijri. It is interesting that *Ishq* is not recorded in an earlier source on spirituality like *Qut al-Qulub* by Abu Talib al-Makki (d. 386 H) except once in reference to the denounced love of the world. The possibilities are: (1) the term gained currency only after al-Makki's death (from 386 to 405 H); (2) it was not popular in Baghdad where he lived but known in Nishapur (Northeastern Iran) where al-Daqqaq and al-Qushayri رَحِمَهُ ٱللَّهُ lived; or that Abu Talib al-Makki purposely ignored it. His use of it to describe the intense and harmful love of the world suggests that the term had negative connotations.

Scholars like Ibn al-Jawzi رَحِمَهُ ٱللَّهُ and Ibn Taymiyyah رَحِمَهُ ٱللَّهُ agreed. They were critical of the use of this term on several grounds. For Ibn al-Jawzi رَحِمَهُ ٱللَّهُ, the term is flawed when used with Allah (*Talbis Iblis*, p. 153). First, *Ishq* linguistically means love with sexual desire for intercourse. Second, the attributes of Allah are revealed (i.e. handed down to us), and humans do not assign it to Him. The Quran and Sunnah tell us that Allah loves and is loved (*hubb*), but *Ishq* is never used in connection to Allah in the Quran or Sunnah. Third, *Ishq* occurs between beings of similar nature: their compatibility allows them to find comfort with each other (*Talbis Iblis*, p. 219). Allah, on the other hand, is above all and thus deserves glorification and awe (*Talbis Iblis*, p. 203). Ibn Taymiyyah رَحِمَهُ ٱللَّهُ, echoing al-Daqqaq, added that *Ishq* is excessive love that is negative because of its extremism, and is thus blameworthy (*Majmu' al-Fatawa*, vol. 10, p. 131). If one is in a state of *Ishq* (excessive love) with a human, this will push love to transgress the limits set by Allah and the rights of others. Also, no one can love Allah enough, let alone for their love of Allah to be excessive. No matter how much we love Allah, there is no end limit to loving Him. Ibn Taymiyyah رَحِمَهُ ٱللَّهُ also agreed with Ibn al-Jawzi رَحِمَهُ ٱللَّهُ that *Ishq* is sexual love, often illicit. This term, he contended, is not used in loving homelands, family, wealth, the Prophets, and the pious. It is thus inappropriate to describe how we feel about Allah.

The Prophet ﷺ loved Allah the most, but nowhere does he describe this love as *Ishq*. So, either we discovered a level of love that the Prophet ﷺ did not know about, or we are using the wrong terminology to talk about Allah.

Unconditional love

This is one of the terms used to describe divine love. Popular in Christian circles, the claim is made that God loves unconditionally. This notion has migrated to human love. Unconditional human love became the sublimest love, the romance all need and should seek. But what does unconditional love mean? Love without expectations? Or selfless love? The two are not precisely the same.

At a basic level, we are seeking something when we love. There is something we want to gain from this experience. As discussed before, we love to exist and love everything that secures and enhances this existence. This means that a large chunk of what we love brings us some sort of benefit (see *Hadith* Six). And the greater the benefit, the greater the love. This is why we do not love everything, and of the things we love, we do not love them equally. We may say that this is a selfish love, but I would argue that it is not. A selfish pursuit pays no regard to the wellbeing of others, and it sacrifices their rights for personal gains. When we seek to benefit from our love, we are expressing our human need. No one would say that working for pay to buy food is selfish. We need to eat. It is selfish only when we eat and deprive others. Similarly, love that expects something in return is not selfish. It is only selfish when we allow it to deprive others of their rights.

What kind of return do we expect and need from our love? We love to be loved back and understood. We want our beloved to be kind, forgiving, and helpful. We want to give love and care and to receive love and care. It is clear that we gain something from our romantic love: I am not in it simply to make someone else happy; I want to be happy as well. And we are looking for something in return when we marry. We expect fidelity, kindness, care, and so on. If we receive nothing back from this marriage, it will dissolve. And if we gain nothing from our romantic love, it will fizzle out. If there are no conditions on this love and union, anyone could behave in whatever way they desired and still claim the right to our full love. This is untenable.

We can love without any return and benefit, but this does not characterize most of what we love. Once love has secured our needs, we can move to love without expectations. If I am starving, my love for food is aimed at consuming it. Once I am full, I can appreciate and love the creation of a masterful chef solely for the sake of its beauty and not because I want to eat it. I can help others and expect nothing in return from them. But there has to be a love in my life to make this possible. And this love must satisfy me in ways that make sacrifices possible. We can love a few things without expectation, but not everything.

We cannot love unconditionally where the behavior of the beloved—no matter what it is—does not alter how much love we have for them. Our love for another increases and decreases based on their actions. This is the first sense of unconditional love. Additionally, we cannot love unconditionally in the sense of having no expectations or desiring no benefit from our love. There are few exceptions to this second sense, but they are exceptions. If all of this is true, we should not expect or seek unconditional love. It is just a fantasy.

What confirms this assertion is Allah's love. Allah does not love unconditionally in the first sense of the word. Allah's love for us increases and decreases based on piety, *Iman*, and striving. But once we love Him, we will find that His love for us is greater than our love for Him. He rewards us plentifully for the smallest things we do—even a good intention—and forgives us great sins with mere repentance. He multiplies our good deeds up to seven hundred times and more, and each sin is recorded as one. He rewards us with eternal life in Jannah despite us never doing enough to earn it. When one gains His love, they will see from His favors and love what is beyond their wildest dreams.

In the second sense, Allah's love is unconditional. Allah does not gain anything from our love. Allah commands us for our own good, not His. And He is the only One who does this. Everyone else approaches you because they need something from you. Allah wants to benefit you without needing anything from you. Allah's love is as unique as He is, and we will not experience another love like His. Just as seeing Him in Jannah is greater than all of its other blessings, experiencing His love is greater than all other loves combined. There is no one like Him, may He be praised for eternity.

The Christian scripture and doctrine do not support the claim that God's love is unconditional (in the first sense). If it were, there would be no laws and punishment. Does God love you the same whether you sin or not? What if you do not have faith? Is not belief a condition to receive God's love and salvation? If love is unconditional, who is Hell for? It is a claim that contradicts the rest of what they preach.

Is a mother's love greater than Allah's?

What proponents of unconditional love may point to is that a mother will always love her children no matter what they do. *Hadith Fifteen* compares the love of a mother for her child to Allah's love, stating that Allah does not punish His beloveds. If a mother's love is unconditional, is it greater than Allah's love?

First, no human love can ever be compared to Allah's love. Allah granted each woman the love and mercy she has for her child. Her love cannot exceed that of the One who created and keeps love in her heart. The combined love of all women for their children is only a tiny fraction of the love of Allah.

Second, a mother's love is not truly unconditional, at least not all women and not at all times. Her love will fluctuate based on behavior. The kinder the child, the more beloved they are. Can we say that a mother will love her child the same no matter what they do? Even if they are extremely abusive to her and her other children? If you imagine the worst crime possible, would a mother love that offending child the same as another who is righteous and kind?

Third, a mother's love is an extension of her love for herself. She loves the child that she carried for months, came out of her, and nursed. The love she feels is not universal; it is limited to her children. Does she have the same intense love for children in other families? A mother typically puts her children's needs ahead of other children. In some cases, she may benefit her children at the expense of others. This, of course, is not intended to belittle mothers, their sacrifices, and their incredible love. It is to say that mothers are humans, and their love does not escape the flaws of human love.

Fourth, Allah's beloveds are like a mother's offspring. A mother does not have that intense love for all, only her children. And when the pious gain the love of Allah, He will take care of them better than a mother with her child. Allah does not offer this to everyone, and a mother similarly limits her special love to her children.

Finally, we believe that what we know about Allah is only a small fraction of His Greatness, Power, Wisdom, and Love. As we mature in knowledge and experience, we will understand Him better. And when we pass on to the next life, many of our questions will be answered, and many marvels will be revealed. The love of Allah is greater than we can imagine. The love of Allah encompasses the heavens and the earth.

APPENDIX II
Love and Hate

Does love exist as pure emotion, unmixed with other emotions? Though this question seems theoretical, it has momentous practical consequences. These consequences become apparent when we hear some expressing their religious and philosophical beliefs in terms of pure love, with no hate at all. Have you heard of "Love for all, hate for none?" Some move to describe the divine as pure love (God is love), suggesting that God only acts with love and without judgment or condemnation. These statements are attractive. But how true are they? And are they helpful?

Love is complex. Nothing complex exists in a vacuum. It is part of a web of multiple emotions, ideas, and interactions. Hence, love is interwoven with other emotions, including hate. But before we proceed any further, we need to clarify what we mean by hate.

In popular western vernacular, hate is dark and destructive, sometimes irrational, emotion directed unjustly at others. Examples include racism, jingoism, and hatred of refugees and immigrants. These venomous beliefs and ideologies are not the hate under discussion here, even though they would not exist without love, as we shall see shortly. The hate under consideration is simply the opposite of love. One may hate certain foods, seasons, illness, and death. Conversely, they love other types of food, other seasons, health, and life. One's hatred of these things may motivate simple avoidance (not eating the food we hate) or an attempt at eradication (fighting diseases and illness). Hate can distance us from harm. We hate sickness, so we avoid its causes and triggers. We plan and pursue our dreams because we hate failure. This type of hate, or whatever we decide to call it, is not inherently negative. Love would not exist without it. To understand this better, let us examine some universal moral principles.

We love honesty. Do we hate its opposite? Do we not hate

lying, betrayal, and deception? We love justice and abhor tyranny and inequality. Are we neutral about rape, sexual harassment, pedophilia, and mass murder? Why do we hate them? Is it not because we love their opposite: sexual relations based on consent, respect, and the sanctity of human life? Is it possible to love something and not hate its opposite? Or is loving something part of hating its opposite, and hating something part of loving its opposite?

Love and hate are intertwined, and the presence of each is essential in the constitution of the other. The venomous hate of racism and jingoism is fed by extreme and misguided love of one's ethnicity, nation, and self: every hate requires a form of love. Had this extreme love not existed, its accompanying hatred would not exist as well. Racial supremacy is based on love, albeit a faulty one. Legitimate love feeds legitimate hate, and illegitimate love feeds illegitimate hate.

Allah teaches us in the Quran that not all love is legitimate and appropriate. He said:

وَمِنَ ٱلنَّاسِ مَن يَتَّخِذُ مِن دُونِ ٱللَّهِ أَندَادًا يُحِبُّونَهُمْ كَحُبِّ ٱللَّهِ... ١٦٥

And among people are those who adopt rivals to Allah, loving them as they love Allah.

Al-Baqarah (Q2:165)

The love that these people give to their *andad* (rivals to Allah) is misguided and blameworthy. Sometimes, love is blind, wrong, and destructive. To speak of love as a universal good sacrifices nuance and conveys the erroneous and dangerous impression that as long as what we are feeling is love, it justifies everything. Love is not always good, and hatred, equally, is not always wrong.

We love because we hate and hate because we love. When our love is intense, so is our hate for its opposite. And when our hate is intense, so is our love for its opposite. For example, our passionate love for an individual makes us hate separating from them. If we dig deeper, we will find that the crux of this love is our aversion to being alone. If solitude were not distasteful and unbearable, we would not seek companionship. Our hatred and aversion to something push us to find its opposite. Because we hate injustice, we move to establish justice. We eat because we hate hunger, collect money because we hate poverty, and try to live healthy because we hate sickness and death. If we love something, there is no escaping the fact that we must hate its opposite.

Love and hate even coexist simultaneously in much of what we like. We usually do not purely love or hate something but have mixed emotions about it. We may love summer more than winter, but we do not love everything about summer nor hate everything about winter. We love sweets but hate the weight gain. We love our spouses and children, but not every small detail about them. There are things to like and dislike about everything in this world. Sometimes love dominates, and sometimes hate does. The percentage of each determines how much we love or hate something. This realization grounds our experiences in reality. Love is not a pure emotion that is untinged with dislikes and discomfort.

Love exists as part of a complex array of human emotions, all connected and interdependent. Consider hope in relation to fear as a case in point. Ibn Taymiyyah رَحِمَهُ ٱللَّهُ wrote:

إذا لم يقترن بالخوف رجاءٌ لم يكن خوفًا وإنما هو يأسٌ وقُنوطٌ...
ومتى لم يقترن بالرجاء خوفٌ لم يكن رجاءً وإنما هو أمنٌ.

جامع المسائل (المجموعة التاسعة ص ١٤٠ دار عالم الفوائد)

If hope does not accompany fear, it would not be fear but hopelessness and despair... And when fear does not accompany hope, it would not be hope, but it would be [complete] safety.

Jami' al-Masa'il (vol. 9, p. 140, Dar 'Alam al-Fawa'id)

Ibn Taymiyyah رَحِمَهُ ٱللَّهُ rightfully argued that hope and fear fashion each other and head off the extreme. If one fears Allah with no hope at all, they will despair of His Mercy. This would not be a fruitful type of fear. One proceeds to take an exam despite their anxiety because of the hope that they will pass. If they lost that hope, their anxiety becomes despair, and the exam meaningless. If one's fear of Allah leads to loss of all hope for forgiveness, worship ceases to be useful and attractive. Similarly, if hope for Jannah is not tempered with the fear of Hell, salvation would seem guaranteed and worship unnecessary. Proper and healthy hope needs fear, and fear needs hope: they are part of each other. A couple of pages later (p. 142), Ibn Taymiyyah رَحِمَهُ ٱللَّهُ pointed to the fact that hope and fear are based upon love and hate. This is so clear that it's almost intuitive. We hope for something because we love it and hate its opposite; we fear something because we hate it and love its opposite. It is impossible to hope and fear without love and hate. And it is impossible to love and hate without hope and fear.

Some describe God as love. But what does this mean? Does it mean that God is the emotion of love? Or is it saying that God only loves and does not hate? If it means that God is an emotion, then He is no longer a personal God who creates, but only the feeling of love that all of us have. Does this make us divine because God is in all of us? And what about love when it is harmful and misguided? Is it divine as well? Is all love, no matter what I love and how I love it, divine? This can hardly be true. The other more likely possibility is that God loves and does not hate. Theoretically and practically, this cannot be true. Does God love murder and rape? Does He love sin? If God loves something, He must hate its opposite. This is why He loves and hates.

Describing God as love is popular in some Christian circles. Let us examine this. Did the God of the Old Testament hate? God in the Old Testament smote people and wiped them off the face of the earth, punished left and right, and commanded the faithful to punish the unfaithful. Isn't He the same God as the God of the New Testament? Or did His nature change and become incapable of hate in the New Testament? If God is eternal, this change in nature would be impossible: it would mean that God became something that He was not before. The only possible answer is that God decided not to hate in the New Testament. But if so, who is Hell for in the New Testament? It cannot be for those whom God loves. If the Book of Revelation is a literal foretelling of the end of times, and if Jesus عَلَيْهِ ٱلسَّلَامُ will return to earth to stand in judgment over its people and separate the righteous from the wicked, sending the latter with the devil to Hell, if this is all true, then how can God love and not hate? The Jewish and Christian scriptures do not support the mantra of "God is love." I do not mean that there is no love in the Bible, but that God loves and hates in the Judeo-Christian scriptures. "God is love" is an oversimplification that is divorced from Christian and Jewish scriptures.

"God is love" also runs the risk of becoming a carte blanche that justifies everything. If God is love, then He allows everything. Or more accurately, He allows everything we happen to love. "God is love" becomes the tool to justify what we like. If we love something and God is all for love, then it must be right.

The question to ask here is: does God decide what He loves, or we? If we decide, then we have assumed His role and have become God ourselves. If God decides, then His decisions are not always going to match what we love. We cannot even get another human to love everything we love. If that is impossible on the human level, how do we expect God to love everything we do? Either God must change to match us, or we must change to match Him. In our world today, "God is love" is changing Him to fit our needs. The Quran teaches us the opposite: we must change to please Him.

This brings us to the following important realization: we should learn love from Allah, not proceed to teach it to Him. The last part of the sentence may sound outrageous, but this is what we do when we object to His Will. When we protest the law and punishment in the name of love, when we reject the idea of Hell, and when we question the utility of suffering, we are instructing the Creator of love on what love is. The irony is that we do not have a handle on our own emotions, so how can we give anyone else advice? We are often extreme in our love and hate. Our vision is often obstructed, and we fail to see the whole picture. We are biased, weak, and ignorant. How can we fully understand and encompass what Allah, the First and the Last, is doing? How can we think that we can love and be merciful more than He?

We are imbalanced in our emotions and reactions. Some of us exaggerate love and eliminate the boundaries between good and bad, beneficial and harmful. Some tilt more towards hate and enmity. We need love and hate for balance. This, after all, is how we structure our personal lives and societies. We do not build a nation on love alone. We outlaw the harmful and punish violators to keep evil at bay. We individually distance ourselves from dangerous people, objects, and places. If we erase these limits in the name of love, we will invite pain and chaos. We need hate to protect love. There can be no love without hate.

APPENDIX III

Can Muslims love non-Muslims?

One of the main objectives of this book is to demonstrate the centrality of love in Islam. The superiority of love in Allah's revelation also makes love essential in the Muslims' interactions with Allah's creation. The question that naturally follows from this assertion is: can Muslims even love non-Muslims? To answer this question with a flat "yes" or "no" sidesteps the nuanced Quranic position on the issue and conflates the different categories of love and the different categories of non-Muslims.

In the Quran, several *ayahs* shed light on this issue. Below, I discuss the most relevant to our question.

(1)

لَّا تَجِدُ قَوْمًا يُؤْمِنُونَ بِٱللَّهِ وَٱلْيَوْمِ ٱلْءَاخِرِ يُوَآدُّونَ مَنْ حَآدَّ ٱللَّهَ وَرَسُولَهُۥ وَلَوْ كَانُوٓا۟ ءَابَآءَهُمْ أَوْ أَبْنَآءَهُمْ أَوْ إِخْوَٰنَهُمْ أَوْ عَشِيرَتَهُمْ... ﴿٢٢﴾

You will not find those who have Iman in Allah and the Last Day loving and being loyal to those who oppose Allah and His Messenger, even if they were their parents, children, brothers, or relatives.

Al-Mujadilah (Q58:22)

Allah explains in this *ayah* that *Iman* prevents one from love and loyalty towards those who oppose Allah and His Messenger ﷺ. The two significant words in understanding this *ayah* are *yuwaddun* (يُوَآدُّونَ) and *hādda* (حَآدَّ).

The first word *yuwaddun* (يُوَآدُّونَ) means love. Some Quranic exegetes, like al-Baghawi and al-Qurtubi رَحِمَهُمَاٱللَّهُ, added loyalty, aid, and championing hostile nonbelievers. These additional meanings are probably based on the supposition that the *ayah* was revealed in reference to Hatib ibn Abi Balta'ah's tip to Quraysh, before the liberation of Makkah, that the Prophet ﷺ was moving his army towards them. Other cited reasons for the revelation of the *ayah* are reports that some Companions killed some of their nonbelieving family members in combat. The exegetes, Ibn 'Atiyyah and Ibn 'Ashur رَحِمَهُمَاٱللَّهُ, explained that the sequence of the *ayah*s makes them instead about hypocrites who are loyal to combatants from the People of the Book. This view is the stronger one since there is no authentic narration connecting the *ayah* to Hatib ibn Abi Balta'ah, while the reports about the Companions facing and killing family members on the battlefield are weak. According to Ibn 'Atiyyah رَحِمَهُٱللَّهُ, the *ayah* prohibits the exchange of love between Muslims and non-Muslims, or it specifically prohibits loving those who oppose Allah because of their opposition to Allah. As we shall see, it is more likely the latter.

The second word *hādda* (حَآدَّ) is opposition, stubborn rejection, exaggerating the limits, and enmity. It is either derived from the edge of the sword or from occupying an opposite space to that of another person (*Al-Durr al-Masun* by al-Samin al-Halabi, vol. 6, p. 79, Dar al-Qalam). The word, and thus the *ayah* itself, describes those who are actively fighting Islam and opposing it. Al-Tabari رَحِمَهُٱللَّهُ explained this *ayah* with a report from Qatadah that it is concerning "those who show enmity to Allah and His Messenger."

مَنْ حَآدَّ ٱللَّهَ وَرَسُولَهُ أي مَنْ عَادَى ٱللَّهَ وَرَسُولَهُ

Ibn Kathir رَحِمَهُٱللَّهُ explained that the word in question is about nonbelievers who are "stubbornly opposing Allah."

الكفار المعاندين المحادين لله ورسوله

In another manuscript of Tafsir Ibn Kathir, it reads "Stubbornly fighting Allah and His Messenger" (*Tafsir Ibn Kathir* by Dar Taibah).

الكفار المعاندين المحاربين لله ورسوله

تفسير ابن كثير طبعة دار طيبة

In a nutshell, this *ayah* prohibits giving love, loyalty, and support to those who are combating and attacking Islam and

Muslims. Whether we consider the incidents of Hatib ibn Abi Balta'ah and some Companions' opposition to their families on the battlefield as reasons for revelation or—more accurately—as examples of what the *ayah* intends, they both point to those who are hostile and wage war against Muslims.

(2)

يَٰٓأَيُّهَا ٱلَّذِينَ ءَامَنُواْ لَا تَتَّخِذُواْ ٱلْيَهُودَ وَٱلنَّصَٰرَىٰٓ أَوْلِيَآءَ ۘ بَعْضُهُمْ أَوْلِيَآءُ بَعْضٍ ۚ وَمَن يَتَوَلَّهُم مِّنكُمْ فَإِنَّهُۥ مِنْهُمْ ۗ إِنَّ ٱللَّهَ لَا يَهْدِي ٱلْقَوْمَ ٱلظَّٰلِمِينَ ﴿٥١﴾

O you who believe, do not take the Jews and Christians as allies. They are each other's allies. And if anyone among you takes them as an ally, he becomes one of them. Allah does not guide the transgressors.

Al-Ma'idah (Q5:51)

The pivotal word in understanding this and similar *ayahs* is *awliya'* (أَوْلِيَاءُ), which is the plural of *wali* (وَلِيّ). Linguistically, it means proximity, where two things are close to each other (*Mu'jam Maqayis al-Lughah*) (see also *Hadith Forty-One*). *Wali* (وَلِيّ) also carries in it the meanings of love and support. This is so because love is either the cause of this proximity or is its consequence. Common experience shows that we stay close to what we love or grow to love what we are close to. And when there is love, it in turn breeds support for what we love. So, wil*ayah* (i.e. being a *wali*) is built on love and support (i.e. to protect, champion, and help what we love. See *Tafsir Ibn 'Ashur ayah* 51 from al-Ma'idah, *al-Qawl al-Mufid* by Ibn Othaymin, vol. 2, p. 56).

Al-Tabari رَحِمَهُ ٱللَّهُ in his Tafsir commented on this *ayah* by writing:

إن الله تعالى ذكره نهى المؤمنين جميعا أن يتخذوا اليهود والنصارى أنصارًا وحلفاءَ على أهل الإيمان بالله ورسوله وأخبر أنه من اتخذهم

نصيرًا وحليفًا ووليًّا من دون الله ورسوله والمؤمنين فإنه منهم في التحزُّب على الله وعلى رسوله والمؤمنين.

Allah the Exalted forbade all the believers from adopting Jews and Christians as helpers and allies against the Believers in Allah and His Messenger. And Allah said that the one who takes them as helpers and allies and *awliya'* rather than Allah and His Messenger and the believers becomes one of them in uniting against Allah and His Messenger and the believers.

According to al-Tabari رَحِمَهُ ٱللَّهُ, the *ayah* addresses those who align themselves with the enemies of the believers and support them in their fight against Allah and His Messenger. He further explained that the one who takes the nonbelievers as allies and helps them against the believers has, in effect, become one of the nonbelievers: one fights the believers and champions their adversaries only when he is pleased with their religion. And if one is happy with their religion, he is, in effect, one of them. Embedded in all this is the prohibition of loving a nonbeliever because of their disbelief, akin to loving a sinner because of their sin.

If we look at the sequence of the *ayahs* in Surah al-Ma'idah—always important in understanding the meaning of the *ayahs*—we will find that they refer to those who ally themselves with the enemies of Allah. Ayah (52) states:

فَتَرَى ٱلَّذِينَ فِي قُلُوبِهِم مَّرَضٌ يُسَٰرِعُونَ فِيهِمْ يَقُولُونَ نَخْشَىٰٓ أَن تُصِيبَنَا دَآئِرَةٌ فَعَسَى ٱللَّهُ أَن يَأْتِيَ بِٱلْفَتْحِ أَوْ أَمْرٍ مِّنْ عِندِهِۦ فَيُصْبِحُوا۟ عَلَىٰ مَآ أَسَرُّوا۟ فِيٓ أَنفُسِهِمْ نَٰدِمِينَ ﴿٥٢﴾

But you see those diseased in heart rushing to them, saying, "We are afraid that we will be hit by a reversal of fortune." But perhaps

Allah will bring about a victory or a matter from Himself, and
they will regret what they concealed in their hearts.

Al-Ma'idah (Q5:52)

Allah described the hypocrites and those with diseased hearts as seeking alliances with the enemies of Allah to secure favor with them in case they triumph. The *ayahs* that follow, including *ayah* (57) below, are in the context of alliances with active enemies who are plotting, fighting, and ridiculing Islam.

يَـٰٓأَيُّهَا ٱلَّذِينَ ءَامَنُوا۟ لَا تَتَّخِذُوا۟ ٱلَّذِينَ ٱتَّخَذُوا۟ دِينَكُمْ هُزُوًا وَلَعِبًا مِّنَ
ٱلَّذِينَ أُوتُوا۟ ٱلْكِتَـٰبَ مِن قَبْلِكُمْ وَٱلْكُفَّارَ أَوْلِيَآءَ ۚ وَٱتَّقُوا۟ ٱللَّهَ إِن كُنتُم
مُّؤْمِنِينَ ﴿٥٧﴾

O you who believe, do not take those who ridicule and mock
your religion from the People of the Book and the disbelievers as
awliya'. And have taqwa of Allah if you are believers.

Al-Ma'idah (Q5:57)

The *ayahs* under consideration here, also al-Mujadilah (22), denounce love and support given to those who are in open conflict with Muslims. They also emphasize that a Muslim cannot be motivated to love a nonbeliever because of their disbelief. As we shall see, it does not preclude loving a nonbeliever due to worldly reasons.

(3)

لَّا يَنْهَىٰكُمُ ٱللَّهُ عَنِ ٱلَّذِينَ لَمْ يُقَـٰتِلُوكُمْ فِى ٱلدِّينِ وَلَمْ يُخْرِجُوكُم مِّن
دِيَـٰرِكُمْ أَن تَبَرُّوهُمْ وَتُقْسِطُوٓا۟ إِلَيْهِمْ ۚ إِنَّ ٱللَّهَ يُحِبُّ ٱلْمُقْسِطِينَ ﴿٨﴾
إِنَّمَا يَنْهَىٰكُمُ ٱللَّهُ عَنِ ٱلَّذِينَ قَـٰتَلُوكُمْ فِى ٱلدِّينِ وَأَخْرَجُوكُم مِّن
دِيَـٰرِكُمْ وَظَـٰهَرُوا۟ عَلَىٰٓ إِخْرَاجِكُمْ أَن تَوَلَّوْهُمْ ۚ وَمَن يَتَوَلَّهُمْ فَأُو۟لَـٰٓئِكَ هُمُ

ٱلظَّٰلِمُونَ ۝٩

Allah does not forbid you to deal kindly and justly with those who did not fight you because of religion and drive you out of your homes. Indeed, Allah loves the just. Allah only forbids you to take as allies those who fought you because of religion, drove you out of your homes, and helped others to drive you out. And whoever among you takes them as allies are the transgressors.

Al-Mumtahanah (Q60:8–9)

There are two categories of nonbelievers: combatants and non-combatants (or hostiles and non-hostiles). The *ayah* defines the non-combatants as those who did not seek to harm Muslims on account of their religion: they did not fight them, did not expel them from their homes, and did not aid others in an expulsion. In dealing with this group, Allah allows Muslims to be kind and just. This does not mean that injustice is allowed with combatant nonbelievers. Ayahs 2 and 8 from Surah al-Ma'idah obligate justice with the enemy even when they transgress. What Al-Mumtahinah (8) is conveying is that mere differences in religion should not stop Muslims from kindness. The *ayah* then moves on to define the second group of nonbelievers as the combatants who fought Muslims because of their Islam and expelled them from their lands or aided in their expulsion. Allah prohibits *wilayah* of this group: giving them love, loyalty, support.

Though the Quran prohibits loving those actively attacking Islam and Muslims (the second group), it is silent on love towards the first group: it neither commands nor forbids it. One could say that it hints at allowing natural affection towards this category of nonbelievers since it does not come out categorically against it. Kindness is impossible without affection. Kindness is founded on sympathy and shared experiences. When we see the pain and need of others, we rush to help because we have experienced and understand pain and need. Being kind without having or developing feelings for a person is unimaginable.

The incident quoted as the cause of the revelation of the *ayah* explains this. Al-Bukhari (5978) reported that the nonbelieving mother of Asma' bintu Abi Bakr رَضِيَ ٱللَّهُ عَنْهَا came to visit her. Asma' رَضِيَ ٱللَّهُ عَنْهَا consulted the Prophet ﷺ on the limits of what she can do. Her mother came to reconnect with her. In another narration in Musnad Ahmad (16111), she came bearing gifts. The Prophet ﷺ allowed her to receive her mother, accept her gifts, and reciprocate. It is impossible to accept gifts from someone or gift them while feeling nothing for them or even hating them. And the mother-child relationship, even when the two belong to different faiths, cannot be emptied of love. Similarly, Allah permits Muslim men to marry women from the People of the Book (al-Ma'idah: 5), and it is impossible for this type of relationship not to produce love and affection. The explanation of the next *ayah* will clarify this further.

(4)

إِنَّكَ لَا تَهْدِي مَنْ أَحْبَبْتَ وَلَٰكِنَّ ٱللَّهَ يَهْدِي مَن يَشَآءُ ۚ وَهُوَ أَعْلَمُ
بِٱلْمُهْتَدِينَ ﴿٥٦﴾

You do not guide those whom you love, but Allah guides whomever He wishes. And He knows the guided.

Al-Qasas (Q28:56)

This *ayah* was revealed about Abu Talib, the uncle of the Prophet ﷺ. As Bukhari (3884) and Muslim (39) reported, when Abu Talib was on his death bed, he rejected the invitation of the Prophet ﷺ to accept Islam and died a nonbeliever. The critical question is: did the Prophet ﷺ love his uncle? The Quranic exegetes recorded two opinions. The first is that the Prophet ﷺ loved him because he was kin, while the second was that he only loved that he be guided (see for example al-Wahidi's *al-Tafsir al-Basit*). Ibn Othaymin رَحِمَهُ ٱللَّهُ explained why "loved him" and not "loved for him to be guided" is the accurate meaning of the *ayah*. He said:

وقوله ﴿إِنَّكَ لَا تَهْدِي مَنْ أَحْبَبْتَ﴾ المفسر قدّره بقوله (هدايته)، ﴿مَنْ أَحْبَبْتَ﴾ هدايته، والصواب من أحببته ﴿إِنَّكَ لَا تَهْدِي مَنْ أحببته﴾ وقد عدل المفسر رحمه الله إلى تقدير أحببت هدايته لأن الرسول لا يمكن أن يحب أبا طالب وهو كافر، فإن المؤمن لا يُحِب الكافرين. ولكننا نقول الحب الطبيعي لا ينافي الإيمان، فالإنسان يحب مثلًا قريبَه ولو كان كافرًا، لكنَّها محبة طبيعية كما تُحِب الأمُّ ولدها. فالمحبة الدينية لا تجوز بين المؤمن والكافر، قال تعالى ﴿لَا تَجِدُ قَوْمًا يُؤْمِنُونَ بِاللَّهِ وَالْيَوْمِ الْآخِرِ يُوَادُّونَ مَنْ حَادَّ اللَّهَ وَرَسُولَهُ وَلَوْ كَانُوا آبَاءَهُمْ أَوْ أَبْنَاءَهُمْ أَوْ إِخْوَانَهُمْ﴾ [المجادلة ٢٢]. أيضا المفسر يقول ﴿مَنْ أَحْبَبْتَ﴾ هدايته ولو أننا حملناها على ما قال المفسر لكانت هذه تعم كلَّ الناس؛ لأن الرسول يحِب أن يهدي كلَّ الناس وليس أبا طالب فقط. لكن ﴿من أحببته﴾ هذا يختص بأبي طالب أو غيره من أقاربه... وأما ما لاحظه المفسر من أن الرسول ﷺ لا يمكن أن يحب أبا طالب، فالجواب عليه أن المحبة نوعان: محبة طبيعية ومحبة شرعية، فالمحبة الطبيعية لا تنافي المحبة الشرعية، قد تجتمع معها وقد تنفرد. فإذا كان المؤمن قريبًا لك اجتمع فيه المحبتان، وإذا كان بعيدًا منك وُجِد فيه محبة واحدة وهي الشرعية، وإذا كان قريبًا وهو غير مؤمن ففيه محبة واحدة وهي المحبة الطبيعية.

تفسير سورة القصص (ص٢٧٨-٢٧٩. مؤسسة ابن عثيمين الخيرية)

And as far as the saying of Allah, "You do not guide the one that you love," the exegete [in Tafsir al-Jalalayn] assumed the ellipted "guidance," so it becomes "that you love his guidance." But the accurate interpretation is "the one that you love," [so it is] "you do not guide the one that you love." The exegete

> chose to assume [the ellipsis] "love his guidance" because the Prophet ﷺ cannot love Abu Talib because he is a *kafir*, since the believer does not love the nonbelievers. But we say that natural love does not contradict Iman. One could love their relative while a nonbeliever, as a mother loves her child. Religious love is impermissible between believers and nonbelievers. Allah, the Highest, said, ﴾You will not find those who have Iman in Allah and the Last Day loving and being loyal to those who oppose Allah and His Messenger, even if they were their parents, children, brothers, or relatives.﴿ [Al-Mujadilah 22]. In addition, the exegete said, "The one whom you loved to be guided," but if we accept what the exegete said, it would include all people because the Prophet loves the guidance of all people and not only Abu Talib. But "the one that you love" is specific to Abu Talib or others from [the Prophet's] relatives... As for what the exegete noted that the Prophet ﷺ cannot love Abu Talib, the answer to this is that love is of two kinds: natural love and religious love. Natural love does not contradict religious love, and they could be combined or exist independently. If you have a relative who is a believer, they will have both of these loves. If they are unrelated, they will have one love, which is the religious one. And if they are a relative who is a nonbeliever, they will have one love, which is the natural love.
>
> *Tafsir Surah al-Qasas* (pp. 278–279, Mu'assasat Ibn Othaymin al-Khayriyyah)

The Prophet ﷺ loved his uncle for natural reasons, and so Muslims are allowed to love non-Muslims for natural reasons. These reasons include loving a relative, loving those who do us a favor, and loving those with noble qualities like honesty and altruism for the sake of these qualities. Religious love, however, is reserved for Muslims. In discussing the *ayah* in question, Ibn Kathir رَحِمَهُ ٱللَّهُ made the distinction between these two types of love. He wrote about Abu Talib:

وَقَدْ كَانَ يَحوطُه وَيَنْصُرُهُ وَيَقُومُ فِي صَفِّهِ وَيُحِبُّهُ حُبًّا شَدِيدًا طَبْعِيًّا لَا شَرْعِيًّا.

And he [Abu Talib] used to protect him [the Prophet], champion him, stand with him, and love him immensely, naturally but not religiously.

This remark from Ibn Kathir رَحِمَهُ ٱللَّهُ is important because it illustrates that distinguishing between natural and religious love is part of the traditional scholarly understanding of relations with non-Muslims. It is also important because it helps us understand non-Muslims' attitudes and reactions. Had Abu Talib loved the Prophet ﷺ religiously, he would have loved him as a Prophet and would have accepted Islam. Non-Muslims, similarly, do not love Muslims religiously—or else they would embrace Islam—but could very well have natural (worldly) affection towards some or many Muslims. Religious differences preclude religious love—even though one could still admire certain parts in the other's faith. But religious love does not prevent natural (worldly) love.

The quote also highlights another reason why the Prophet ﷺ loved Abu Talib: it was all the help he offered. The hearts are naturally inclined towards those who offer it kindness and assistance. Al-Ghazali رَحِمَهُ ٱللَّهُ wrote:

حب القلب للمحسن اضطرار لا يستطاع دفعه وهو جبلة وفطرة لا سبيل إلى تغييرها.

إحياء علوم الدين (ج٦ ص١٣)

The heart's love for a benefactor is a necessary [feeling] that cannot be eliminated. It is innate and a fitrah, and there is no way to change it.

Ihya' 'Ulum al-Din (vol. 6, p. 13)

It is thus impossible to ask a Muslim to develop no natural feelings for a kind non-Muslim.

Another scholar who pointed to the permissibility of loving a non-Muslim was Ibn al-Wazir in his famous book *'Ithar al-Haqq 'Ala al-Khalq*. He wrote:

الْمُوَالَاة الْمُحرمَة بالاجماع هِيَ أَن تحب الْكَافِر لكفره والعاصي لمعصيته لَا لسَبَب آخر من جلب نفع أَو دفع ضَرَر أَو خصْلَة خير فِيهِ.

إيثار الحق على الخلق (ج٢ ص٥٢٢) دار الصميعي

The forbidden *wilayah* [allegiance], by consensus, is to love the nonbeliever because of their disbelief and the sinner because of their sin, not because of another reason such as bringing benefit [to you] or protecting [you] from harm or because of a good quality in them.

'Ithar al-Haqq 'Ala al-Khalq (v.2, p. 522)

Loving a non-Muslim because of the benefit they bring, the harm they eliminate, or the good that is in them is permissible.

Some scholars, past and present, prohibit loving any non-Muslim. But as Ibn Othaymin noted above, they do not distinguish between natural and religious love and so outlaw both. They may also be fearful of natural love leading to religious love and consequently to the abandonment of Islam. So, they forbid both. True enough, natural love should not be allowed to turn into religious love. But demanding that there be no love between parents and their children or between spouses is unrealistic. Even asking one to dislike a non-Muslim who was kind and helpful is very difficult, if not impossible. The proper response is to strike a balance between preserving Islam and allowing natural love to persist. This can be done by explaining the different types of love, their different motivations, and the importance of keeping them separate. If we don't, then either natural love will turn into religious love and lead to disbelief, or religious distinctions will lead to cruelty, abuse, and mayhem.

For more fatwas on the permissibility of natural love towards non-Muslims, please see:

- Fatwa on Islamqa.info (answer 257654)
- Fatwa on islamweb (https://fatwa.islamweb.net/ar/fatwa/219466/)
- Fatwa by Sh. Abdulrahman al-Barrak (http://almoslim.net/node/268708)
- Fatwa by Sh. Lutfallah Khojah (http://www.islamtoday.net/bohooth/artshow-86-9244.htm)
- *Mawsu'at al-'Aqidah wa al-Adyan, wa al-Firaq wa al-Madhahib al-Mu'asirah* (The Encyclopedia of Aqidah, Religions, Sects, and Contemporary Ideologies) (Dar al-Tawhid: 2018), vol. 6, p. 3170.

Do we love the best for all?

This is *Hadith Twenty-Two* in the book:

قَالَ رَسُولُ اللَّهِ ﷺ «وَالَّذِي نَفْسِي بِيَدِهِ لَا يُؤْمِنُ أحدكم حَتَّى يُحِبَّ لِأَخِيهِ مَا يُحِبُّ لِنَفْسِهِ مِنَ الْخَيْرِ.»

رواه أحمد (١٣١٤٦) والبخاري (١٣) ومسلم (٤٥) واللفظ لأحمد

> The Messenger ﷺ said, «I swear by the One in Whose Hand is my soul, one of you does not believe until they love good for their brother as they love it for themselves.»
>
> Reported by Ahmad (13146), al-Bukhari (13), and Muslim (45). The wording is that of Ahmad

Does "their brother" refer to Muslims alone, or does it include non-Muslims? Some scholars restrict the brotherhood mentioned in the *hadith* to Muslims (religious brotherhood). In contrast, other scholars expand it to mean all humans (human brotherhood) (see Sh. Atiyyah Salim's, Sh. Abdul Karim al-Khudayr's, and Sh. Abdul Muhsin al-Abbad's commentaries on the *Hadith* of the chapter in their respective explanations of the *Forty Hadith Nawawi*).

Two *hadiths* shed more light on this. The first is:

«لَا يُؤْمِنُ عَبْدٌ حَتَّى يُحِبَّ لِأَخِيهِ الْمُسْلِمِ مَا يُحِبُّهُ لِنَفْسِهِ مِنَ الْخَيْرِ.»

رواه أحمد (١٣٦٢٩) وصححه شعيب الأرناؤوط

«One of you does not believe until they love for their Muslim brother good that they love for themselves.»

Reported by Ahmad (13629) and Shu'ayb al-Arna'ut declared it sahih

In this *hadith*, it is restricted to Muslims. But in another *hadith*:

«لَا يَبْلُغُ عَبْدٌ حَقِيقَةَ الْإِيمَانِ حَتَّى يُحِبَّ لِلنَّاسِ مَا يُحِبُّ لِنَفْسِهِ مِنَ الخير.»

رواه ابن حبان (٢٣٥) وصححه الألباني (التعليقات الحسان على صحيح ابن حبان ٢٣٥)

«One does not reach the reality of Iman until they love good for people as they love it for themselves.»

Reported by Ibn Hibban (235) and al-Albani declared it sahih (*al-Ta'liqat al-Hisan*, 235)

Either "people" in the *hadith* refers exclusively to Muslims, allowing the first *hadith* to restrict the meaning of the second, or the second *hadith* expands the category in the first *hadith* and extends loving the good to all people. Al-Qastallani رَحِمَهُ ٱللَّهُ presented the two possibilities in his famous commentary on *Sahih al-Bukhari*. He wrote commenting on a chapter heading in it:

(مِنَ الإِيمَانِ أَنْ يُحِبَّ لأَخِيهِ) المسلم وكذا المسلمة أو أعمُّ.

إرشاد الساري (ج١ ص٩٥)

"It is from Iman to love for his brother" [meaning] Muslim men and women or it is more general.

Irshad al-Sari (vol. 1, p. 95)

He then wrote:

ويحتمل أن يكون قوله (أخيه) شاملًا للذِّمِّيِّ أيضًا بأن يحبَّ له الإسلام مثلًا ويؤيِّده حديث أبي هريرة رضي الله عنه قال: قال رسول الله صلى الله عليه وسلم «من يأخذ عنِّي هؤلاء الكلمات فيعمل بهنَّ، أو يُعلِّم من يعمل بهنَّ؟» فقال أبو هريرة رضي الله عنه: قلت: أنا يا رسول الله فأخذ بيدي فعدَّ خمسًا قال «اتَّقِ المحارم تكنْ أعبدَ النَّاس وارضَ بما قسم الله لك تكنْ أغنى النَّاس وأحسِنْ إلى جارك تكنْ مؤمنًا وأحبَّ للنَّاس ما تحبُّ لنفسك تكن مسلمًا» الحديثَ رواه التِّرمذيُّ وغيره.

إرشاد الساري (ج١ ص٩٦)

And it is also possible that his statement "his brother" be inclusive of the *dhimmi* [i.e. non-Muslim living in Muslim lands] such as, for instance, loving Islam for him. What supports this [interpretation] is the hadith of Abu Hurayrah رَضِيَ اللَّهُ عَنْهُ where he stated that the Messenger ﷺ said, «Who would take these statements from me and apply them or teach them to someone who will apply them?» I said, "I will, O Messenger of Allah." So, he held my hand and enumerated five and said, «Avoid sins and you will be the best worshipper, be happy with what Allah portioned for you and you will be the richest person, be kind to your neighbor and you will be a believer, and love for people what you love for yourself and you will be a Muslim.» This hadith is reported by al-Tirmidhi and others.

Irshad al-Sari (vol. 1, p. 96)

In *Manar al-Qari*, a commentary on a summary of *Sahih al-Bukhari*, Hamzah Muhammad Qasim رَحِمَهُ اللَّهُ wrote:

وقال ابن العماد: الأولى أن يحمل قوله (حتى يحب لأخيه) على عموم الأخوة حتى يشمل الكافر والمسلم فيحب لأخيه الكافر ما يحب لنفسه من الدخول في الإسلام ولذلك ندب الدعاء له بالهداية، وقد كان النبي صلى الله عليه وسلم يدعو لكفار قريش

بالخير ويحبه لهم ويقول «اللهم اهد قومي فإنهم لا يعلمون» ومما يؤكد أن المراد محبة الخير للناس جميعاً لا فرق بين مسلم وكافر قوله صلى الله عليه وسلم «أفضل الإيمان أن تحب للناس ما تحب لنفسك وتكره لهم ما تكره لنفسك» أخرجه أحمد في مسنده ولكن هذا إذا لم يكن في الخير الذي يصيبهم مَضَرَّة للمسلمين وإلّا دخل ذلك في موالاة أعداء الله.

منار القاري شرح مختصر صحيح البخاري (ج١ ص٩٠)

Ibn al-'Imad said, "It is more proper to interpret his saying 'until he loves for his brother' to mean general brotherhood so that it includes the nonbeliever and the Muslim. So, he loves for his disbelieving brother what he loves for himself in terms of acceptance of Islam, and this is why it is recommended to pray for him to be guided." The Prophet ﷺ used to pray for the disbelievers of Quraysh to receive what is good; he loved that for them and would say, «O Allah, guide my people, for they do not know.» And what confirms that the meaning is loving what is good for all people, without differentiating between a Muslim and a disbeliever, is his saying ﷺ, «The best of Iman is to love for people what you love for yourself and to hate for them what you hate for yourself,» reported by Ahmad in his Musnad. But this is only if the good they receive does not harm Muslims, or else this would fall under taking the enemies of Allah as allies.

Manar al-Qari Sharh Mukhtasar Sahih al-Bukhari (vol. 1, p. 90)

The *hadith* is also narrated with the word "neighbor":

«وَالَّذِي نَفْسِي بِيَدِهِ لَا يُؤْمِنُ عَبْدٌ حَتَّى يُحِبَّ لِجَارِهِ أَوْ قَالَ لِأَخِيه مَا يُحِبُّ لِنَفْسِهِ.»

رواه مسلم (٧٢)

«By the One in Whose Hand is my soul, one does not believe

until they love for their neighbor—or he said brother—what they love for themselves.»

Reported by Muslim (72)

Al-San'ani رَحِمَهُ ٱللَّهُ was of the opinion that the "neighbor" designation is inclusive of non-Muslims. He wrote:

وَرِوَايَةُ الْجَارِ عَامَّةٌ لِلْمُسْلِمِ وَالْكَافِرِ وَالْفَاسِقِ وَالصِّدِّيقِ وَالْعَدُوِّ وَالْقَرِيبِ وَالْأَجْنَبِيِّ وَالْأَقْرَبِ جِوَارًا وَالْأَبْعَدِ... فَإِنْ كَانَ الْجَارُ أَخًا أَحَبَّ لَهُ مَا يُحِبُّ لِنَفْسِهِ وَإِنْ كَانَ كَافِرًا أَحَبَّ لَهُ الدُّخُولَ فِي الْإِيمَانِ مَعَ مَا يُحِبُّ لِنَفْسِهِ مِنْ الْمَنَافِعِ بِشَرْطِ الْإِيمَانِ.

سبل السلام (ج٢ ص٦٣٣-٦٣٤)

The "neighbor" narration is general for a Muslim, a disbeliever, a sinner, a friend, an enemy, a relative, a nonrelative, the physically close, and the physically distant... If the neighbor was a [Muslim] brother, he loves for him what he loves for himself. And if he was a disbeliever, he loves for him to embrace Islam in addition to [loving for him] the benefits that he loves for himself, on the condition that he has Iman.

Subul al-Salam (vol. 2, pp. 633–634)

Loving the best for non-Muslims is what fuels the work of *da'wah*. There is also nothing wrong with wishing them and their families peace and prosperity, even if they do not end up embracing Islam. The following piece of wisdom from a Companion illustrates this.

مر عقبة بن عامر الجهني رضي الله عنه برجل هيأته هيأة مُسْلِمٍ فَسَلَّمَ فَرَدَّ عَلَيْهِ: وَعَلَيْكَ وَرَحْمَةُ اللَّهِ وَبَرَكَاتُهُ، فَقَالَ له الْغُلَامُ إِنَّهُ نَصْرَانِيٌّ، فَقَامَ عُقْبَةُ فَتَبِعَهُ حَتَّى أَدْرَكَهُ فَقَالَ: إِنَّ رَحْمَةَ اللَّهِ وَبَرَكَاتَهُ عَلَى الْمُؤْمِنِينَ لَكِنْ أَطَالَ اللَّهُ حياتك وأكثر مالك وولدك.

رواه البخاري في الأدب المفرد (١١١٢) وحسنه الألباني (صحيح الأدب المفرد ٨٥١)

'Uqbah ibn 'Amir al-Juhani رَضِيَ ٱللَّهُ عَنْهُ passed by a man who looked

> like a Muslim and the man greeted him with Salam, so he replied with *wa alayka wa rahmatu Allahi wa barakatuh*. But then his servant informed him that the man was Christian, so 'Uqbah followed him until he caught up with him and said, "The Mercy of Allah and His blessings are for the believers, but may Allah give you long life and multiply your wealth and children."
>
> Reported by al-Bukhari in *al-Adab al-Mufrad* (1112) and al-Albani declared it hasan (*Sahih al-Adab al-Mufrad*, 851)

This is the balance, justice, and mercy of Islam. The religious Salam is reserved for Muslims, but kindness belongs to all.